THE NEW COLOSSUS

Not like the brazen giant of Greek fame,
With conquering limbs astride from land to land;
Here at our sea-washed, sunset gates shall stand
A mighty woman with a torch, whose flame
Is the imprisoned lightning, and her name
Mother of Exiles. From her beacon-hand
Glows world-wide welcome; her mild eyes command
The air-bridged harbor that twin cities frame.
"Keep, ancient lands, your storied pomp!" cries she
With silent lips. "Give me your tired, your poor,
Your huddled masses yearning to breathe free,
The wretched refuse of your teeming shore.
Send these, the homeless, tempest-tost to me,
I lift my lamp beside the golden door!"

-Emma Lazarus

Dedicated to the memory
of Jose Boris Voloj Ramirez
(1948-2023)

First edition published in 2024 by Nobrow, an imprint
of Flying Eye Books Ltd. 27 Westgate Street, London, E8 3RL.

Text © Julian Voloj 2024
Illustrations © Jörg Hartmann 2024

Rights arranged through Nicolas Grivel Agency. Julian Voloj and Jörg Hartmann have asserted their rights under the Copyright, Designs and Patents Act, 1988, to be identified as the Author and Illustrator of this Work.

All rights reserved. No part of this publication may be reproduced or transmitted in any form or by any means, electronic or mechanical, including photocopying, recording or by any information and storage retrieval system, without prior written consent from the publisher.

1 3 5 7 9 10 8 6 4 2

Published in the US by Flying Eye Books Ltd.
Printed in Poland on FSC® certified paper.

ISBN: 978-1-91312-305-5
www.nobrow.net

LIBERTY

Julian Voloj · Jörg Hartmann

NOBROW

WHO IS WHO
In Order of Appearance:

Frédéric-Auguste Bartholdi
(1834-1904)
French sculptor and painter, best known for designing "Liberty Enlightening the World", commonly known as the Statue of Liberty.

Isma'il Pasha
(1830-1895)
Known as Isma'il the Magnificent, he was the Khedive of Egypt and ruler of Sudan (1863-1879). During his reign, he modernized Egypt and Sudan by investing in industrial development and urbanization.

Augusta Charlotte Bartholdi
(1801-1891)
Mother of Frédéric-Auguste and his older brother Jean-Charles. After her husband Jean-Charles Bartholdi died she moved from Colmar to Paris, but maintained ownership of their house in Alsace, which in 1922 became the Bartholdi Museum.

Édouard de Laboulaye
(1811-1883)
French lawyer, writer, and anti-slavery activist. He introduced the idea of the Statue of Liberty as a present from the people of France to the United States.

Oscar du Motier de Lafayette
(1815-1881)
French soldier and politician whose grandfather was George Washington's comrade-in-arms.

Charles de Rémusat
(1797-1875)
French politician and writer whose father was the chamberlain to Napoleon Bonaparte. He was married to one of Lafayette's granddaughters.

Hippolyte de Tocqueville
(1797-1877)
French writer and philosopher who traveled to the United States in 1831 with his brother Alexis where they accidentally separated and never saw each other again.

Mary Louise Booth
(1831-1889)
American editor, translator and writer. She was the first editor-in-chief of the women's fashion magazine "Harper's Bazaar," and the translator of Laboulaye's books into English.

Charles Sumner
(1811-1874)
American lawyer and politician who was a leading advocate for the abolition of slavery. In 1856, he was viciously attacked on the Senate floor by Representative Preston Brooks, making him a symbol for the anti-slavery cause. He chaired the Senate Foreign Relations Committee from 1861 to 1871.

Ulysses Grant
(1822-1885)
American military officer and politician who served as the 18th president of the United States (1869-1877). As Commanding General, he led the Union Army to victory during the American Civil War.

John W. Forney
(1817-1881)
American newspaper publisher and politician who served as secretary of the U.S. Senate (1861-1868). He was an earnest promoter of the Centennial Exposition of 1876 held in Philadelphia, where parts of the Statue of Liberty were displayed.

John La Farge
(1835-1910)

American artist, born to wealthy French parents in New York City. He designed stained glass.

Carl Schurz
(1829-1906)

German revolutionary and American journalist. He came to the United States after the German Revolutions of 1848-1849. In Missouri, he established the "Westliche Post" and became the first German-American elected to the U.S. Senate.

Eugene Viollet-le-Duc
(1814-1879)

French architect known for his restoration of prominent medieval landmarks in France such as Notre-Dame de Paris and the Basilica of Saint Denis. He designed a brick pier within the Statue of Liberty, to which copper sheets would be anchored.

Alexandre-Gustave Eiffel
(1832-1923)

French civil engineer best known for the Eiffel Tower he designed and built for the 1889 World Exposition in Paris. Contacted in 1881 by Augusta Bartholdi, he designed the interior structure of the Statue of Liberty.

Richard Morris Hunt
(1827-1895)

American architect who designed the pedestal of the Statue of Liberty as well as the entrance facade of the Metropolitan Museum of Art.

Levi P. Morton
(1824-1920)

American politician who served as the U.S. Minister to France (1881-1885). He attended the dedication of the Statue of Liberty and would later become the 22nd Vice President of the United States (1889-1893).

Joseph Pulitzer
(1847-1911)

American newspaper publisher who started his newspaper career at the German language daily "Westliche Post." He eventually became publisher of the "St. Louis Post-Dispatch" and "The New York World." He is best known for the Pulitzer Prize established in 1917 as a result of his endowment to Columbia University.

Victor Hugo
(1802-1885)

French writer and politician, best known for his novels "The Hunchback of Notre-Dame" (1831) and "Les MisÉrables" (1862). He campaigned for social causes such as the abolition of capital punishment and slavery.

Emma Lazarus
(1849-1887)

American poet and translator. Her poem "The New Colossus" (1883) was inspired by the Statue of Liberty and is inscribed on a bronze plaque on the pedestal of the statue, installed in 1903.

William Evarts
(1818-1901)

American lawyer and politician who served as U.S. Secretary of State and attended the dedication ceremony of the Statue of Liberty.

Grover Cleveland
(1837-1908)

American politician who served as the 22nd and 24th president of the United States (1885-1889 and 1893-1897). He had vetoed funding for the pedestal of the Statue of Liberty, but nevertheless attended its dedication ceremony.

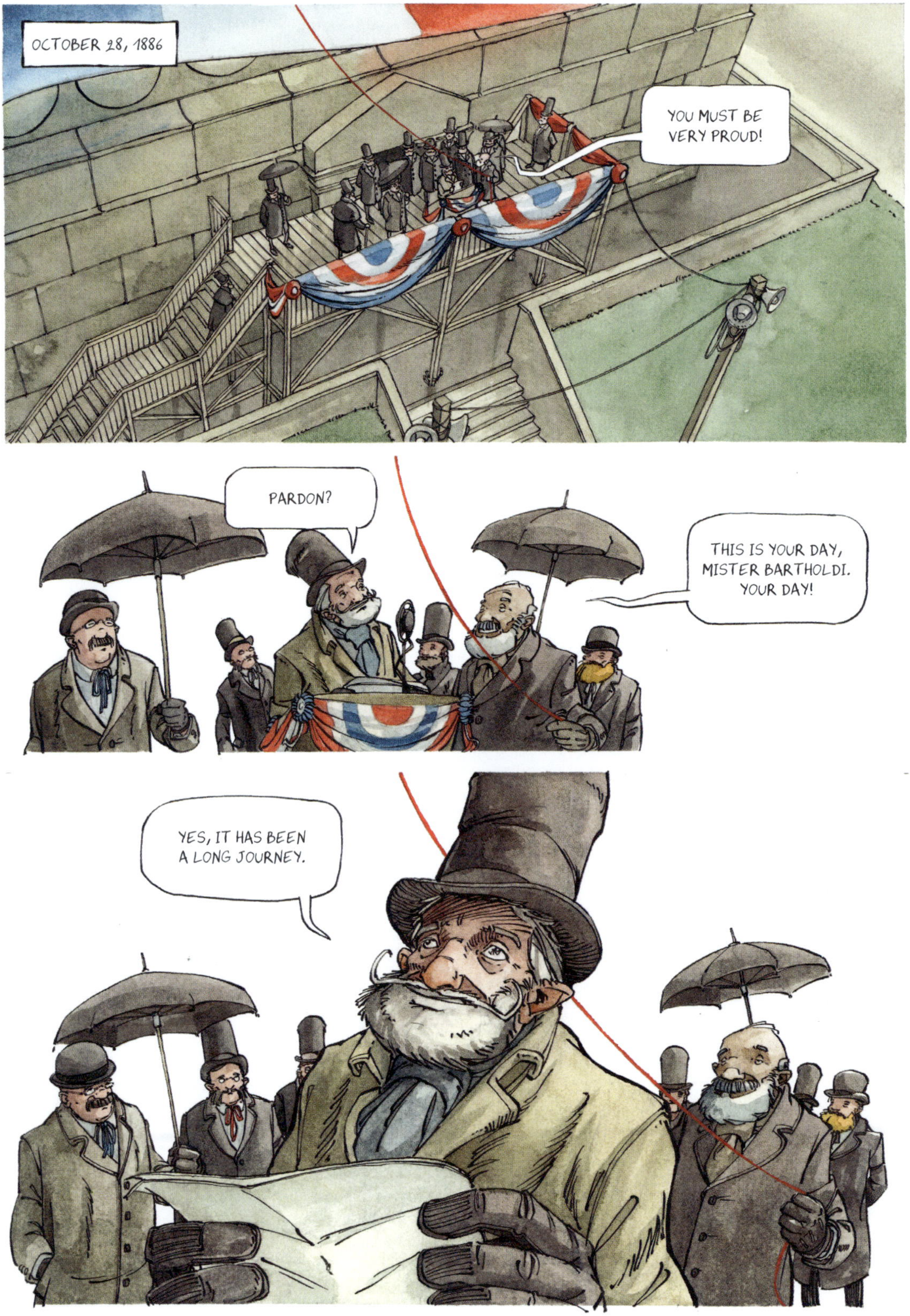
OCTOBER 28, 1886
YOU MUST BE VERY PROUD!
PARDON?
THIS IS YOUR DAY, MISTER BARTHOLDI. YOUR DAY!
YES, IT HAS BEEN A LONG JOURNEY.

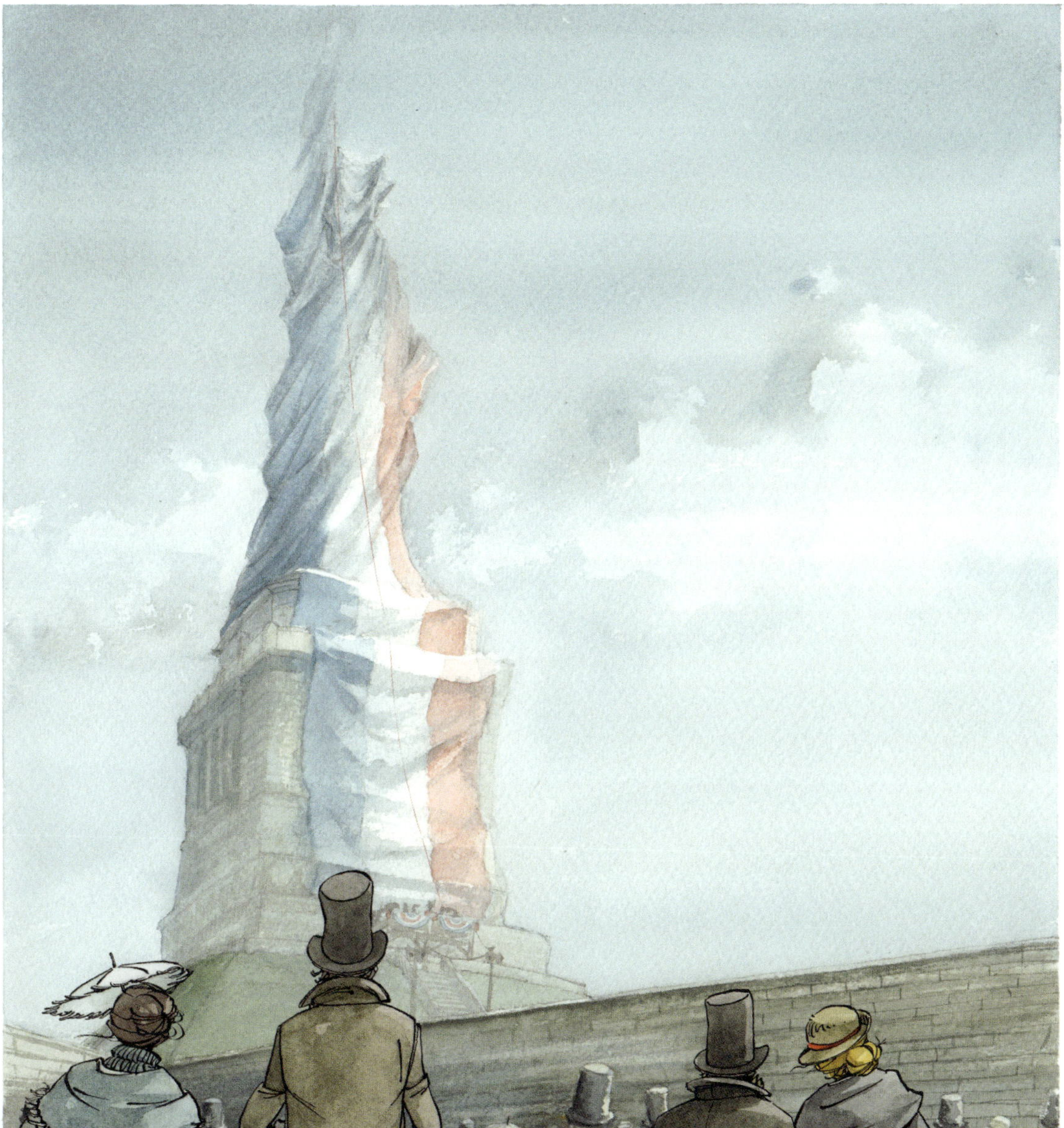

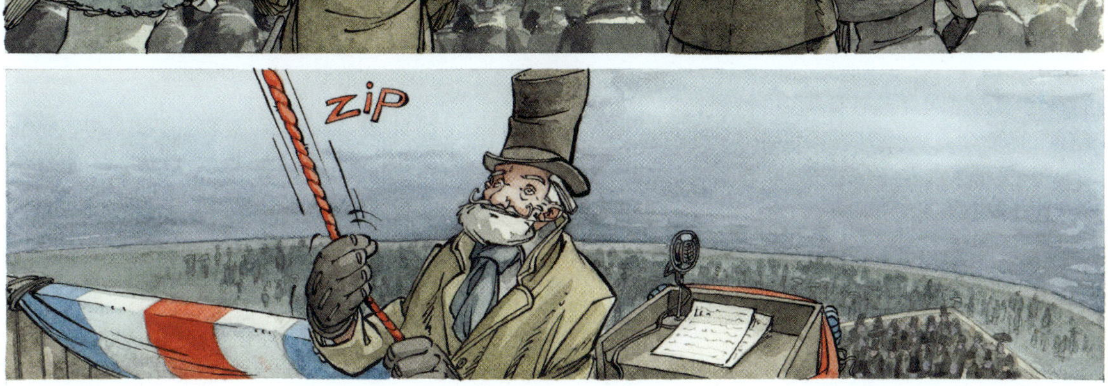
ZIP

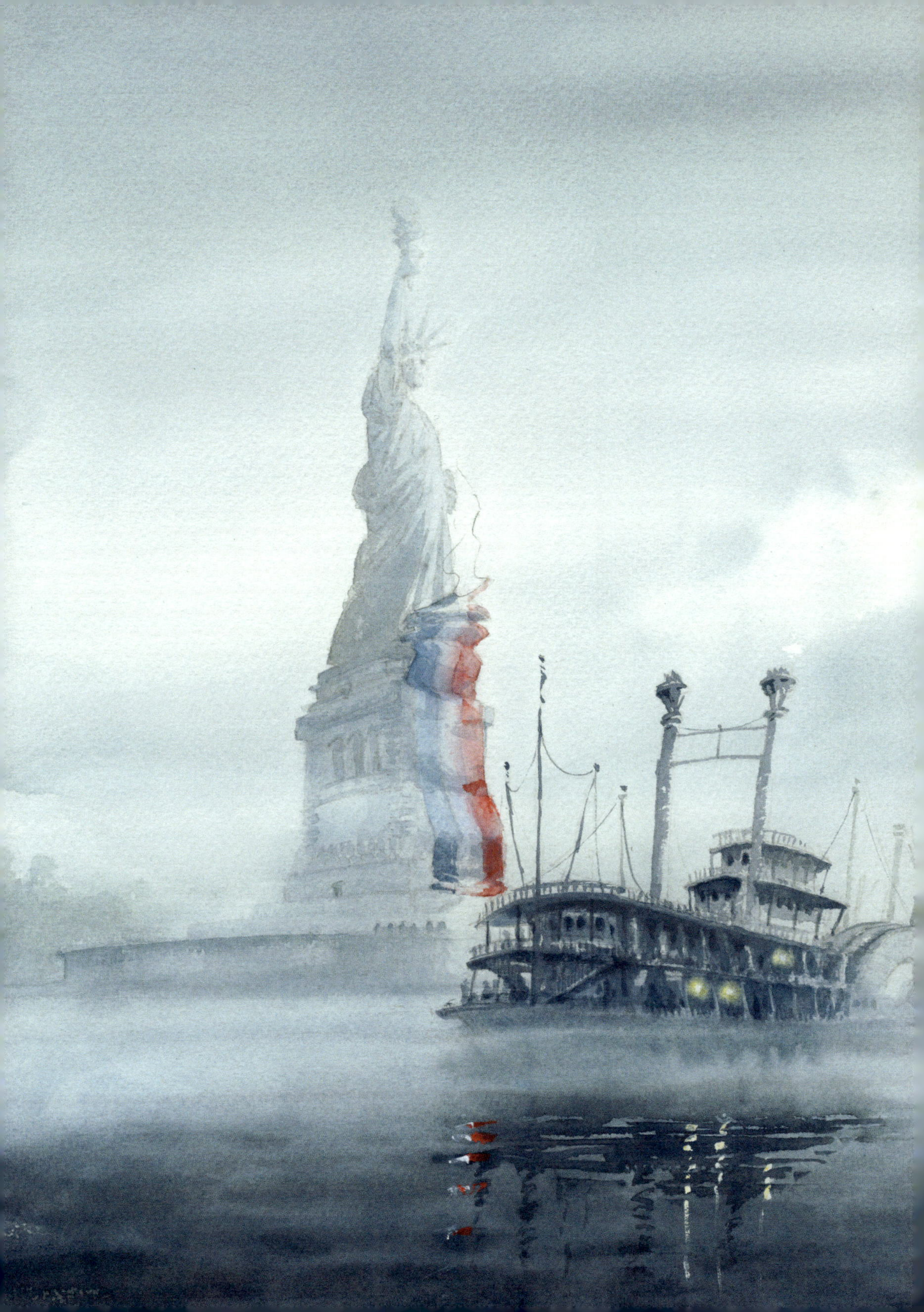

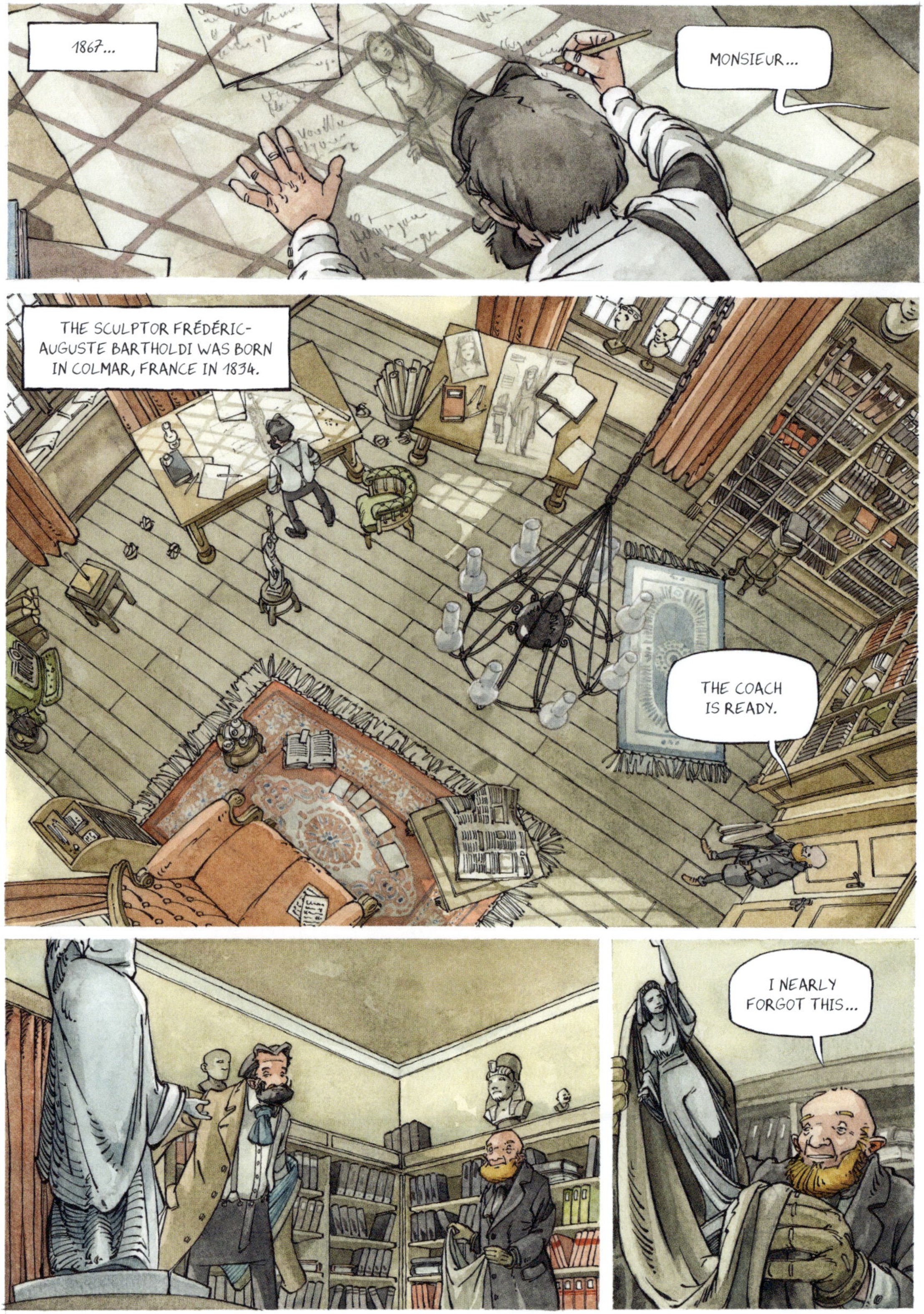
1867...
MONSIEUR...
THE SCULPTOR FRÉDÉRIC-AUGUSTE BARTHOLDI WAS BORN IN COLMAR, FRANCE IN 1834.
THE COACH IS READY.
I NEARLY FORGOT THIS...

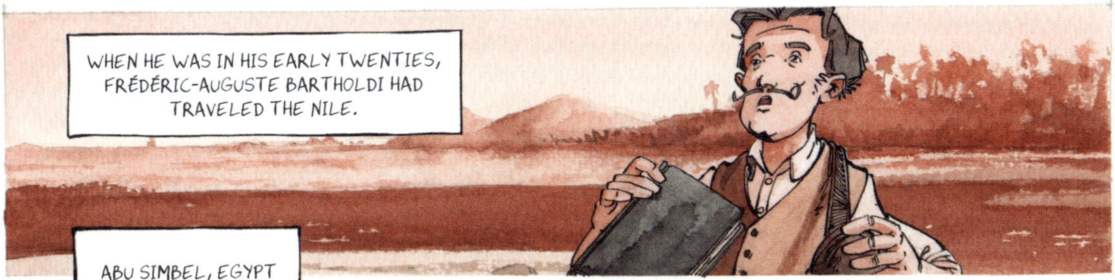
WHEN HE WAS IN HIS EARLY TWENTIES, FRÉDÉRIC-AUGUSTE BARTHOLDI HAD TRAVELED THE NILE.

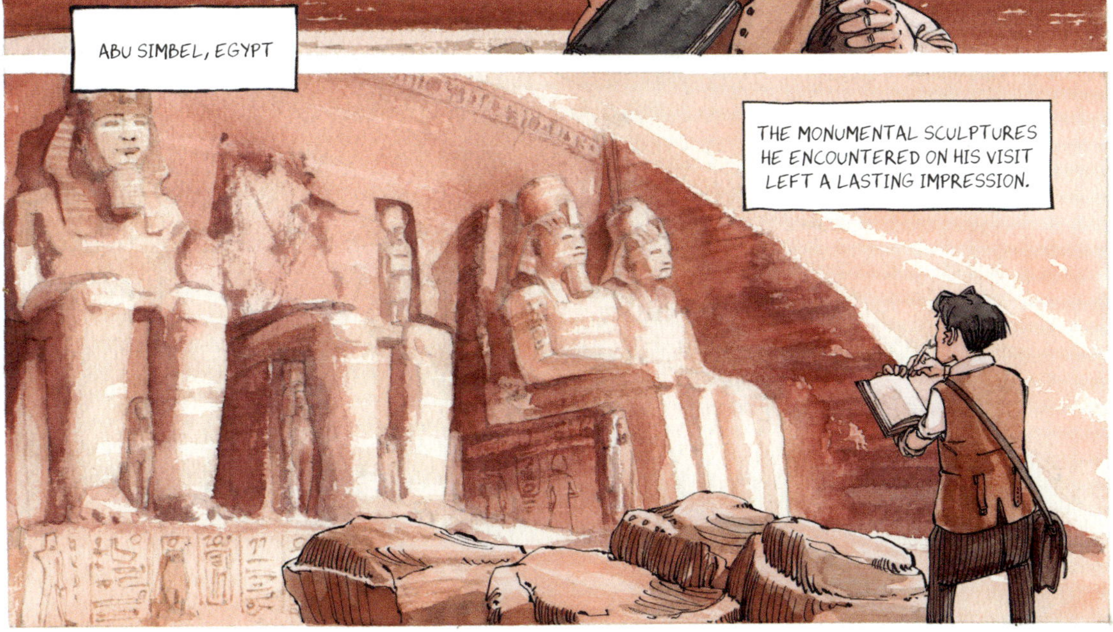
ABU SIMBEL, EGYPT
THE MONUMENTAL SCULPTURES HE ENCOUNTERED ON HIS VISIT LEFT A LASTING IMPRESSION.

A DECADE LATER, HE WAS ABOUT TO PROPOSE A COLOSSAL STATUE INSPIRED BY HIS TRIP.

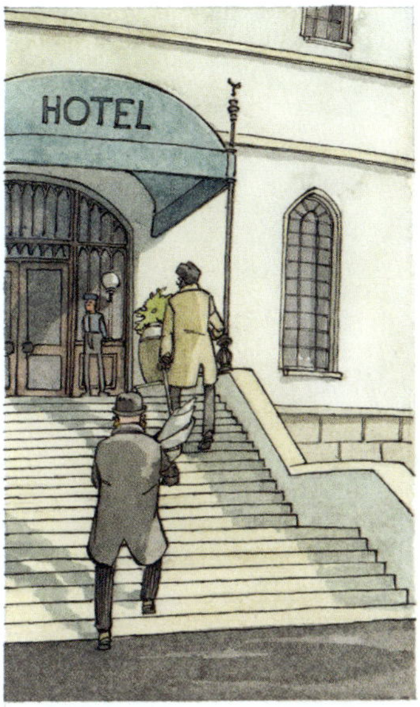
HOTEL

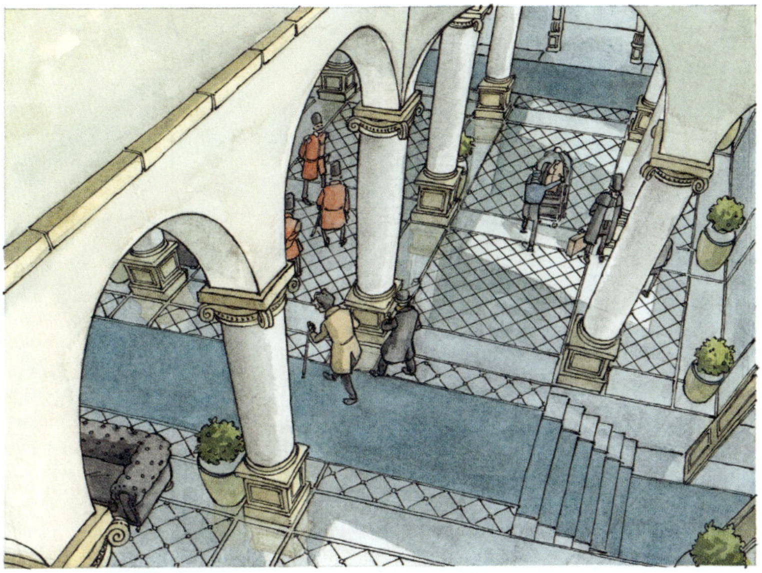

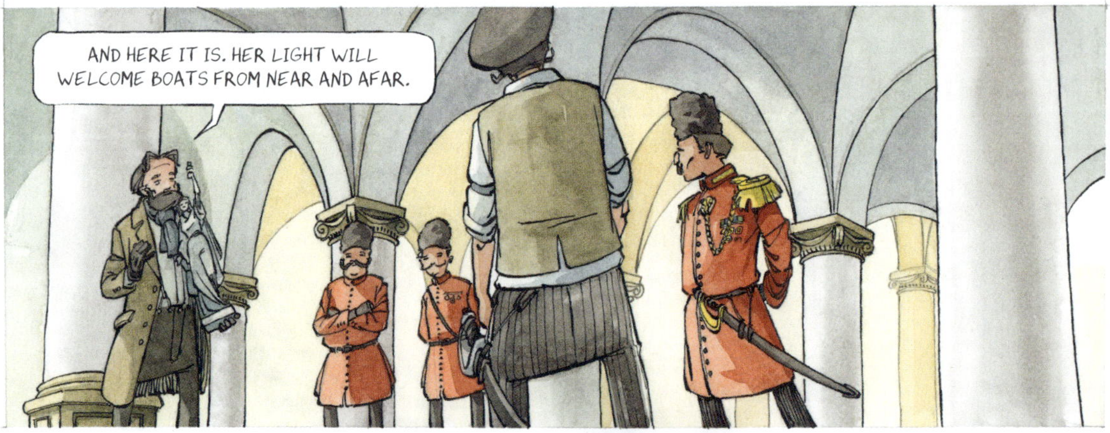
AND HERE IT IS. HER LIGHT WILL WELCOME BOATS FROM NEAR AND AFAR.

FRÉDÉRIC-AUGUSTE HAD SECURED A MEETING WITH ISMA'IL PASHA, THE RULER OF EGYPT, WHO WAS VISITING THE EXPOSITION UNIVERSELLE IN PARIS. THE SUEZ CANAL WAS NEAR COMPLETION, AND BARTHOLDI PROPOSED A LIGHTHOUSE RECALLING THE ANCIENT PHAROS OF ALEXANDRIA.

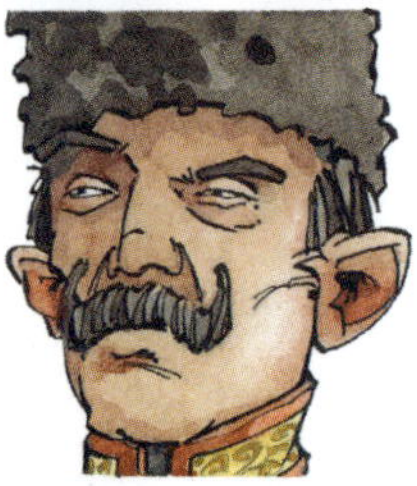

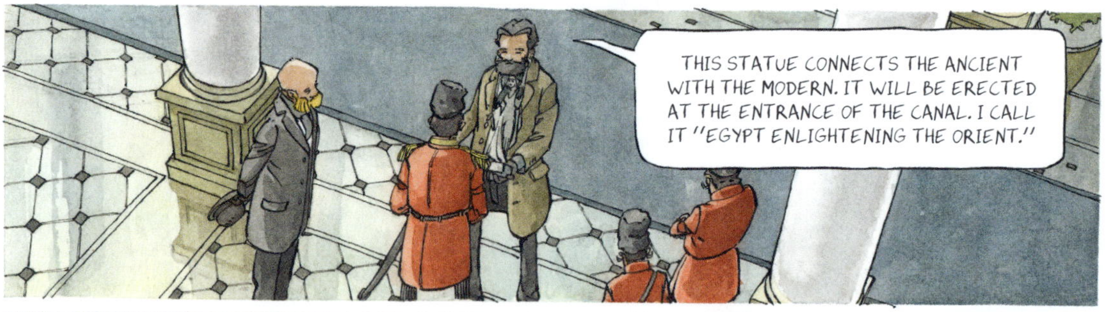
THIS STATUE CONNECTS THE ANCIENT WITH THE MODERN. IT WILL BE ERECTED AT THE ENTRANCE OF THE CANAL. I CALL IT "EGYPT ENLIGHTENING THE ORIENT."

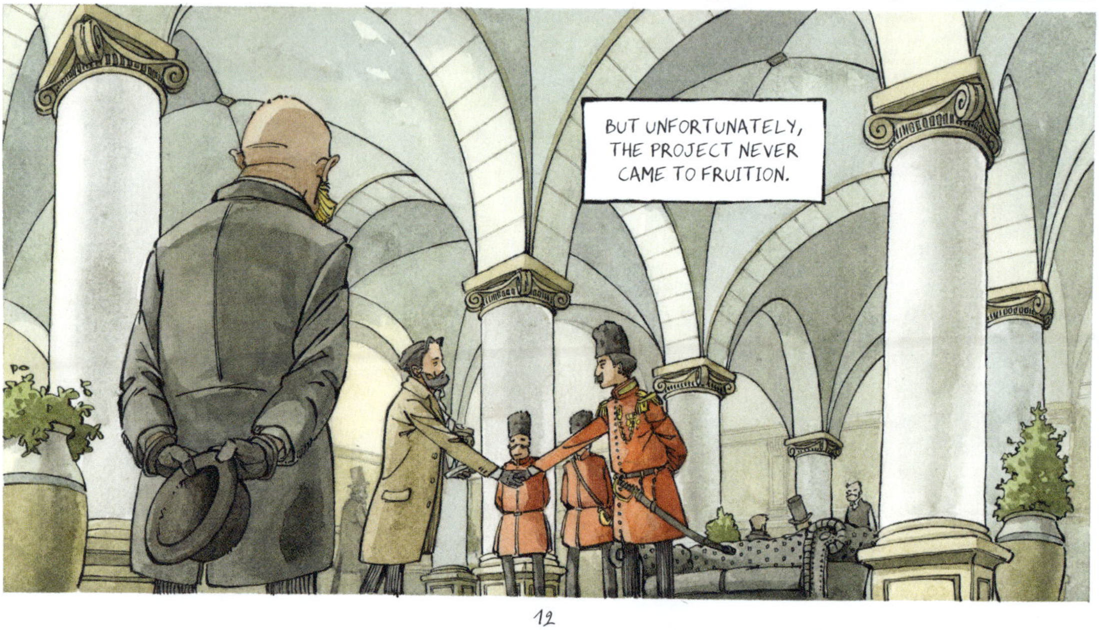
BUT UNFORTUNATELY, THE PROJECT NEVER CAME TO FRUITION.

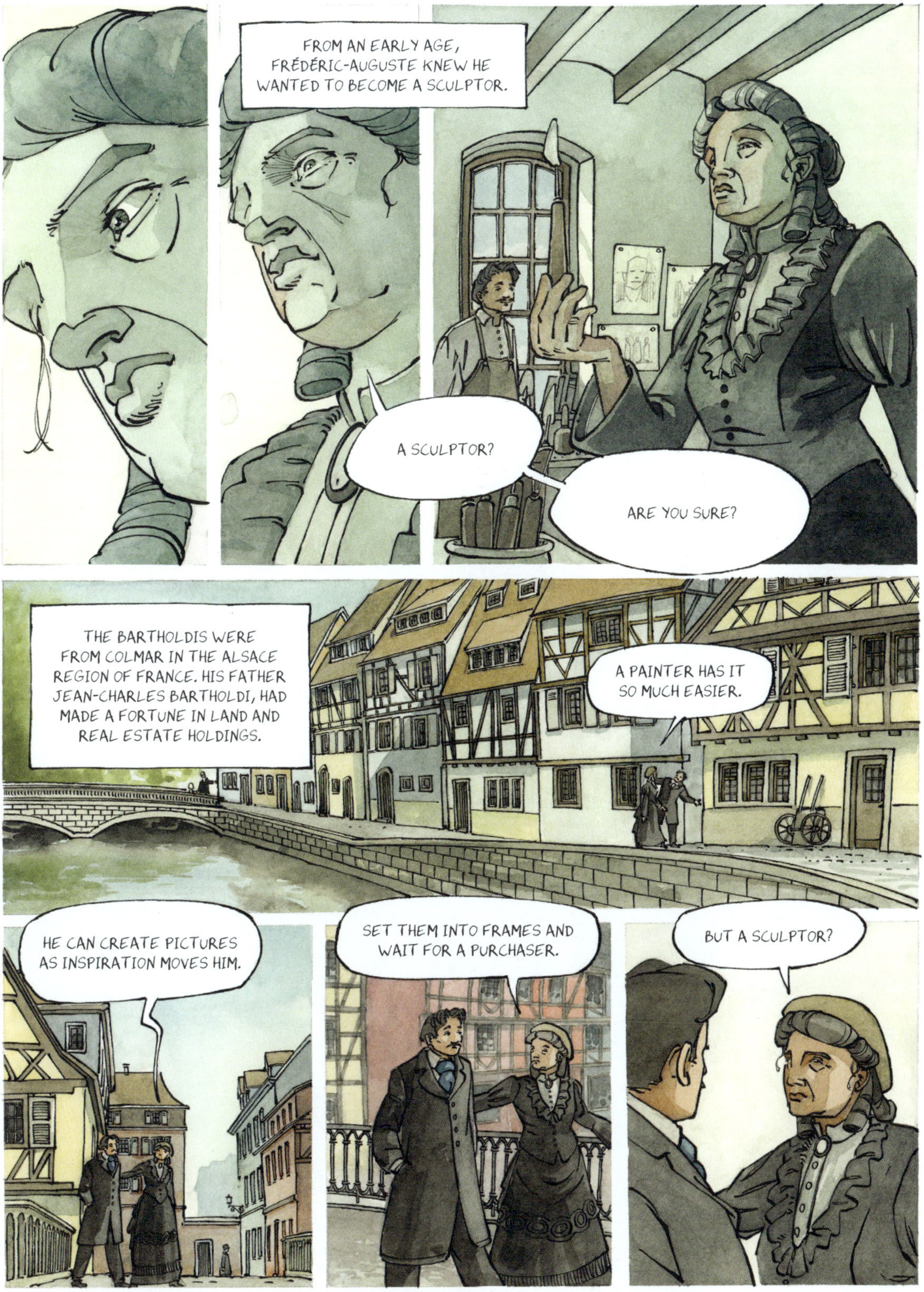
FROM AN EARLY AGE, FRÉDÉRIC-AUGUSTE KNEW HE WANTED TO BECOME A SCULPTOR.
A SCULPTOR?
ARE YOU SURE?
THE BARTHOLDIS WERE FROM COLMAR IN THE ALSACE REGION OF FRANCE. HIS FATHER JEAN-CHARLES BARTHOLDI, HAD MADE A FORTUNE IN LAND AND REAL ESTATE HOLDINGS.
A PAINTER HAS IT SO MUCH EASIER.
HE CAN CREATE PICTURES AS INSPIRATION MOVES HIM.
SET THEM INTO FRAMES AND WAIT FOR A PURCHASER.
BUT A SCULPTOR?

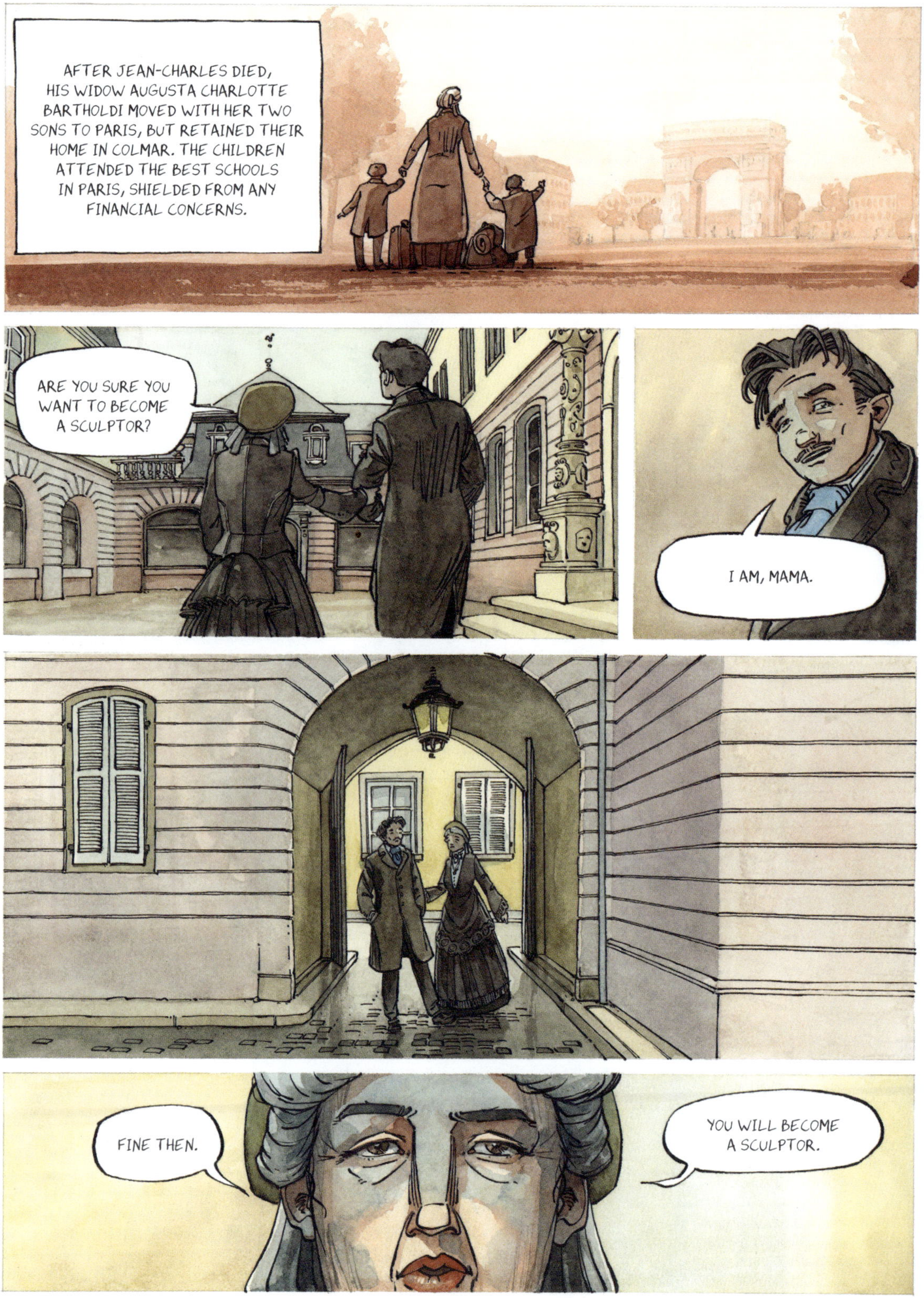

AFTER JEAN-CHARLES DIED, HIS WIDOW AUGUSTA CHARLOTTE BARTHOLDI MOVED WITH HER TWO SONS TO PARIS, BUT RETAINED THEIR HOME IN COLMAR. THE CHILDREN ATTENDED THE BEST SCHOOLS IN PARIS, SHIELDED FROM ANY FINANCIAL CONCERNS.
ARE YOU SURE YOU WANT TO BECOME A SCULPTOR?
I AM, MAMA.
FINE THEN.
YOU WILL BECOME A SCULPTOR.

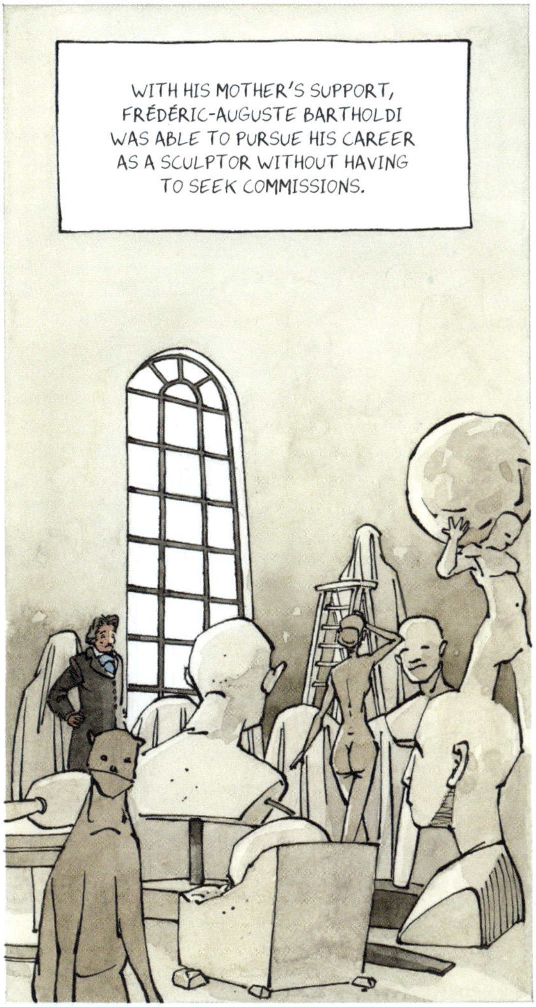
WITH HIS MOTHER'S SUPPORT, FRÉDÉRIC-AUGUSTE BARTHOLDI WAS ABLE TO PURSUE HIS CAREER AS A SCULPTOR WITHOUT HAVING TO SEEK COMMISSIONS.

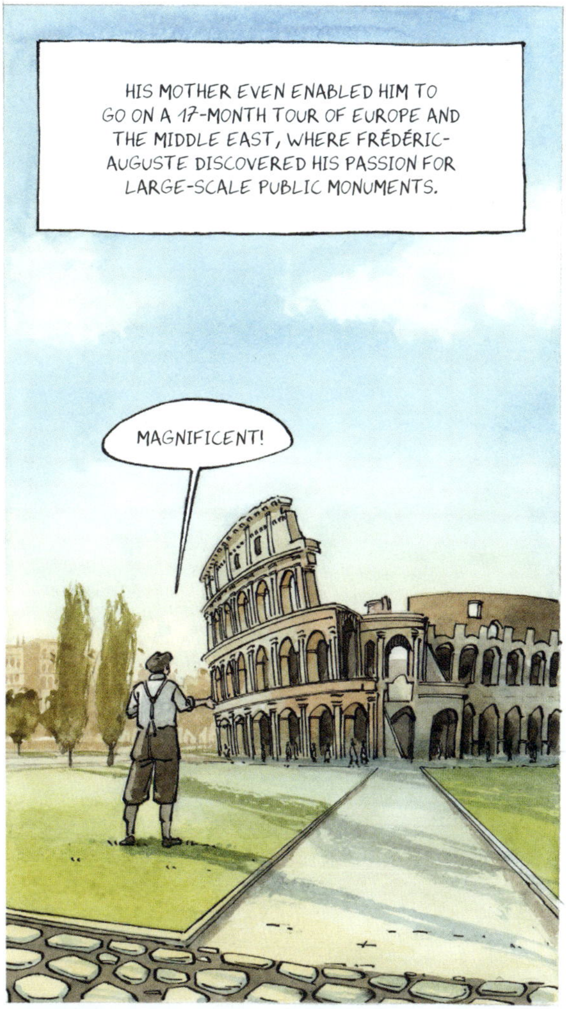
HIS MOTHER EVEN ENABLED HIM TO GO ON A 17-MONTH TOUR OF EUROPE AND THE MIDDLE EAST, WHERE FRÉDÉRIC-AUGUSTE DISCOVERED HIS PASSION FOR LARGE-SCALE PUBLIC MONUMENTS.
MAGNIFICENT!

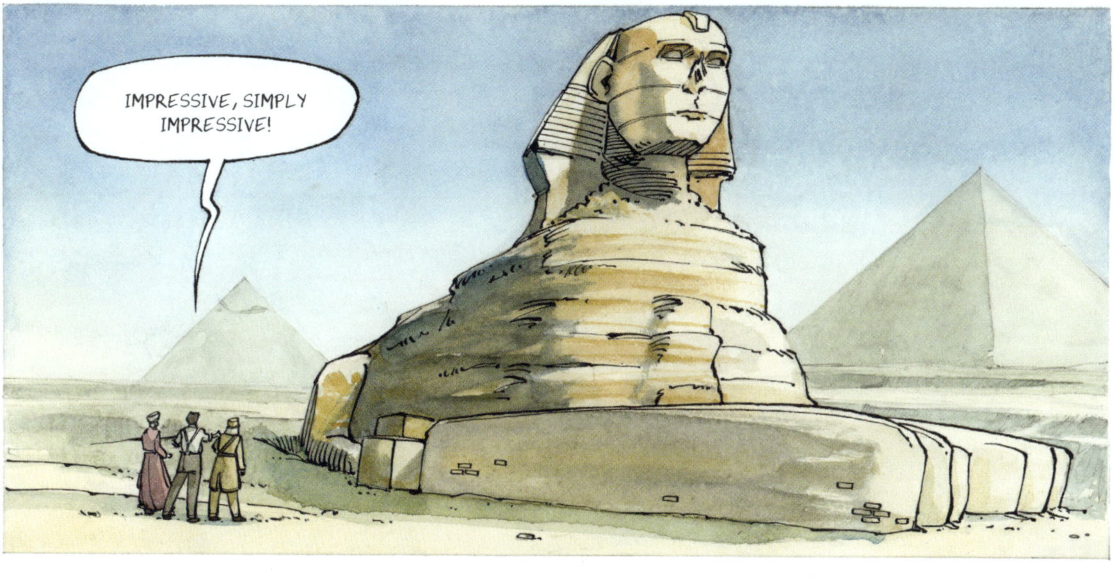
IMPRESSIVE, SIMPLY IMPRESSIVE!

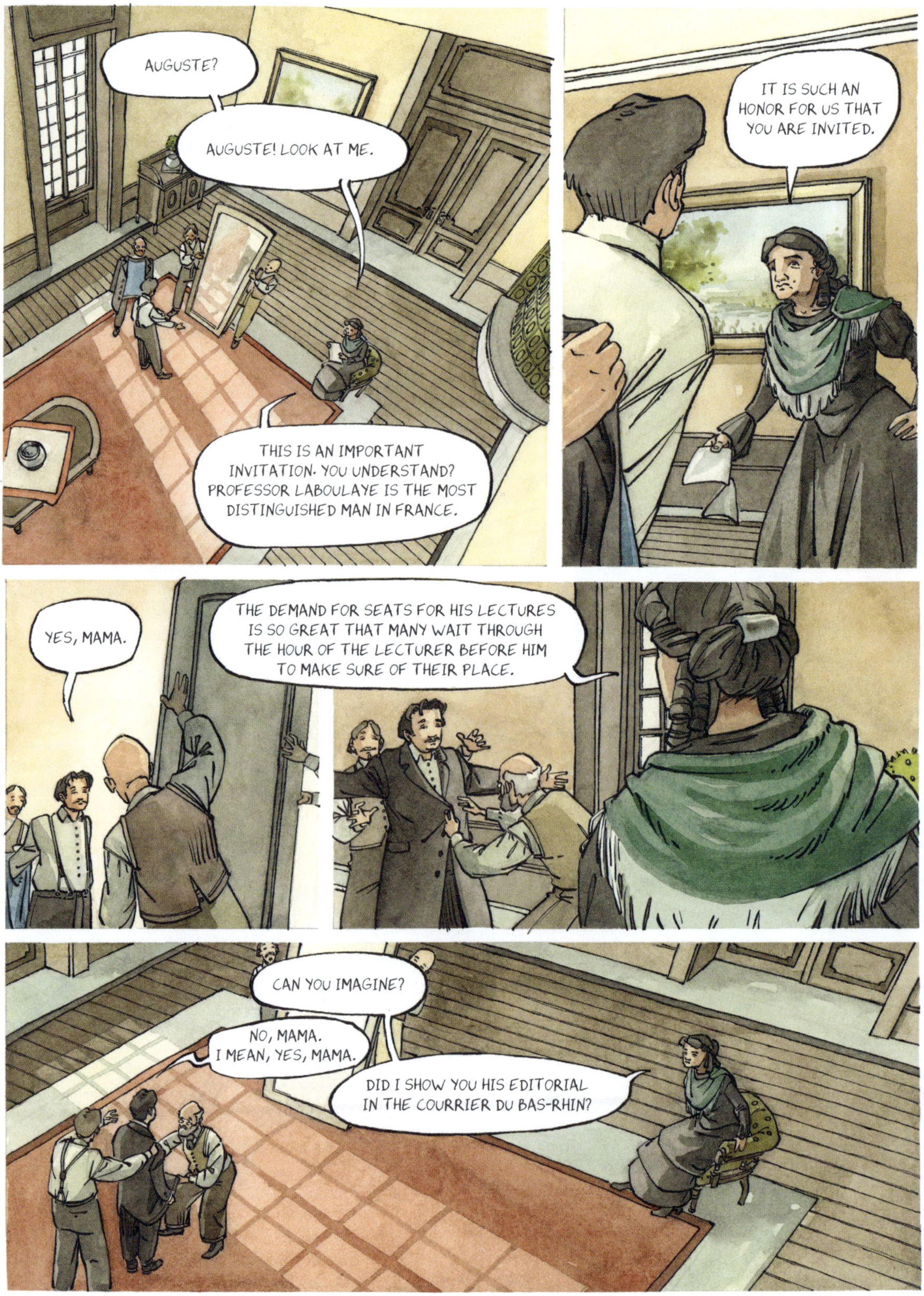
AUGUSTE?
AUGUSTE! LOOK AT ME.
THIS IS AN IMPORTANT INVITATION. YOU UNDERSTAND? PROFESSOR LABOULAYE IS THE MOST DISTINGUISHED MAN IN FRANCE.
IT IS SUCH AN HONOR FOR US THAT YOU ARE INVITED.
YES, MAMA.
THE DEMAND FOR SEATS FOR HIS LECTURES IS SO GREAT THAT MANY WAIT THROUGH THE HOUR OF THE LECTURER BEFORE HIM TO MAKE SURE OF THEIR PLACE.
CAN YOU IMAGINE?
NO, MAMA. I MEAN, YES, MAMA.
DID I SHOW YOU HIS EDITORIAL IN THE COURRIER DU BAS-RHIN?

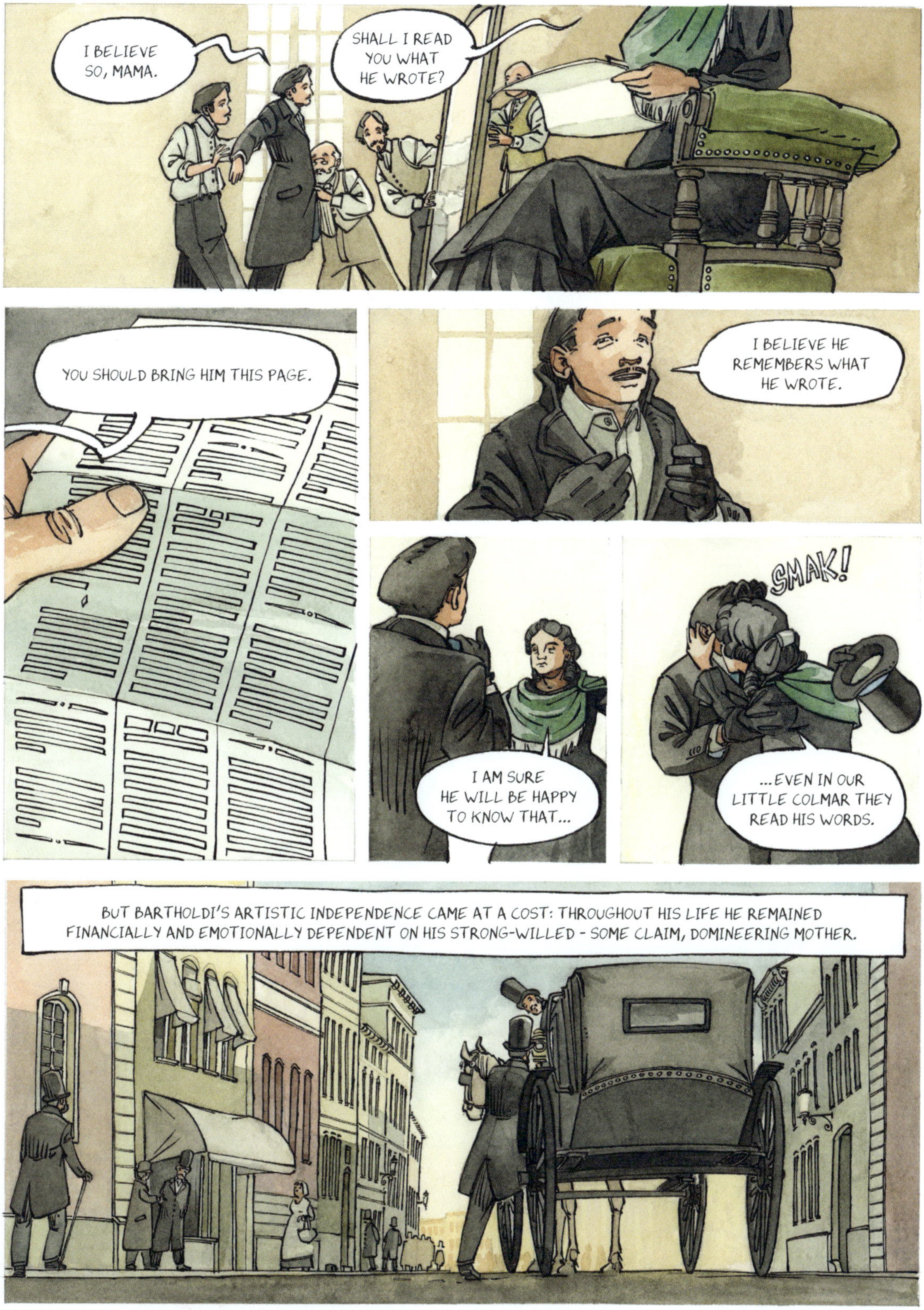
I BELIEVE SO, MAMA.
SHALL I READ YOU WHAT HE WROTE?
YOU SHOULD BRING HIM THIS PAGE.
I BELIEVE HE REMEMBERS WHAT HE WROTE.
I AM SURE HE WILL BE HAPPY TO KNOW THAT...
SMAK!
...EVEN IN OUR LITTLE COLMAR THEY READ HIS WORDS.
BUT BARTHOLDI'S ARTISTIC INDEPENDENCE CAME AT A COST: THROUGHOUT HIS LIFE HE REMAINED FINANCIALLY AND EMOTIONALLY DEPENDENT ON HIS STRONG-WILLED - SOME CLAIM, DOMINEERING MOTHER.

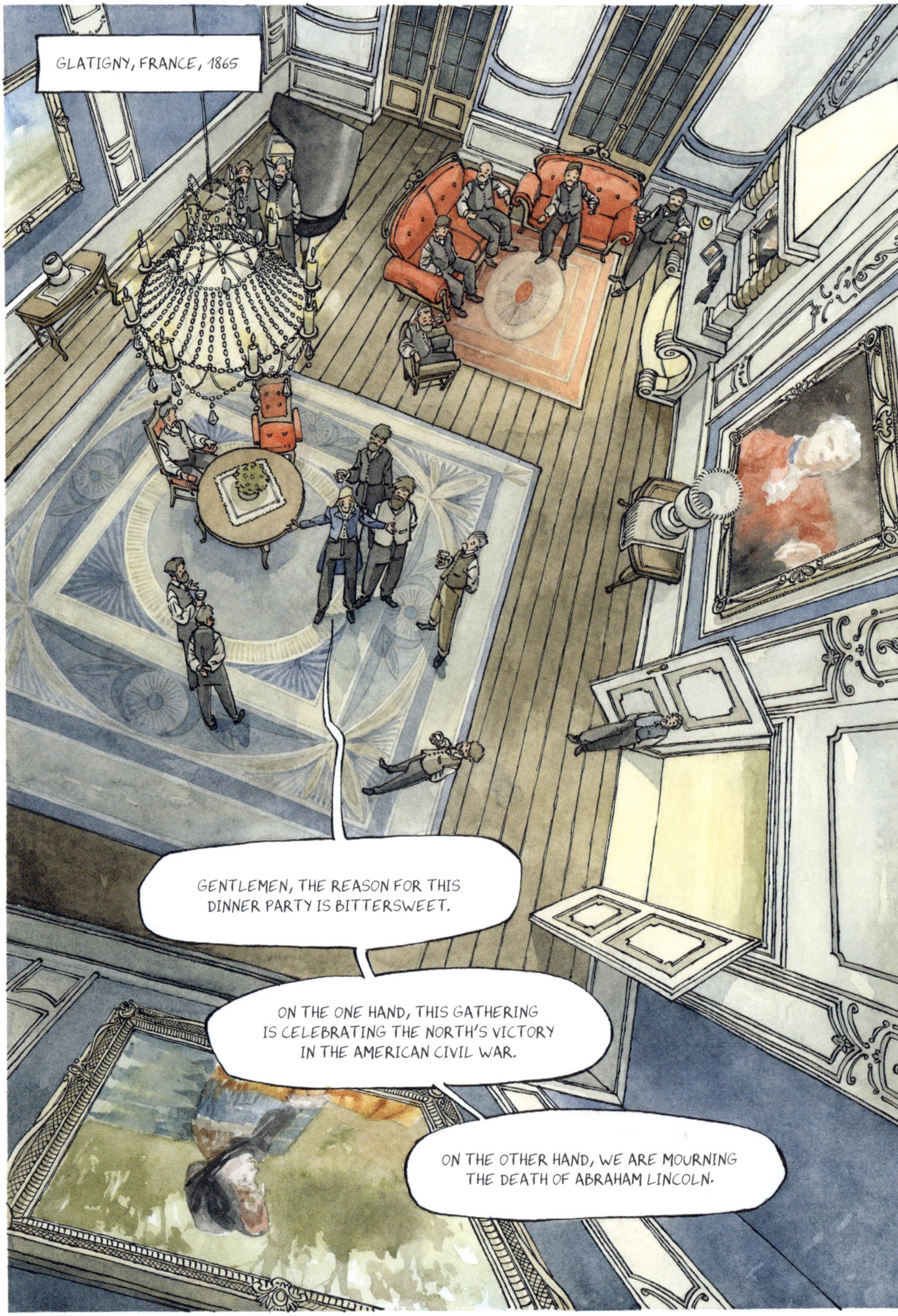
GLATIGNY, FRANCE, 1865
GENTLEMEN, THE REASON FOR THIS DINNER PARTY IS BITTERSWEET.
ON THE ONE HAND, THIS GATHERING IS CELEBRATING THE NORTH'S VICTORY IN THE AMERICAN CIVIL WAR.
ON THE OTHER HAND, WE ARE MOURNING THE DEATH OF ABRAHAM LINCOLN.

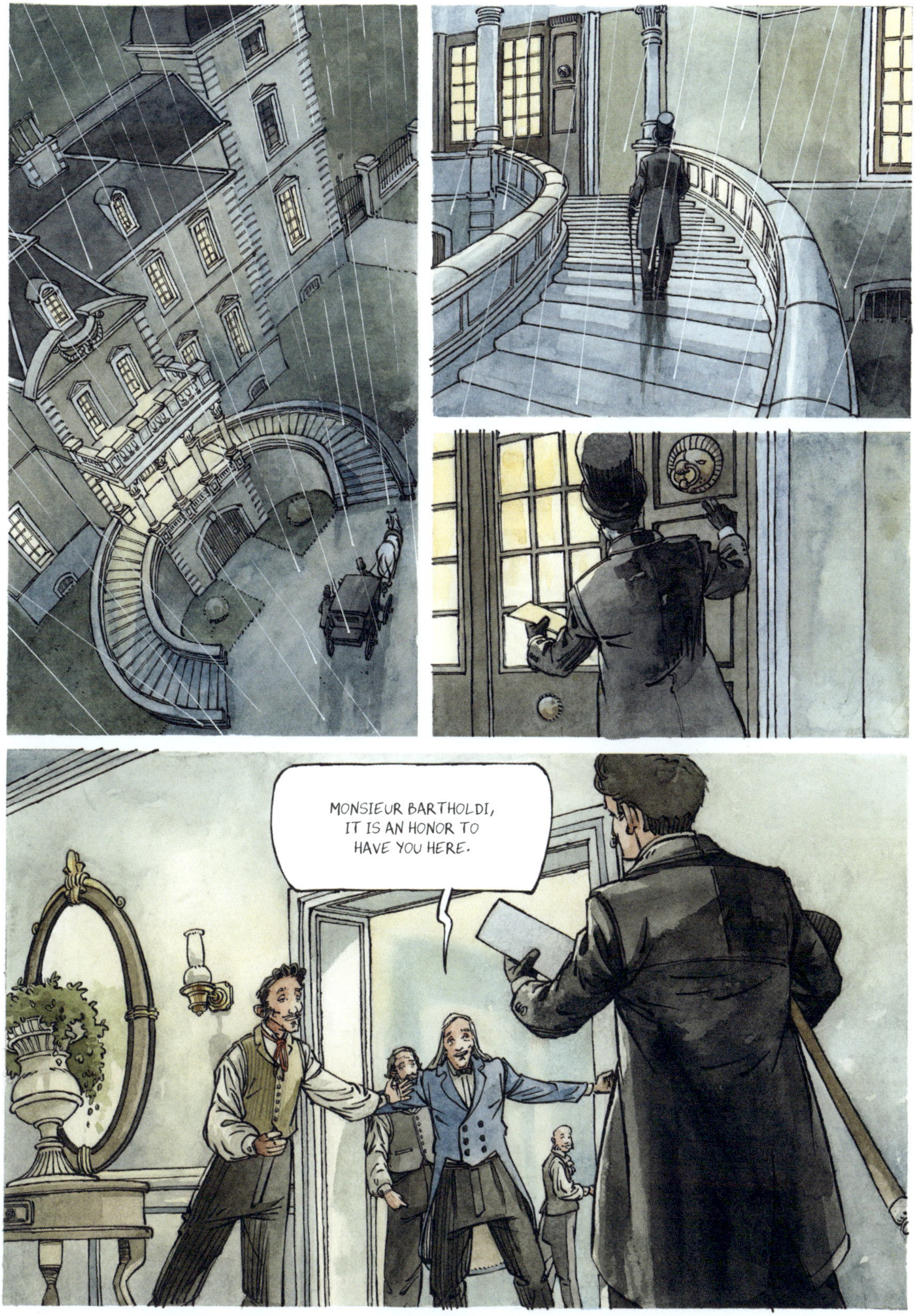
MONSIEUR BARTHOLDI, IT IS AN HONOR TO HAVE YOU HERE.

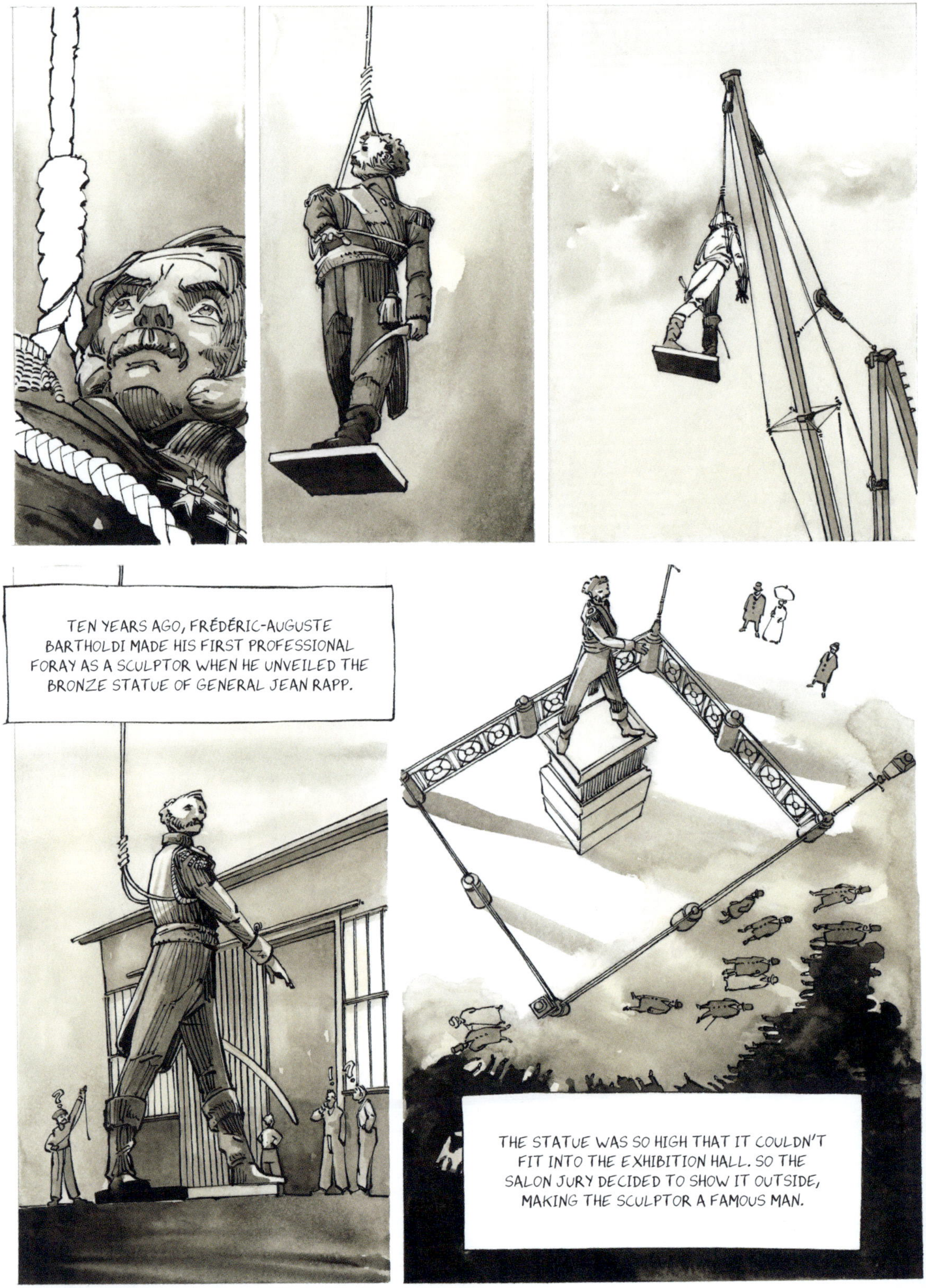
TEN YEARS AGO, FRÉDÉRIC-AUGUSTE BARTHOLDI MADE HIS FIRST PROFESSIONAL FORAY AS A SCULPTOR WHEN HE UNVEILED THE BRONZE STATUE OF GENERAL JEAN RAPP.
THE STATUE WAS SO HIGH THAT IT COULDN'T FIT INTO THE EXHIBITION HALL. SO THE SALON JURY DECIDED TO SHOW IT OUTSIDE, MAKING THE SCULPTOR A FAMOUS MAN.

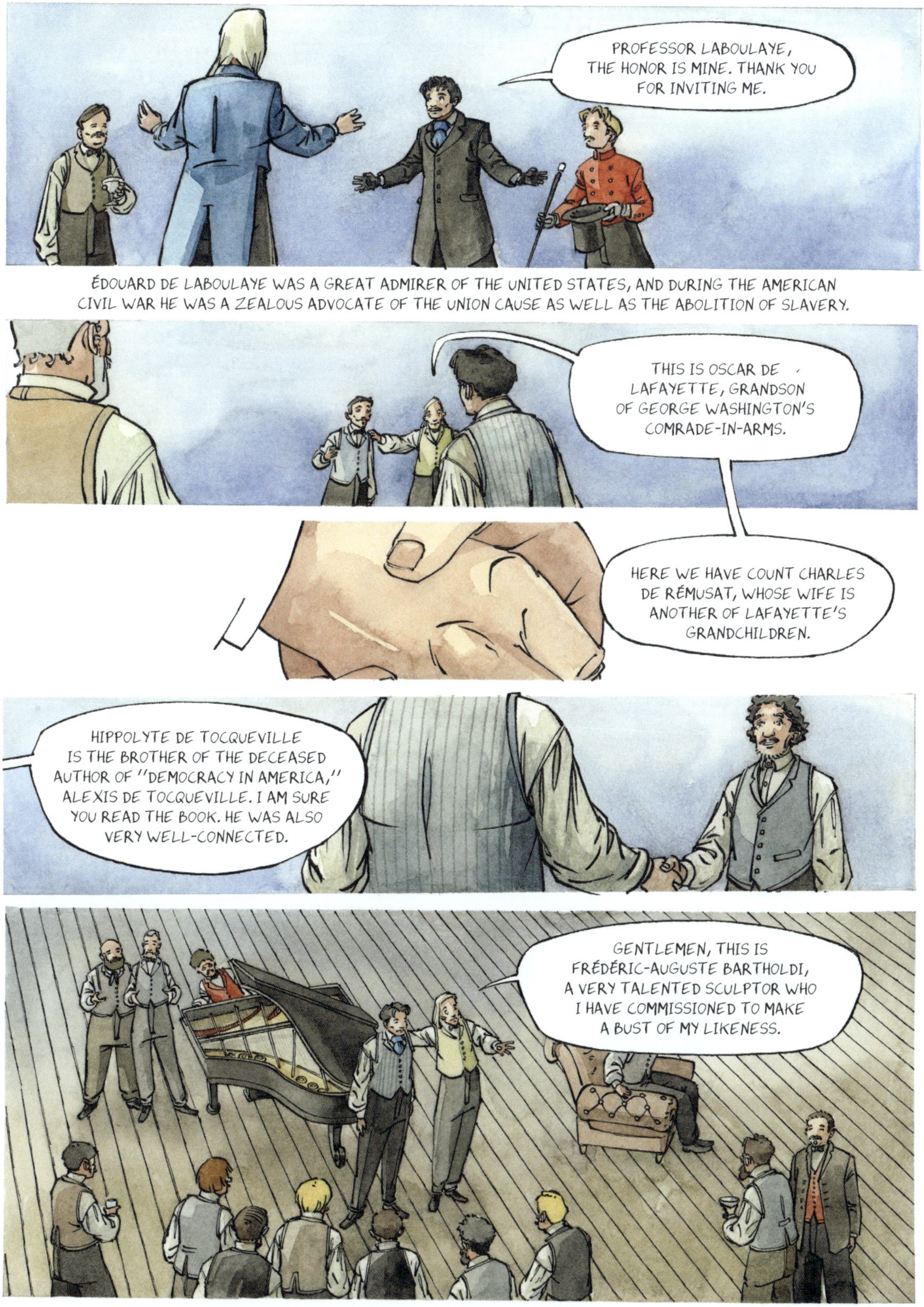
PROFESSOR LABOULAYE, THE HONOR IS MINE. THANK YOU FOR INVITING ME.
ÉDOUARD DE LABOULAYE WAS A GREAT ADMIRER OF THE UNITED STATES, AND DURING THE AMERICAN CIVIL WAR HE WAS A ZEALOUS ADVOCATE OF THE UNION CAUSE AS WELL AS THE ABOLITION OF SLAVERY.
THIS IS OSCAR DE LAFAYETTE, GRANDSON OF GEORGE WASHINGTON'S COMRADE-IN-ARMS.
HERE WE HAVE COUNT CHARLES DE RÉMUSAT, WHOSE WIFE IS ANOTHER OF LAFAYETTE'S GRANDCHILDREN.
HIPPOLYTE DE TOCQUEVILLE IS THE BROTHER OF THE DECEASED AUTHOR OF "DEMOCRACY IN AMERICA," ALEXIS DE TOCQUEVILLE. I AM SURE YOU READ THE BOOK. HE WAS ALSO VERY WELL-CONNECTED.
GENTLEMEN, THIS IS FRÉDÉRIC-AUGUSTE BARTHOLDI, A VERY TALENTED SCULPTOR WHO I HAVE COMMISSIONED TO MAKE A BUST OF MY LIKENESS.

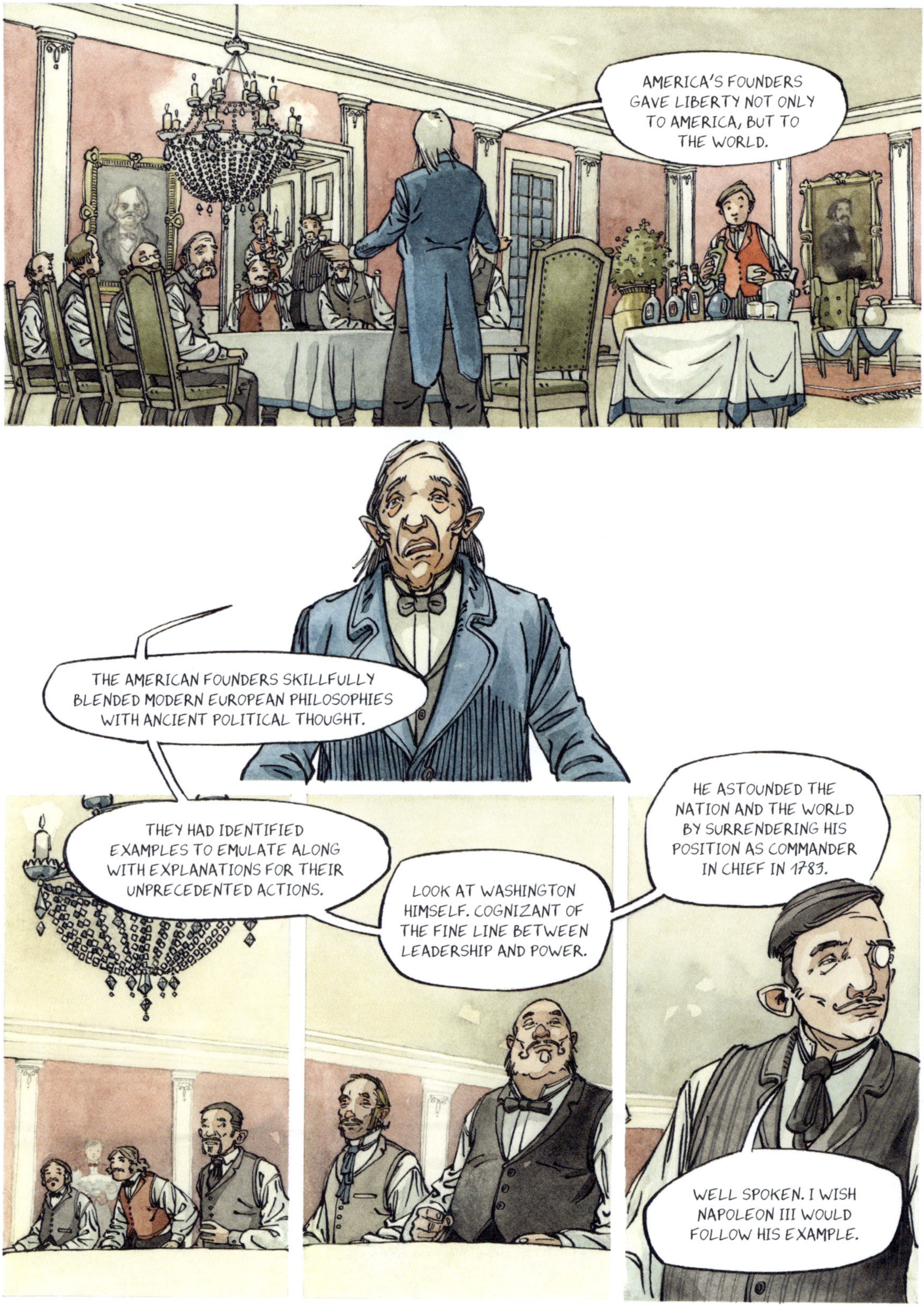
AMERICA'S FOUNDERS GAVE LIBERTY NOT ONLY TO AMERICA, BUT TO THE WORLD.
THE AMERICAN FOUNDERS SKILLFULLY BLENDED MODERN EUROPEAN PHILOSOPHIES WITH ANCIENT POLITICAL THOUGHT.
THEY HAD IDENTIFIED EXAMPLES TO EMULATE ALONG WITH EXPLANATIONS FOR THEIR UNPRECEDENTED ACTIONS.
LOOK AT WASHINGTON HIMSELF. COGNIZANT OF THE FINE LINE BETWEEN LEADERSHIP AND POWER.
HE ASTOUNDED THE NATION AND THE WORLD BY SURRENDERING HIS POSITION AS COMMANDER IN CHIEF IN 1783.
WELL SPOKEN. I WISH NAPOLEON III WOULD FOLLOW HIS EXAMPLE.

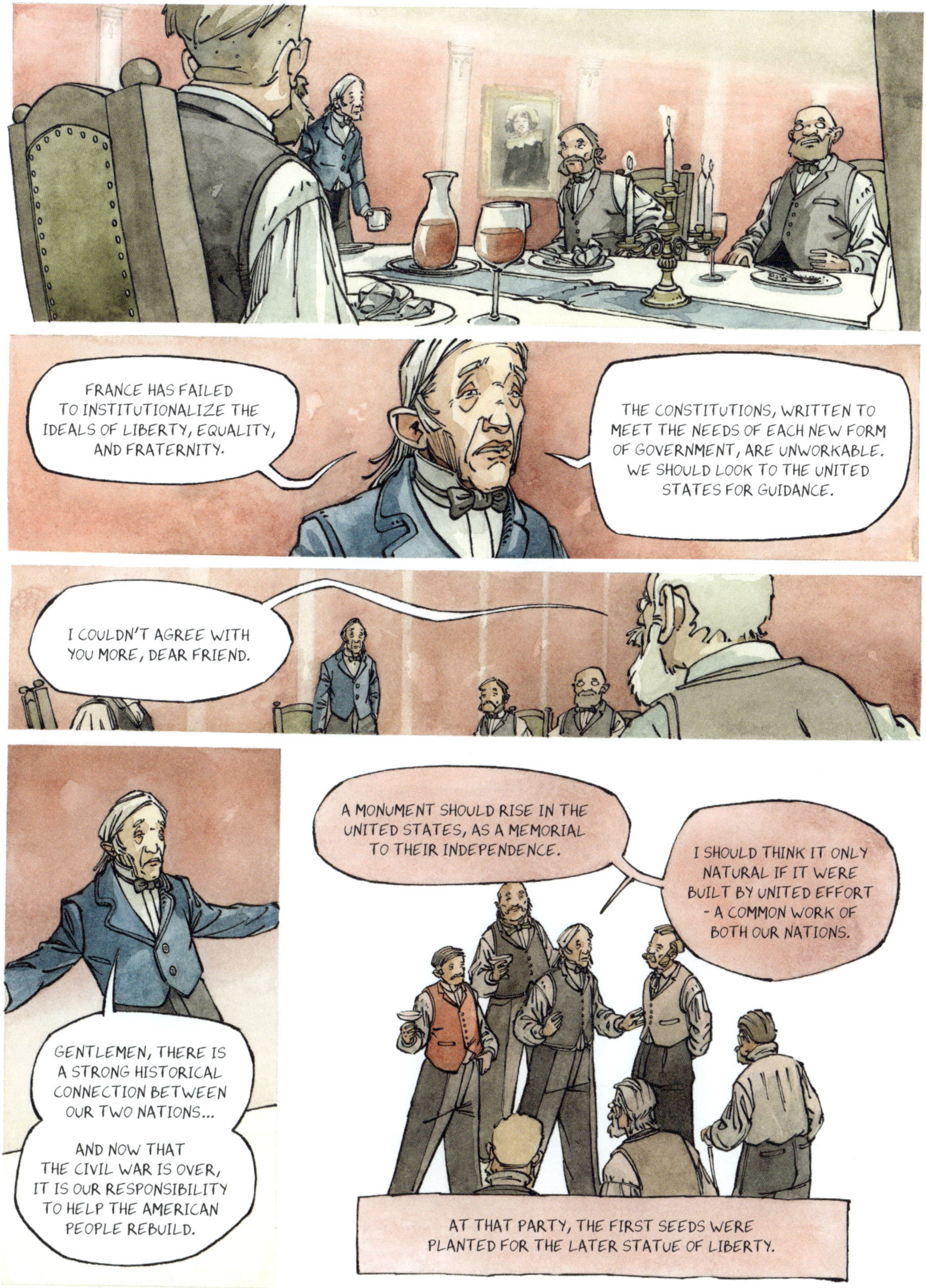
FRANCE HAS FAILED TO INSTITUTIONALIZE THE IDEALS OF LIBERTY, EQUALITY, AND FRATERNITY.
THE CONSTITUTIONS, WRITTEN TO MEET THE NEEDS OF EACH NEW FORM OF GOVERNMENT, ARE UNWORKABLE. WE SHOULD LOOK TO THE UNITED STATES FOR GUIDANCE.
I COULDN'T AGREE WITH YOU MORE, DEAR FRIEND.
GENTLEMEN, THERE IS A STRONG HISTORICAL CONNECTION BETWEEN OUR TWO NATIONS...
AND NOW THAT THE CIVIL WAR IS OVER, IT IS OUR RESPONSIBILITY TO HELP THE AMERICAN PEOPLE REBUILD.
A MONUMENT SHOULD RISE IN THE UNITED STATES, AS A MEMORIAL TO THEIR INDEPENDENCE.
I SHOULD THINK IT ONLY NATURAL IF IT WERE BUILT BY UNITED EFFORT - A COMMON WORK OF BOTH OUR NATIONS.
AT THAT PARTY, THE FIRST SEEDS WERE PLANTED FOR THE LATER STATUE OF LIBERTY.

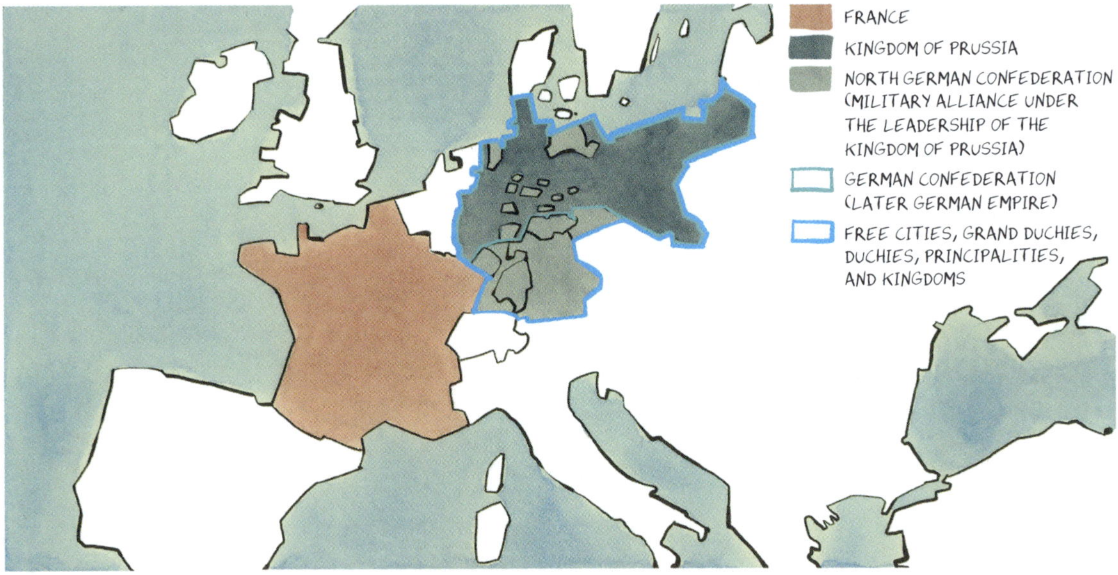
FRANCE
KINGDOM OF PRUSSIA
NORTH GERMAN CONFEDERATION (MILITARY ALLIANCE UNDER THE LEADERSHIP OF THE KINGDOM OF PRUSSIA)
GERMAN CONFEDERATION (LATER GERMAN EMPIRE)
FREE CITIES, GRAND DUCHIES, DUCHIES, PRINCIPALITIES, AND KINGDOMS

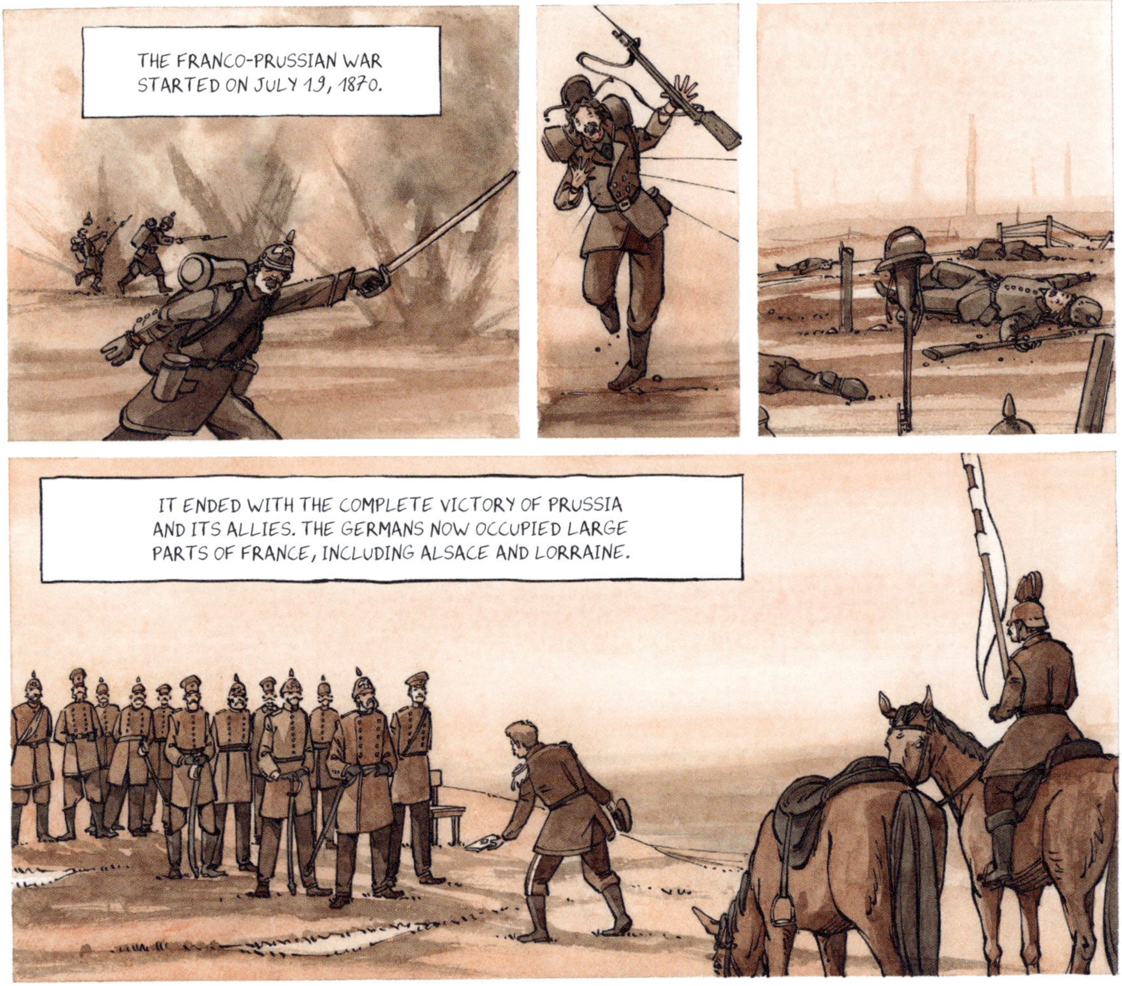
THE FRANCO-PRUSSIAN WAR STARTED ON JULY 19, 1870.
IT ENDED WITH THE COMPLETE VICTORY OF PRUSSIA AND ITS ALLIES. THE GERMANS NOW OCCUPIED LARGE PARTS OF FRANCE, INCLUDING ALSACE AND LORRAINE.

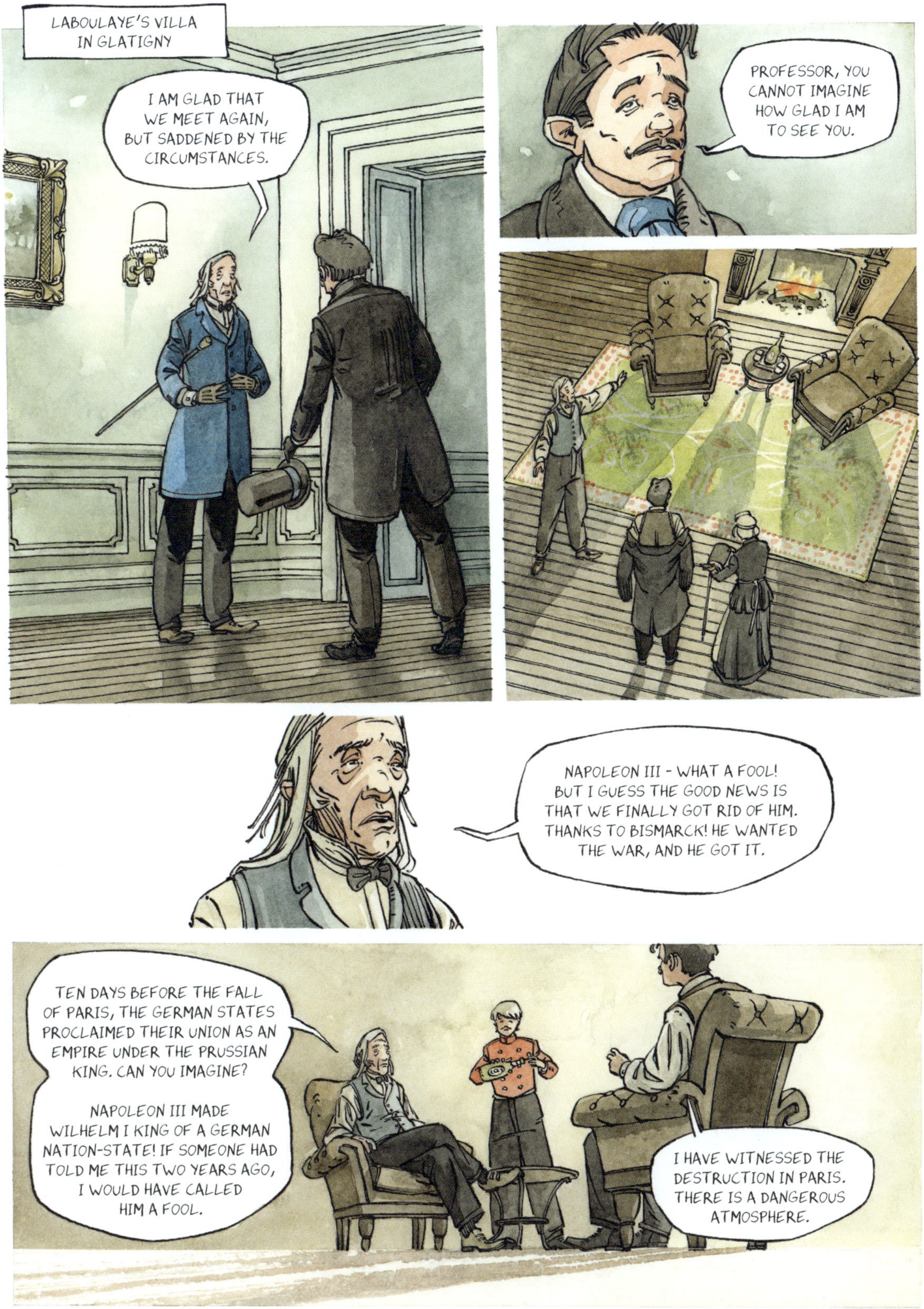
LABOULAYE'S VILLA IN GLATIGNY
I AM GLAD THAT WE MEET AGAIN, BUT SADDENED BY THE CIRCUMSTANCES.
PROFESSOR, YOU CANNOT IMAGINE HOW GLAD I AM TO SEE YOU.
NAPOLEON III - WHAT A FOOL! BUT I GUESS THE GOOD NEWS IS THAT WE FINALLY GOT RID OF HIM. THANKS TO BISMARCK! HE WANTED THE WAR, AND HE GOT IT.
TEN DAYS BEFORE THE FALL OF PARIS, THE GERMAN STATES PROCLAIMED THEIR UNION AS AN EMPIRE UNDER THE PRUSSIAN KING. CAN YOU IMAGINE?
NAPOLEON III MADE WILHELM I KING OF A GERMAN NATION-STATE! IF SOMEONE HAD TOLD ME THIS TWO YEARS AGO, I WOULD HAVE CALLED HIM A FOOL.
I HAVE WITNESSED THE DESTRUCTION IN PARIS. THERE IS A DANGEROUS ATMOSPHERE.

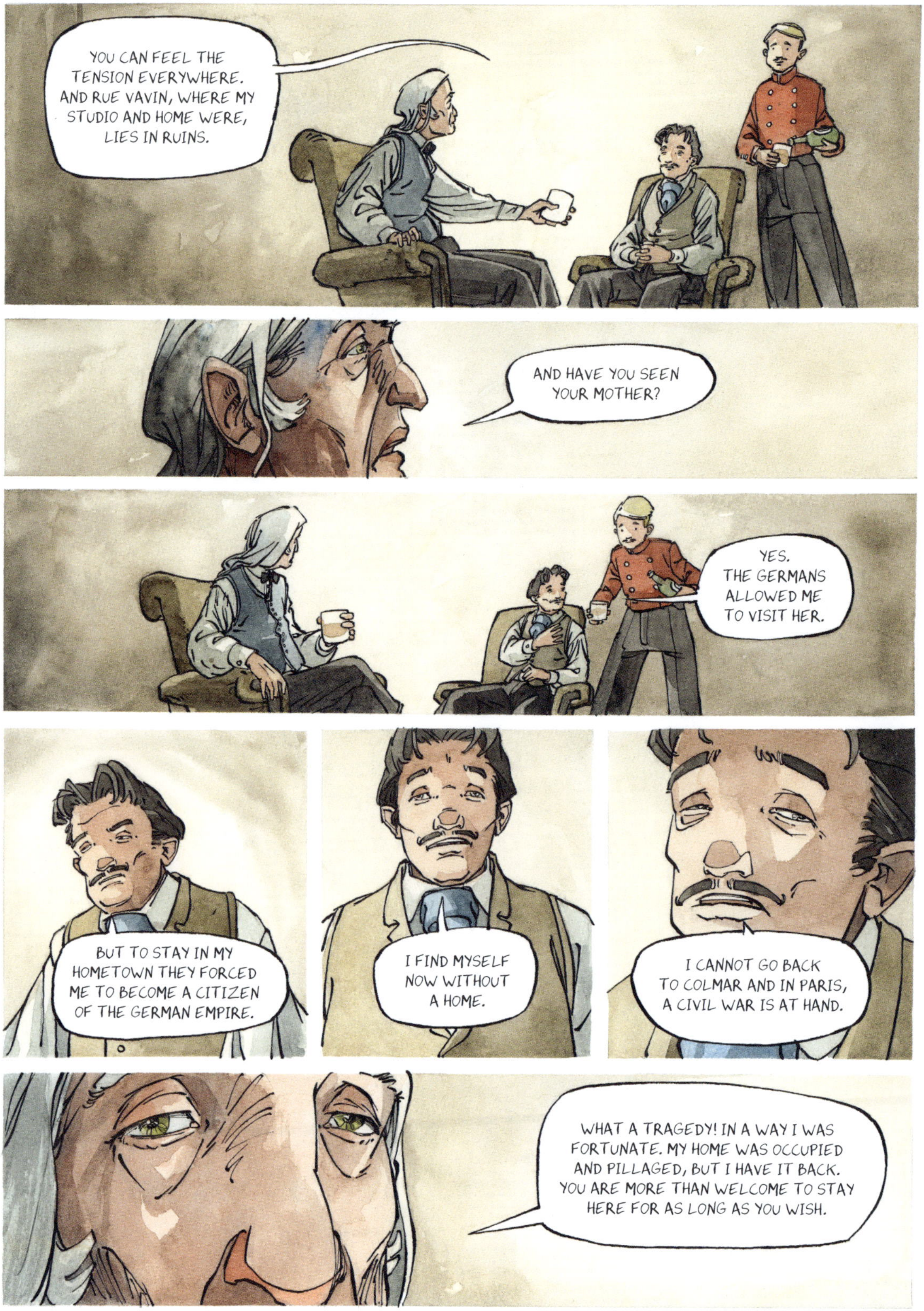

YOU CAN FEEL THE TENSION EVERYWHERE. AND RUE VAVIN, WHERE MY STUDIO AND HOME WERE, LIES IN RUINS.
AND HAVE YOU SEEN YOUR MOTHER?
YES. THE GERMANS ALLOWED ME TO VISIT HER.
BUT TO STAY IN MY HOMETOWN THEY FORCED ME TO BECOME A CITIZEN OF THE GERMAN EMPIRE.
I FIND MYSELF NOW WITHOUT A HOME.
I CANNOT GO BACK TO COLMAR AND IN PARIS, A CIVIL WAR IS AT HAND.
WHAT A TRAGEDY! IN A WAY I WAS FORTUNATE. MY HOME WAS OCCUPIED AND PILLAGED, BUT I HAVE IT BACK. YOU ARE MORE THAN WELCOME TO STAY HERE FOR AS LONG AS YOU WISH.

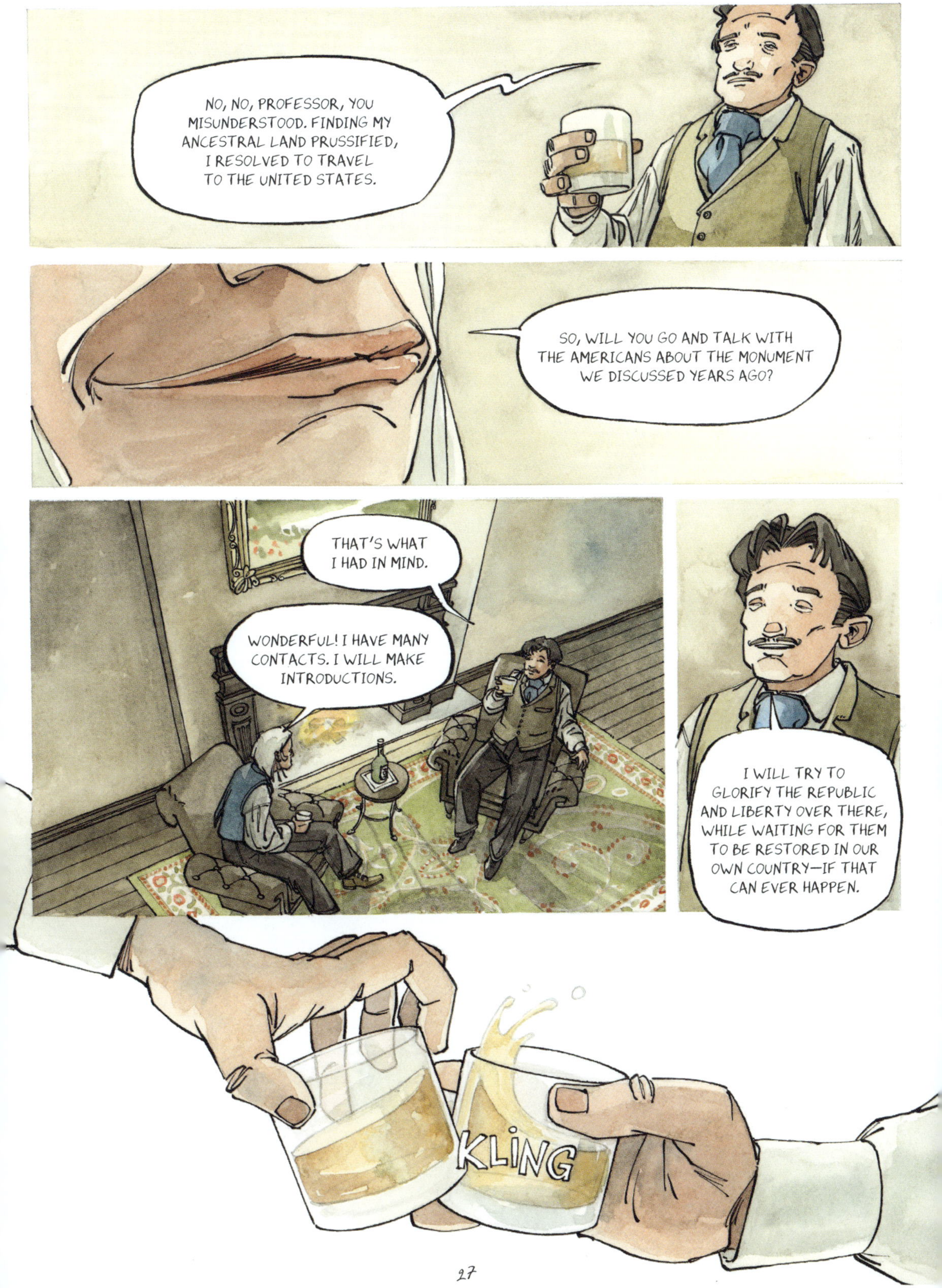
NO, NO, PROFESSOR, YOU MISUNDERSTOOD. FINDING MY ANCESTRAL LAND PRUSSIFIED, I RESOLVED TO TRAVEL TO THE UNITED STATES.
SO, WILL YOU GO AND TALK WITH THE AMERICANS ABOUT THE MONUMENT WE DISCUSSED YEARS AGO?
THAT'S WHAT I HAD IN MIND.
WONDERFUL! I HAVE MANY CONTACTS. I WILL MAKE INTRODUCTIONS.
I WILL TRY TO GLORIFY THE REPUBLIC AND LIBERTY OVER THERE, WHILE WAITING FOR THEM TO BE RESTORED IN OUR OWN COUNTRY—IF THAT CAN EVER HAPPEN.
KLING

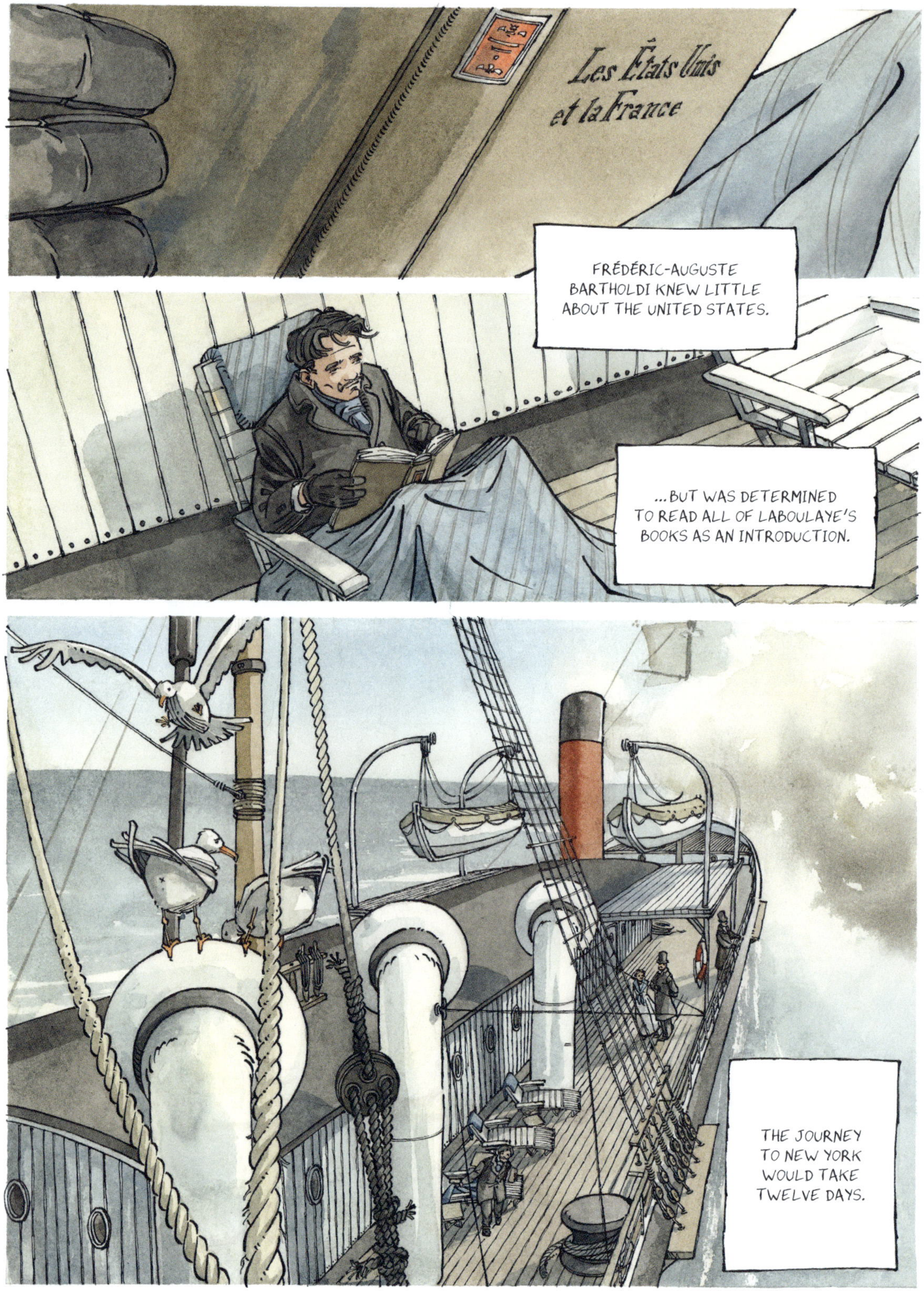

Les États Unis et la France
FRÉDÉRIC-AUGUSTE BARTHOLDI KNEW LITTLE ABOUT THE UNITED STATES.
...BUT WAS DETERMINED TO READ ALL OF LABOULAYE'S BOOKS AS AN INTRODUCTION.
THE JOURNEY TO NEW YORK WOULD TAKE TWELVE DAYS.

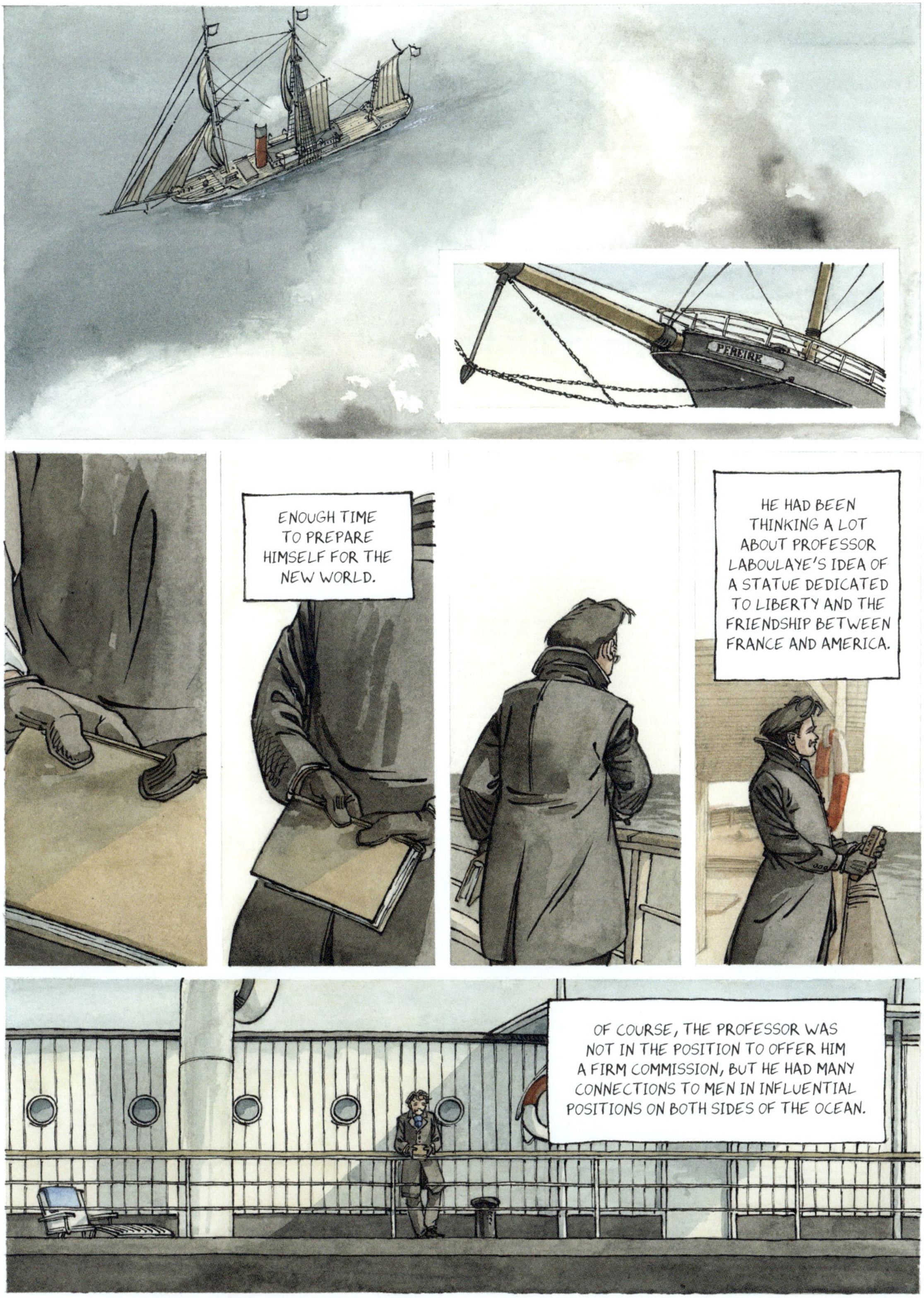

PEREIRE
ENOUGH TIME TO PREPARE HIMSELF FOR THE NEW WORLD.
HE HAD BEEN THINKING A LOT ABOUT PROFESSOR LABOULAYE'S IDEA OF A STATUE DEDICATED TO LIBERTY AND THE FRIENDSHIP BETWEEN FRANCE AND AMERICA.
OF COURSE, THE PROFESSOR WAS NOT IN THE POSITION TO OFFER HIM A FIRM COMMISSION, BUT HE HAD MANY CONNECTIONS TO MEN IN INFLUENTIAL POSITIONS ON BOTH SIDES OF THE OCEAN.

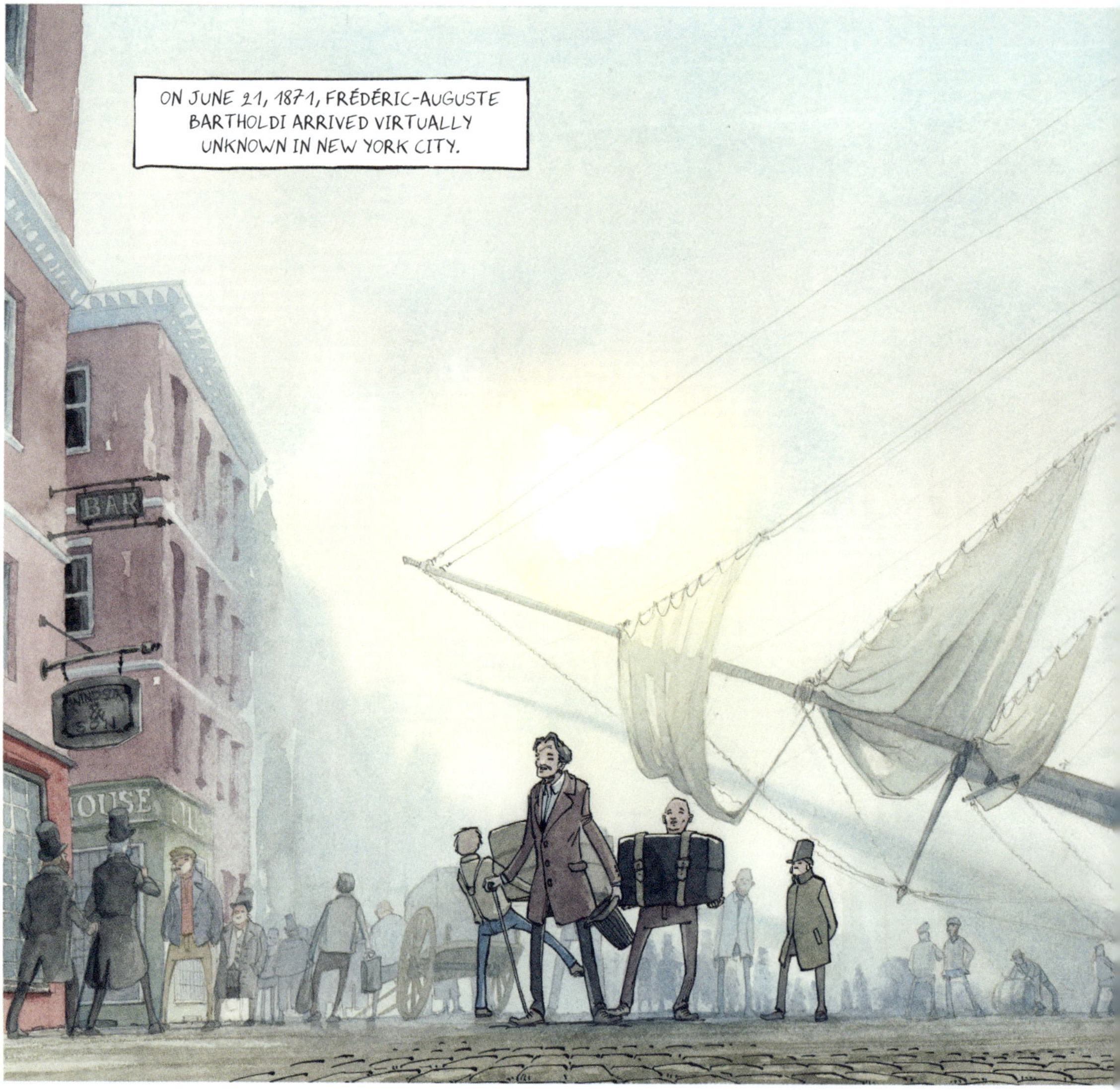
ON JUNE 21, 1871, FRÉDÉRIC-AUGUSTE BARTHOLDI ARRIVED VIRTUALLY UNKNOWN IN NEW YORK CITY.
BAR
OUSE

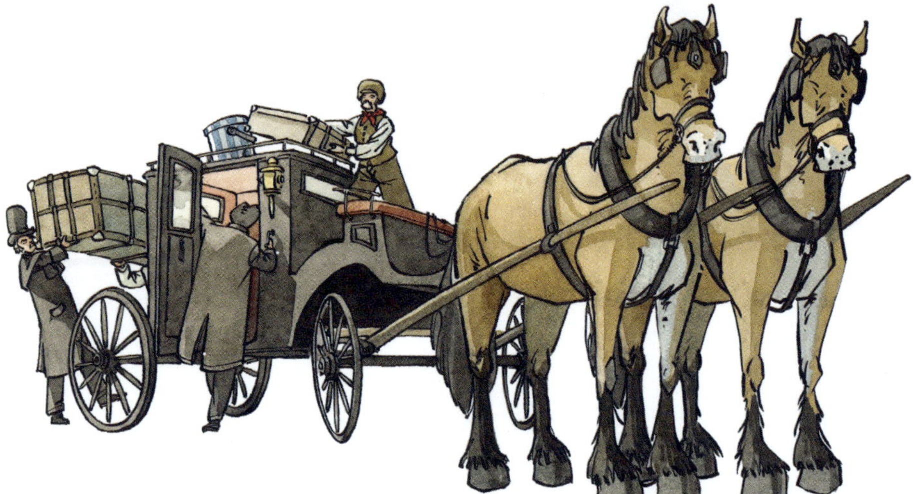

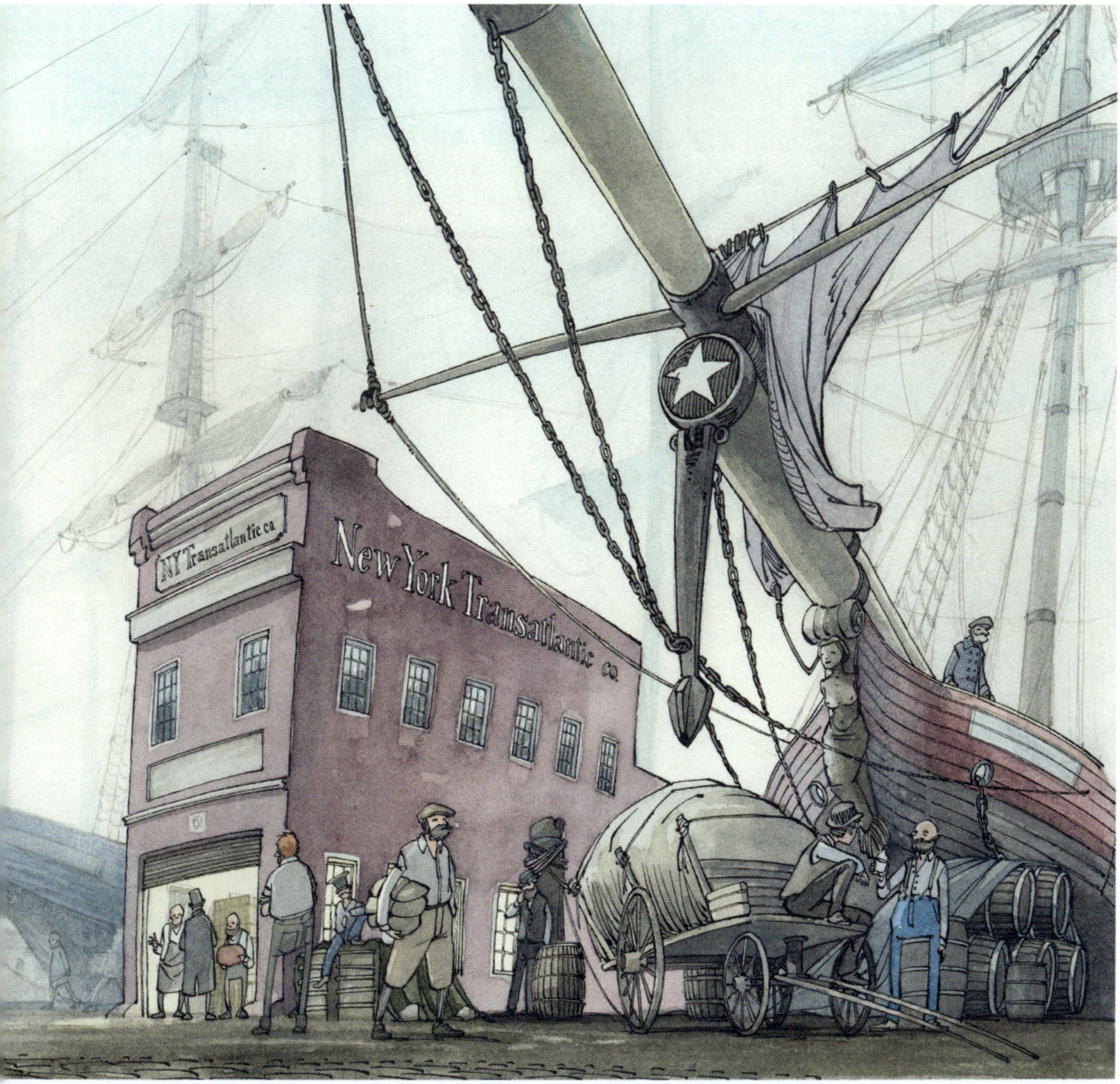
NY Transatlantic co
New York Transatlantic co.

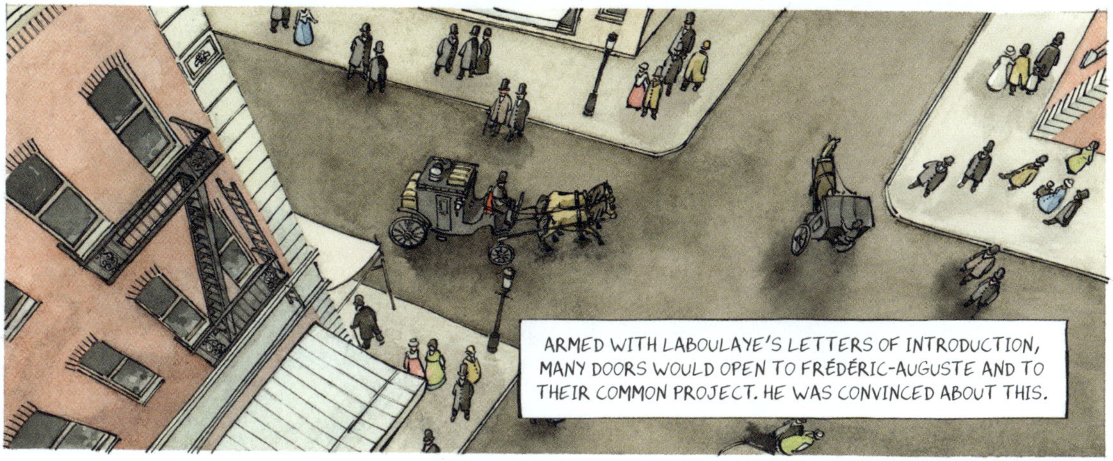
ARMED WITH LABOULAYE'S LETTERS OF INTRODUCTION, MANY DOORS WOULD OPEN TO FRÉDÉRIC-AUGUSTE AND TO THEIR COMMON PROJECT. HE WAS CONVINCED ABOUT THIS.

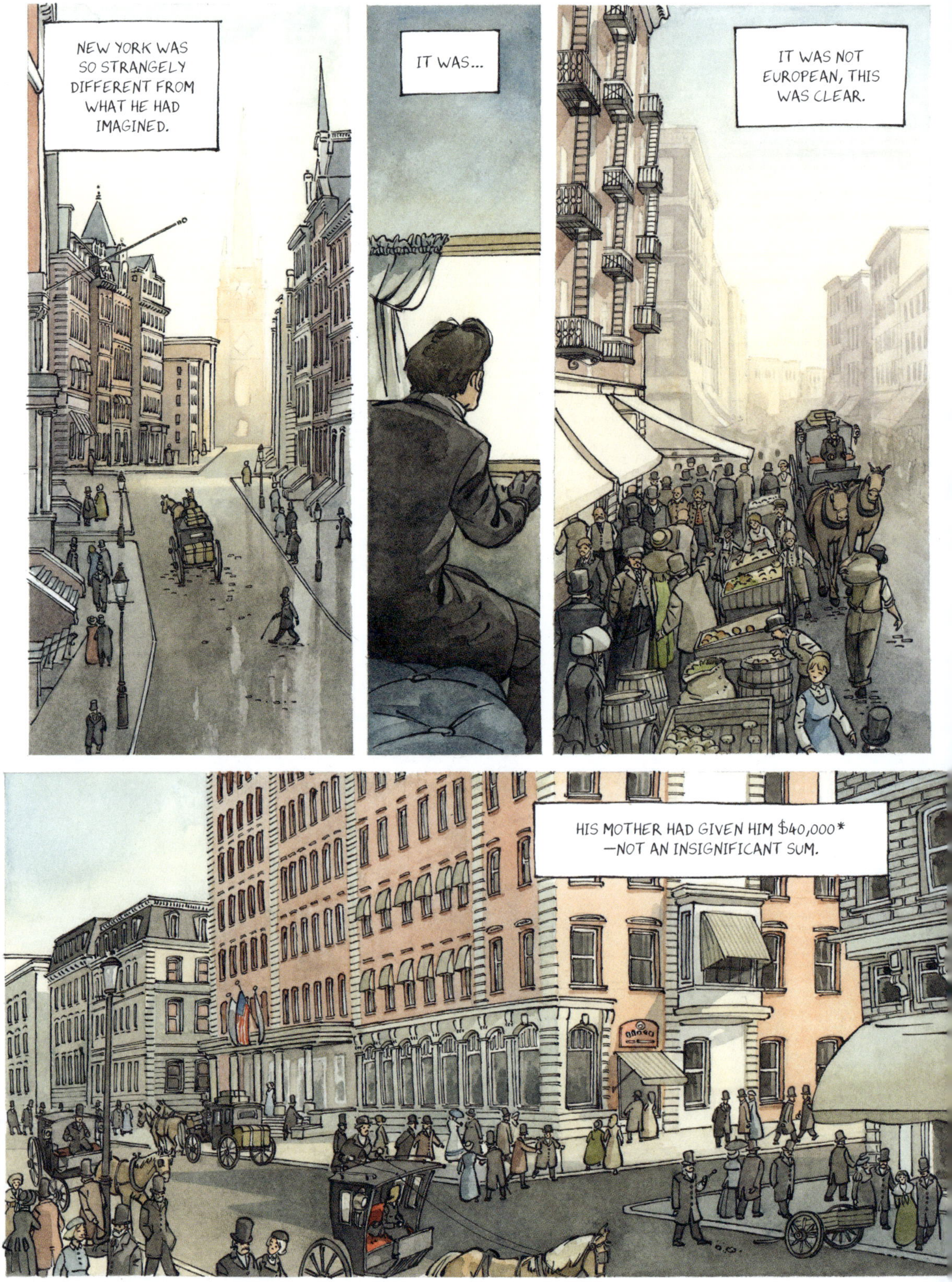
NEW YORK WAS SO STRANGELY DIFFERENT FROM WHAT HE HAD IMAGINED.
IT WAS...
IT WAS NOT EUROPEAN, THIS WAS CLEAR.
HIS MOTHER HAD GIVEN HIM $40,000* —NOT AN INSIGNIFICANT SUM.

*A MIDDLE-CLASS OFFICE WORKER EARNED ABOUT $2,000 PER YEAR.

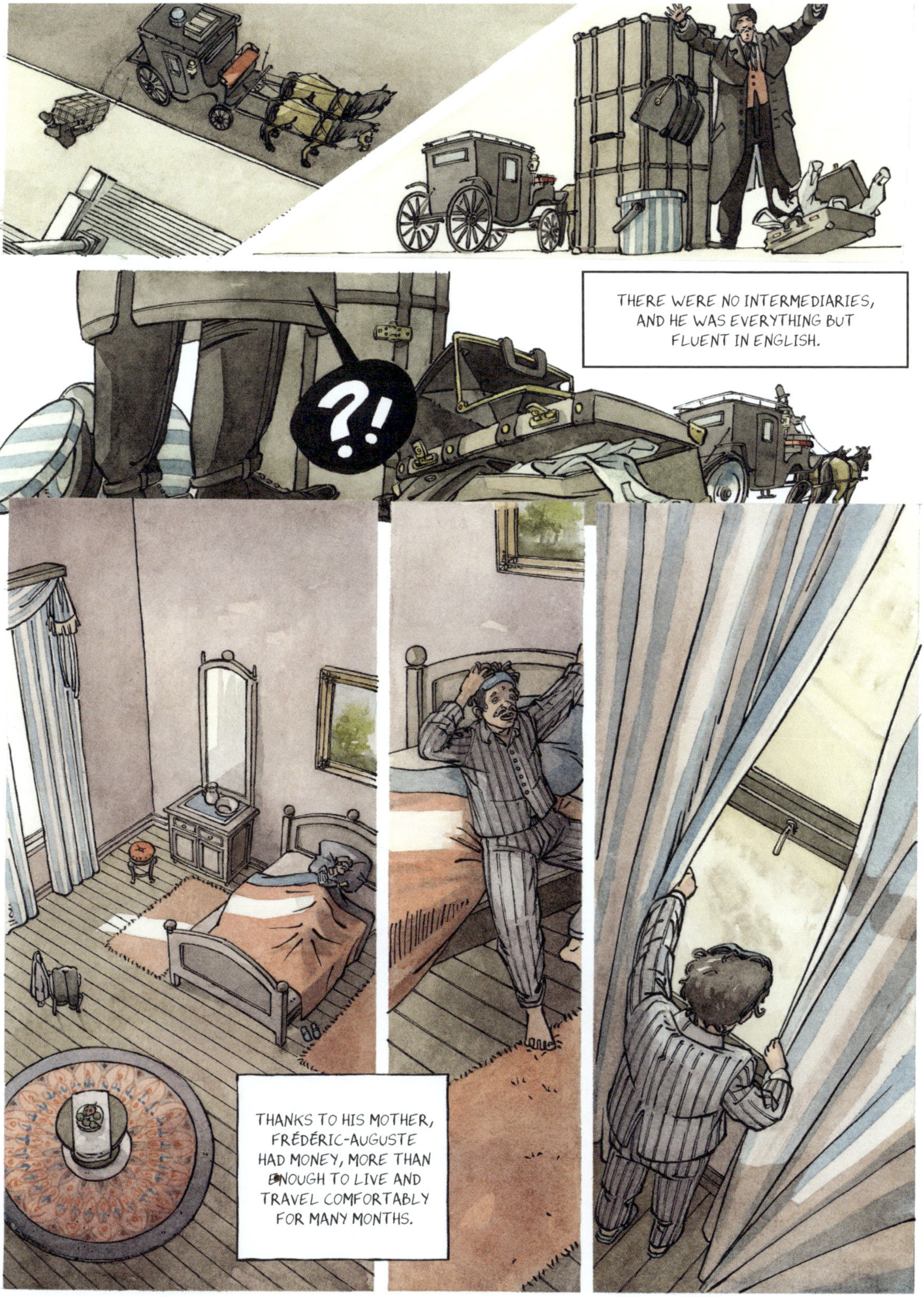
THERE WERE NO INTERMEDIARIES, AND HE WAS EVERYTHING BUT FLUENT IN ENGLISH.
?!
THANKS TO HIS MOTHER, FRÉDÉRIC-AUGUSTE HAD MONEY, MORE THAN ENOUGH TO LIVE AND TRAVEL COMFORTABLY FOR MANY MONTHS.

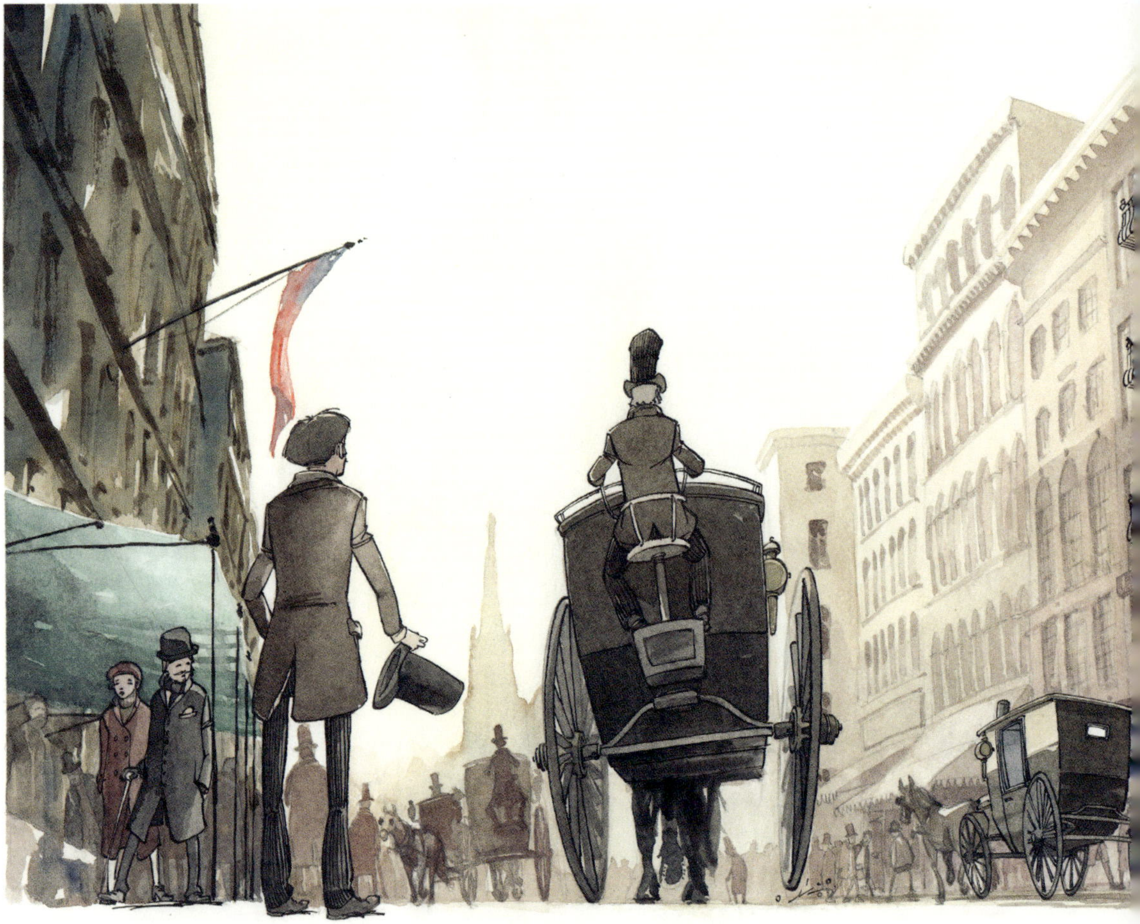

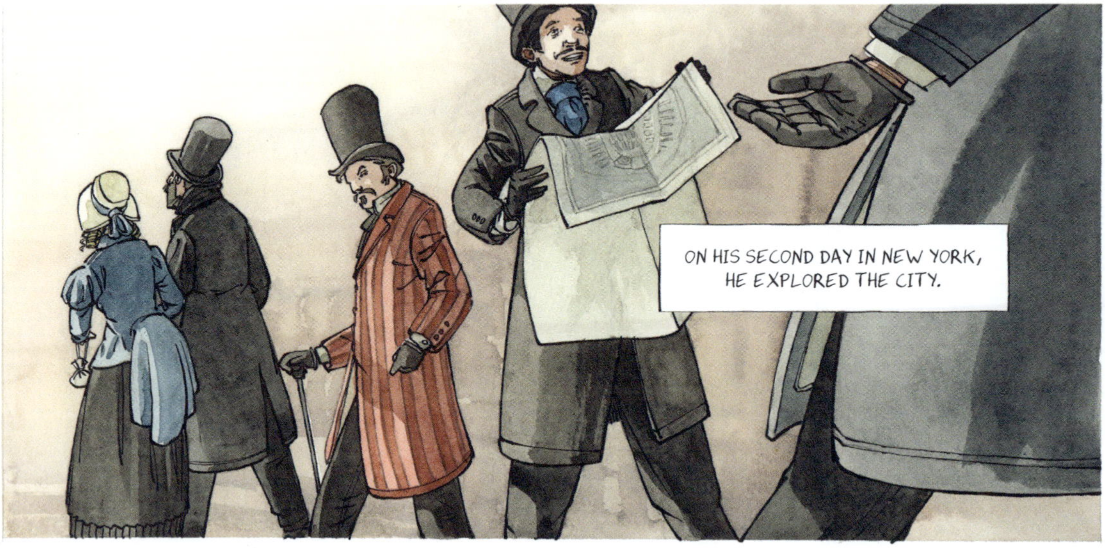
ON HIS SECOND DAY IN NEW YORK, HE EXPLORED THE CITY.

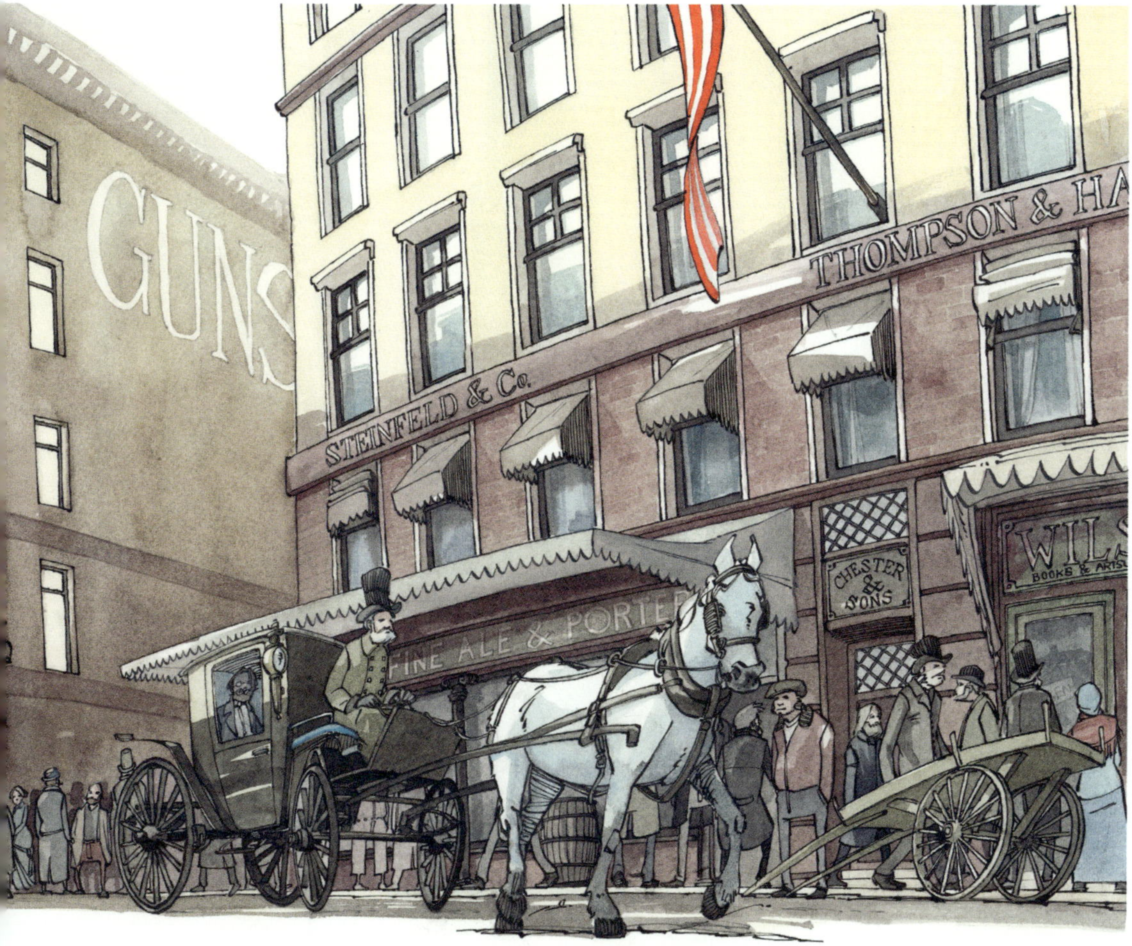
GUNS
THOMPSON & HA
STEINFELD & Co.
FINE ALE & PORTER
CHESTER & SONS
WILS
BOOKS & ARTS

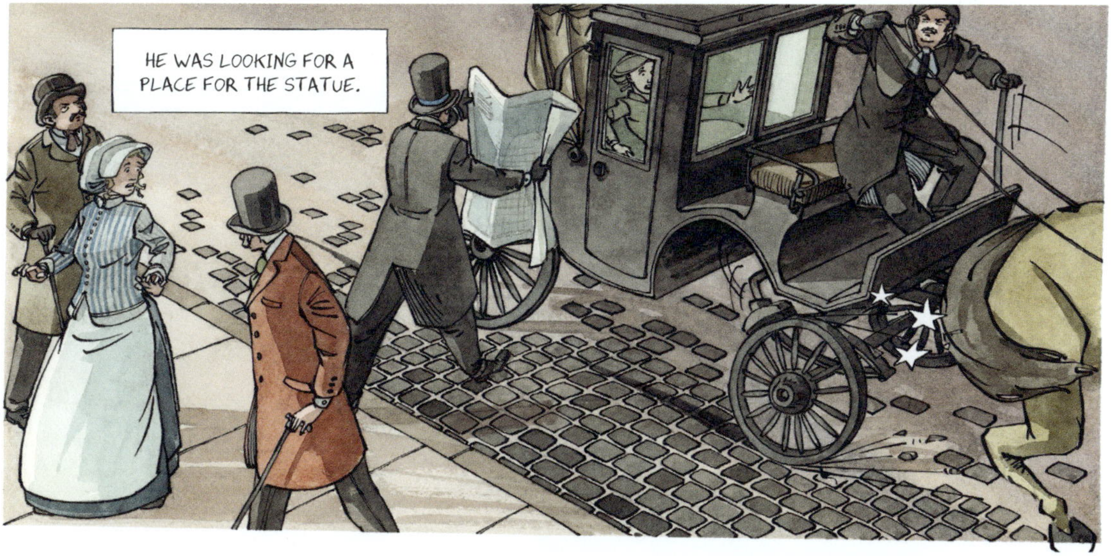
HE WAS LOOKING FOR A PLACE FOR THE STATUE.

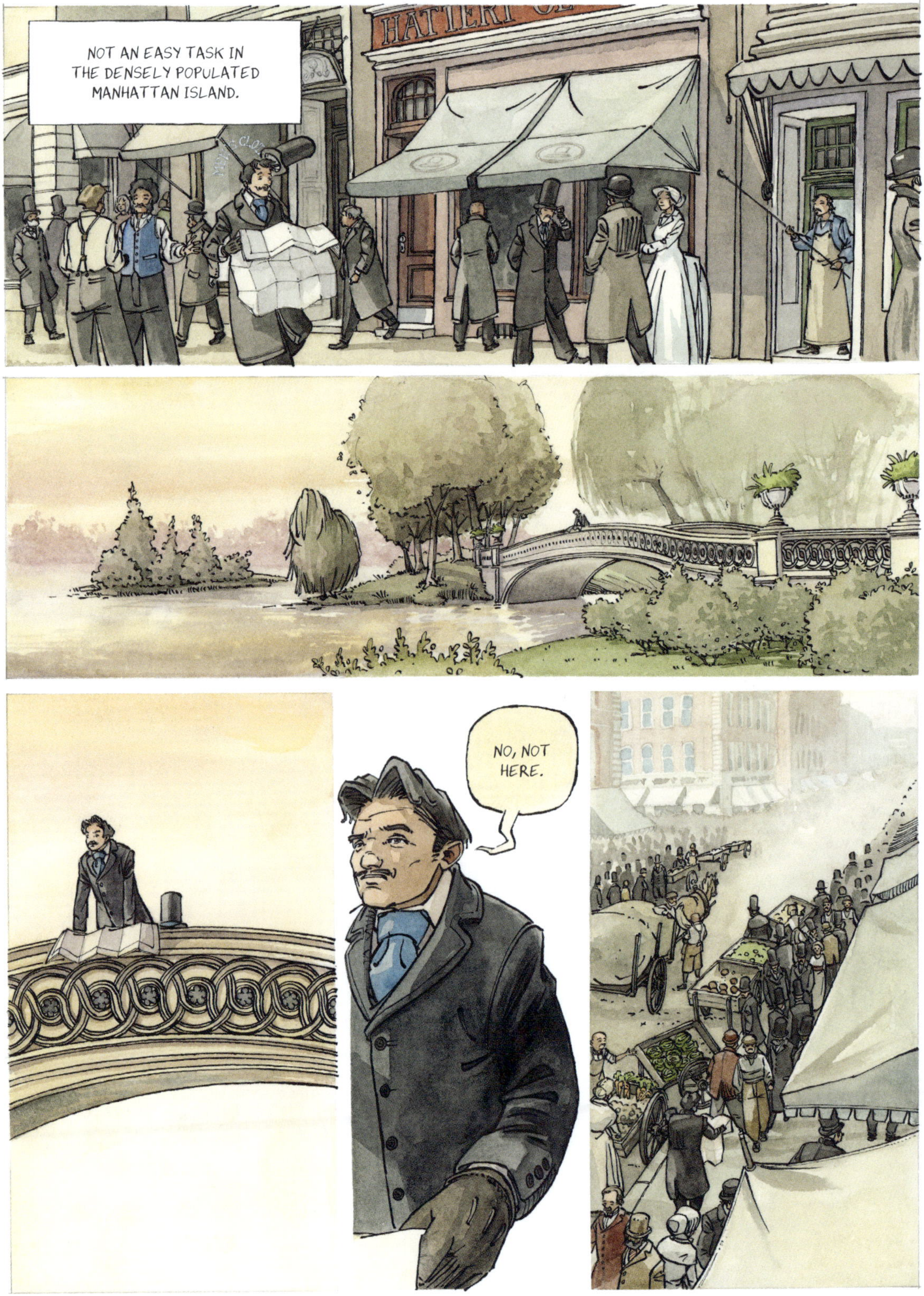
NOT AN EASY TASK IN THE DENSELY POPULATED MANHATTAN ISLAND.
NO, NOT HERE.

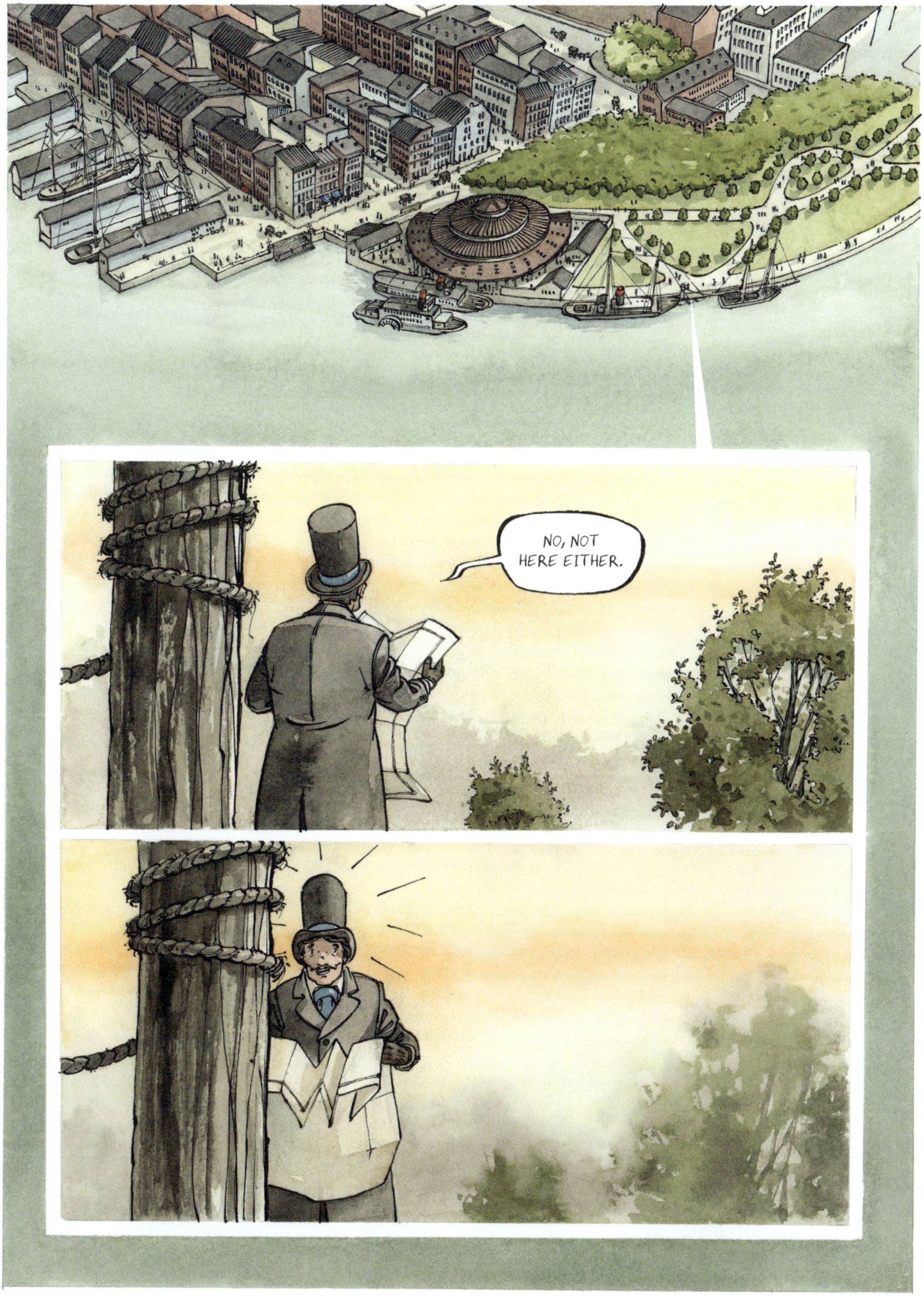
NO, NOT HERE EITHER.

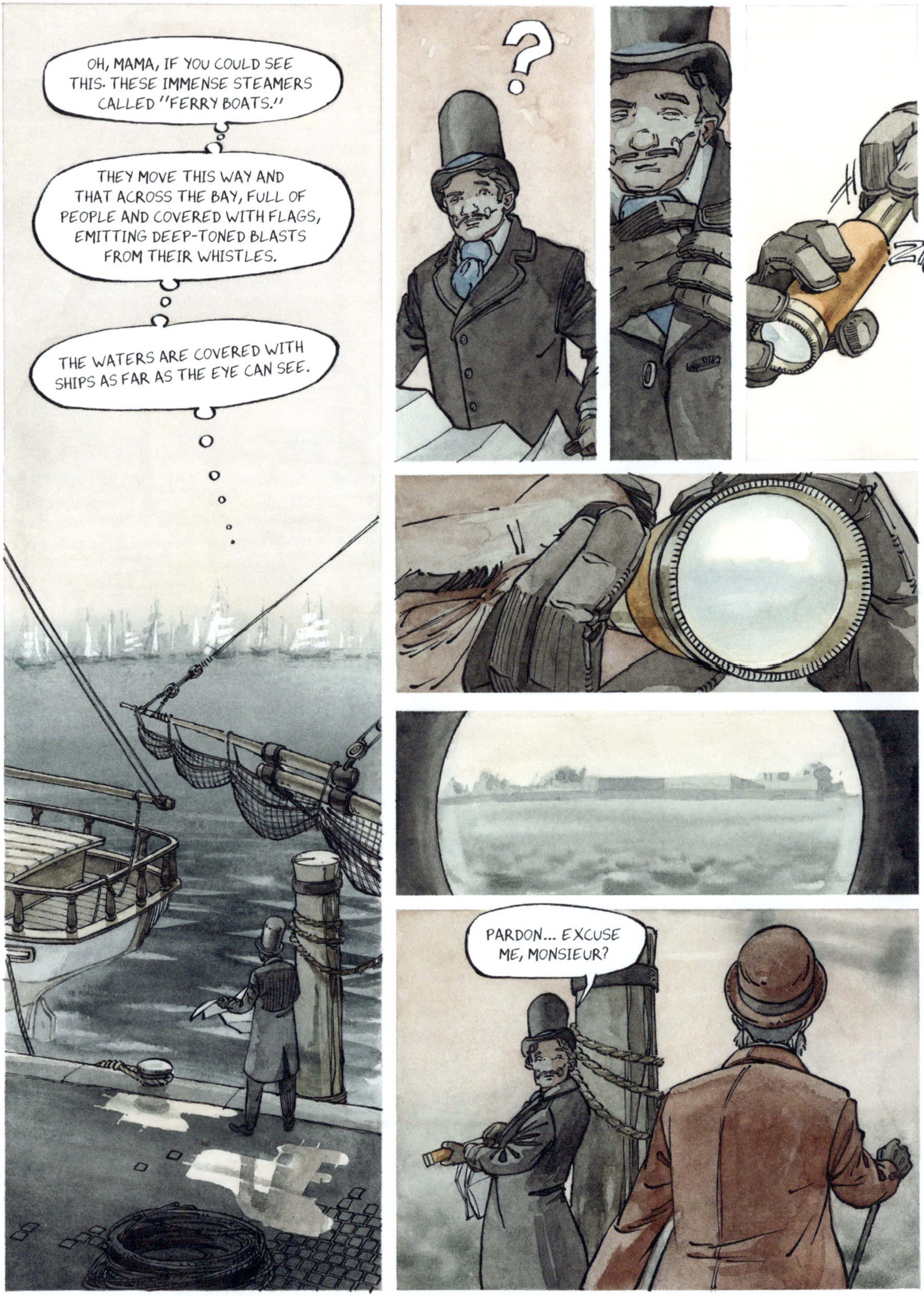
OH, MAMA, IF YOU COULD SEE THIS. THESE IMMENSE STEAMERS CALLED "FERRY BOATS."
THEY MOVE THIS WAY AND THAT ACROSS THE BAY, FULL OF PEOPLE AND COVERED WITH FLAGS, EMITTING DEEP-TONED BLASTS FROM THEIR WHISTLES.
THE WATERS ARE COVERED WITH SHIPS AS FAR AS THE EYE CAN SEE.
?
ZIC
PARDON... EXCUSE ME, MONSIEUR?

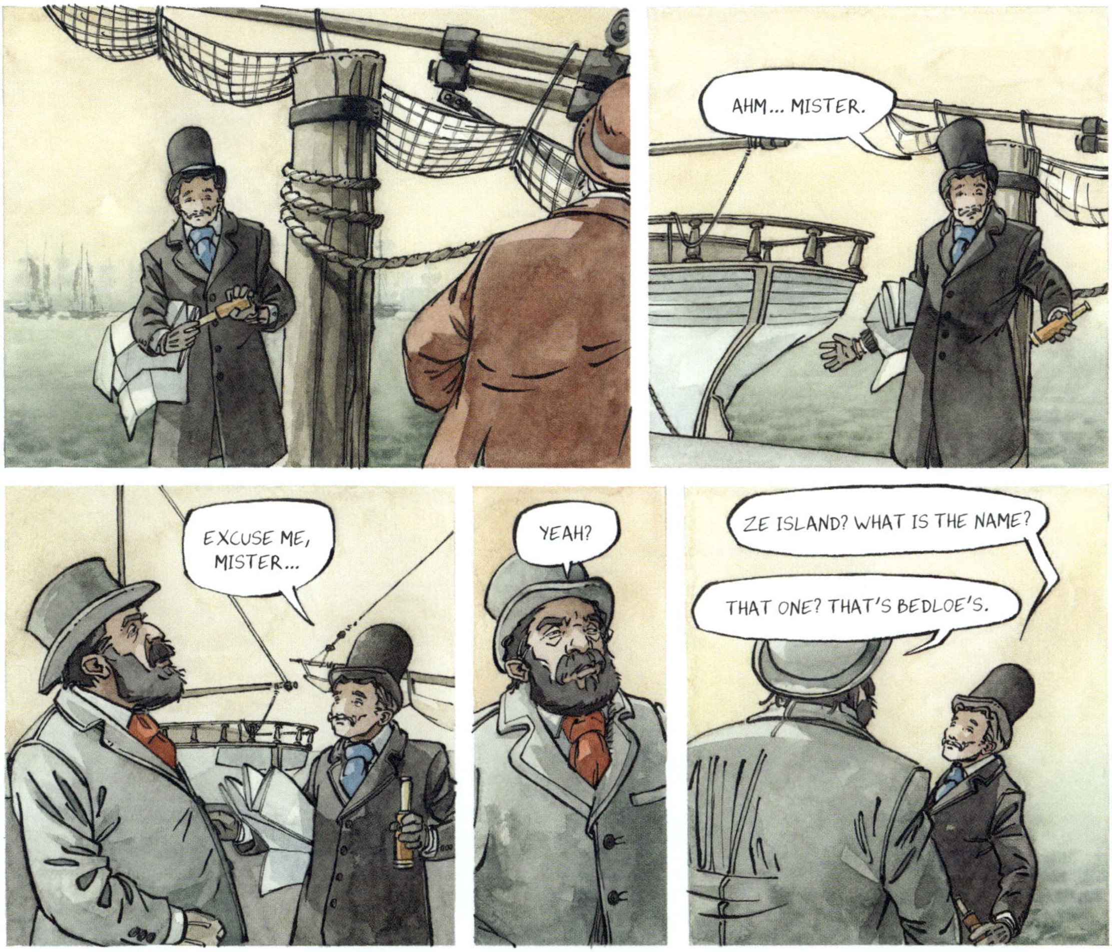
AHM... MISTER.
EXCUSE ME, MISTER...
YEAH?
ZE ISLAND? WHAT IS THE NAME?
THAT ONE? THAT'S BEDLOE'S.

BEDLOE'S ISLAND. THE STATUE WOULD BE VISIBLE FROM THE CITY, THE HARBOR, AND EVERY SHIP COMING FROM THE OLD WORLD TO THE NEW. FRÉDÉRIC-AUGUSTE BARTHOLDI KNEW THAT HE HAD FOUND HIS SPOT.

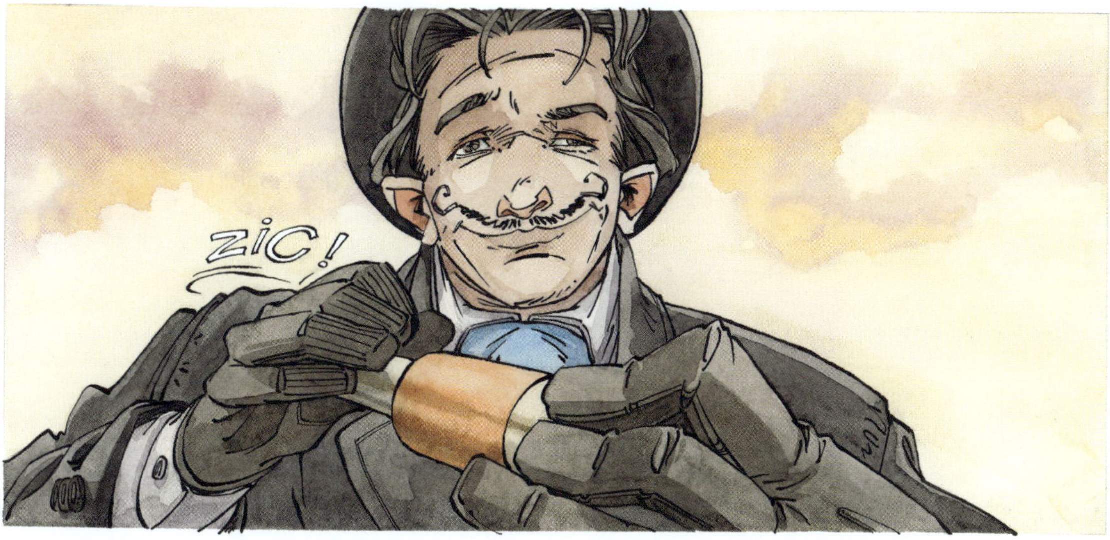
ZIC!

Horrible Murder
Who killed Benjamin Nathan?

PROFESSOR LABOULAYE HAD GIVEN FRÉDÉRIC-AUGUSTE MANY LETTERS OF INTRODUCTION. MARY LOUISE BOOTH WAS THE FIRST PERSON ON HIS LIST.

MISTER BARTHOLDI IS HERE TO SEE YOU.

MARY LOUISE BOOTH WAS THE TRANSLATOR OF LABOULAYE'S BOOKS INTO ENGLISH. HER GRANDFATHER WAS FRENCH AND SHE SPOKE THE LANGUAGE FLUENTLY. SHE WAS ALSO THE FOUNDING EDITOR OF AMERICA'S FIRST FASHION MAGAZINE, "HARPER'S BAZAAR", AND HAD MANY CONNECTIONS IN THE MEDIA WORLD, WHICH WOULD LATER BE IMPORTANT FOR PROMOTING THE IDEA OF THE MONUMENT.

PLEASE LET HIM IN.

IT IS A PLEASURE MAKING YOUR ACQUAINTANCE, MONSIEUR BARTHOLDI. A FRIEND OF EDOUARD IS A FRIEND OF MINE.

SO KIND OF YOU. HE SENDS HIS REGARDS AND REGRETS THAT HE STILL HASN'T BEEN ABLE TO JOURNEY ACROSS THE OCEAN HIMSELF.

I'VE SEEN A SIMILAR HEADLINE IN "LE COURRIER DES ETATS-UNIS."* WHAT HAPPENED?

THE VICE-PRESIDENT OF THE NEW YORK STOCK EXCHANGE WAS BRUTALLY MURDERED. HE WAS ONE OF THE RICHEST PEOPLE IN THIS CITY.

*A FRENCH LANGUAGE PAPER PUBLISHED IN NEW YORK.

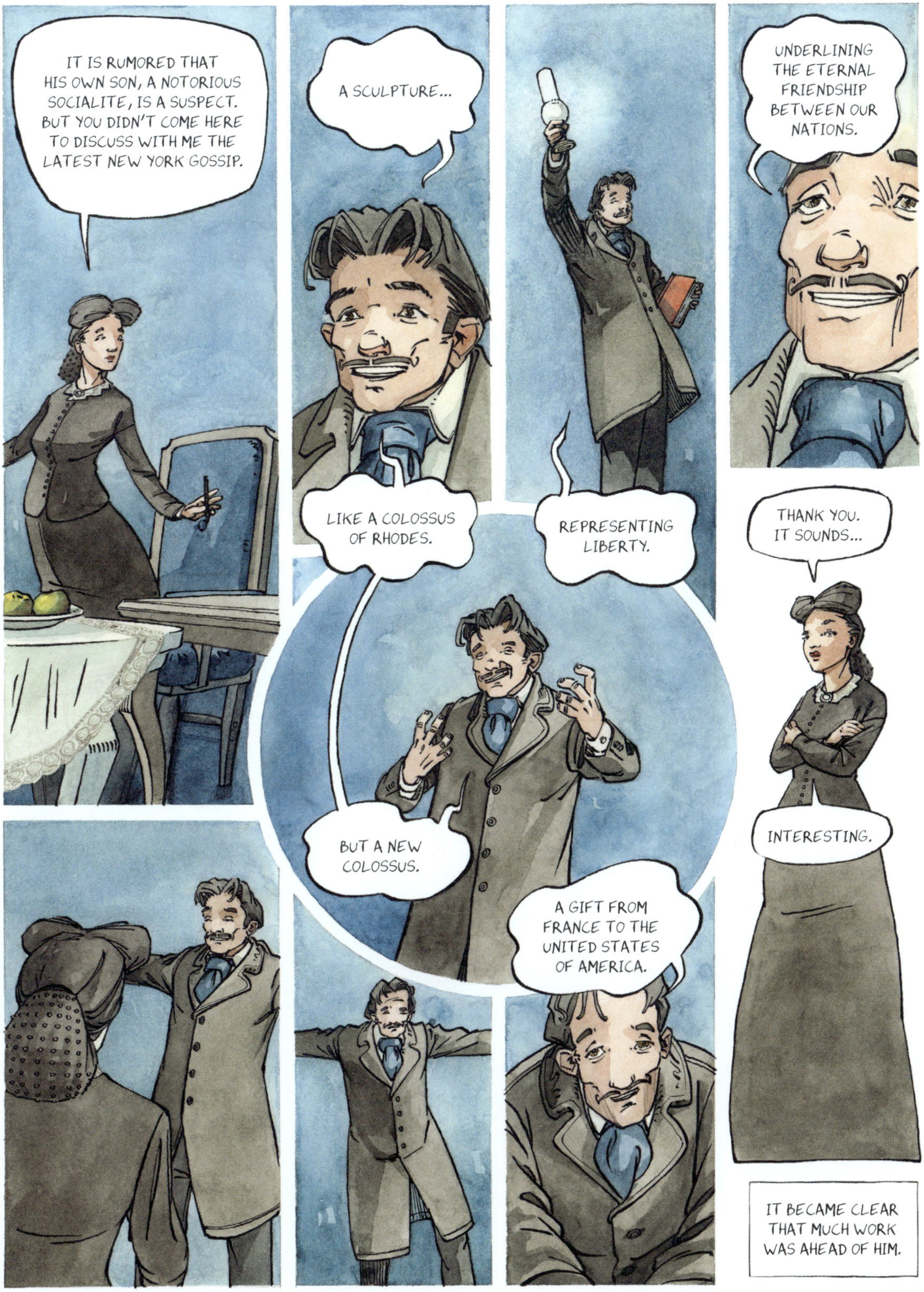
IT IS RUMORED THAT HIS OWN SON, A NOTORIOUS SOCIALITE, IS A SUSPECT. BUT YOU DIDN'T COME HERE TO DISCUSS WITH ME THE LATEST NEW YORK GOSSIP.
A SCULPTURE...
LIKE A COLOSSUS OF RHODES.
REPRESENTING LIBERTY.
UNDERLINING THE ETERNAL FRIENDSHIP BETWEEN OUR NATIONS.
BUT A NEW COLOSSUS.
A GIFT FROM FRANCE TO THE UNITED STATES OF AMERICA.
THANK YOU. IT SOUNDS...
INTERESTING.
IT BECAME CLEAR THAT MUCH WORK WAS AHEAD OF HIM.

IN THE NEXT FEW WEEKS, FRÉDÉRIC-AUGUSTE MET TIRELESSLY WITH LABOULAYE'S MANY CORRESPONDENTS, INTRODUCING THEM TO THE IDEA OF THE STATUE.

HE EVEN MET WITH THE FRENCH CONSUL TO THE UNITED STATES. IT WAS TRUE, LABOULAYE'S NAME OPENED MANY DOORS. THERE WAS POLITE INTEREST.

BUT UNFORTUNATELY, NO ONE SEEMED CONVINCED OF THE IDEA TO BUILD A COLOSSUS DEDICATED TO LIBERTY IN THE NEW YORK HARBOR.

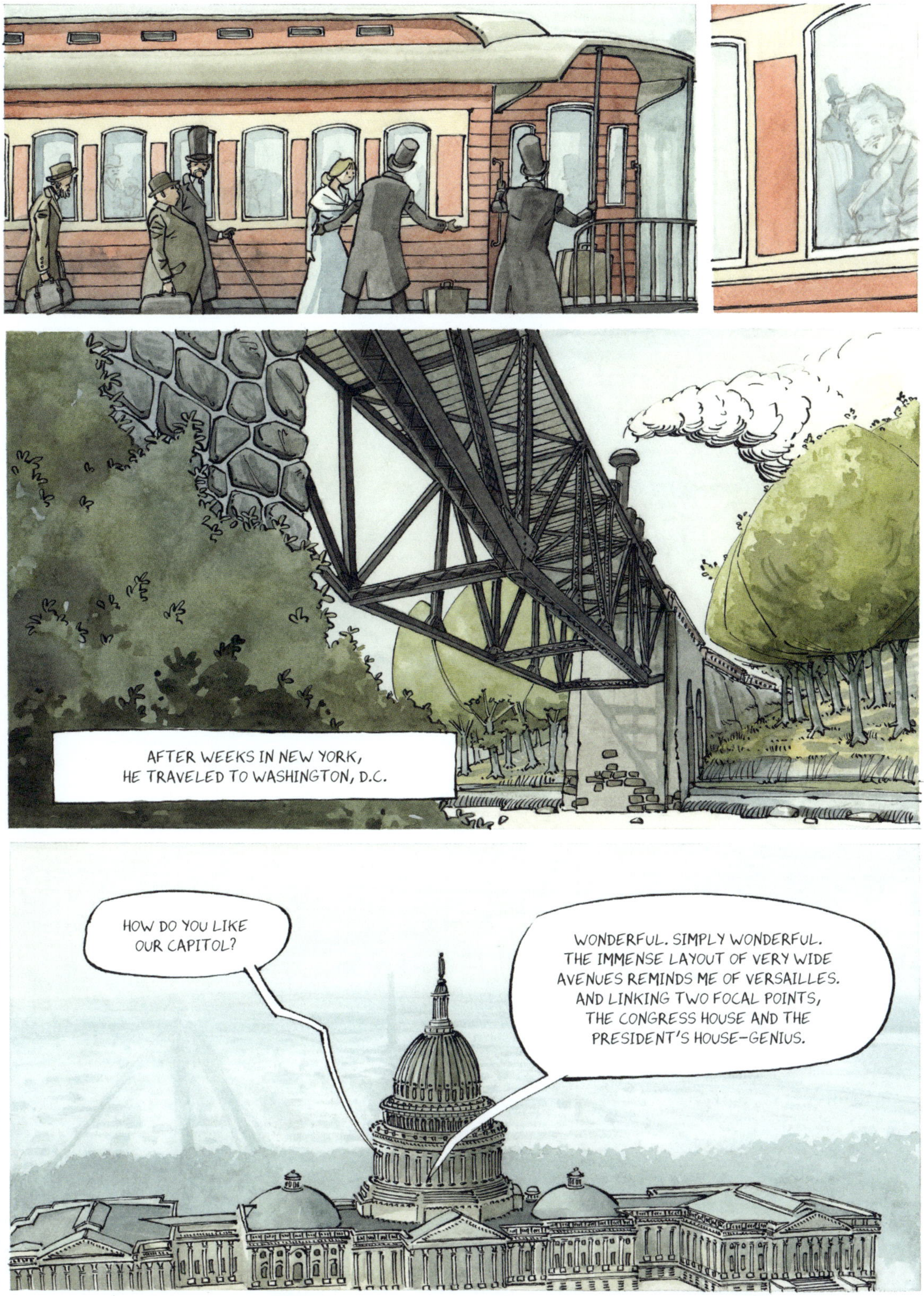
AFTER WEEKS IN NEW YORK,
HE TRAVELED TO WASHINGTON, D.C.
HOW DO YOU LIKE OUR CAPITOL?
WONDERFUL. SIMPLY WONDERFUL. THE IMMENSE LAYOUT OF VERY WIDE AVENUES REMINDS ME OF VERSAILLES. AND LINKING TWO FOCAL POINTS, THE CONGRESS HOUSE AND THE PRESIDENT'S HOUSE—GENIUS.

POTOMAC RIVER

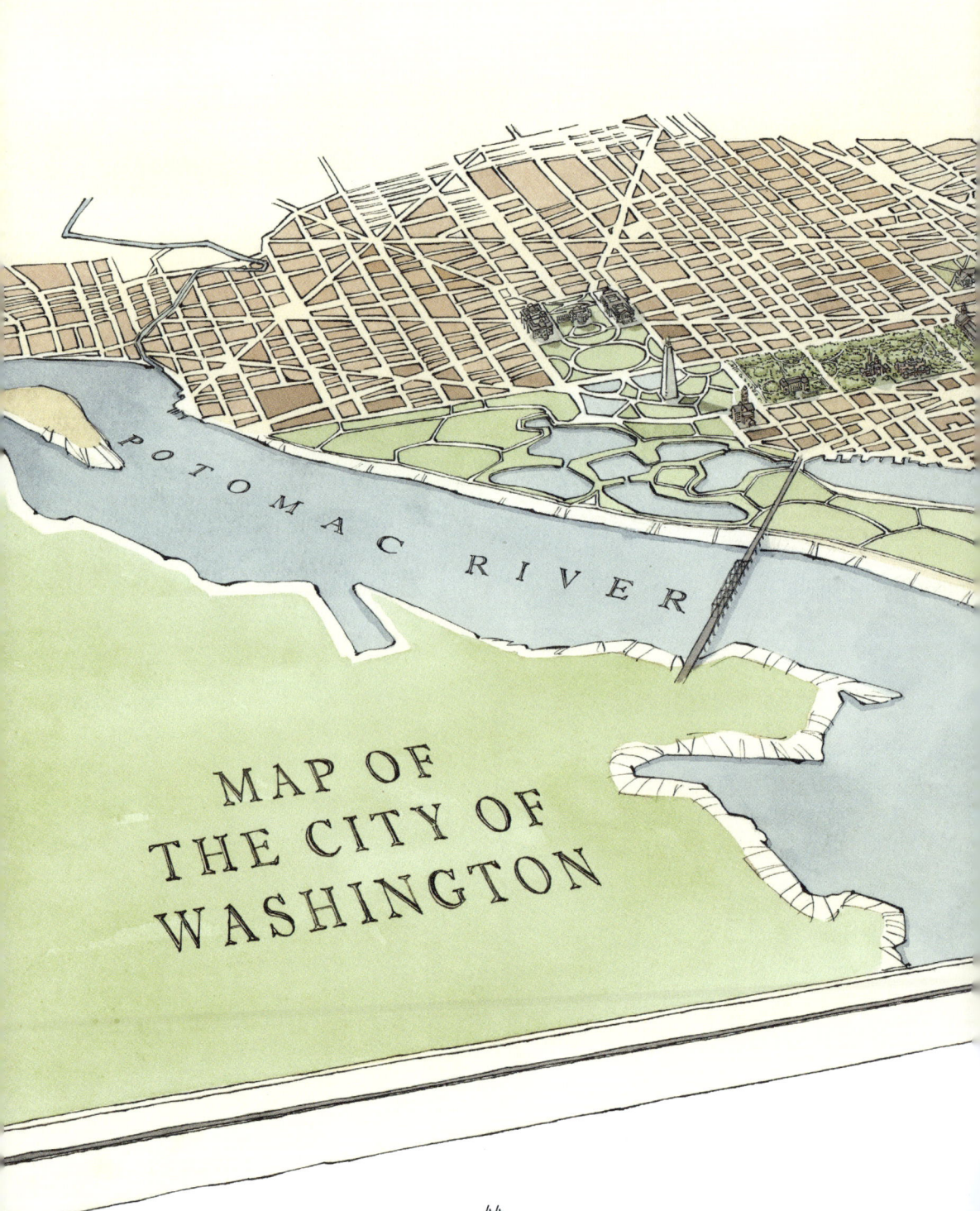

MAP OF
THE CITY OF
WASHINGTON

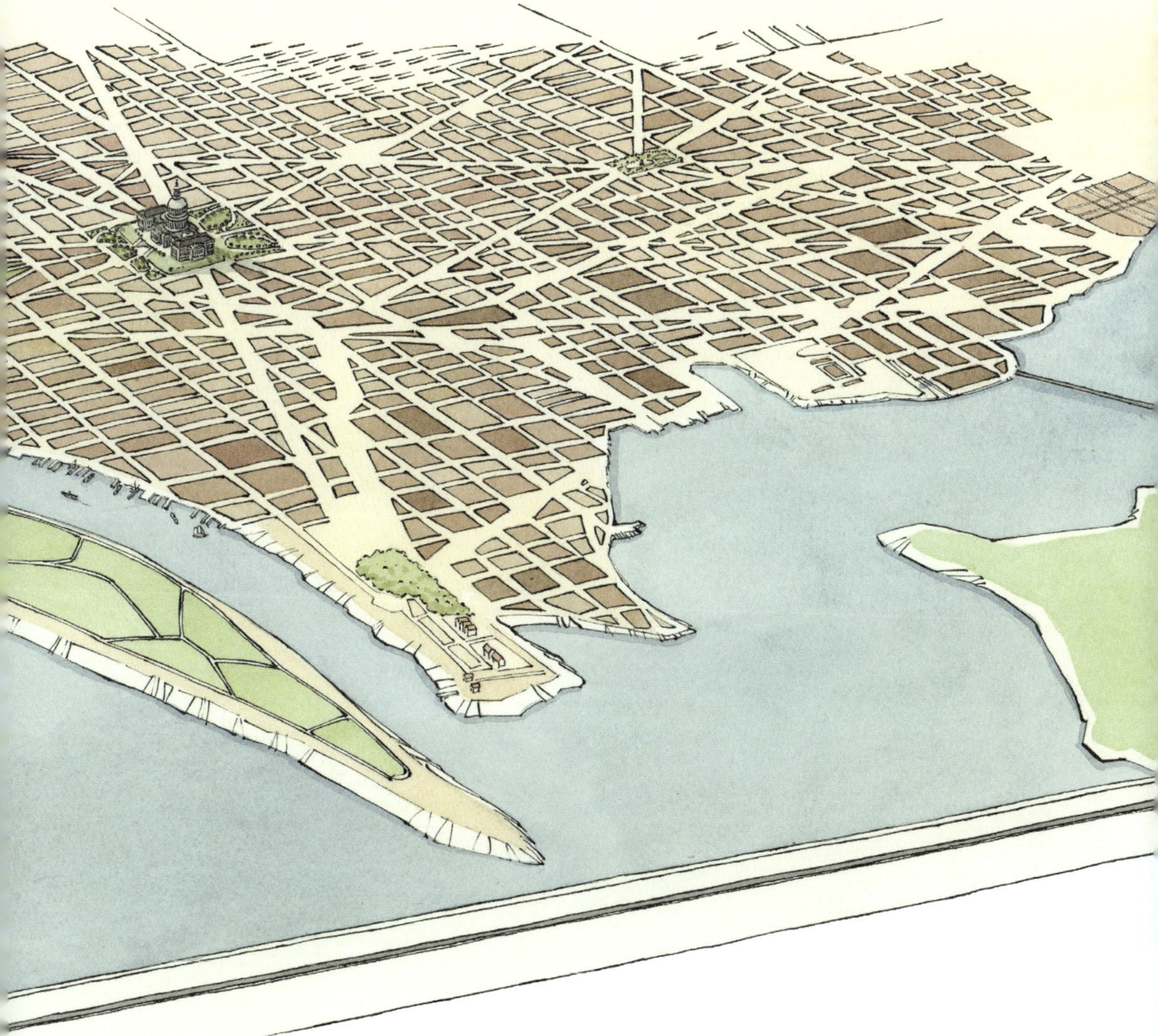

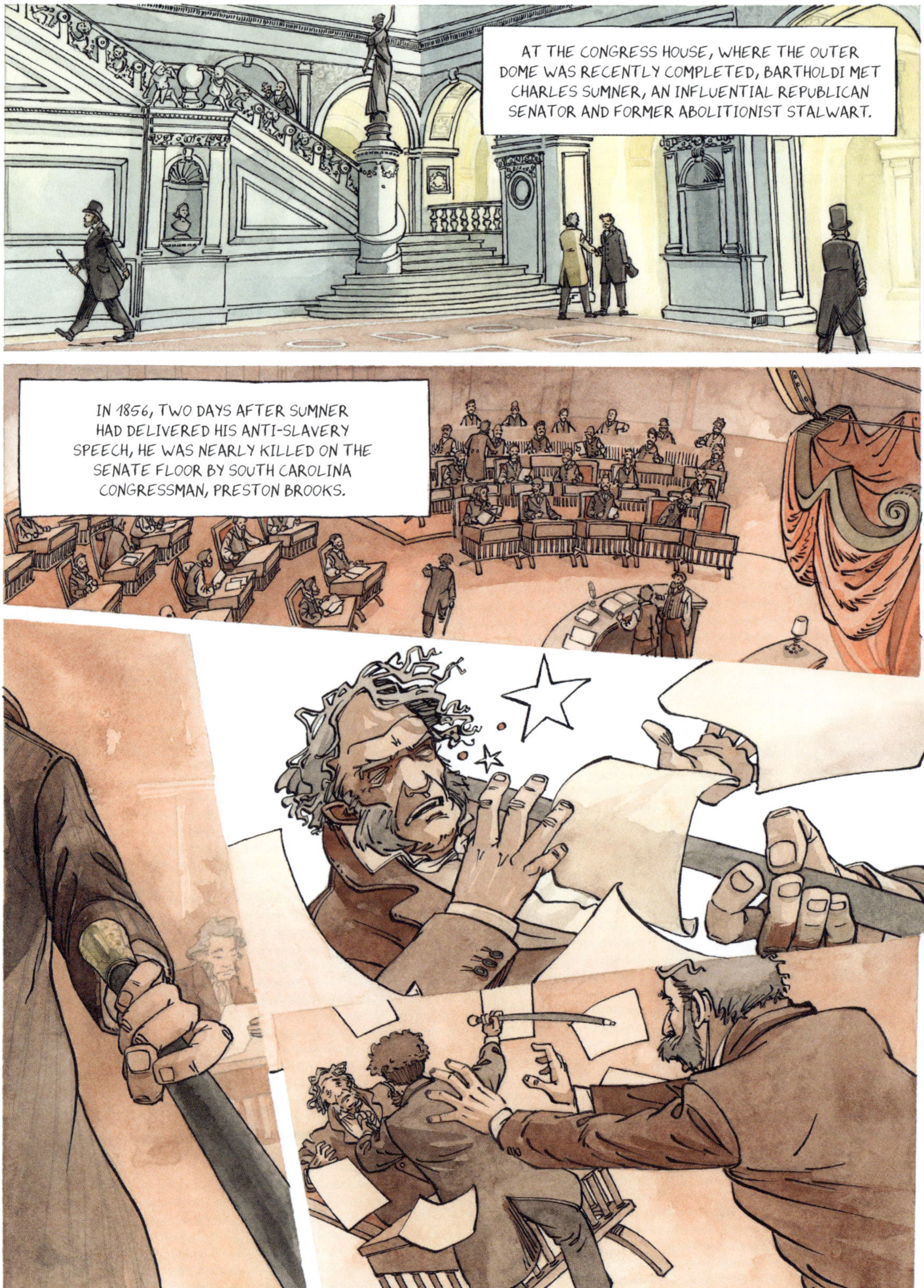
AT THE CONGRESS HOUSE, WHERE THE OUTER DOME WAS RECENTLY COMPLETED, BARTHOLDI MET CHARLES SUMNER, AN INFLUENTIAL REPUBLICAN SENATOR AND FORMER ABOLITIONIST STALWART.
IN 1856, TWO DAYS AFTER SUMNER HAD DELIVERED HIS ANTI-SLAVERY SPEECH, HE WAS NEARLY KILLED ON THE SENATE FLOOR BY SOUTH CAROLINA CONGRESSMAN, PRESTON BROOKS.

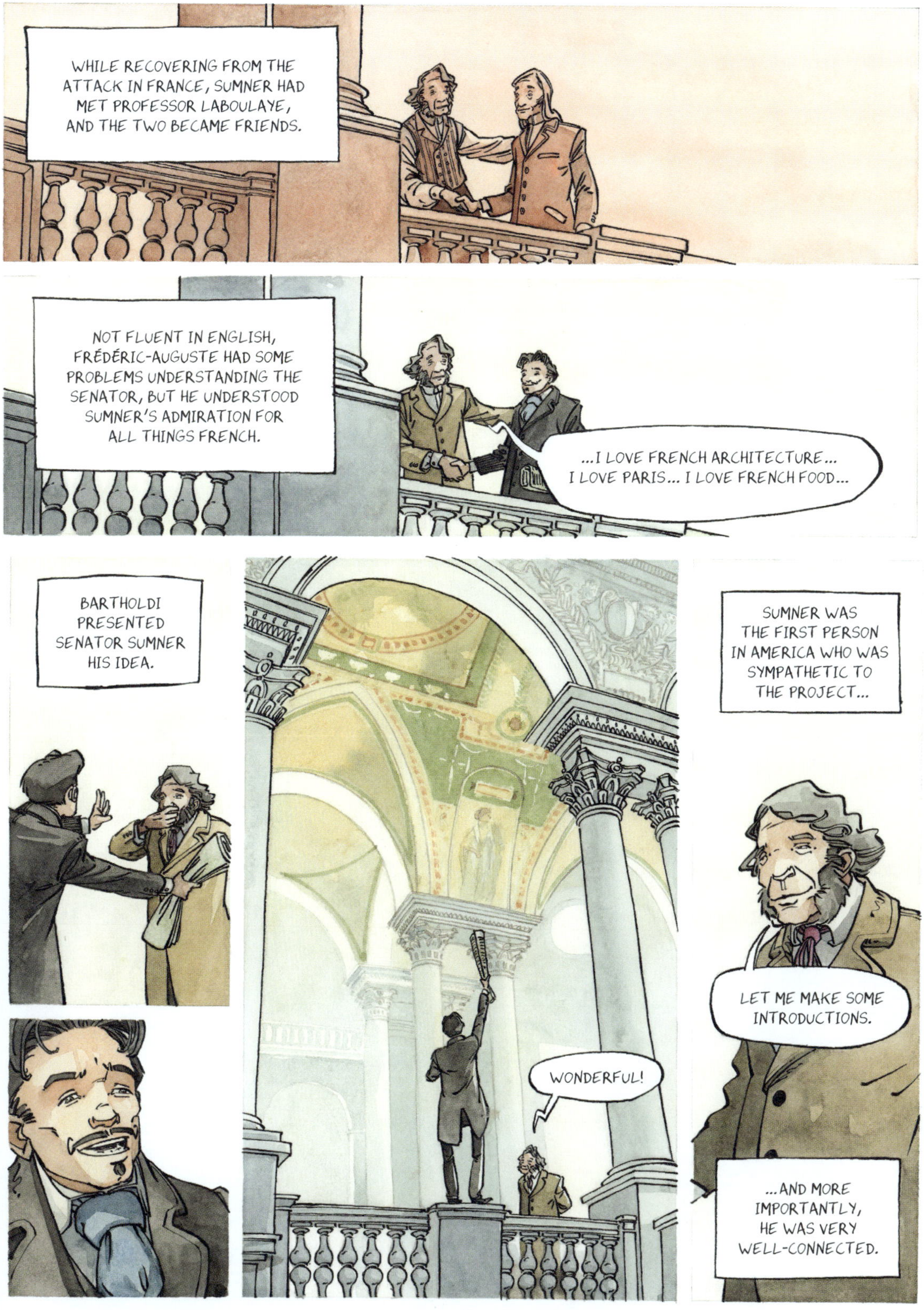
WHILE RECOVERING FROM THE ATTACK IN FRANCE, SUMNER HAD MET PROFESSOR LABOULAYE, AND THE TWO BECAME FRIENDS.
NOT FLUENT IN ENGLISH, FRÉDÉRIC-AUGUSTE HAD SOME PROBLEMS UNDERSTANDING THE SENATOR, BUT HE UNDERSTOOD SUMNER'S ADMIRATION FOR ALL THINGS FRENCH.
...I LOVE FRENCH ARCHITECTURE... I LOVE PARIS... I LOVE FRENCH FOOD...
BARTHOLDI PRESENTED SENATOR SUMNER HIS IDEA.
WONDERFUL!
SUMNER WAS THE FIRST PERSON IN AMERICA WHO WAS SYMPATHETIC TO THE PROJECT...
LET ME MAKE SOME INTRODUCTIONS.
...AND MORE IMPORTANTLY, HE WAS VERY WELL-CONNECTED.

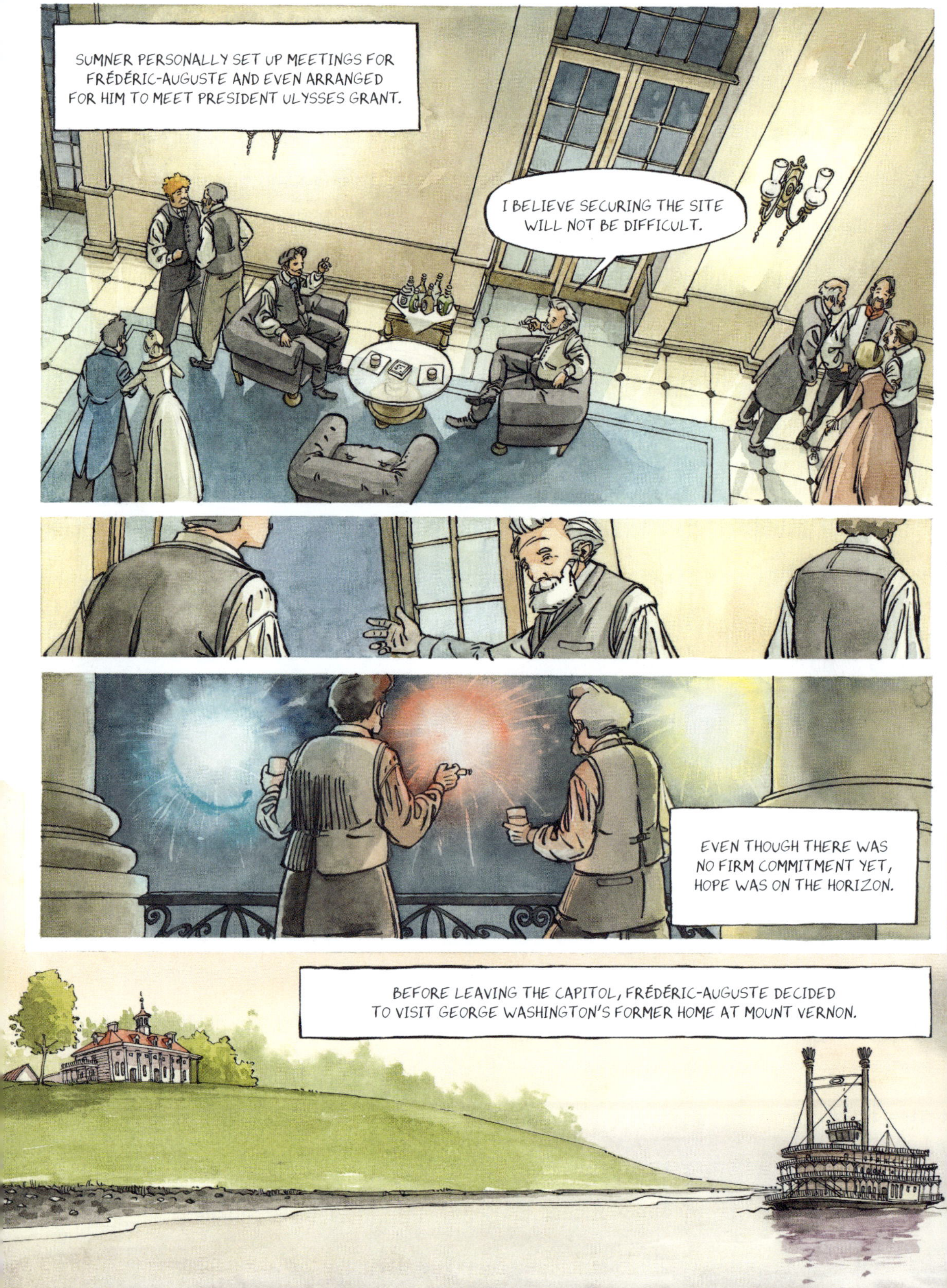
SUMNER PERSONALLY SET UP MEETINGS FOR FRÉDÉRIC-AUGUSTE AND EVEN ARRANGED FOR HIM TO MEET PRESIDENT ULYSSES GRANT.
I BELIEVE SECURING THE SITE WILL NOT BE DIFFICULT.
EVEN THOUGH THERE WAS NO FIRM COMMITMENT YET, HOPE WAS ON THE HORIZON.
BEFORE LEAVING THE CAPITOL, FRÉDÉRIC-AUGUSTE DECIDED TO VISIT GEORGE WASHINGTON'S FORMER HOME AT MOUNT VERNON.

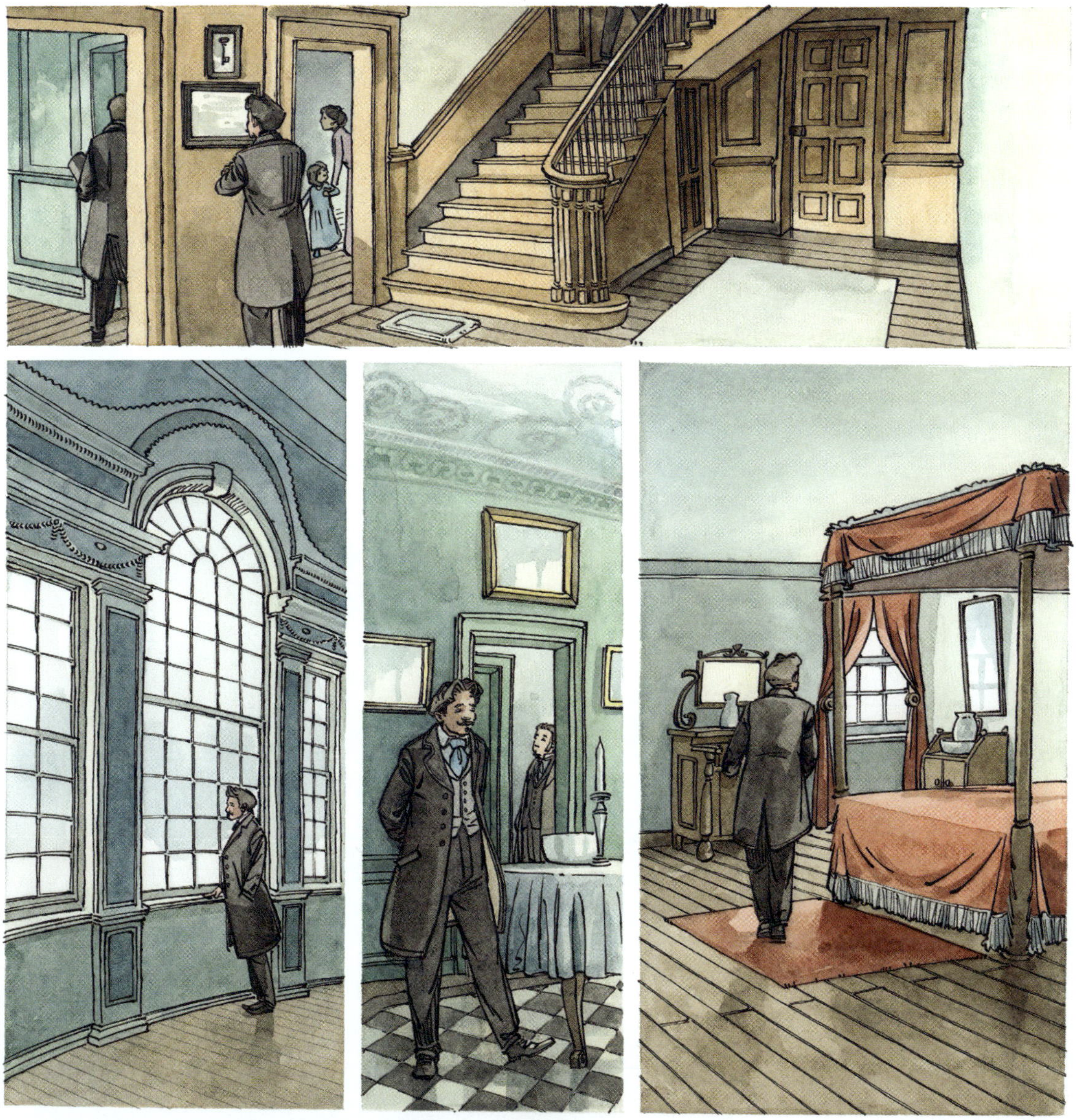

"THE VESTAL FIRE OF FREEDOM IS IN YOUR CUSTODY. MAY THE SOULS OF [THE NATION'S] DEPARTED FOUNDERS NEVER BE CALLED TO WITNESS ITS EXTINCTION BY NEGLECT."*

*EXCERPT FROM A EULOGY FOR LAFAYETTE BY JOHN QUINCY ADAMS, 1834.

PHILADELPHIA

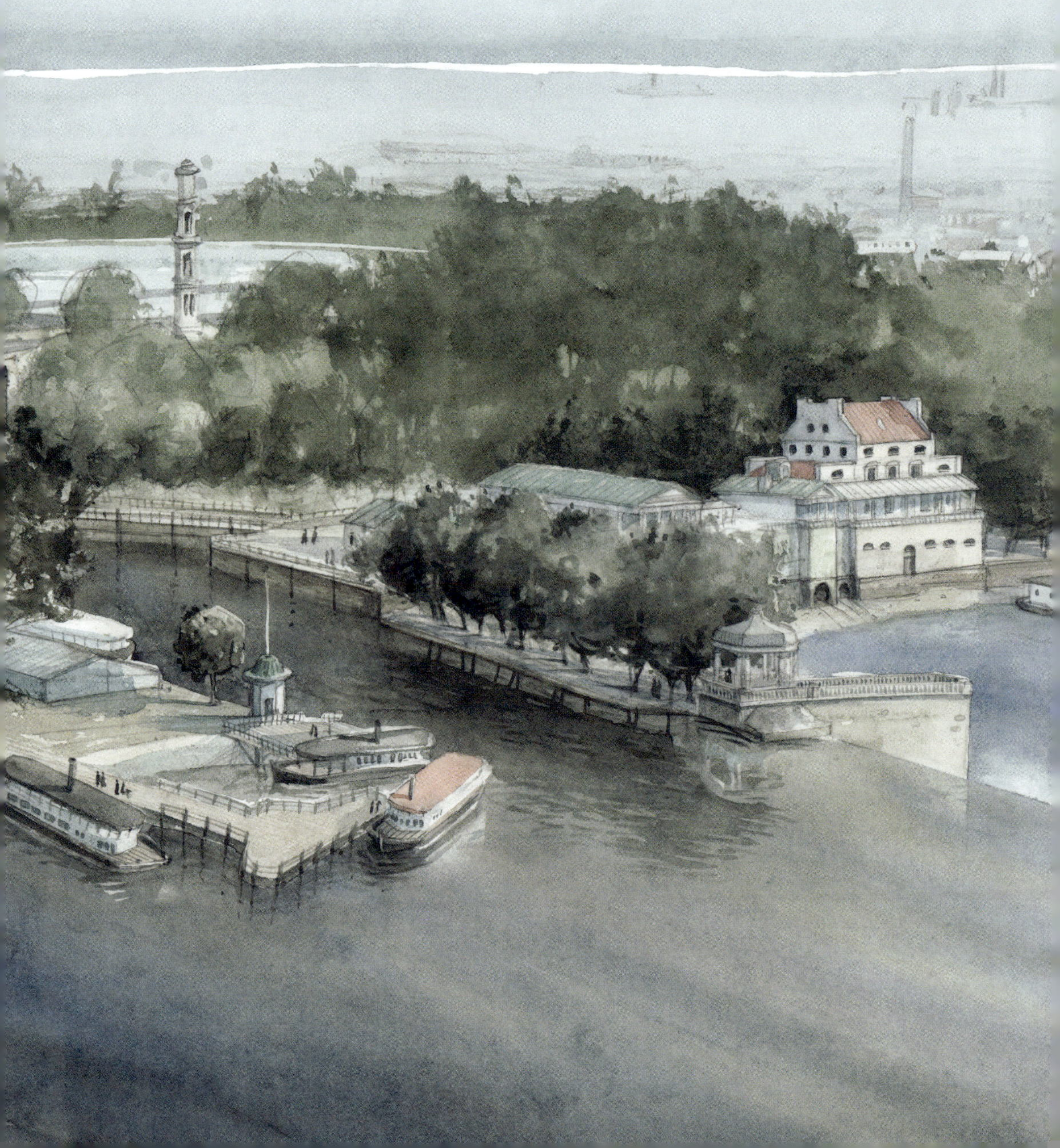

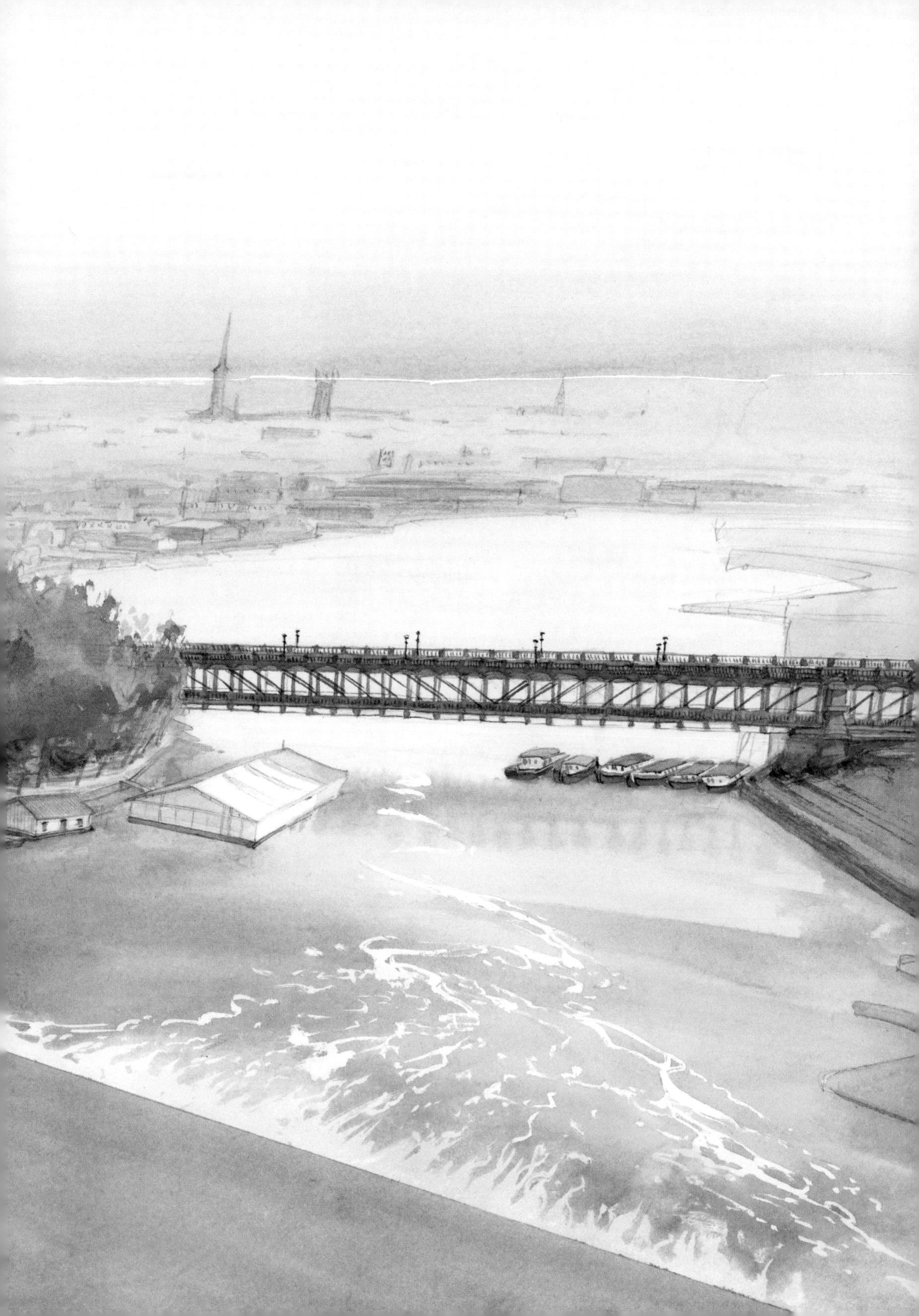

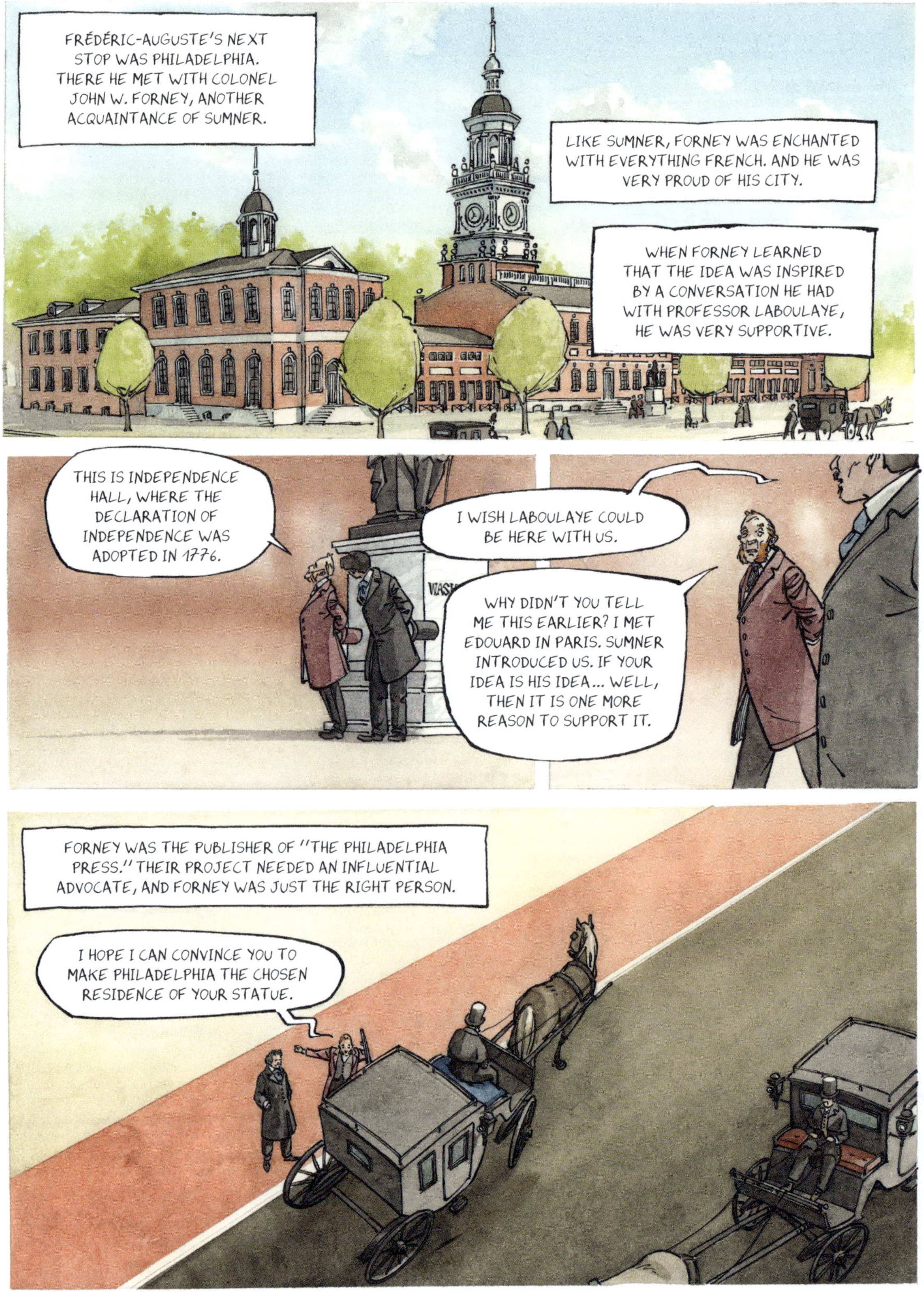
FRÉDÉRIC-AUGUSTE'S NEXT STOP WAS PHILADELPHIA. THERE HE MET WITH COLONEL JOHN W. FORNEY, ANOTHER ACQUAINTANCE OF SUMNER.
LIKE SUMNER, FORNEY WAS ENCHANTED WITH EVERYTHING FRENCH. AND HE WAS VERY PROUD OF HIS CITY.
WHEN FORNEY LEARNED THAT THE IDEA WAS INSPIRED BY A CONVERSATION HE HAD WITH PROFESSOR LABOULAYE, HE WAS VERY SUPPORTIVE.
THIS IS INDEPENDENCE HALL, WHERE THE DECLARATION OF INDEPENDENCE WAS ADOPTED IN 1776.
I WISH LABOULAYE COULD BE HERE WITH US.
WHY DIDN'T YOU TELL ME THIS EARLIER? I MET EDOUARD IN PARIS. SUMNER INTRODUCED US. IF YOUR IDEA IS HIS IDEA... WELL, THEN IT IS ONE MORE REASON TO SUPPORT IT.
FORNEY WAS THE PUBLISHER OF "THE PHILADELPHIA PRESS." THEIR PROJECT NEEDED AN INFLUENTIAL ADVOCATE, AND FORNEY WAS JUST THE RIGHT PERSON.
I HOPE I CAN CONVINCE YOU TO MAKE PHILADELPHIA THE CHOSEN RESIDENCE OF YOUR STATUE.

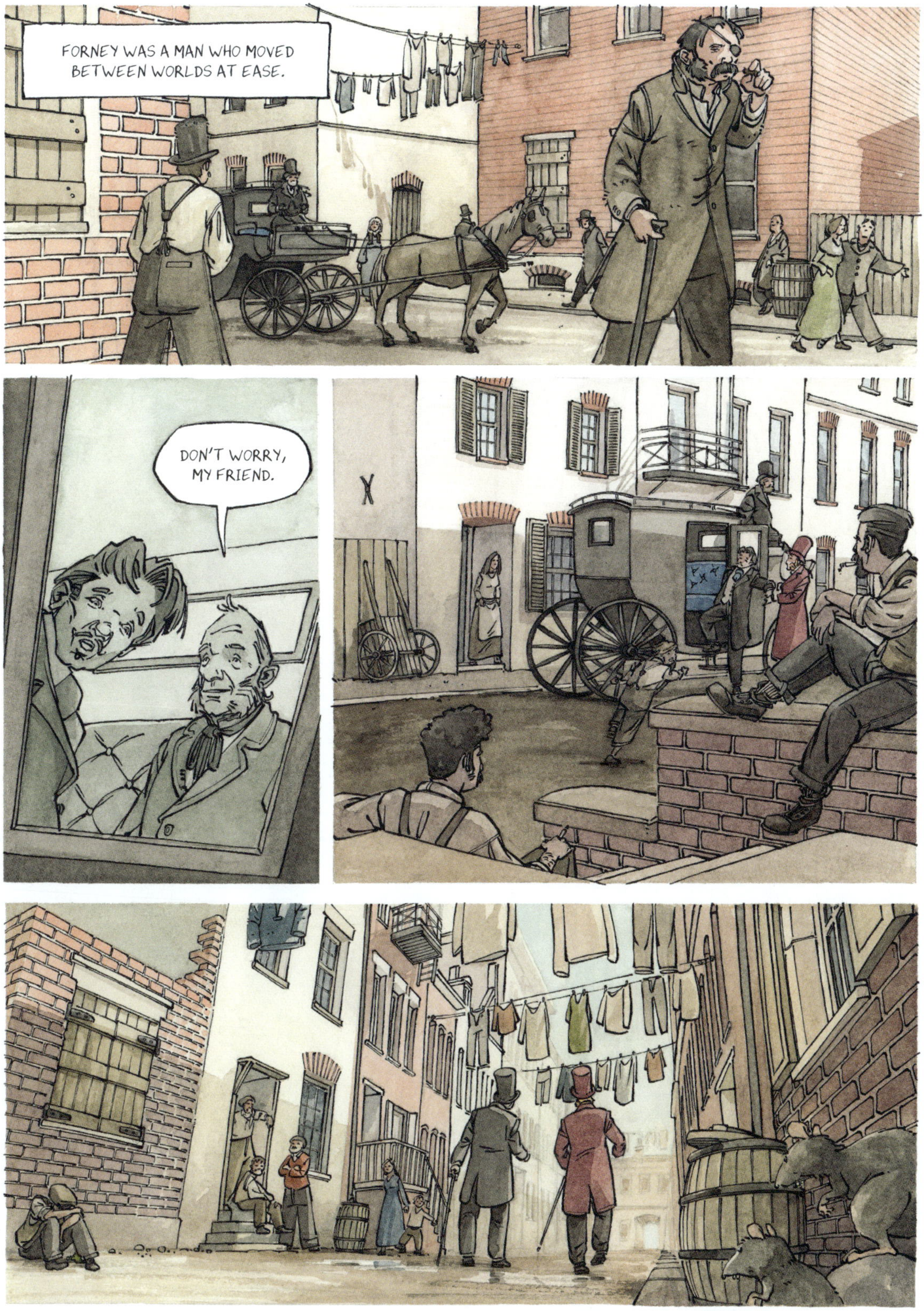
FORNEY WAS A MAN WHO MOVED BETWEEN WORLDS AT EASE.
DON'T WORRY, MY FRIEND.

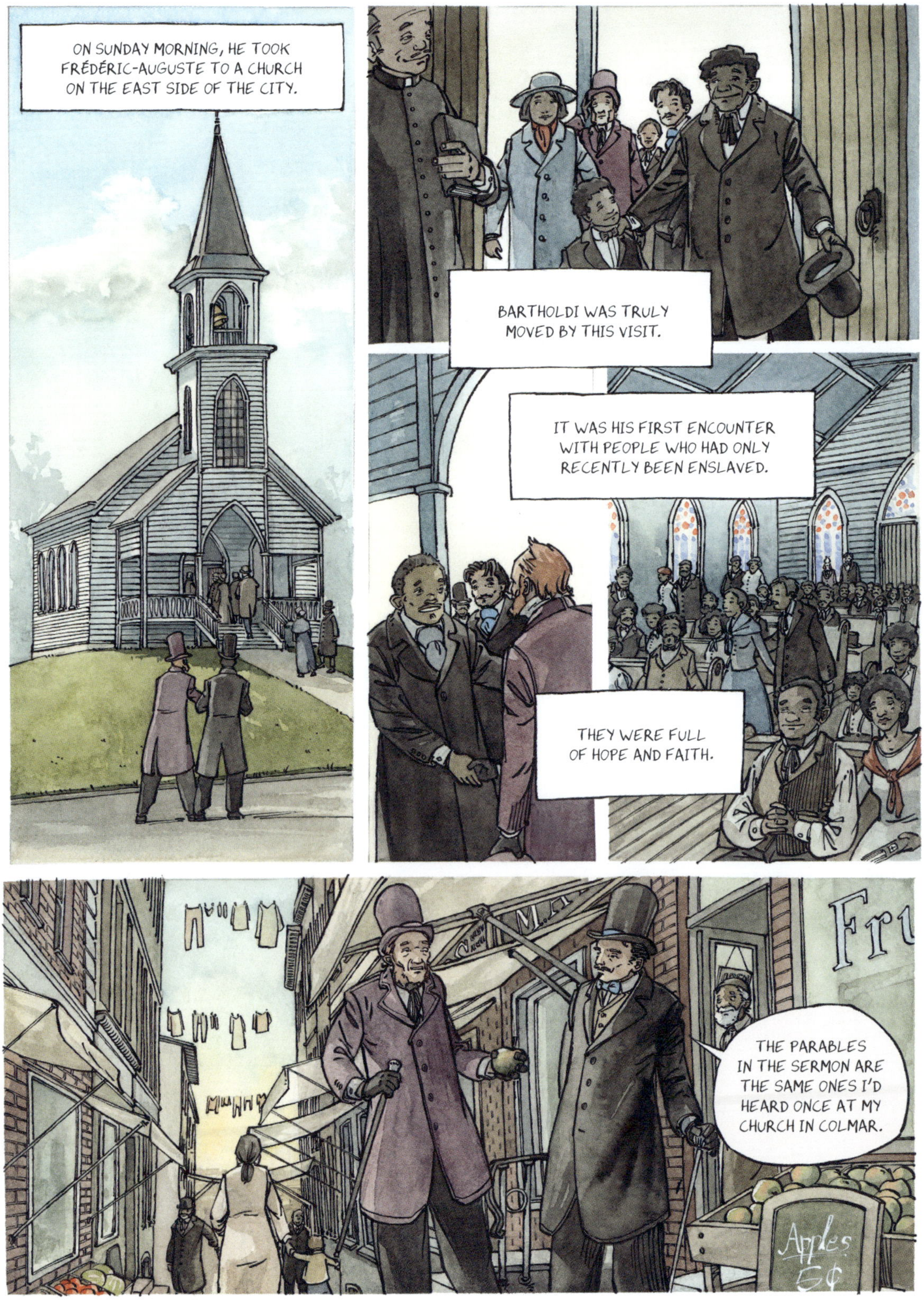
ON SUNDAY MORNING, HE TOOK FRÉDÉRIC-AUGUSTE TO A CHURCH ON THE EAST SIDE OF THE CITY.
BARTHOLDI WAS TRULY MOVED BY THIS VISIT.
IT WAS HIS FIRST ENCOUNTER WITH PEOPLE WHO HAD ONLY RECENTLY BEEN ENSLAVED.
THEY WERE FULL OF HOPE AND FAITH.
Fru
THE PARABLES IN THE SERMON ARE THE SAME ONES I'D HEARD ONCE AT MY CHURCH IN COLMAR.
Apples 5¢

IN THE AFTERNOON, FORNEY INTRODUCED HIM TO THE UNION LEAGUE CLUB, A NETWORK OF WEALTHY LIBERALS.

PHILADELPHIA IS THE PERFECT PLACE FOR YOUR STATUE.

WE WILL BE HOSTING THE WORLD'S FAIR.

AND A CENTENNIAL EXHIBITION!

OF COURSE, THE CENTENNIAL!

PHILADELPHIA IS THE RIGHT PLACE, NOT NEW YORK! SO IF YOU CHANGE YOUR MIND, WE WILL WELCOME YOUR STATUE WITH OPEN ARMS HERE.

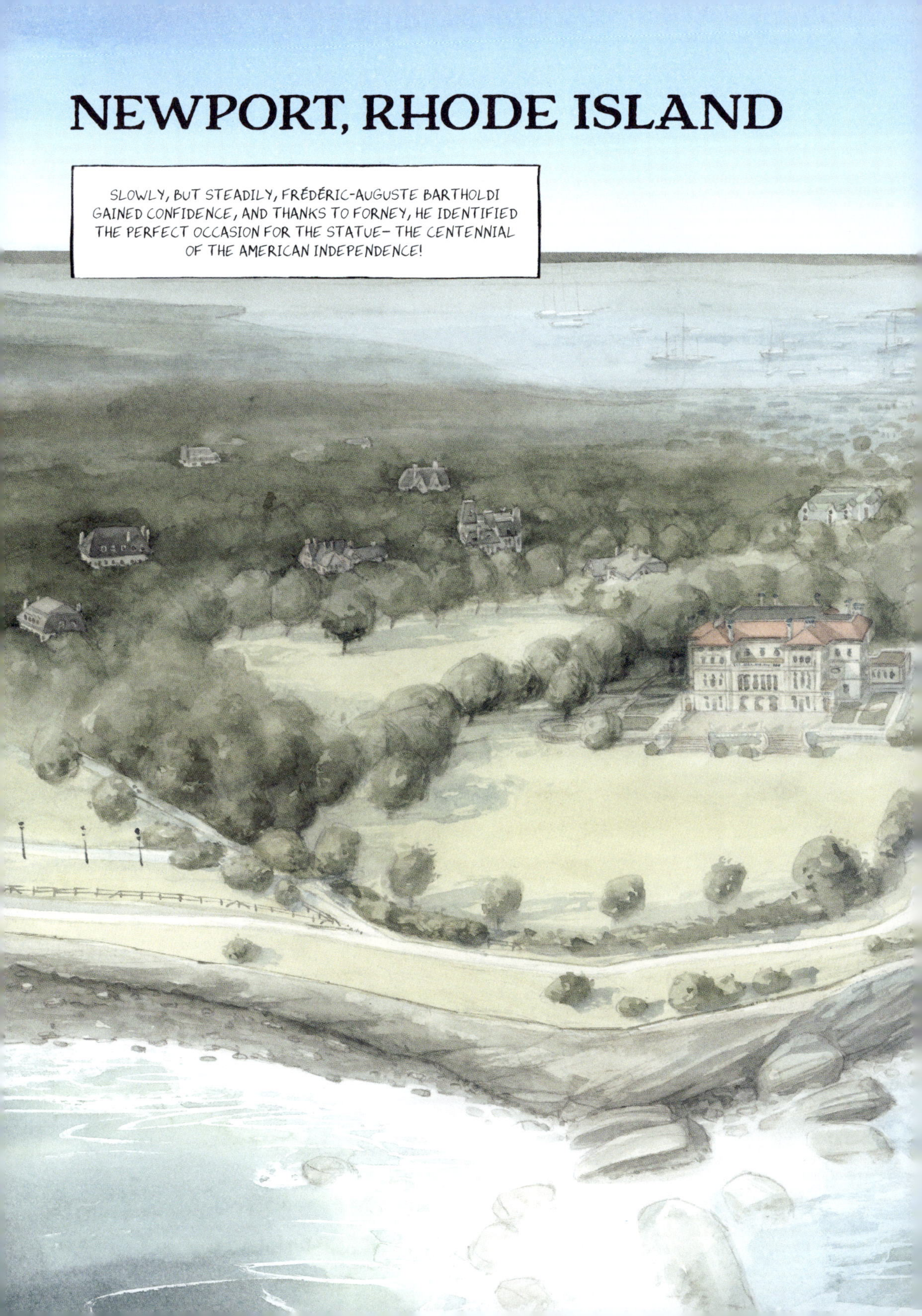
NEWPORT, RHODE ISLAND
SLOWLY, BUT STEADILY, FRÉDÉRIC-AUGUSTE BARTHOLDI GAINED CONFIDENCE, AND THANKS TO FORNEY, HE IDENTIFIED THE PERFECT OCCASION FOR THE STATUE– THE CENTENNIAL OF THE AMERICAN INDEPENDENCE!

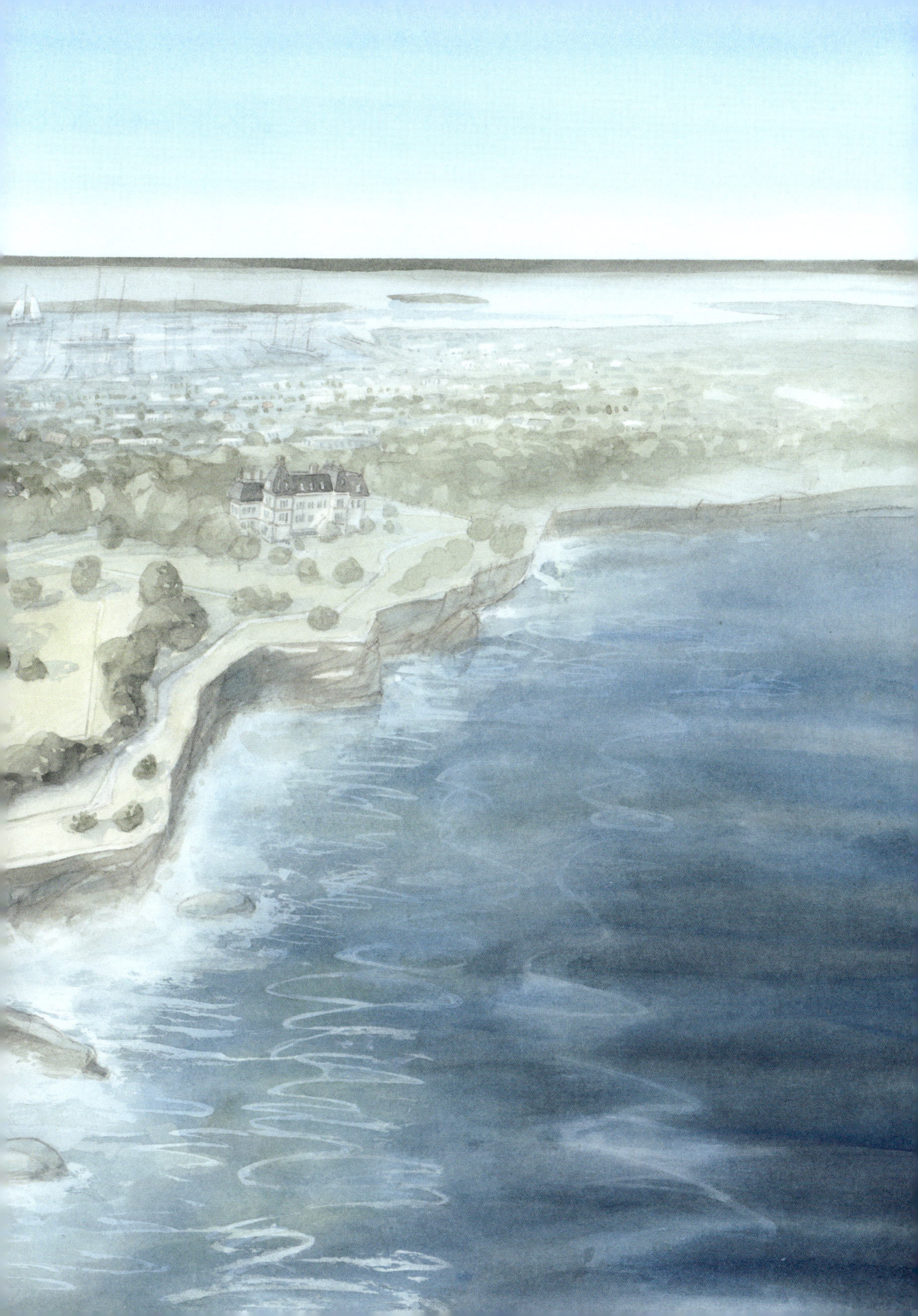

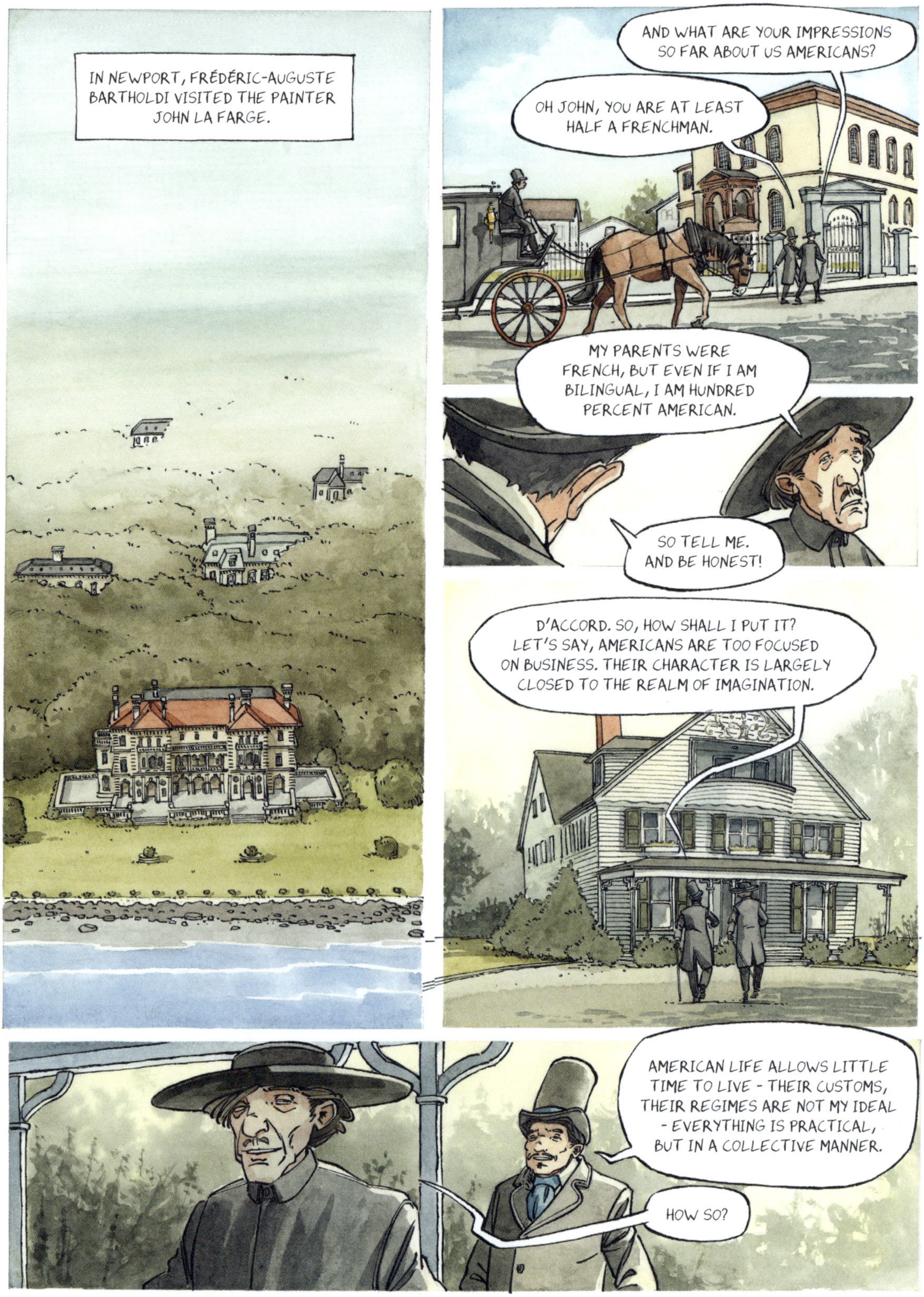
IN NEWPORT, FRÉDÉRIC-AUGUSTE BARTHOLDI VISITED THE PAINTER JOHN LA FARGE.
AND WHAT ARE YOUR IMPRESSIONS SO FAR ABOUT US AMERICANS?
OH JOHN, YOU ARE AT LEAST HALF A FRENCHMAN.
MY PARENTS WERE FRENCH, BUT EVEN IF I AM BILINGUAL, I AM HUNDRED PERCENT AMERICAN.
SO TELL ME. AND BE HONEST!
D'ACCORD. SO, HOW SHALL I PUT IT? LET'S SAY, AMERICANS ARE TOO FOCUSED ON BUSINESS. THEIR CHARACTER IS LARGELY CLOSED TO THE REALM OF IMAGINATION.
AMERICAN LIFE ALLOWS LITTLE TIME TO LIVE - THEIR CUSTOMS, THEIR REGIMES ARE NOT MY IDEAL - EVERYTHING IS PRACTICAL, BUT IN A COLLECTIVE MANNER.
HOW SO?

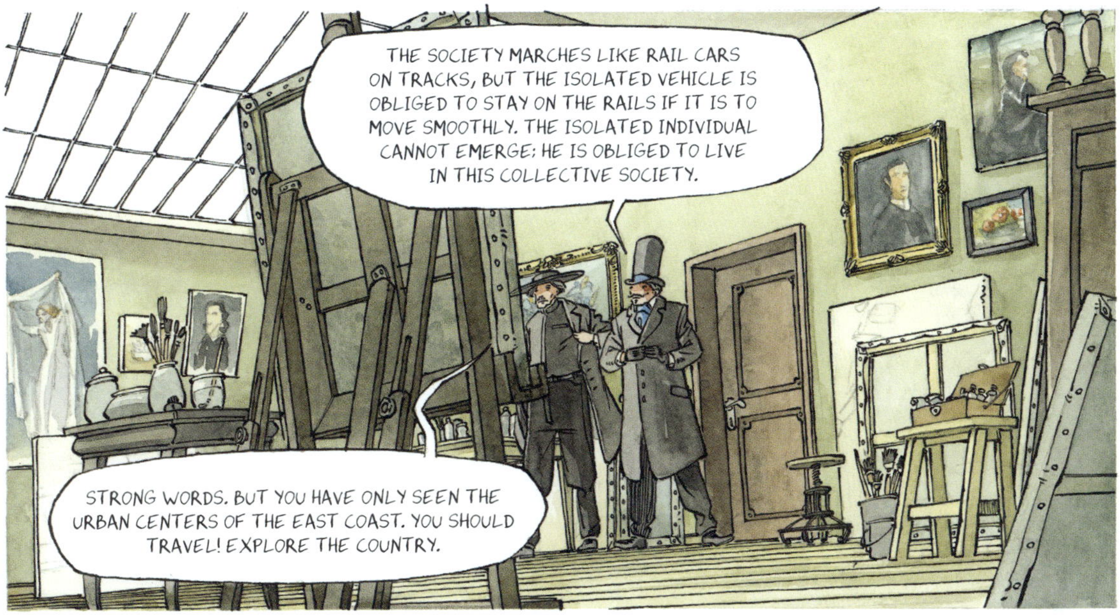

HIS FRIEND WAS RIGHT. TO UNDERSTAND WHAT AMERICA WAS ALL ABOUT, FRÉDÉRIC-AUGUSTE HAD TO SEE THE COUNTRY, MEET ITS PEOPLE.

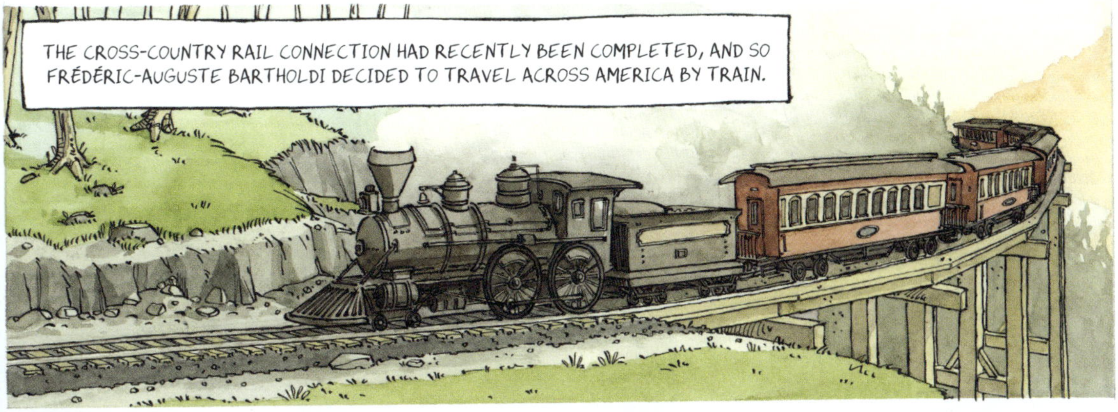

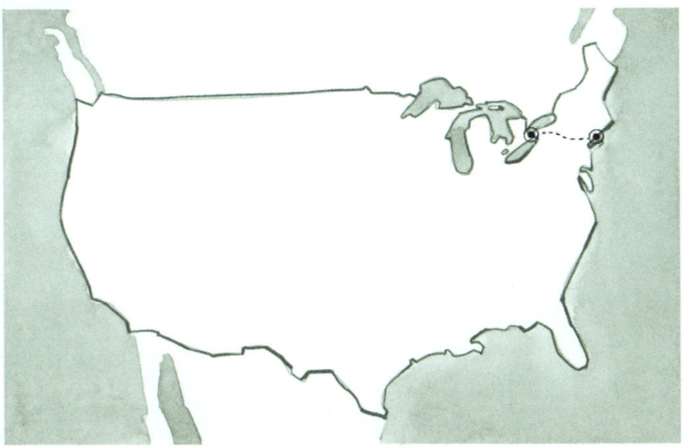

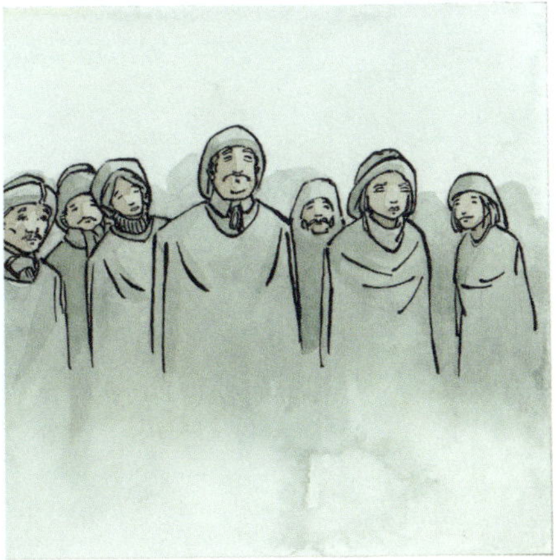

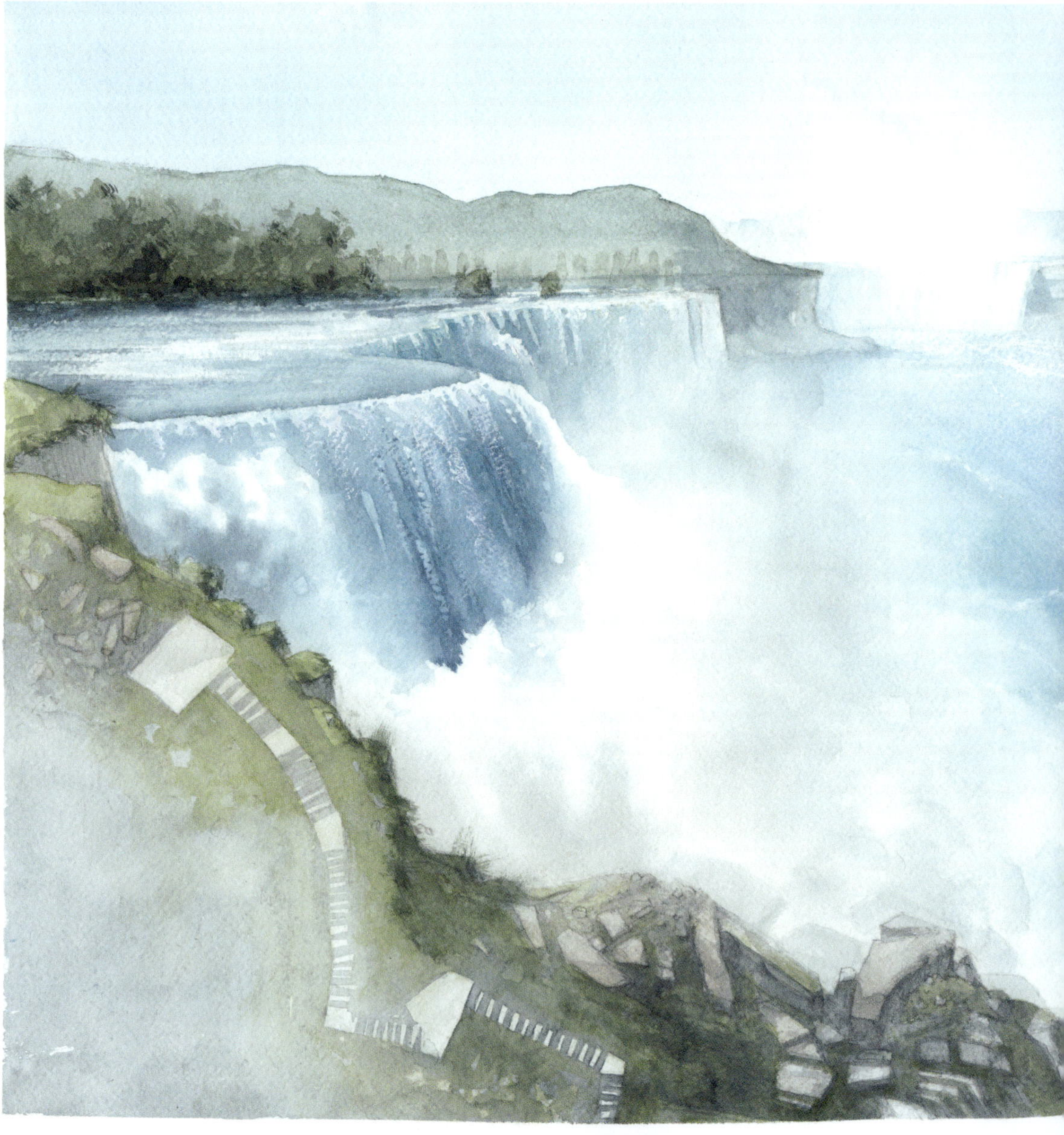

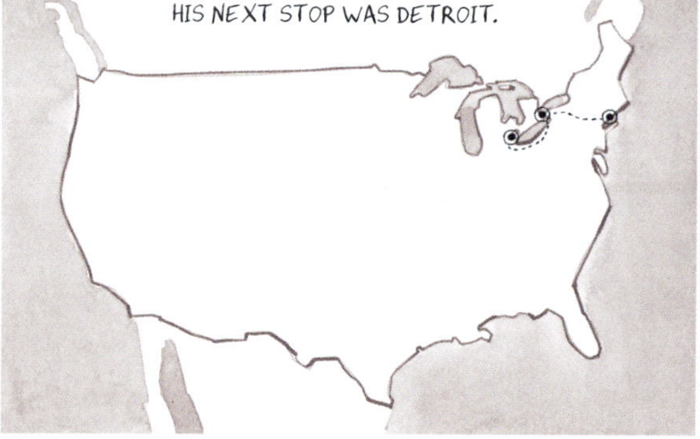
HIS NEXT STOP WAS DETROIT.

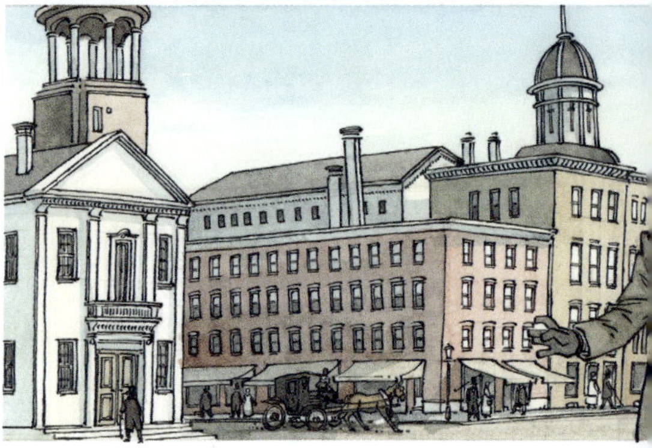

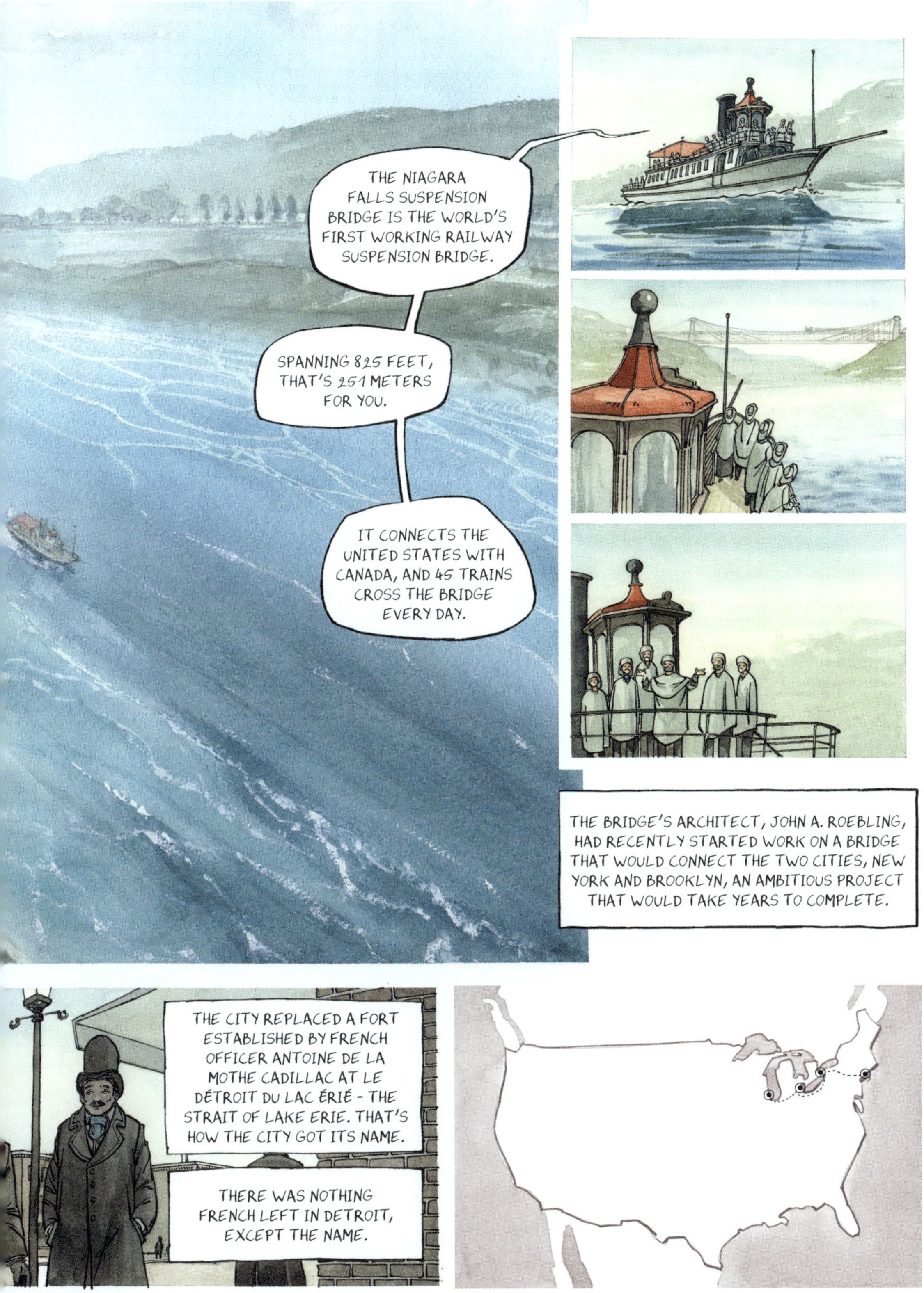
THE NIAGARA FALLS SUSPENSION BRIDGE IS THE WORLD'S FIRST WORKING RAILWAY SUSPENSION BRIDGE.
SPANNING 825 FEET, THAT'S 251 METERS FOR YOU.
IT CONNECTS THE UNITED STATES WITH CANADA, AND 45 TRAINS CROSS THE BRIDGE EVERY DAY.
THE BRIDGE'S ARCHITECT, JOHN A. ROEBLING, HAD RECENTLY STARTED WORK ON A BRIDGE THAT WOULD CONNECT THE TWO CITIES, NEW YORK AND BROOKLYN, AN AMBITIOUS PROJECT THAT WOULD TAKE YEARS TO COMPLETE.
THE CITY REPLACED A FORT ESTABLISHED BY FRENCH OFFICER ANTOINE DE LA MOTHE CADILLAC AT LE DÉTROIT DU LAC ÉRIÉ - THE STRAIT OF LAKE ERIE. THAT'S HOW THE CITY GOT ITS NAME.
THERE WAS NOTHING FRENCH LEFT IN DETROIT, EXCEPT THE NAME.

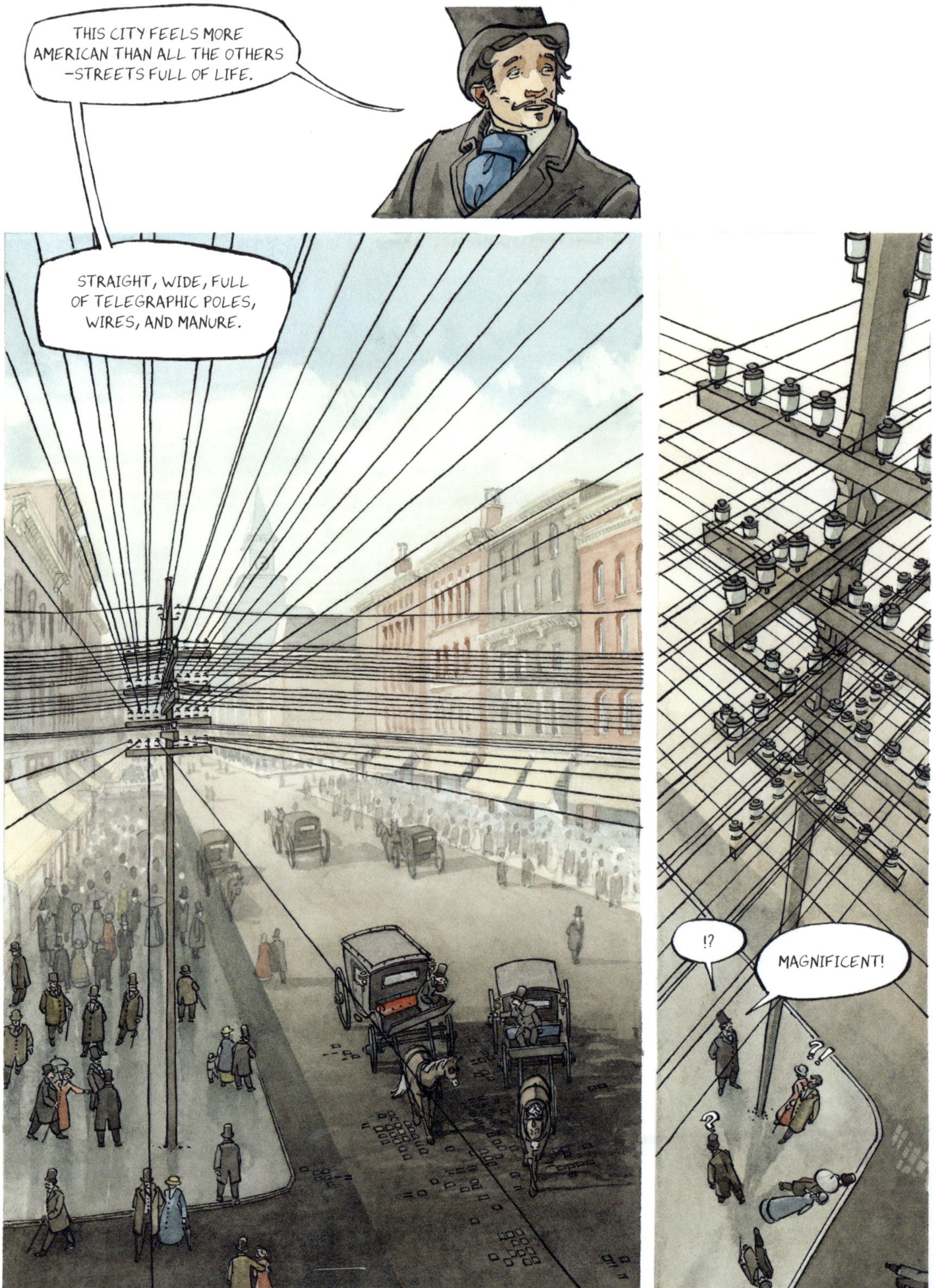
THIS CITY FEELS MORE AMERICAN THAN ALL THE OTHERS –STREETS FULL OF LIFE.
STRAIGHT, WIDE, FULL OF TELEGRAPHIC POLES, WIRES, AND MANURE.
!?
MAGNIFICENT!
?!
?

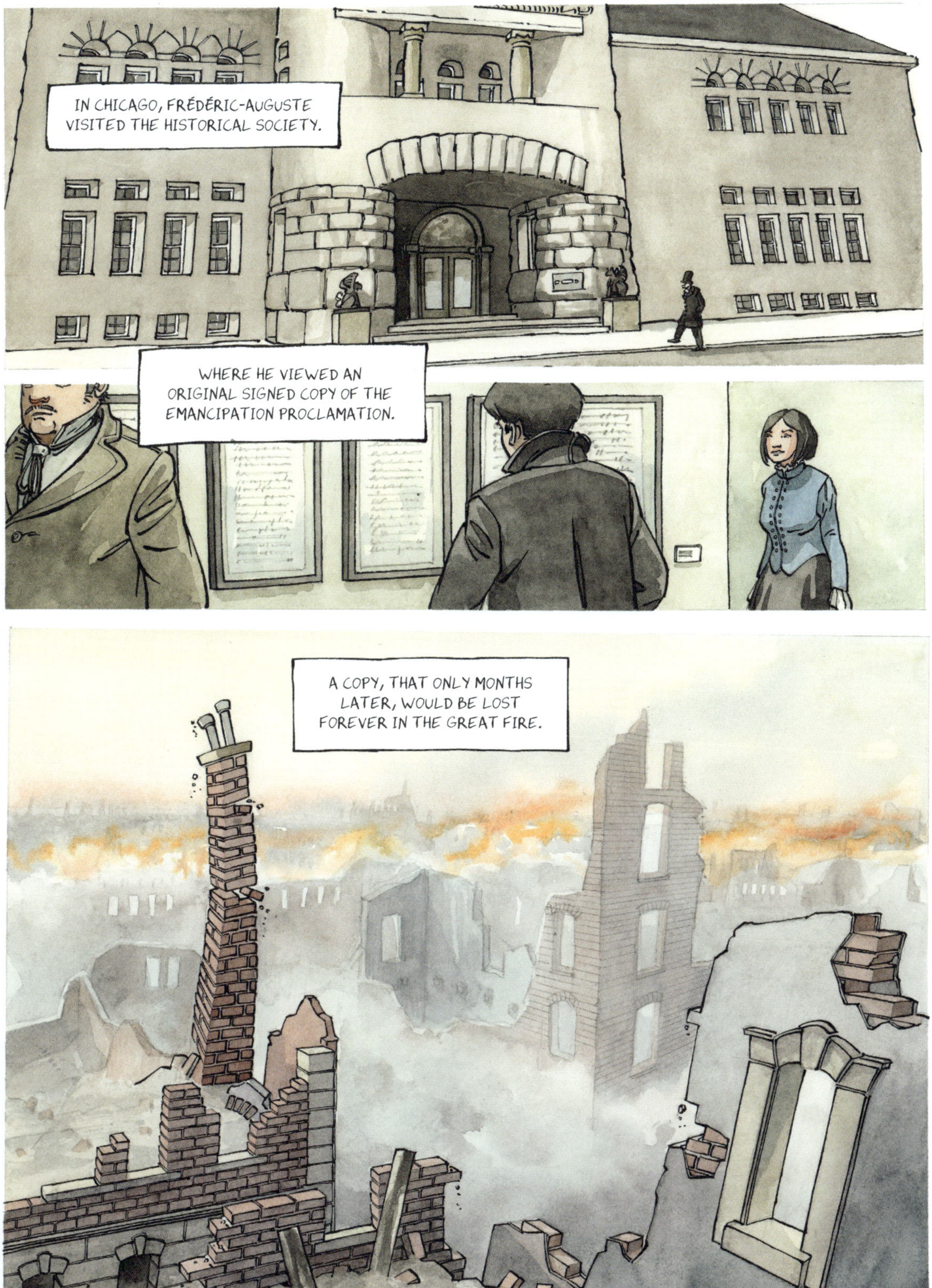
IN CHICAGO, FRÉDÉRIC-AUGUSTE VISITED THE HISTORICAL SOCIETY.
WHERE HE VIEWED AN ORIGINAL SIGNED COPY OF THE EMANCIPATION PROCLAMATION.
A COPY, THAT ONLY MONTHS LATER, WOULD BE LOST FOREVER IN THE GREAT FIRE.

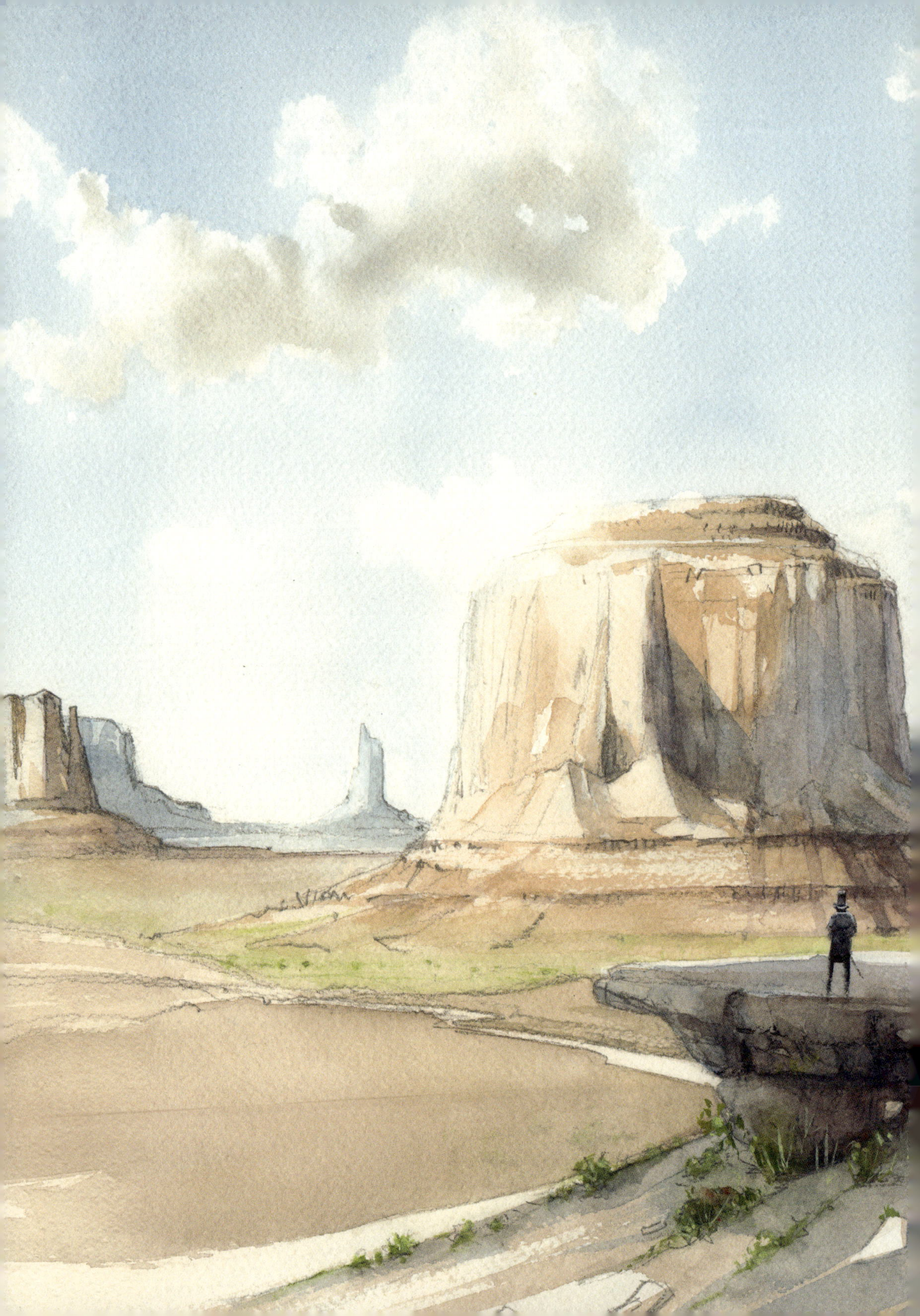

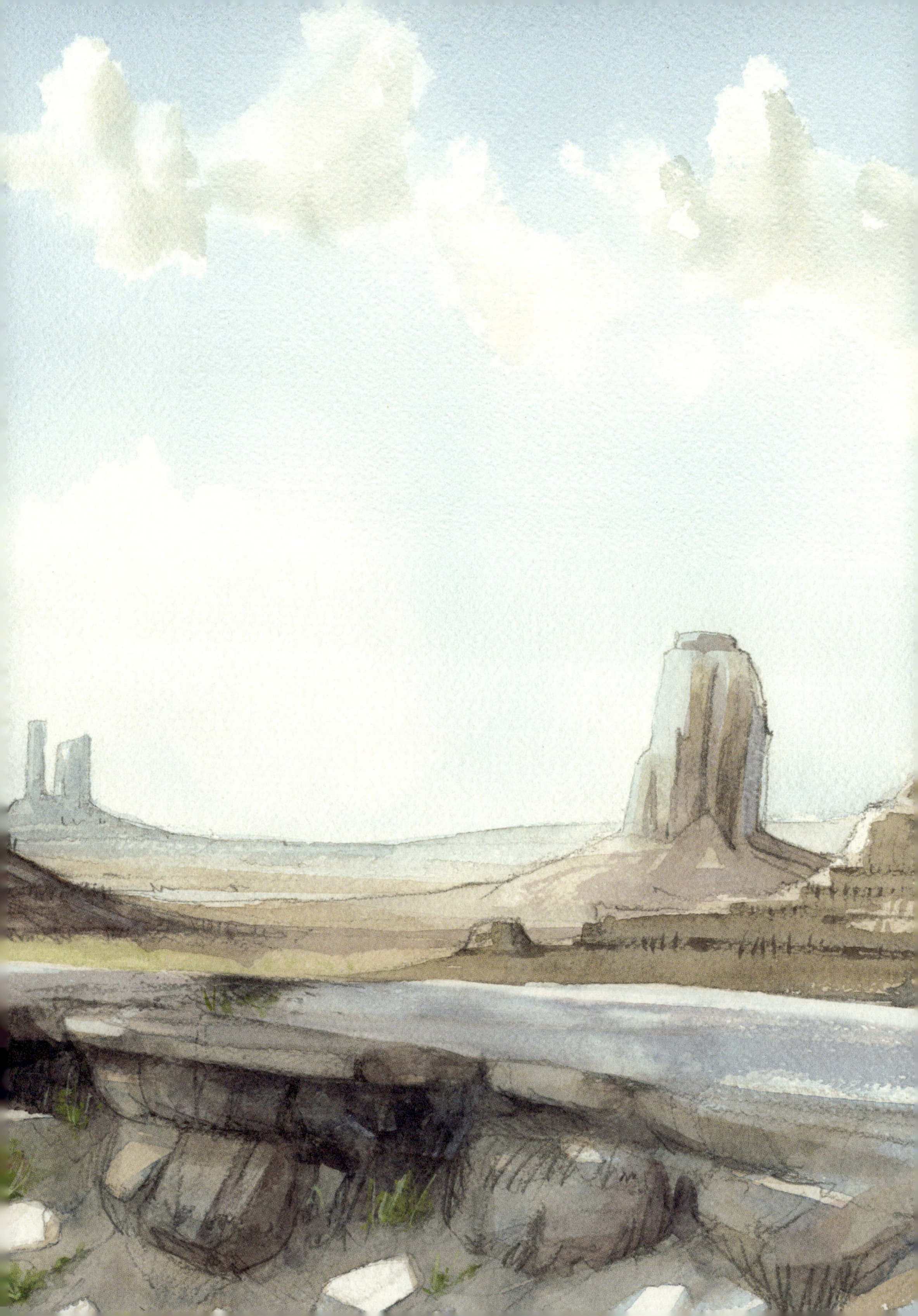

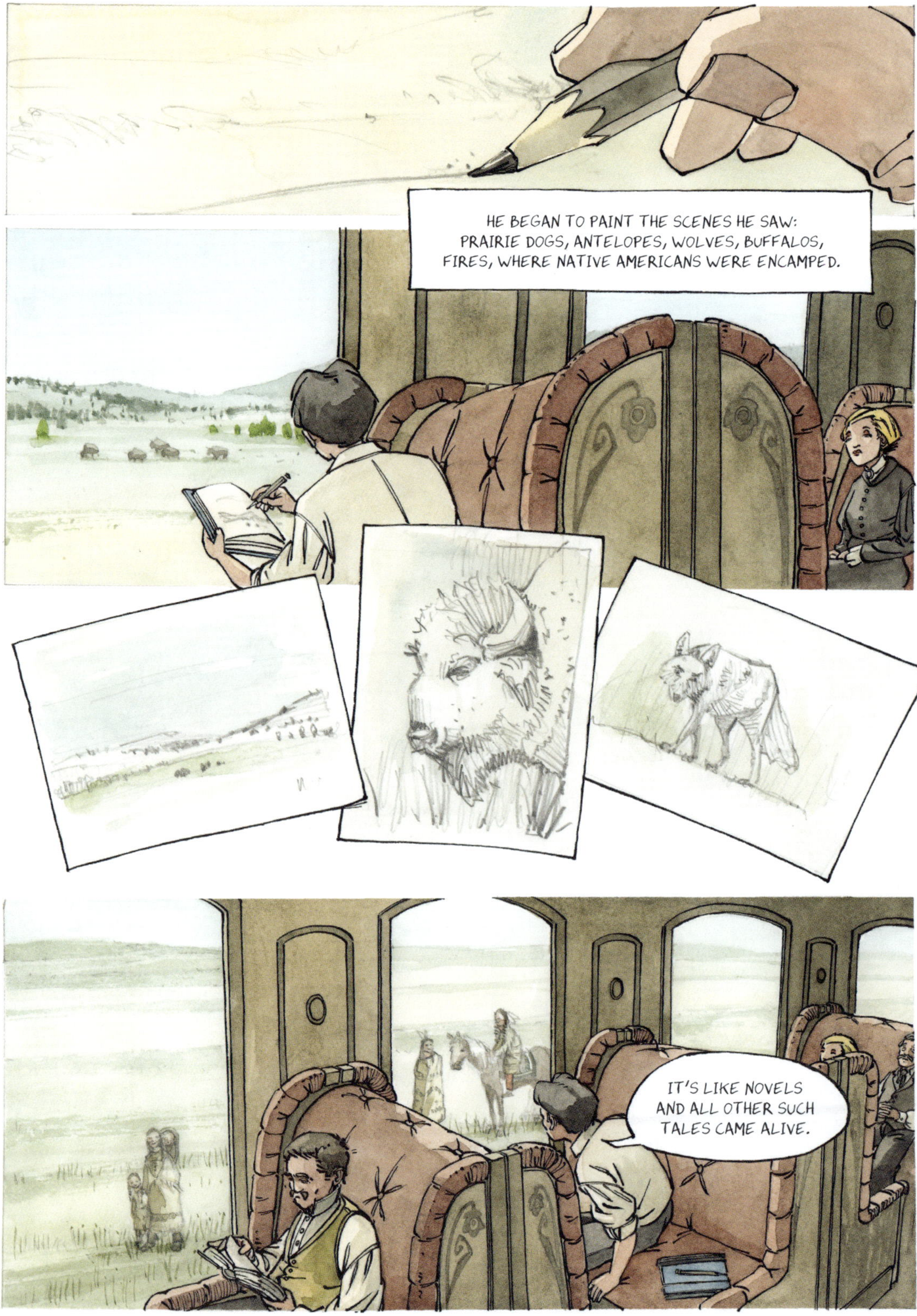
HE BEGAN TO PAINT THE SCENES HE SAW: PRAIRIE DOGS, ANTELOPES, WOLVES, BUFFALOS, FIRES, WHERE NATIVE AMERICANS WERE ENCAMPED.
IT'S LIKE NOVELS AND ALL OTHER SUCH TALES CAME ALIVE.

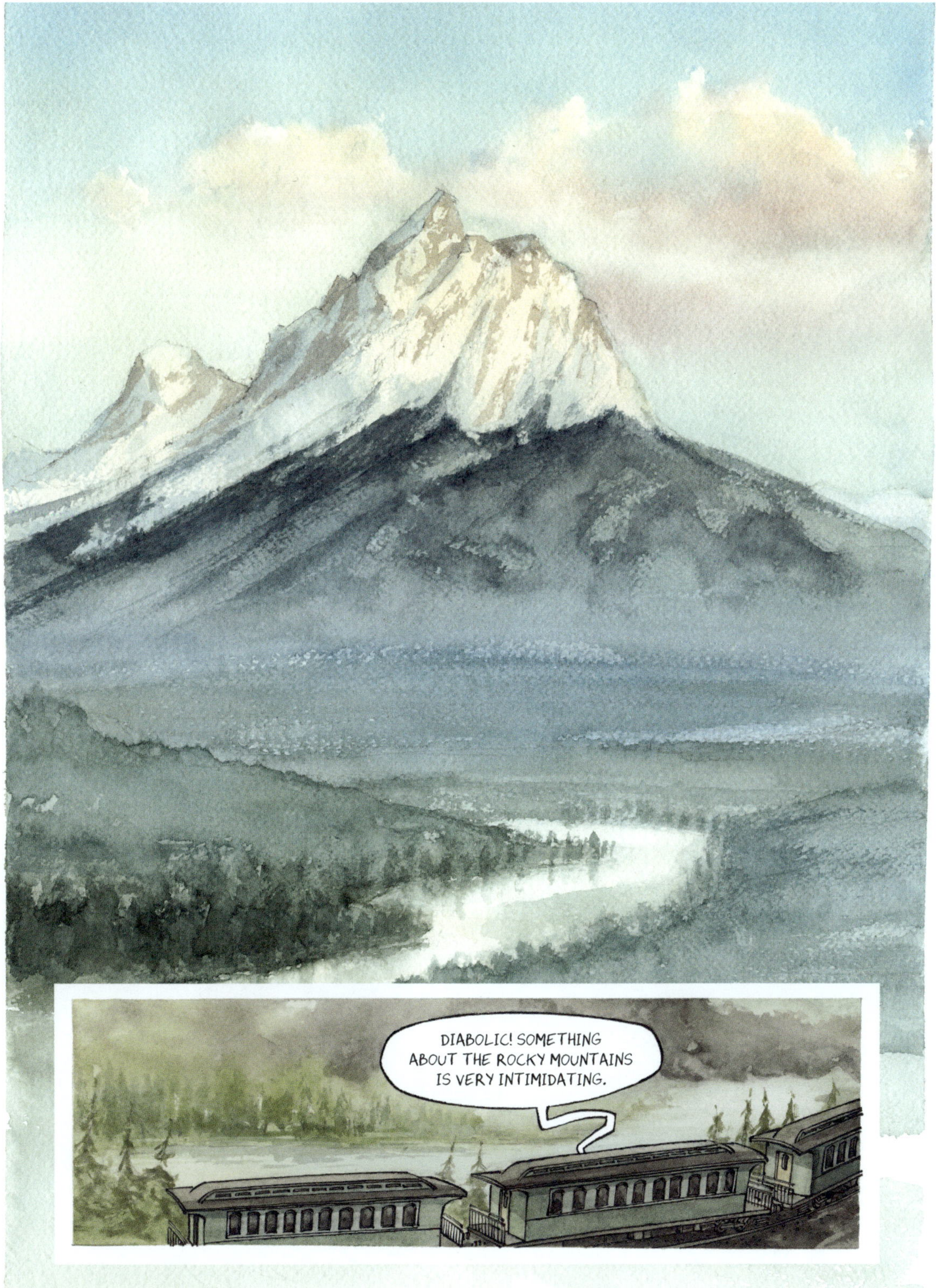
DIABOLIC! SOMETHING ABOUT THE ROCKY MOUNTAINS IS VERY INTIMIDATING.

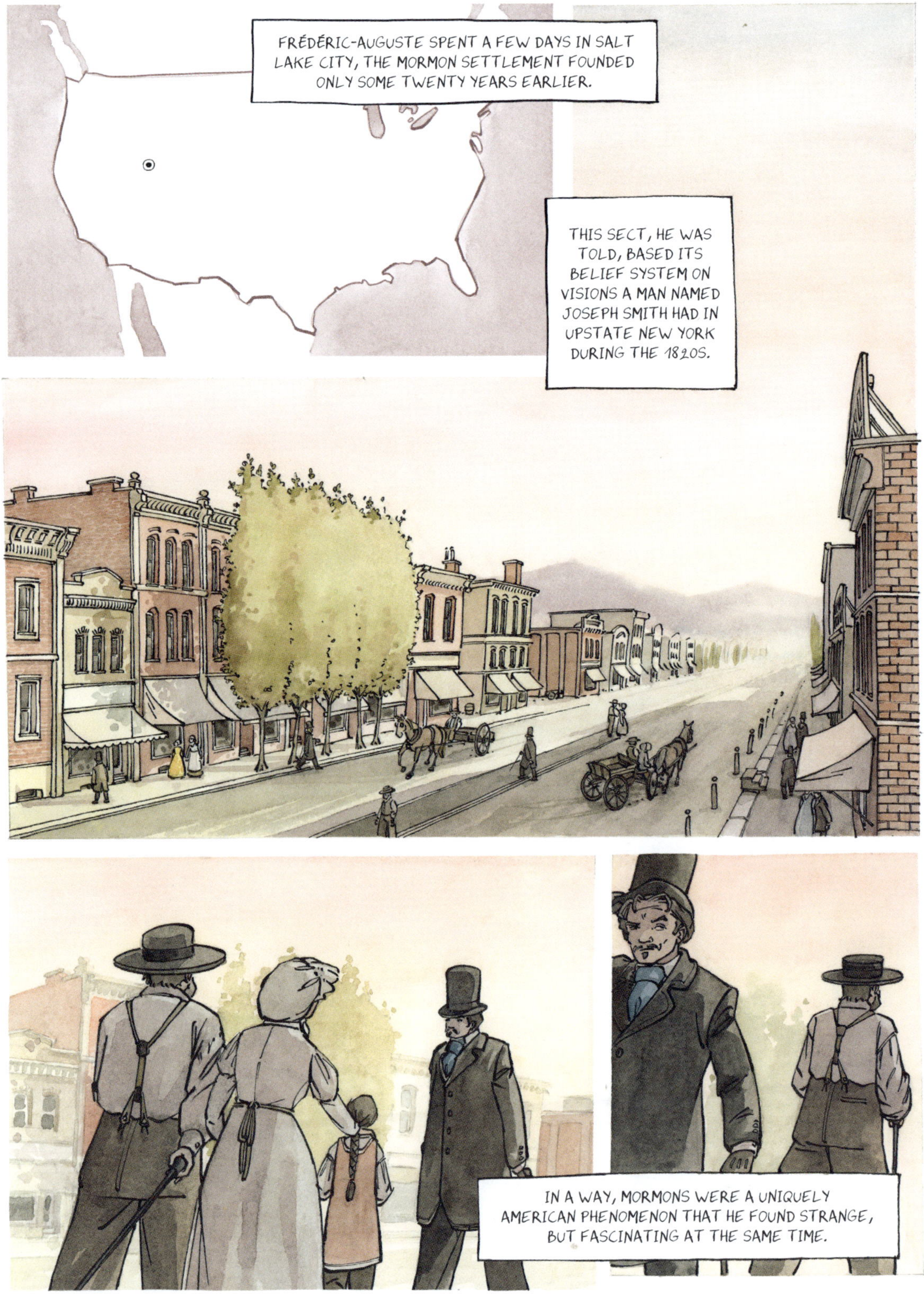
FRÉDÉRIC-AUGUSTE SPENT A FEW DAYS IN SALT LAKE CITY, THE MORMON SETTLEMENT FOUNDED ONLY SOME TWENTY YEARS EARLIER.
THIS SECT, HE WAS TOLD, BASED ITS BELIEF SYSTEM ON VISIONS A MAN NAMED JOSEPH SMITH HAD IN UPSTATE NEW YORK DURING THE 1820S.
IN A WAY, MORMONS WERE A UNIQUELY AMERICAN PHENOMENON THAT HE FOUND STRANGE, BUT FASCINATING AT THE SAME TIME.

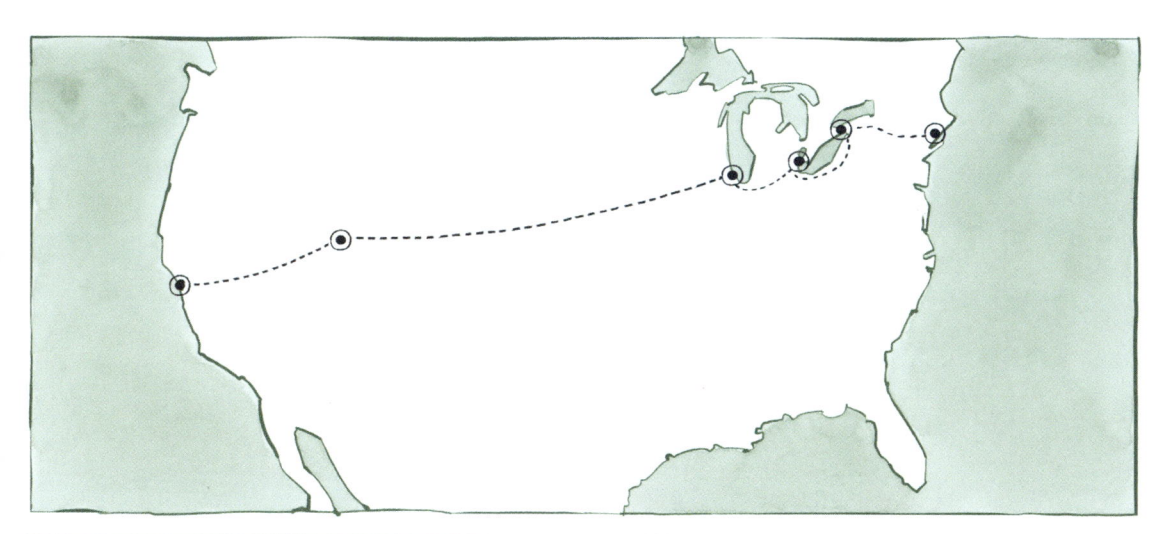

AFTER MONTHS OF TRAVELING, HE REACHED SAN FRANCISCO. FRÉDÉRIC-AUGUSTE BARTHOLDI HAD MADE IT TO THE AMERICAN WEST COAST.

THIS CITY IS A BABEL OF MATERIALISM AND GREED.

HE HAD CROSSED THE WHOLE COUNTRY AND HAD SEEN MORE OF AMERICA THAN ANY OTHER FRENCHMAN BEFORE HIM.

THESE COLOSSI ARE SUPERB!

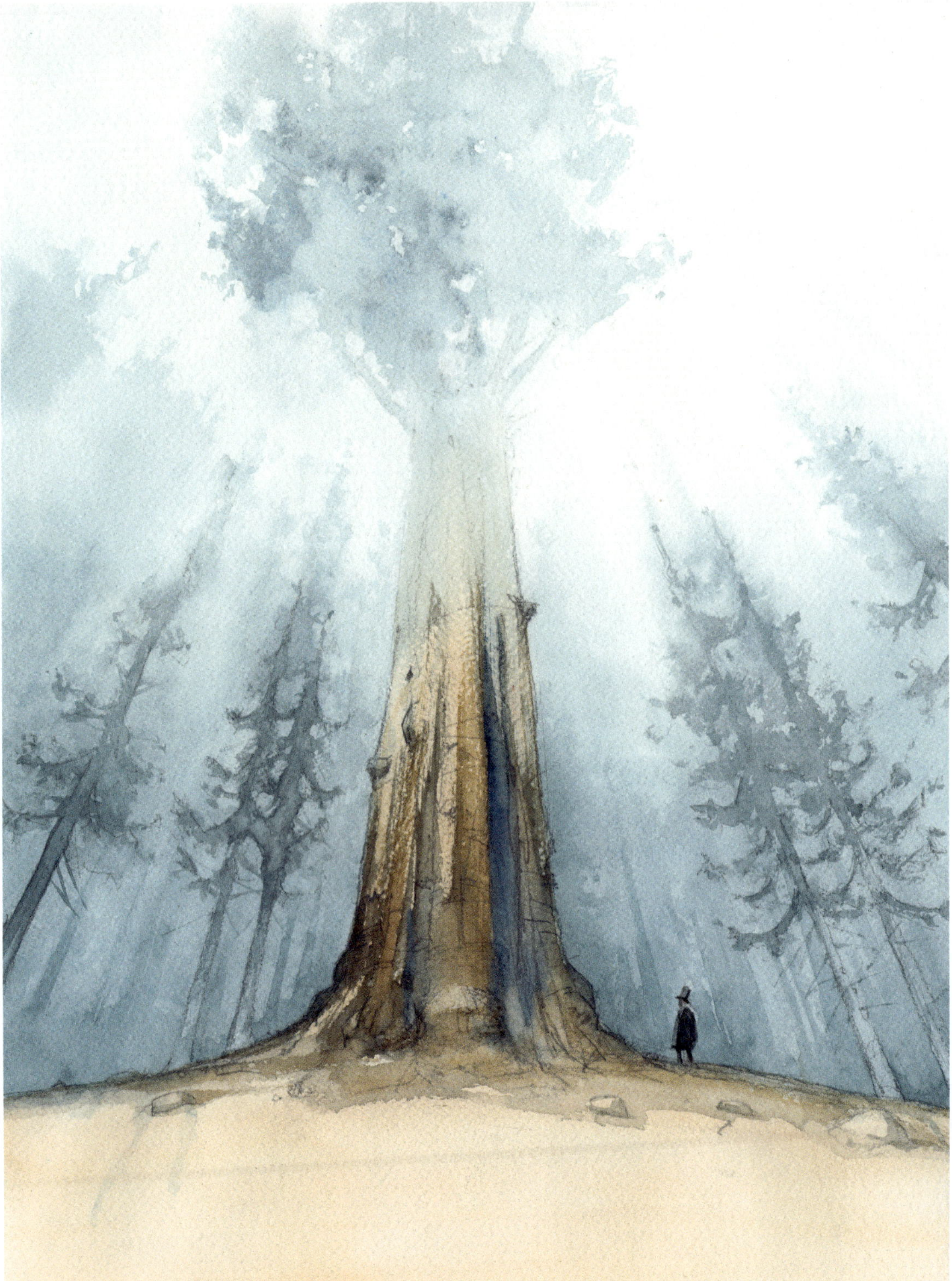

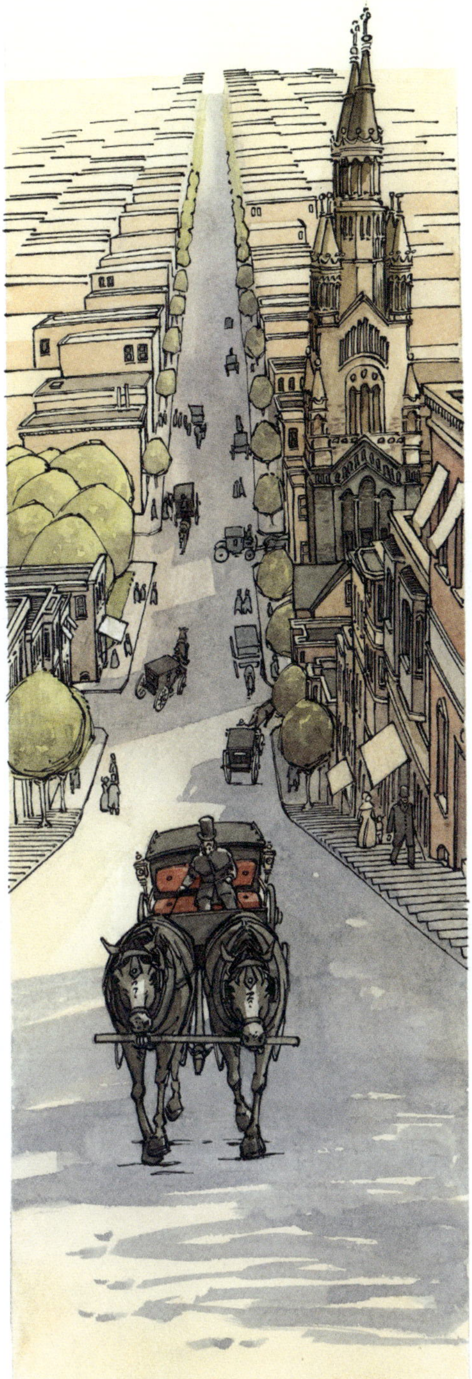

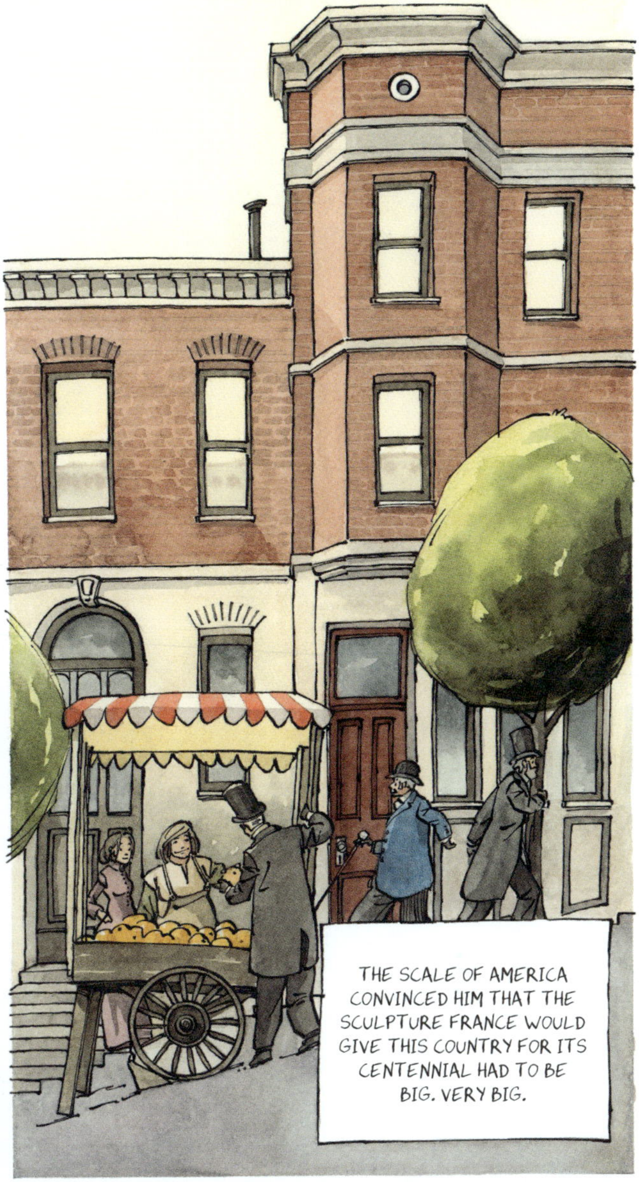

THE SCALE OF AMERICA CONVINCED HIM THAT THE SCULPTURE FRANCE WOULD GIVE THIS COUNTRY FOR ITS CENTENNIAL HAD TO BE BIG. VERY BIG.

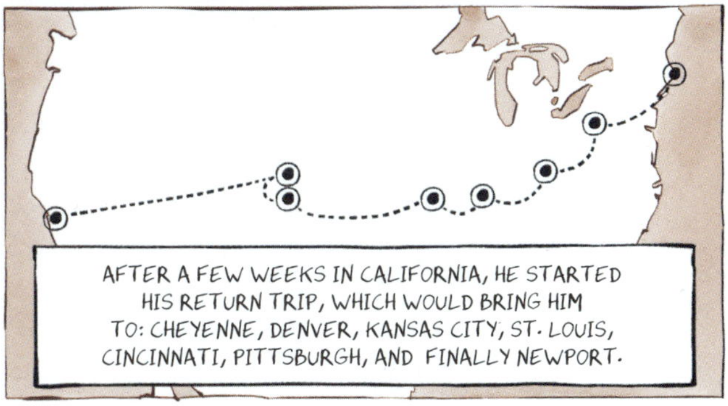

AFTER A FEW WEEKS IN CALIFORNIA, HE STARTED HIS RETURN TRIP, WHICH WOULD BRING HIM TO: CHEYENNE, DENVER, KANSAS CITY, ST. LOUIS, CINCINNATI, PITTSBURGH, AND FINALLY NEWPORT.

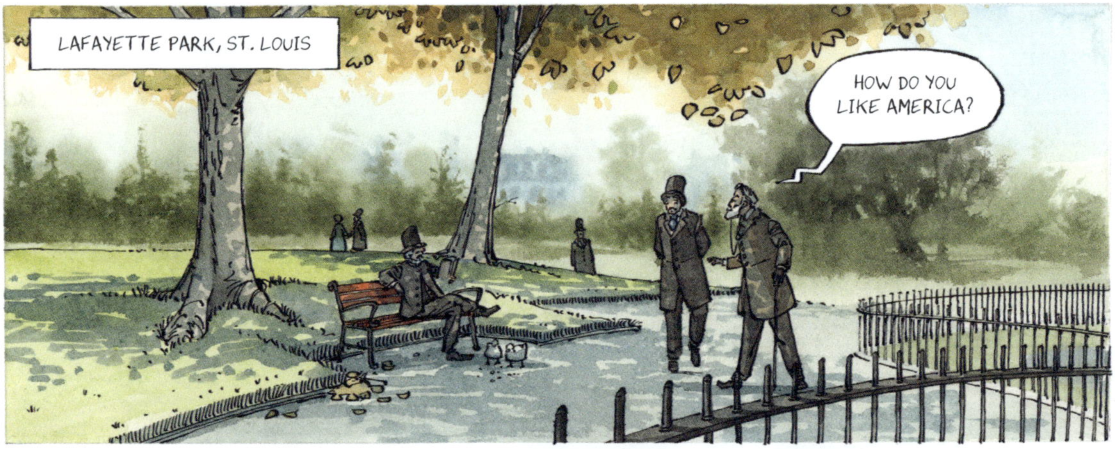
LAFAYETTE PARK, ST. LOUIS
HOW DO YOU LIKE AMERICA?

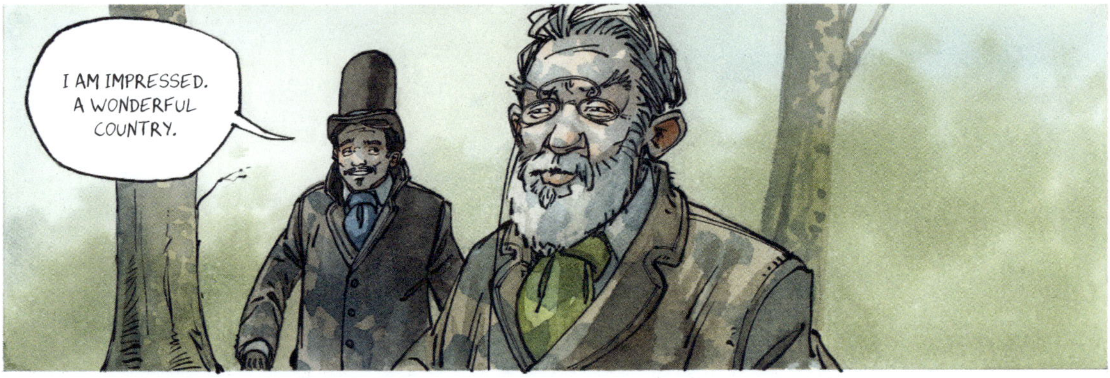
I AM IMPRESSED. A WONDERFUL COUNTRY.

IN ST. LOUIS, FRÉDÉRIC-AUGUSTE MET WITH STATE SENATOR CARL SCHURZ, ANOTHER OF SUMNER'S ACQUAINTANCES. SCHURZ WAR BORN IN GERMANY AND WAS A NATURALIZED CITIZEN. AS ONE OF THE LEADERS OF THE FAILED 1848 REVOLUTION IN GERMANY, HE HAD TO FLEE THE COUNTRY. HE FIRST STAYED IN FRANCE, BUT WHEN THE SECOND REPUBLIC CHANGED TO NAPOLEON III'S SECOND EMPIRE, HE DECIDED TO EMIGRATE TO THE UNITED STATES.

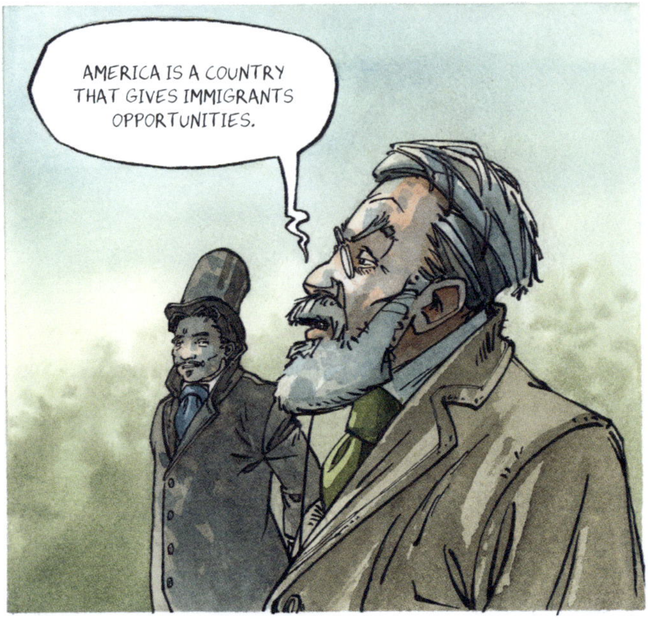
AMERICA IS A COUNTRY THAT GIVES IMMIGRANTS OPPORTUNITIES.

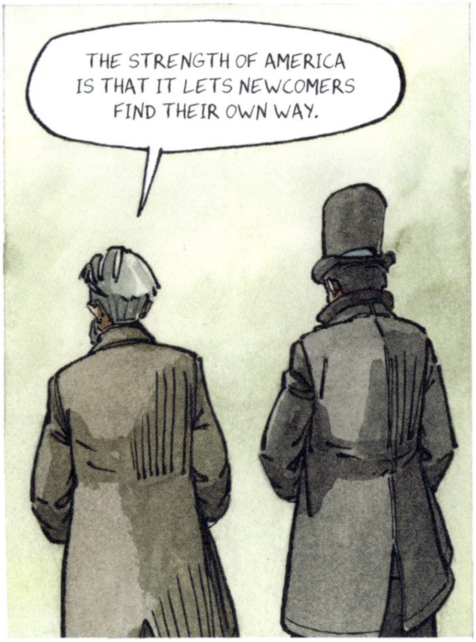
THE STRENGTH OF AMERICA IS THAT IT LETS NEWCOMERS FIND THEIR OWN WAY.

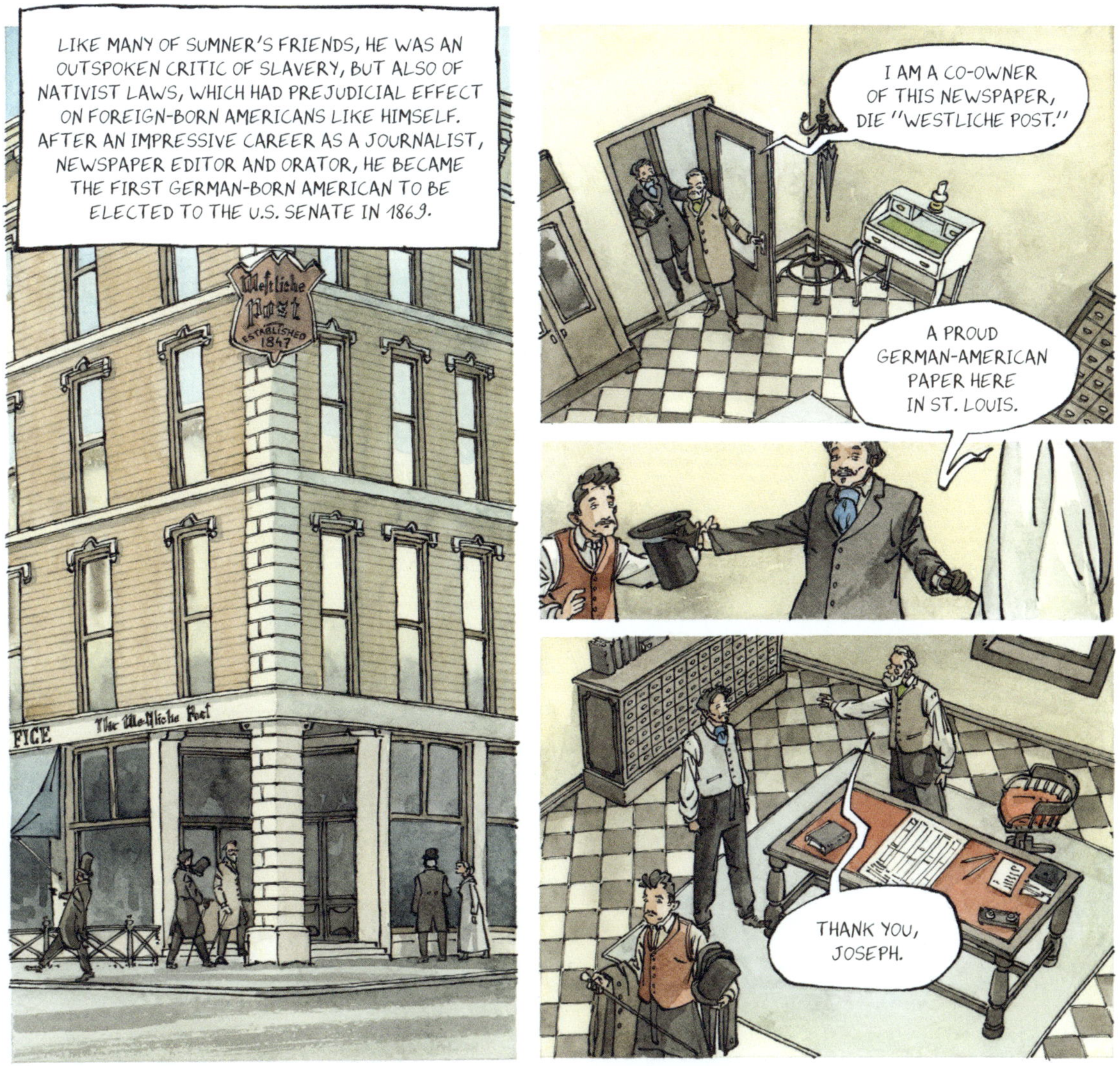
LIKE MANY OF SUMNER'S FRIENDS, HE WAS AN OUTSPOKEN CRITIC OF SLAVERY, BUT ALSO OF NATIVIST LAWS, WHICH HAD PREJUDICIAL EFFECT ON FOREIGN-BORN AMERICANS LIKE HIMSELF. AFTER AN IMPRESSIVE CAREER AS A JOURNALIST, NEWSPAPER EDITOR AND ORATOR, HE BECAME THE FIRST GERMAN-BORN AMERICAN TO BE ELECTED TO THE U.S. SENATE IN 1869.
ESTABLISHED 1847
I AM A CO-OWNER OF THIS NEWSPAPER, DIE "WESTLICHE POST."
A PROUD GERMAN-AMERICAN PAPER HERE IN ST. LOUIS.
THANK YOU, JOSEPH.

SCHURZ WAS IMPRESSED BY THE YOUNG SCULPTOR. FRÉDÉRIC-AUGUSTE WAS AT FIRST CONCERNED THAT AS AN AMERICAN OF GERMAN ORIGIN, SCHURZ WOULD BE OPPOSED TO THE IDEA OF A GIFT AS THE SYMBOL OF FRANCE'S FRIENDSHIP WITH AMERICA. BUT IT WAS QUITE THE OPPOSITE.

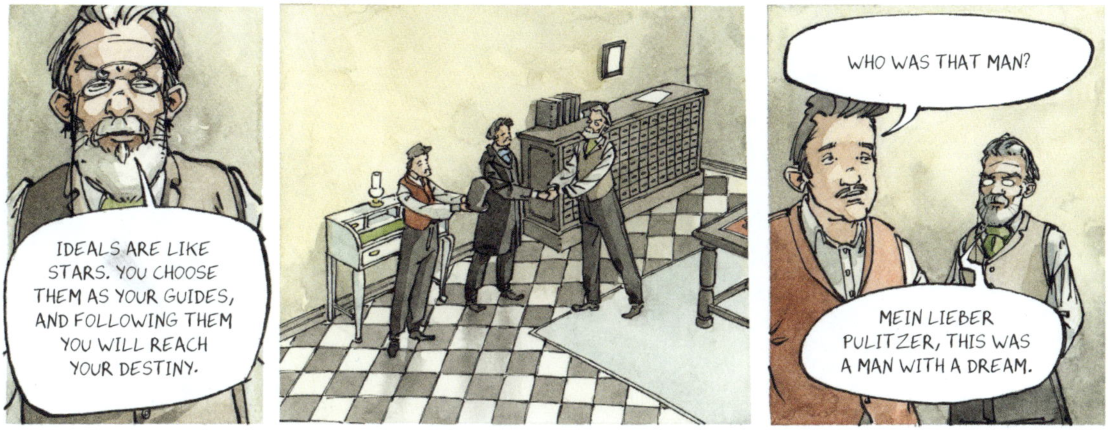
IDEALS ARE LIKE STARS. YOU CHOOSE THEM AS YOUR GUIDES, AND FOLLOWING THEM YOU WILL REACH YOUR DESTINY.
WHO WAS THAT MAN?
MEIN LIEBER PULITZER, THIS WAS A MAN WITH A DREAM.

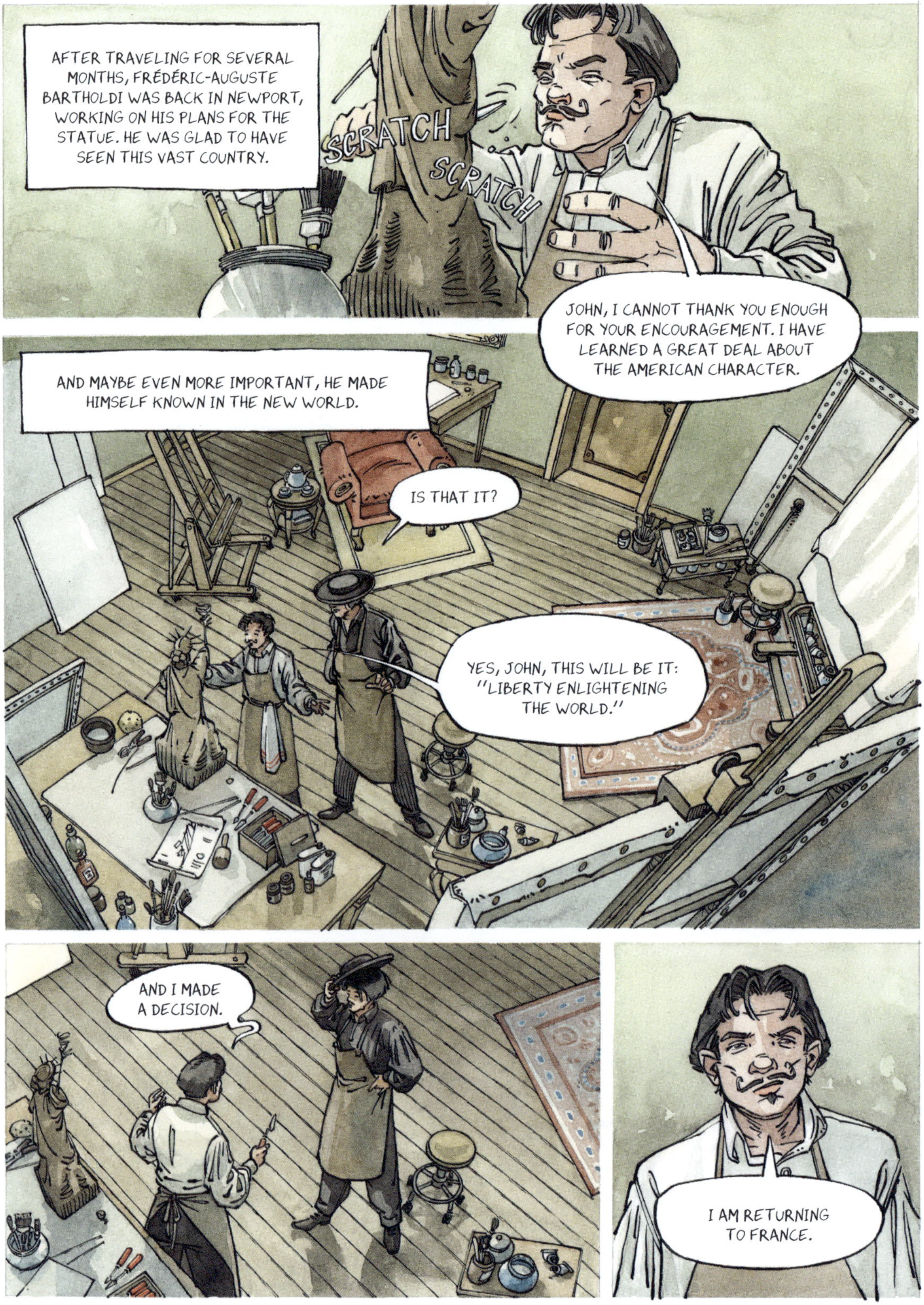
AFTER TRAVELING FOR SEVERAL MONTHS, FRÉDÉRIC-AUGUSTE BARTHOLDI WAS BACK IN NEWPORT, WORKING ON HIS PLANS FOR THE STATUE. HE WAS GLAD TO HAVE SEEN THIS VAST COUNTRY.
SCRATCH
SCRATCH
JOHN, I CANNOT THANK YOU ENOUGH FOR YOUR ENCOURAGEMENT. I HAVE LEARNED A GREAT DEAL ABOUT THE AMERICAN CHARACTER.
AND MAYBE EVEN MORE IMPORTANT, HE MADE HIMSELF KNOWN IN THE NEW WORLD.
IS THAT IT?
YES, JOHN, THIS WILL BE IT: "LIBERTY ENLIGHTENING THE WORLD."
AND I MADE A DECISION.
I AM RETURNING TO FRANCE.

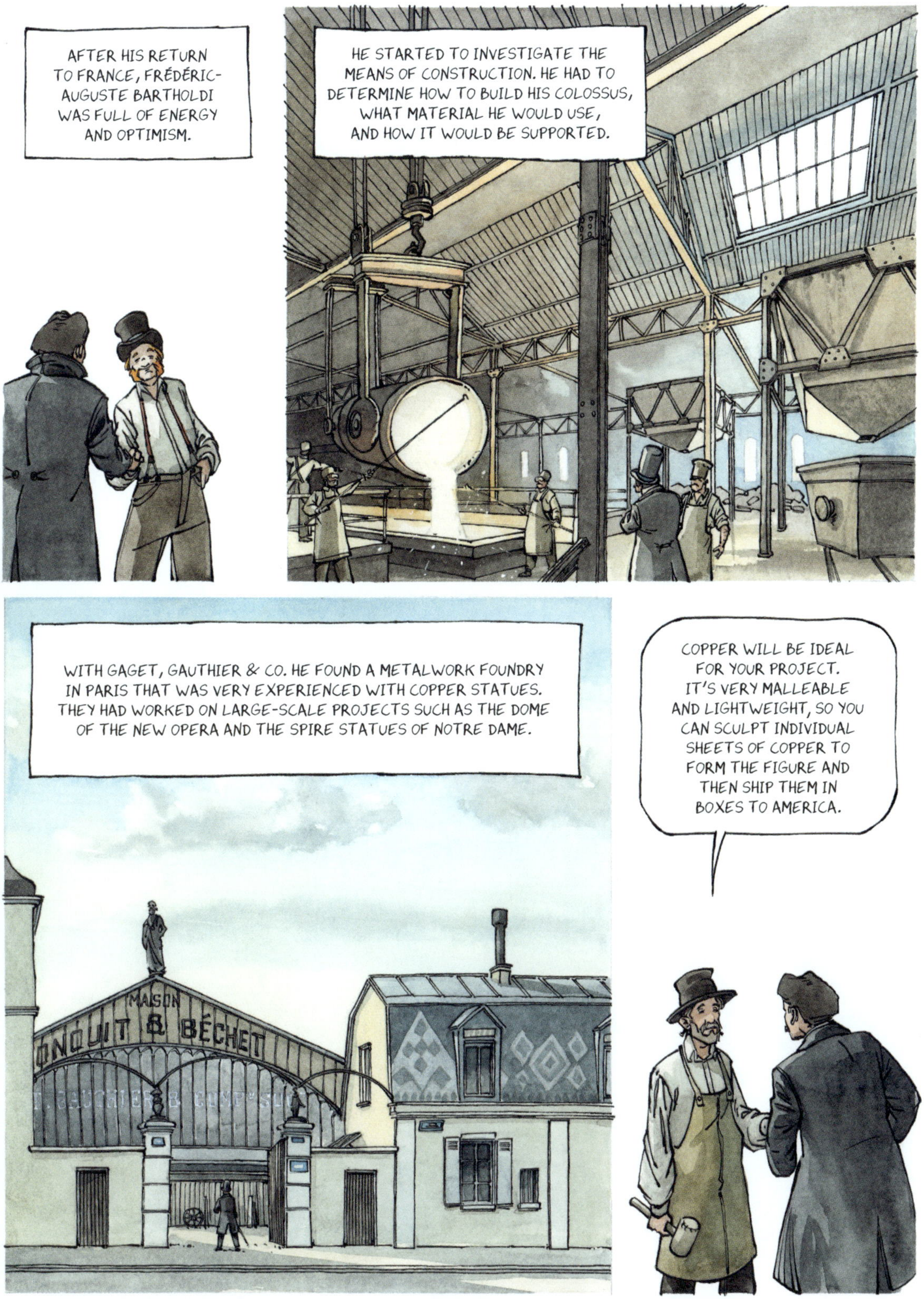
AFTER HIS RETURN TO FRANCE, FRÉDÉRIC-AUGUSTE BARTHOLDI WAS FULL OF ENERGY AND OPTIMISM.
HE STARTED TO INVESTIGATE THE MEANS OF CONSTRUCTION. HE HAD TO DETERMINE HOW TO BUILD HIS COLOSSUS, WHAT MATERIAL HE WOULD USE, AND HOW IT WOULD BE SUPPORTED.
WITH GAGET, GAUTHIER & CO. HE FOUND A METALWORK FOUNDRY IN PARIS THAT WAS VERY EXPERIENCED WITH COPPER STATUES. THEY HAD WORKED ON LARGE-SCALE PROJECTS SUCH AS THE DOME OF THE NEW OPERA AND THE SPIRE STATUES OF NOTRE DAME.
MAISON
BÉCHET
COPPER WILL BE IDEAL FOR YOUR PROJECT. IT'S VERY MALLEABLE AND LIGHTWEIGHT, SO YOU CAN SCULPT INDIVIDUAL SHEETS OF COPPER TO FORM THE FIGURE AND THEN SHIP THEM IN BOXES TO AMERICA.

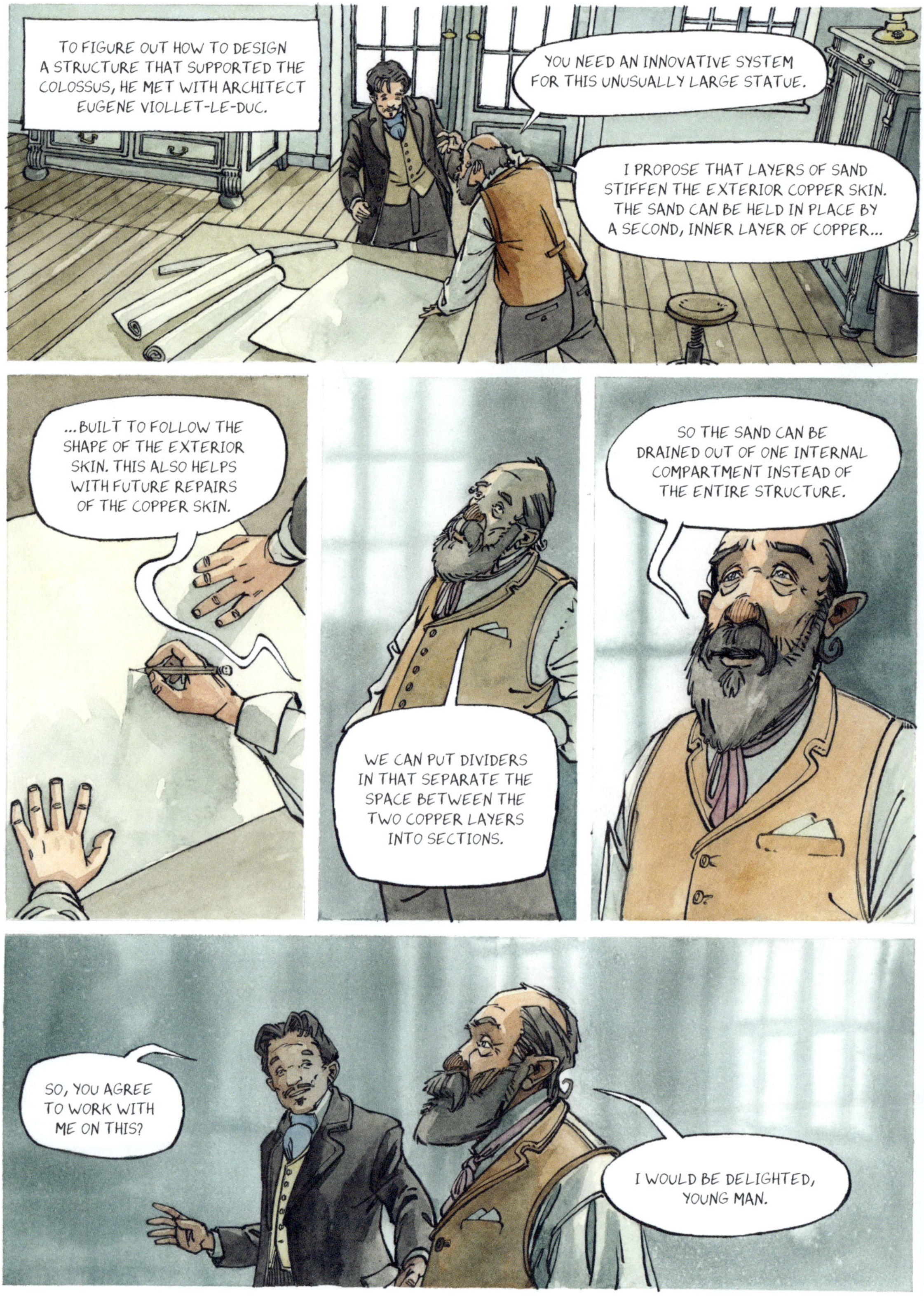
TO FIGURE OUT HOW TO DESIGN A STRUCTURE THAT SUPPORTED THE COLOSSUS, HE MET WITH ARCHITECT EUGENE VIOLLET-LE-DUC.
YOU NEED AN INNOVATIVE SYSTEM FOR THIS UNUSUALLY LARGE STATUE.
I PROPOSE THAT LAYERS OF SAND STIFFEN THE EXTERIOR COPPER SKIN. THE SAND CAN BE HELD IN PLACE BY A SECOND, INNER LAYER OF COPPER...
...BUILT TO FOLLOW THE SHAPE OF THE EXTERIOR SKIN. THIS ALSO HELPS WITH FUTURE REPAIRS OF THE COPPER SKIN.
WE CAN PUT DIVIDERS IN THAT SEPARATE THE SPACE BETWEEN THE TWO COPPER LAYERS INTO SECTIONS.
SO THE SAND CAN BE DRAINED OUT OF ONE INTERNAL COMPARTMENT INSTEAD OF THE ENTIRE STRUCTURE.
SO, YOU AGREE TO WORK WITH ME ON THIS?
I WOULD BE DELIGHTED, YOUNG MAN.

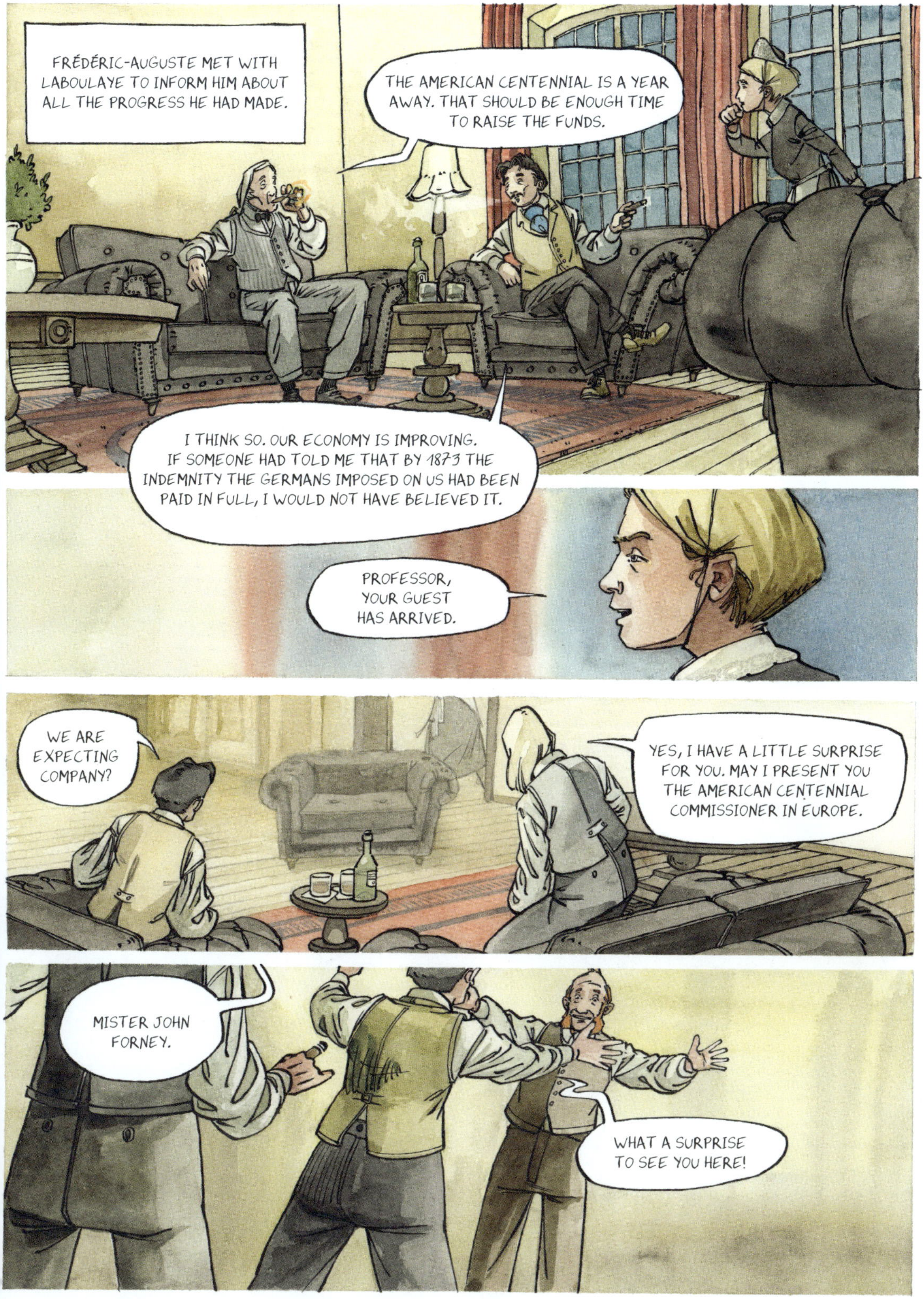
FRÉDÉRIC-AUGUSTE MET WITH LABOULAYE TO INFORM HIM ABOUT ALL THE PROGRESS HE HAD MADE.
THE AMERICAN CENTENNIAL IS A YEAR AWAY. THAT SHOULD BE ENOUGH TIME TO RAISE THE FUNDS.
I THINK SO. OUR ECONOMY IS IMPROVING. IF SOMEONE HAD TOLD ME THAT BY 1873 THE INDEMNITY THE GERMANS IMPOSED ON US HAD BEEN PAID IN FULL, I WOULD NOT HAVE BELIEVED IT.
PROFESSOR, YOUR GUEST HAS ARRIVED.
WE ARE EXPECTING COMPANY?
YES, I HAVE A LITTLE SURPRISE FOR YOU. MAY I PRESENT YOU THE AMERICAN CENTENNIAL COMMISSIONER IN EUROPE.
MISTER JOHN FORNEY.
WHAT A SURPRISE TO SEE YOU HERE!

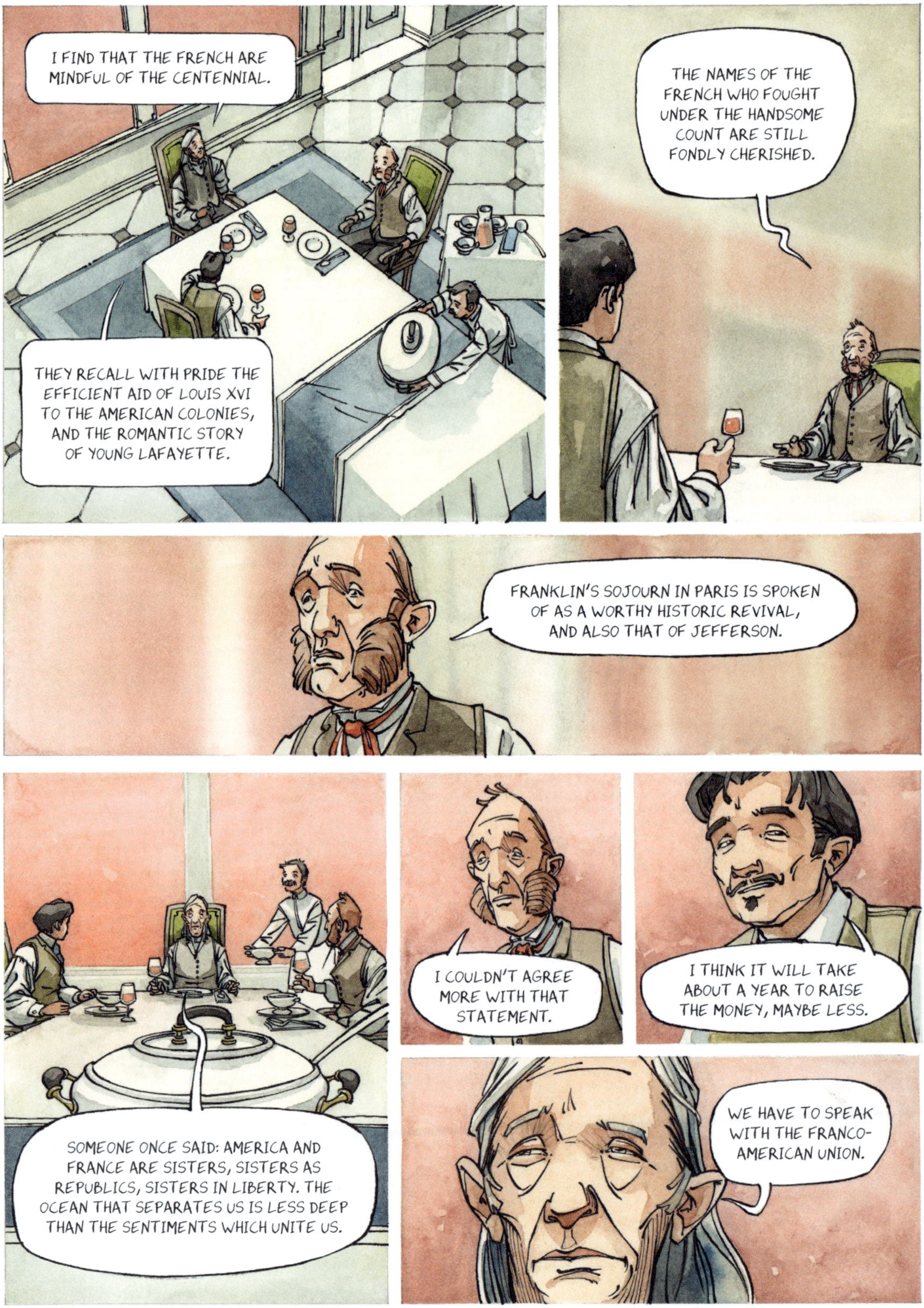
I FIND THAT THE FRENCH ARE MINDFUL OF THE CENTENNIAL.
THEY RECALL WITH PRIDE THE EFFICIENT AID OF LOUIS XVI TO THE AMERICAN COLONIES, AND THE ROMANTIC STORY OF YOUNG LAFAYETTE.
THE NAMES OF THE FRENCH WHO FOUGHT UNDER THE HANDSOME COUNT ARE STILL FONDLY CHERISHED.
FRANKLIN'S SOJOURN IN PARIS IS SPOKEN OF AS A WORTHY HISTORIC REVIVAL, AND ALSO THAT OF JEFFERSON.
SOMEONE ONCE SAID: AMERICA AND FRANCE ARE SISTERS, SISTERS AS REPUBLICS, SISTERS IN LIBERTY. THE OCEAN THAT SEPARATES US IS LESS DEEP THAN THE SENTIMENTS WHICH UNITE US.
I COULDN'T AGREE MORE WITH THAT STATEMENT.
I THINK IT WILL TAKE ABOUT A YEAR TO RAISE THE MONEY, MAYBE LESS.
WE HAVE TO SPEAK WITH THE FRANCO-AMERICAN UNION.

THE FRANCO-AMERICAN UNION RESEMBLED THE AMERICAN UNION LEAGUE CLUB. PROFESSOR LABOULAYE PRESIDED OVER THE GROUP; JOHN FORNAY WAS AN HONORARY MEMBER. ITS MEMBERS, FRENCHMAN AND AMERICANS ALIKE, WERE ALL WEALTHY, LIBERAL, AND EMOTIONALLY ATTACHED TO THE UNITED STATES. MANY OF THEM WERE DESCENDANTS OF FRENCHMEN FAMOUS FOR THEIR TIES TO AMERICA, AMONG THEM WERE OSCAR DE LAFAYETTE, HIPPOLYTE DE TOCQUEVILLE, AS WELL AS PAUL DE REMUSAT, AND JULES DE LASTEYRIE WHO WERE BOTH RELATED TO LAFAYETTE.

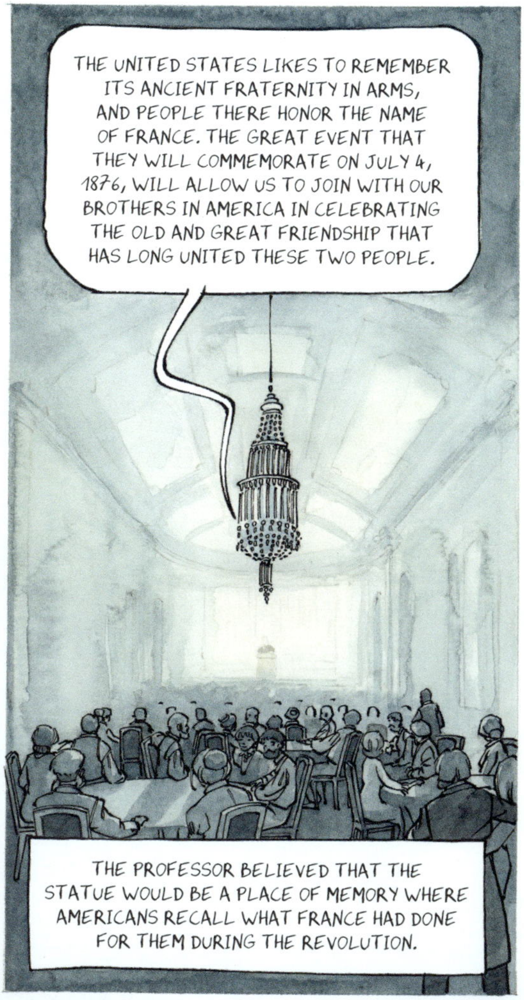
THE UNITED STATES LIKES TO REMEMBER ITS ANCIENT FRATERNITY IN ARMS, AND PEOPLE THERE HONOR THE NAME OF FRANCE. THE GREAT EVENT THAT THEY WILL COMMEMORATE ON JULY 4, 1876, WILL ALLOW US TO JOIN WITH OUR BROTHERS IN AMERICA IN CELEBRATING THE OLD AND GREAT FRIENDSHIP THAT HAS LONG UNITED THESE TWO PEOPLE.

THE PROFESSOR BELIEVED THAT THE STATUE WOULD BE A PLACE OF MEMORY WHERE AMERICANS RECALL WHAT FRANCE HAD DONE FOR THEM DURING THE REVOLUTION.

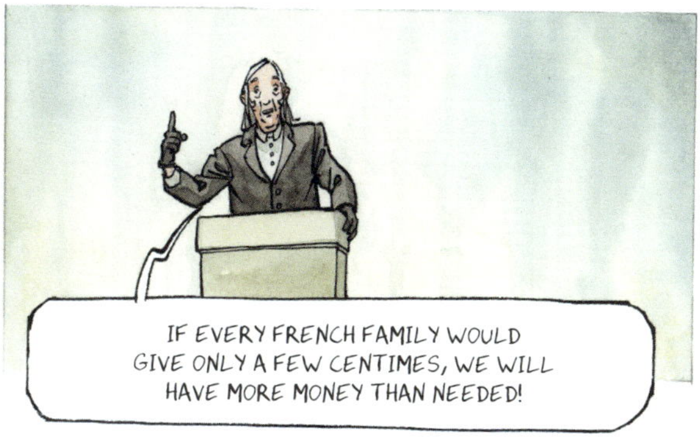
IF EVERY FRENCH FAMILY WOULD GIVE ONLY A FEW CENTIMES, WE WILL HAVE MORE MONEY THAN NEEDED!

IN SEPTEMBER 1875, THE FRANCO-AMERICAN UNION OPENED ITS FUNDRAISING CAMPAIGN WITH A PUBLIC ANNOUNCEMENT OF THE PROJECT. A NOTICE IN NEWSPAPERS THROUGHOUT THE COUNTRY INFORMED THE PUBLIC ABOUT THE STATUE.

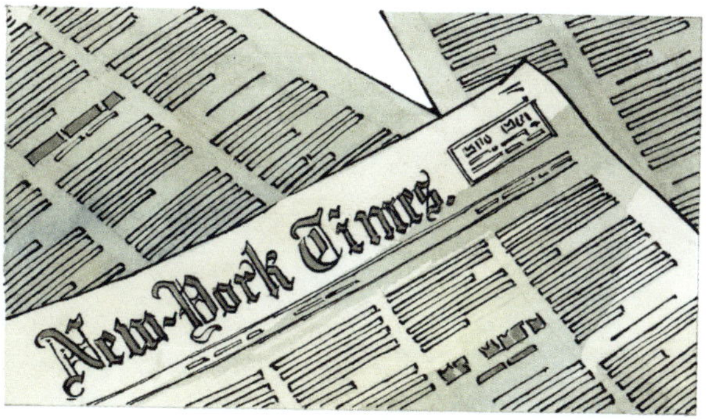
New-York Times.

AT THE SAME TIME, THE UNION APPEALED TO AMERICANS TO ACCEPT THE GIFT AND JOIN "THE FELLOWSHIP OF COLLABORATION" BY PREPARING A SITE AND PEDESTAL FOR THE STATUE. PROFESSOR LABOULAYE WROTE PERSONALLY TO PRESIDENT GRANT AND REQUESTED BEDLOE'S ISLAND, THE LOCATION FRÉDÉRIC-AUGUSTE BARTHOLDI HAD IDENTIFIED DURING HIS VISIT.

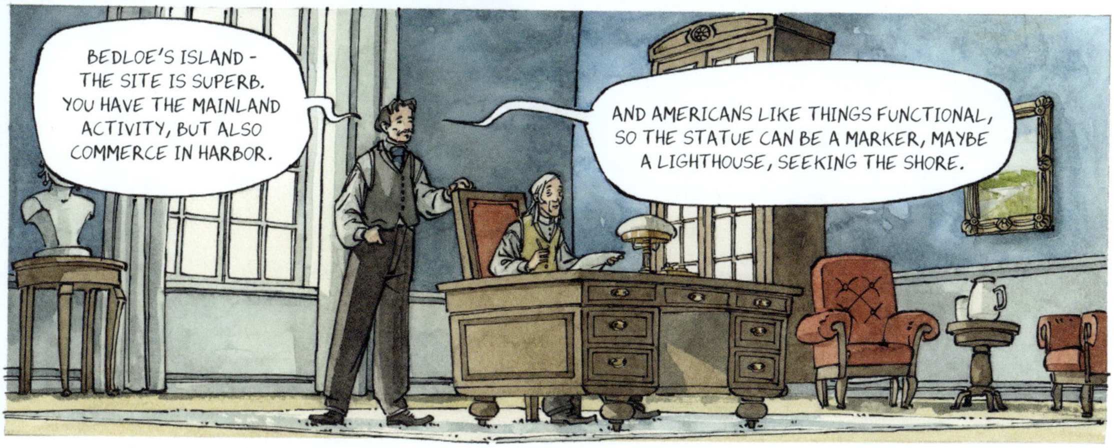
BEDLOE'S ISLAND - THE SITE IS SUPERB. YOU HAVE THE MAINLAND ACTIVITY, BUT ALSO COMMERCE IN HARBOR.
AND AMERICANS LIKE THINGS FUNCTIONAL, SO THE STATUE CAN BE A MARKER, MAYBE A LIGHTHOUSE, SEEKING THE SHORE.

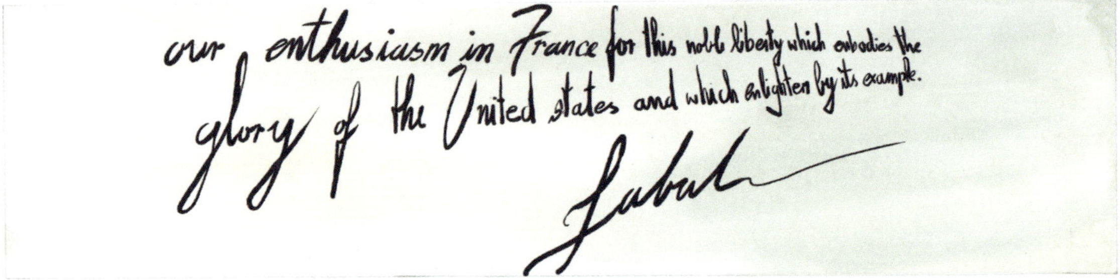
our enthusiasm in France for this noble liberty which embodies the glory of the United states and which enlightens by its example.

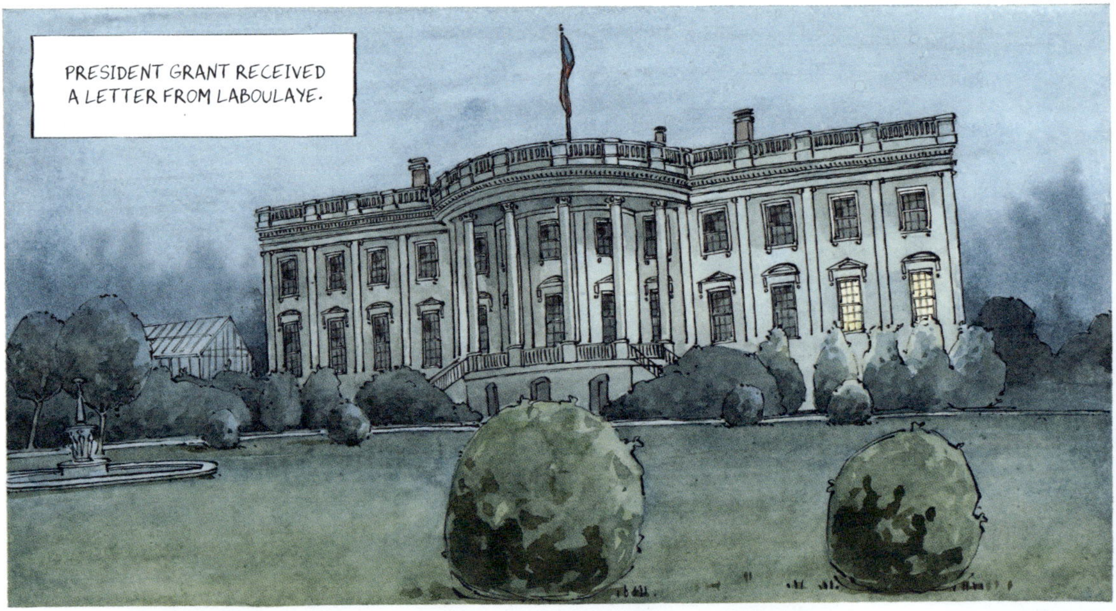
PRESIDENT GRANT RECEIVED A LETTER FROM LABOULAYE.

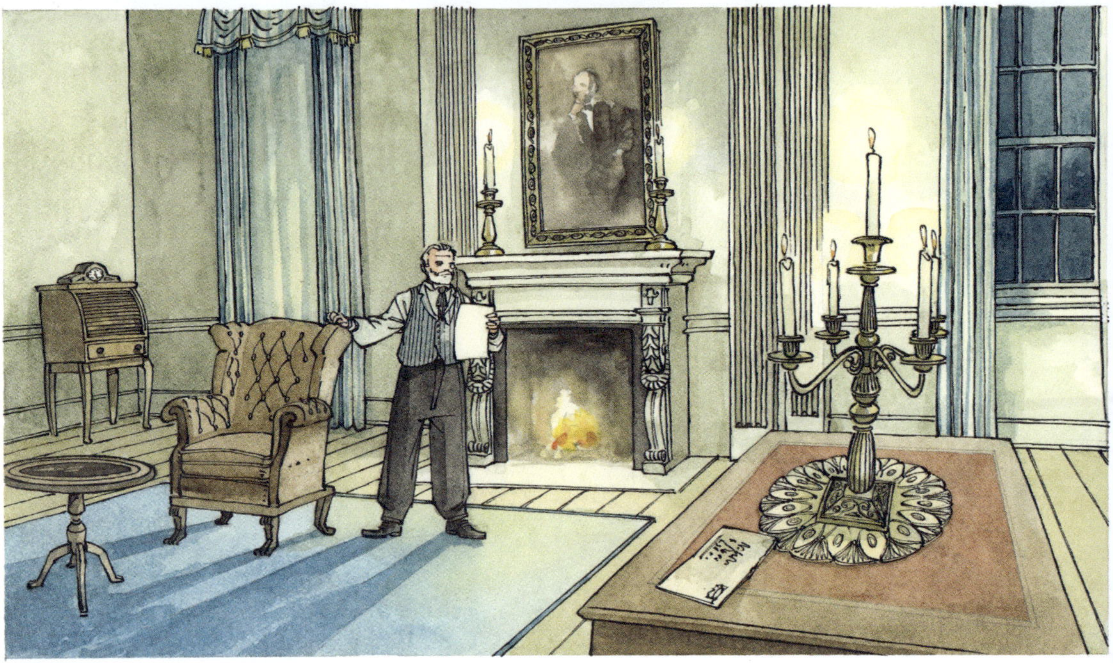

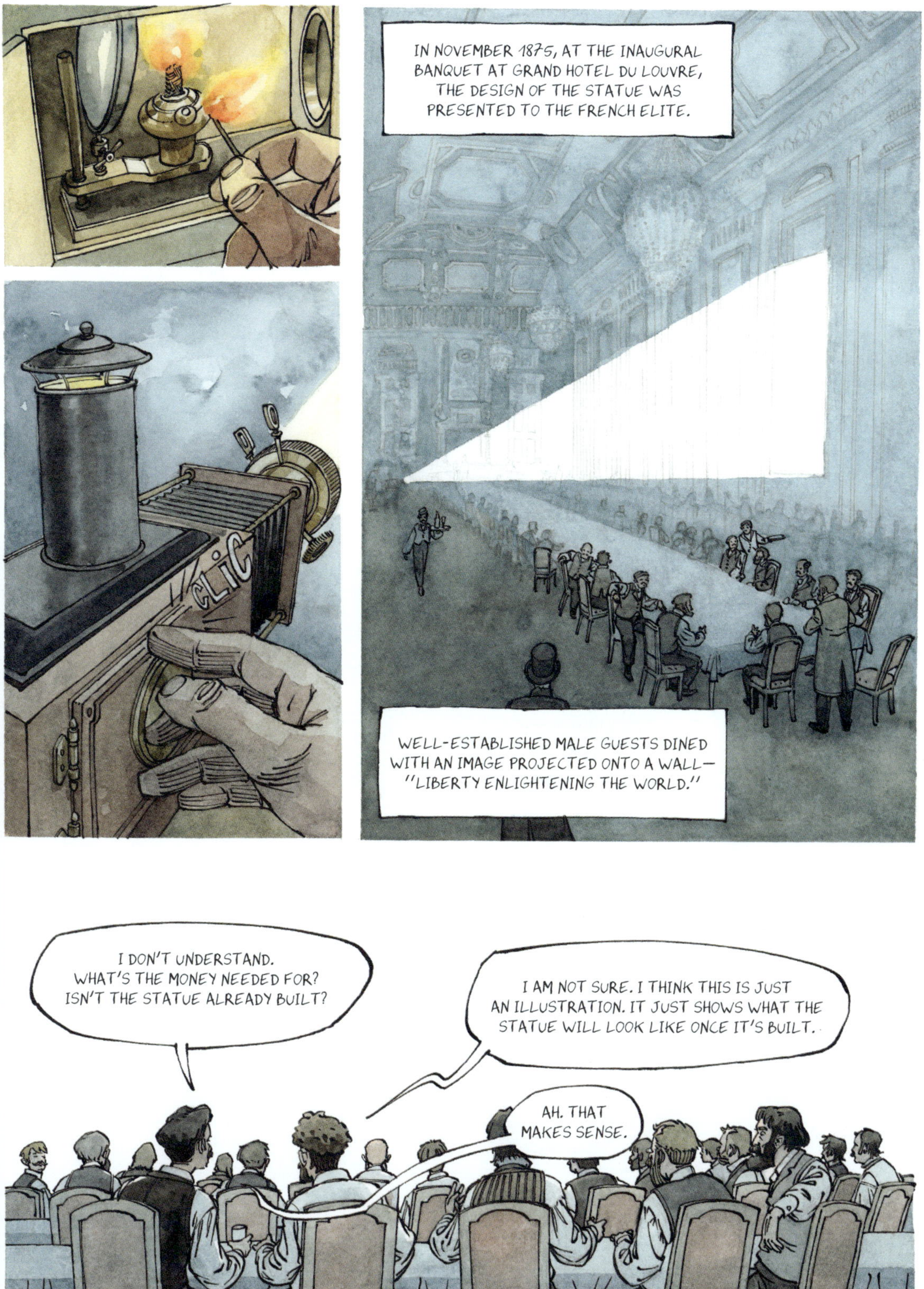
IN NOVEMBER 1875, AT THE INAUGURAL BANQUET AT GRAND HOTEL DU LOUVRE, THE DESIGN OF THE STATUE WAS PRESENTED TO THE FRENCH ELITE.
CLIC
WELL-ESTABLISHED MALE GUESTS DINED WITH AN IMAGE PROJECTED ONTO A WALL— "LIBERTY ENLIGHTENING THE WORLD."
I DON'T UNDERSTAND. WHAT'S THE MONEY NEEDED FOR? ISN'T THE STATUE ALREADY BUILT?
I AM NOT SURE. I THINK THIS IS JUST AN ILLUSTRATION. IT JUST SHOWS WHAT THE STATUE WILL LOOK LIKE ONCE IT'S BUILT.
AH. THAT MAKES SENSE.

"I HEARD PRESIDENT MACMAHON* WAS INVITED."

"IS HE HERE?"

"NO, HE DECLINED."

"TOO BAD."

"OUR PRECIOUS MEMORIES ARE STRONG LINKS BETWEEN OUR TWO NATIONS!"

ANOTHER FUNDRAISING EVENT WAS HELD AT THE OPERA IN PARIS.

"THE STATUE WILL NOT RESEMBLE THOSE BRONZE COLOSSI BOASTED TO HAVE BEEN CAST FROM THE METAL OF CAPTURED CANNONS. ON THE CONTRARY, IT WILL BE DONE IN PRIMARY METAL, THE FRUIT OF LABOR AND PEACE."

*PATRICE DE MACMAHON WAS THE FIRST PRESIDENT OF THE THIRD FRENCH REPUBLIC.

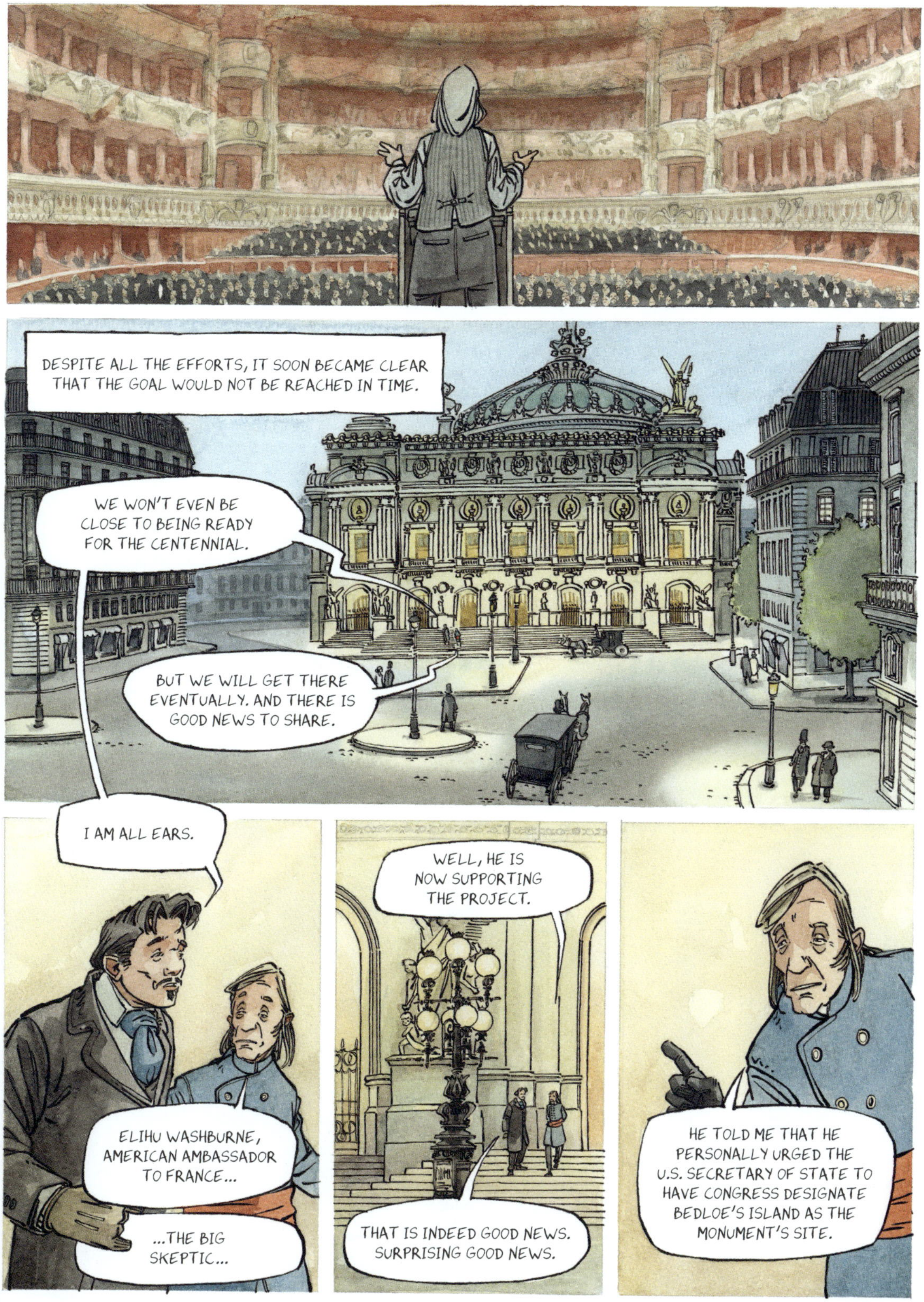
DESPITE ALL THE EFFORTS, IT SOON BECAME CLEAR THAT THE GOAL WOULD NOT BE REACHED IN TIME.
WE WON'T EVEN BE CLOSE TO BEING READY FOR THE CENTENNIAL.
BUT WE WILL GET THERE EVENTUALLY. AND THERE IS GOOD NEWS TO SHARE.
I AM ALL EARS.
ELIHU WASHBURNE, AMERICAN AMBASSADOR TO FRANCE...
...THE BIG SKEPTIC...
WELL, HE IS NOW SUPPORTING THE PROJECT.
THAT IS INDEED GOOD NEWS. SURPRISING GOOD NEWS.
HE TOLD ME THAT HE PERSONALLY URGED THE U.S. SECRETARY OF STATE TO HAVE CONGRESS DESIGNATE BEDLOE'S ISLAND AS THE MONUMENT'S SITE.

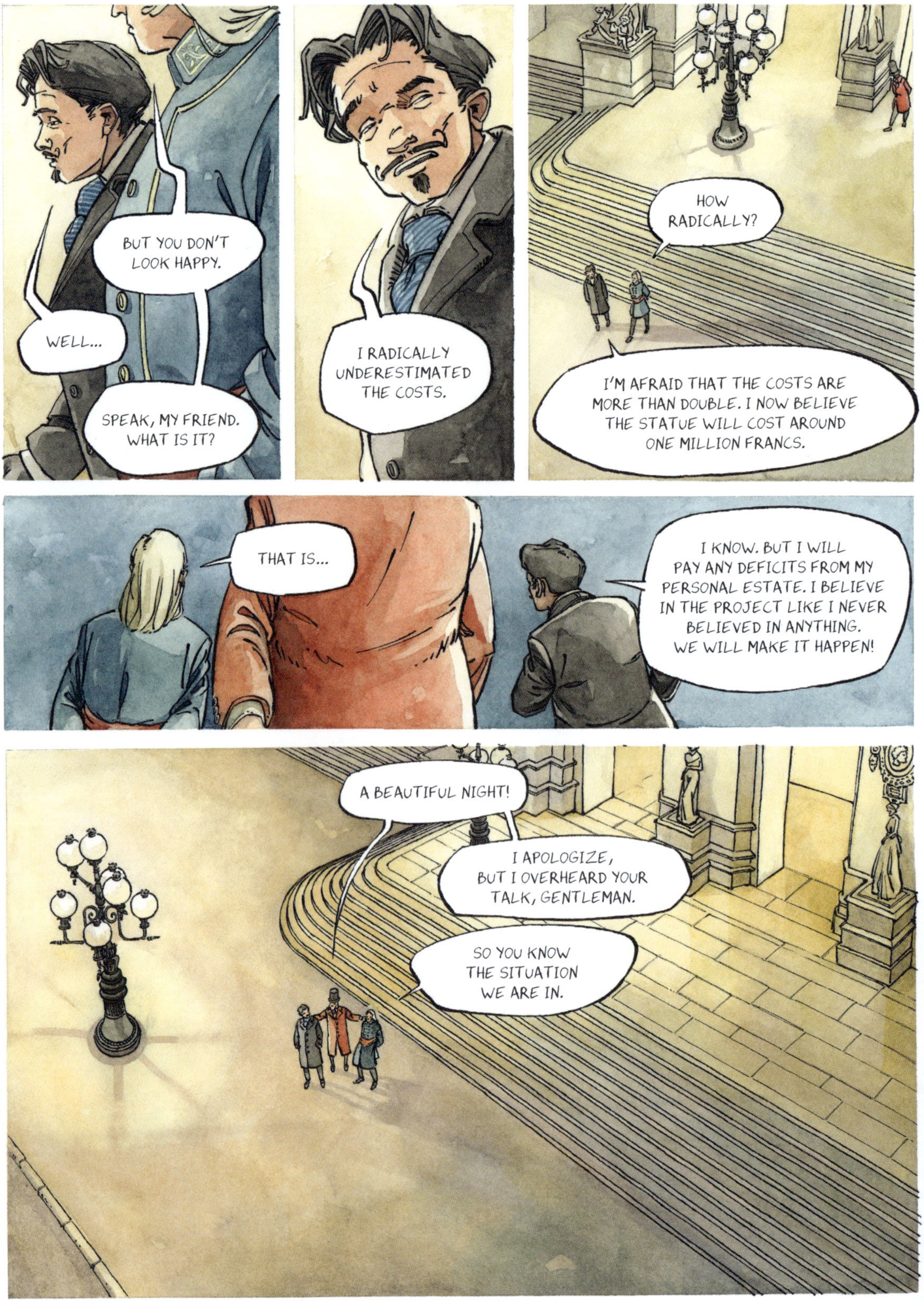
BUT YOU DON'T LOOK HAPPY.
WELL...
SPEAK, MY FRIEND. WHAT IS IT?
I RADICALLY UNDERESTIMATED THE COSTS.
HOW RADICALLY?
I'M AFRAID THAT THE COSTS ARE MORE THAN DOUBLE. I NOW BELIEVE THE STATUE WILL COST AROUND ONE MILLION FRANCS.
THAT IS...
I KNOW. BUT I WILL PAY ANY DEFICITS FROM MY PERSONAL ESTATE. I BELIEVE IN THE PROJECT LIKE I NEVER BELIEVED IN ANYTHING. WE WILL MAKE IT HAPPEN!
A BEAUTIFUL NIGHT!
I APOLOGIZE, BUT I OVERHEARD YOUR TALK, GENTLEMAN.
SO YOU KNOW THE SITUATION WE ARE IN.

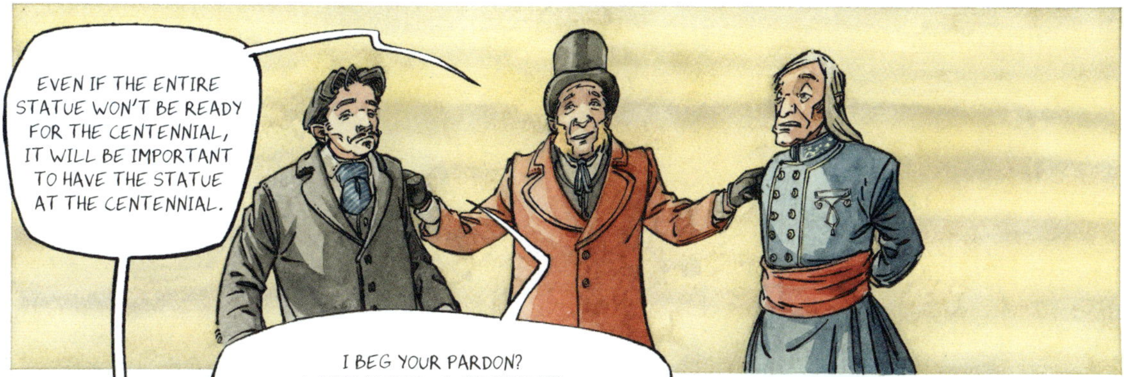
EVEN IF THE ENTIRE STATUE WON'T BE READY FOR THE CENTENNIAL, IT WILL BE IMPORTANT TO HAVE THE STATUE AT THE CENTENNIAL.
I BEG YOUR PARDON? WHAT ARE YOU SUGGESTING?

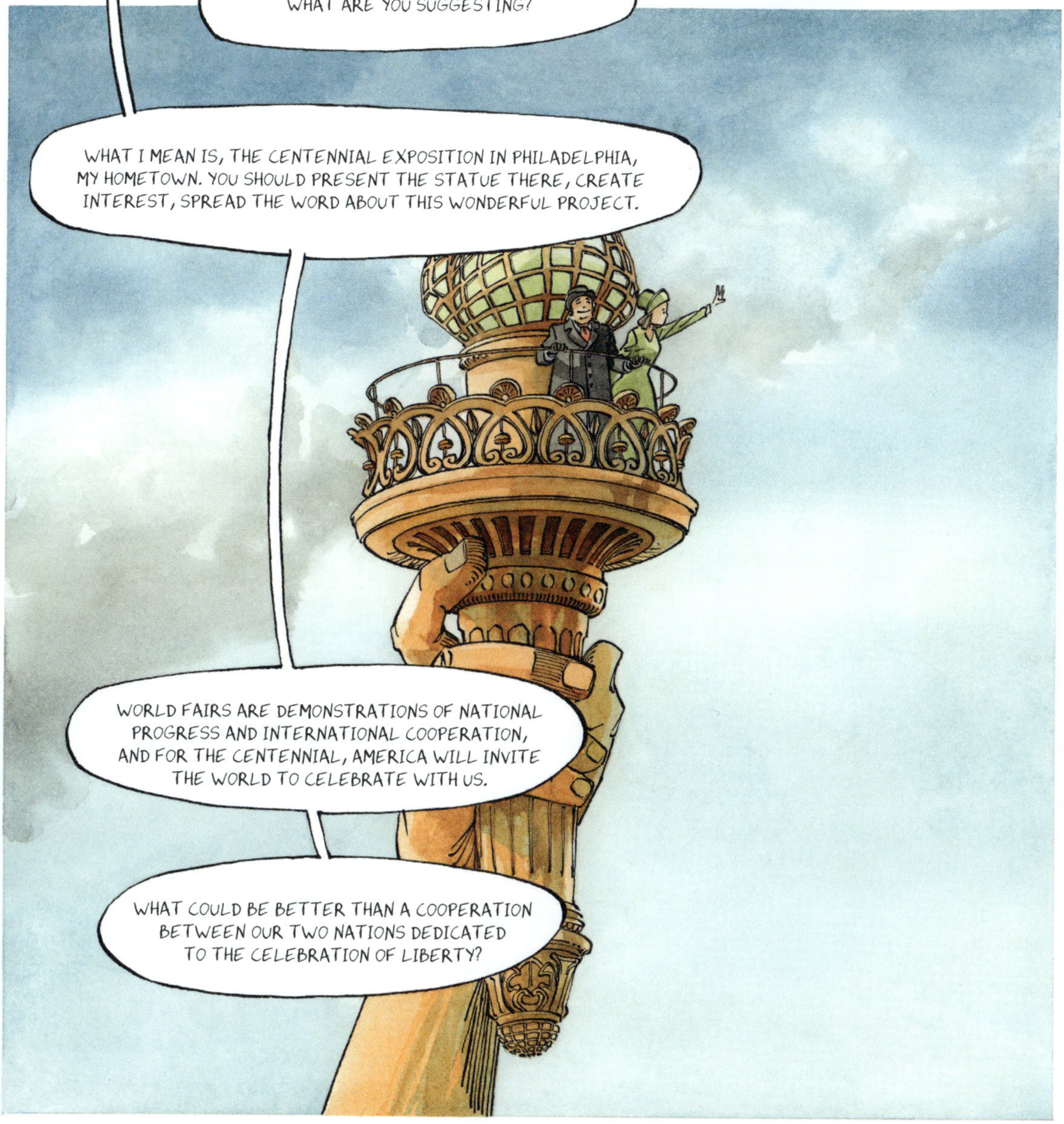
WHAT I MEAN IS, THE CENTENNIAL EXPOSITION IN PHILADELPHIA, MY HOMETOWN. YOU SHOULD PRESENT THE STATUE THERE, CREATE INTEREST, SPREAD THE WORD ABOUT THIS WONDERFUL PROJECT.
WORLD FAIRS ARE DEMONSTRATIONS OF NATIONAL PROGRESS AND INTERNATIONAL COOPERATION, AND FOR THE CENTENNIAL, AMERICA WILL INVITE THE WORLD TO CELEBRATE WITH US.
WHAT COULD BE BETTER THAN A COOPERATION BETWEEN OUR TWO NATIONS DEDICATED TO THE CELEBRATION OF LIBERTY?

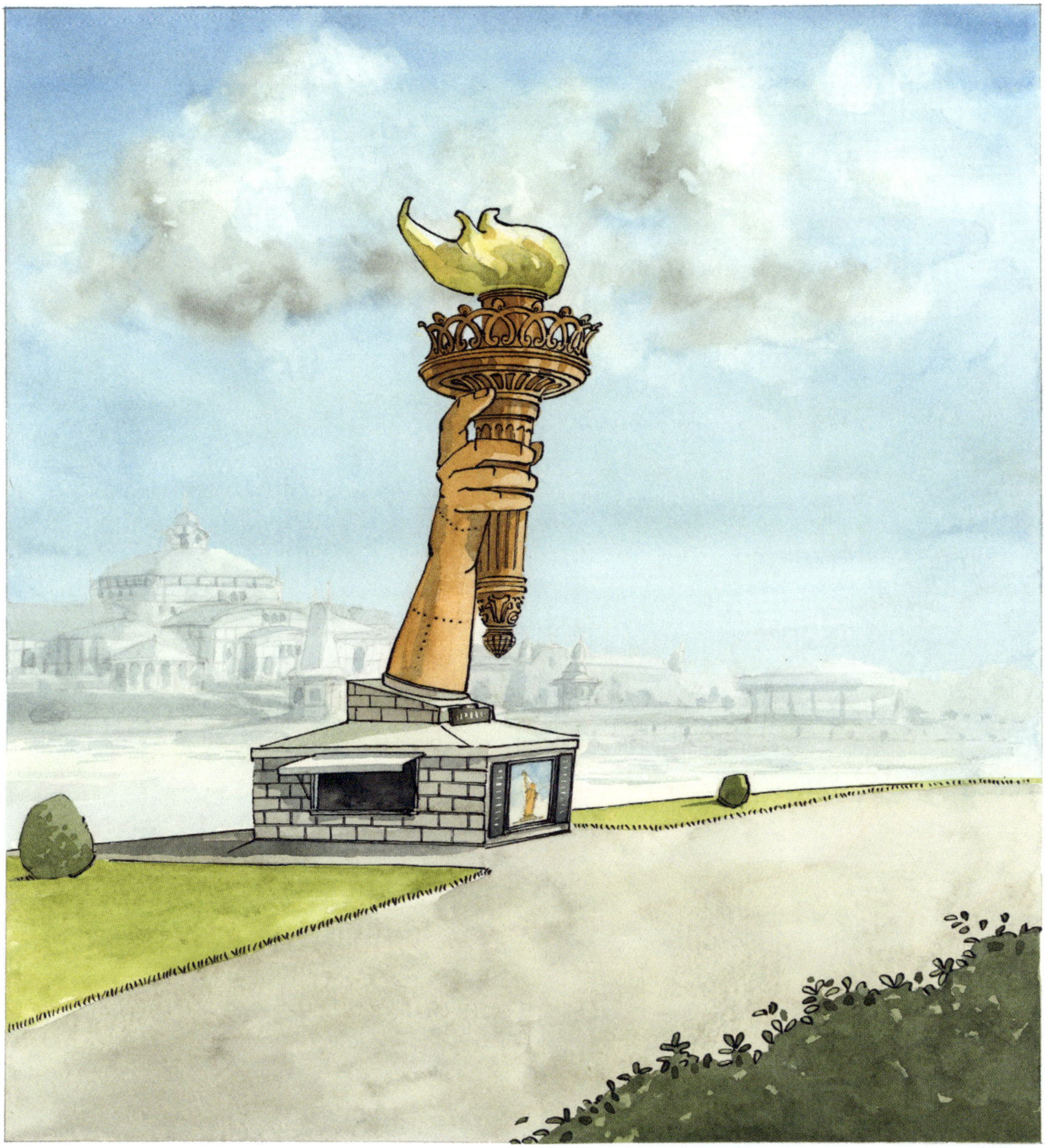

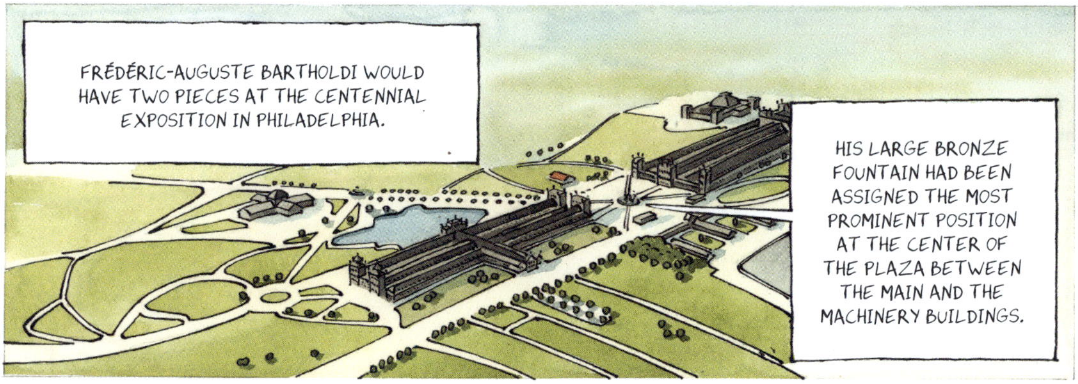
FRÉDÉRIC-AUGUSTE BARTHOLDI WOULD HAVE TWO PIECES AT THE CENTENNIAL EXPOSITION IN PHILADELPHIA.
HIS LARGE BRONZE FOUNTAIN HAD BEEN ASSIGNED THE MOST PROMINENT POSITION AT THE CENTER OF THE PLAZA BETWEEN THE MAIN AND THE MACHINERY BUILDINGS.

BUT HIS MAIN FOCUS WAS, OF COURSE, "LIBERTY ENLIGHTENING THE WORLD," WHICH HE PLANNED TO PRESENT FOR THE FIRST TIME TO THE AMERICAN PUBLIC. CONSTRUCTION ON THE STATUE WAS TAKING MUCH LONGER THAN ANTICIPATED, SO FRÉDÉRIC-AUGUSTE DECIDED TO FOCUS ON TWO PARTS. FOR PHILADELPHIA, THE RIGHT ARM HOLDING A TORCH HAD BEEN PREPARED, AND FOR THE WORLD EXHIBITION IN PARIS IN TWO YEARS, THE HEAD WAS PLANNED TO BE COMPLETED.

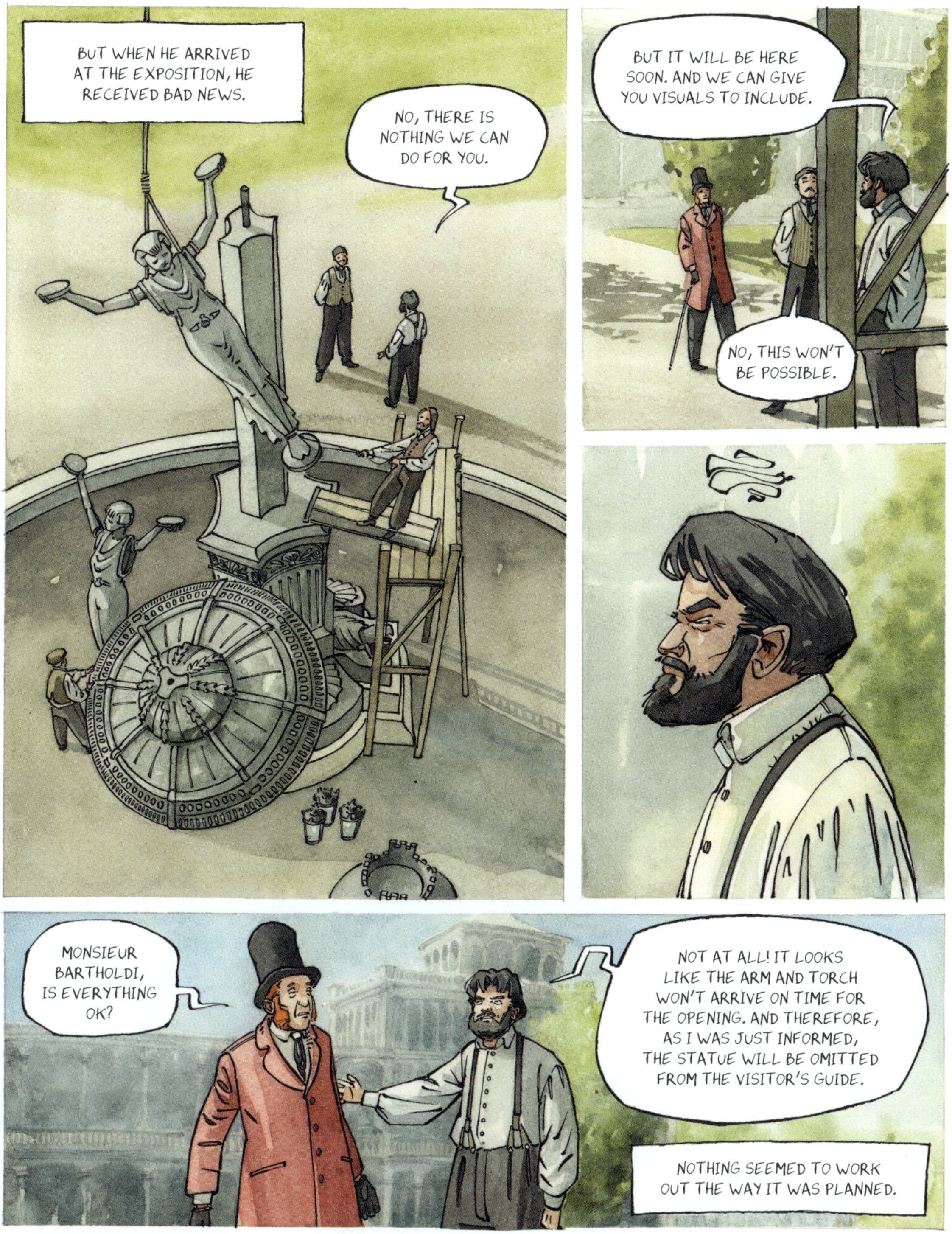

LIBERTY'S ARM ARRIVED A FEW DAYS AFTER THE OPENING. IT WAS JUST ONE OF MANY COLOSSAL WORKS AT THE EXPOSITION.

THERE WERE STATUES REPRESENTING COLUMBUS.

THERE WERE STATUES REPRESENTING WASHINGTON.

AND LINCOLN, OF COURSE.

YES, FRÉDÉRIC-AUGUSTE WAS DISAPPOINTED THAT HIS STATUE DID NOT RECEIVE SPECIAL RECOGNITION.

DID YOU READ THE NEW YORK TIMES? THEY'RE JOKING ABOUT ME!

WHAT DO YOU MEAN?

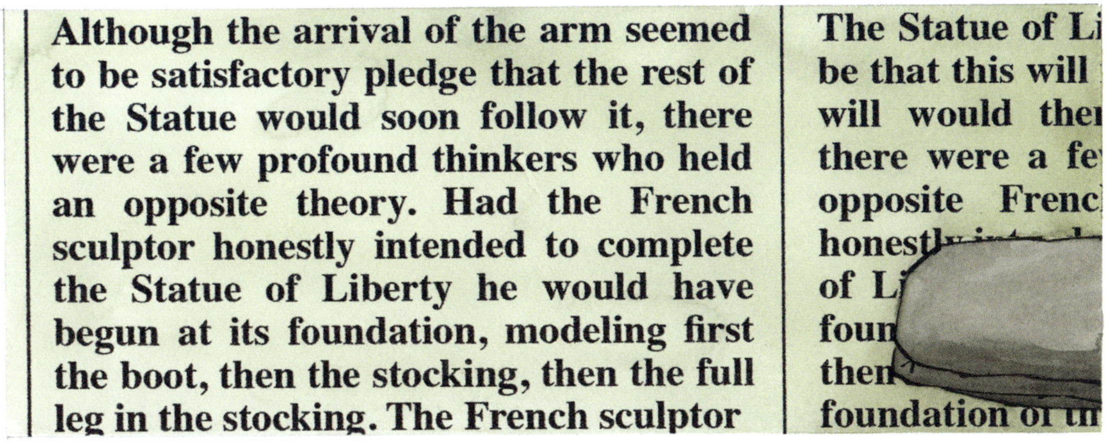
Although the arrival of the arm seemed to be satisfactory pledge that the rest of the Statue would soon follow it, there were a few profound thinkers who held an opposite theory. Had the French sculptor honestly intended to complete the Statue of Liberty he would have begun at its foundation, modeling first the boot, then the stocking, then the full leg in the stocking. The French sculptor
The Statue of Li
be that this will
will would the
there were a fe
opposite Frenc
honest
of L
foun
then
foundation of th

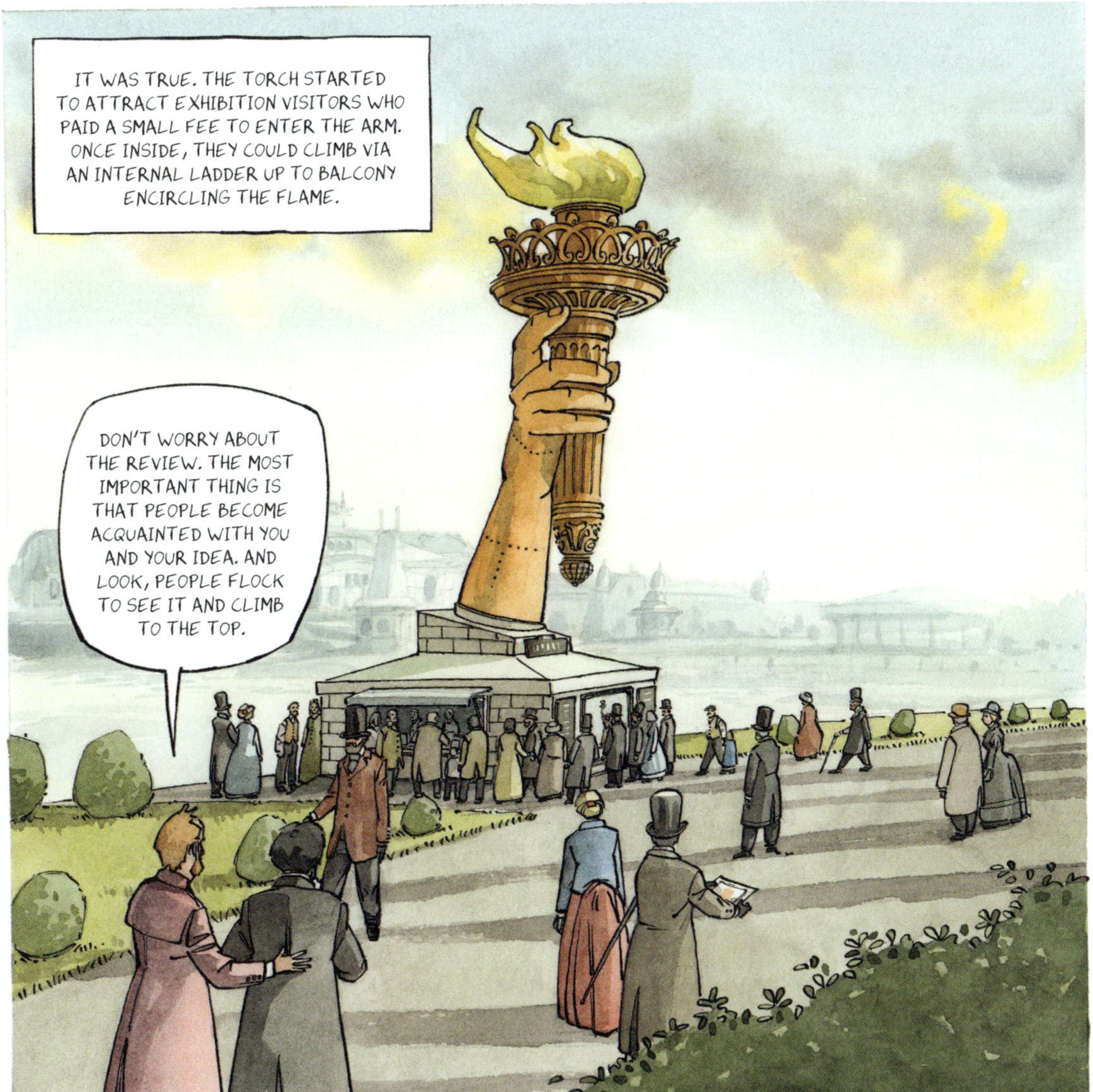
IT WAS TRUE. THE TORCH STARTED TO ATTRACT EXHIBITION VISITORS WHO PAID A SMALL FEE TO ENTER THE ARM. ONCE INSIDE, THEY COULD CLIMB VIA AN INTERNAL LADDER UP TO BALCONY ENCIRCLING THE FLAME.
DON'T WORRY ABOUT THE REVIEW. THE MOST IMPORTANT THING IS THAT PEOPLE BECOME ACQUAINTED WITH YOU AND YOUR IDEA. AND LOOK, PEOPLE FLOCK TO SEE IT AND CLIMB TO THE TOP.

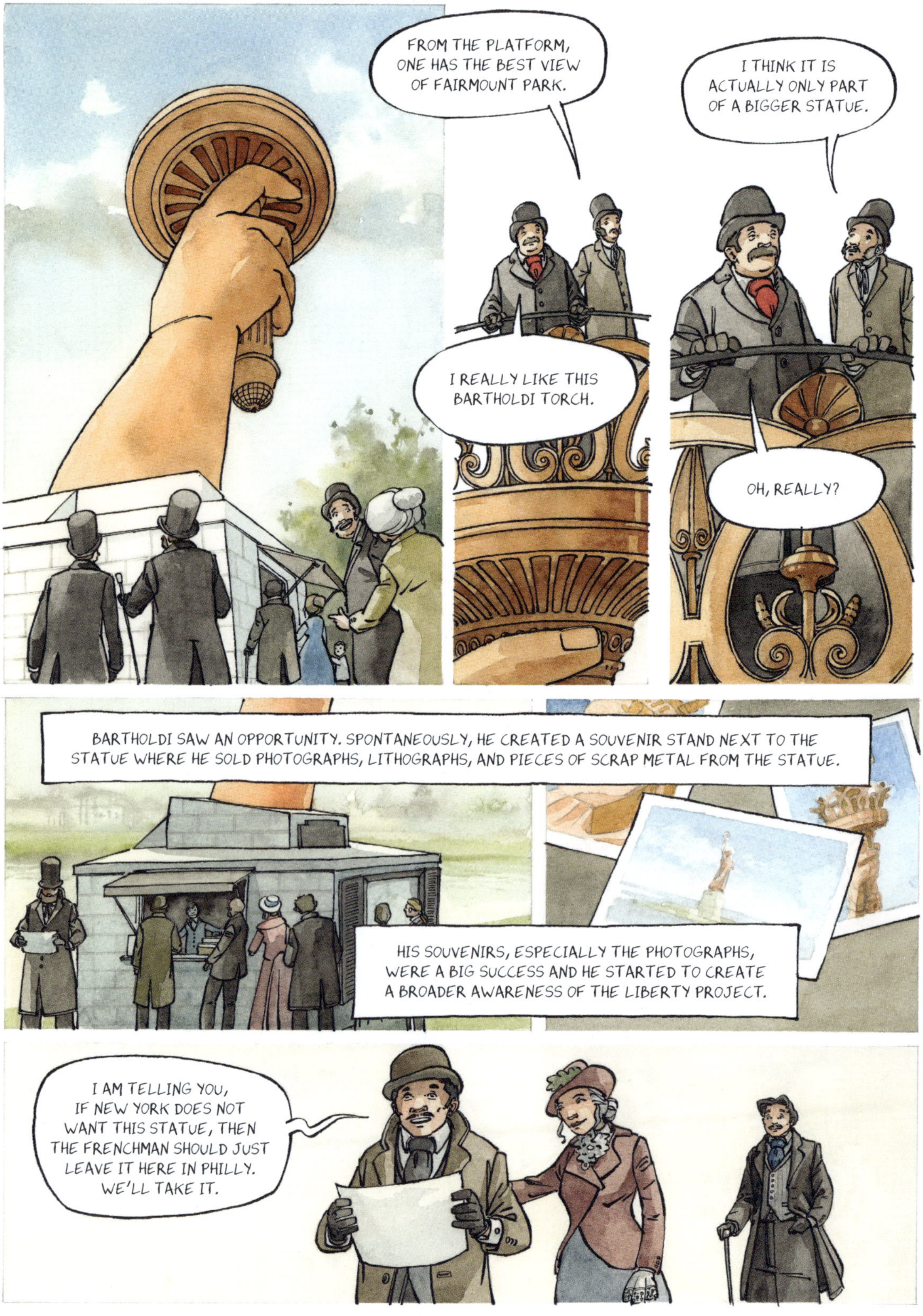
FROM THE PLATFORM, ONE HAS THE BEST VIEW OF FAIRMOUNT PARK.
I REALLY LIKE THIS BARTHOLDI TORCH.
I THINK IT IS ACTUALLY ONLY PART OF A BIGGER STATUE.
OH, REALLY?
BARTHOLDI SAW AN OPPORTUNITY. SPONTANEOUSLY, HE CREATED A SOUVENIR STAND NEXT TO THE STATUE WHERE HE SOLD PHOTOGRAPHS, LITHOGRAPHS, AND PIECES OF SCRAP METAL FROM THE STATUE.
HIS SOUVENIRS, ESPECIALLY THE PHOTOGRAPHS, WERE A BIG SUCCESS AND HE STARTED TO CREATE A BROADER AWARENESS OF THE LIBERTY PROJECT.
I AM TELLING YOU, IF NEW YORK DOES NOT WANT THIS STATUE, THEN THE FRENCHMAN SHOULD JUST LEAVE IT HERE IN PHILLY. WE'LL TAKE IT.

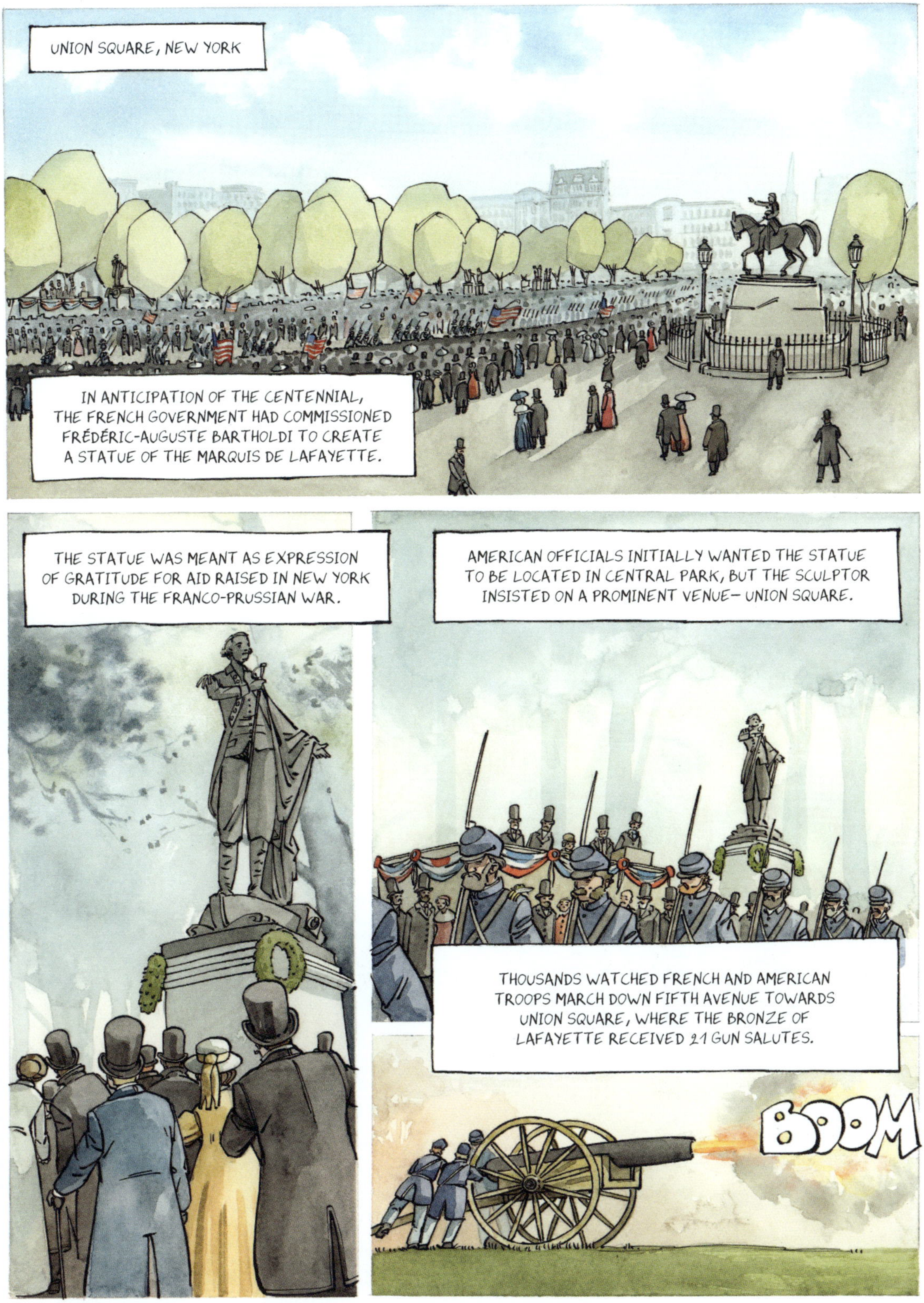
UNION SQUARE, NEW YORK
IN ANTICIPATION OF THE CENTENNIAL, THE FRENCH GOVERNMENT HAD COMMISSIONED FRÉDÉRIC-AUGUSTE BARTHOLDI TO CREATE A STATUE OF THE MARQUIS DE LAFAYETTE.
THE STATUE WAS MEANT AS EXPRESSION OF GRATITUDE FOR AID RAISED IN NEW YORK DURING THE FRANCO-PRUSSIAN WAR.
AMERICAN OFFICIALS INITIALLY WANTED THE STATUE TO BE LOCATED IN CENTRAL PARK, BUT THE SCULPTOR INSISTED ON A PROMINENT VENUE– UNION SQUARE.
THOUSANDS WATCHED FRENCH AND AMERICAN TROOPS MARCH DOWN FIFTH AVENUE TOWARDS UNION SQUARE, WHERE THE BRONZE OF LAFAYETTE RECEIVED 21 GUN SALUTES.
BOOM

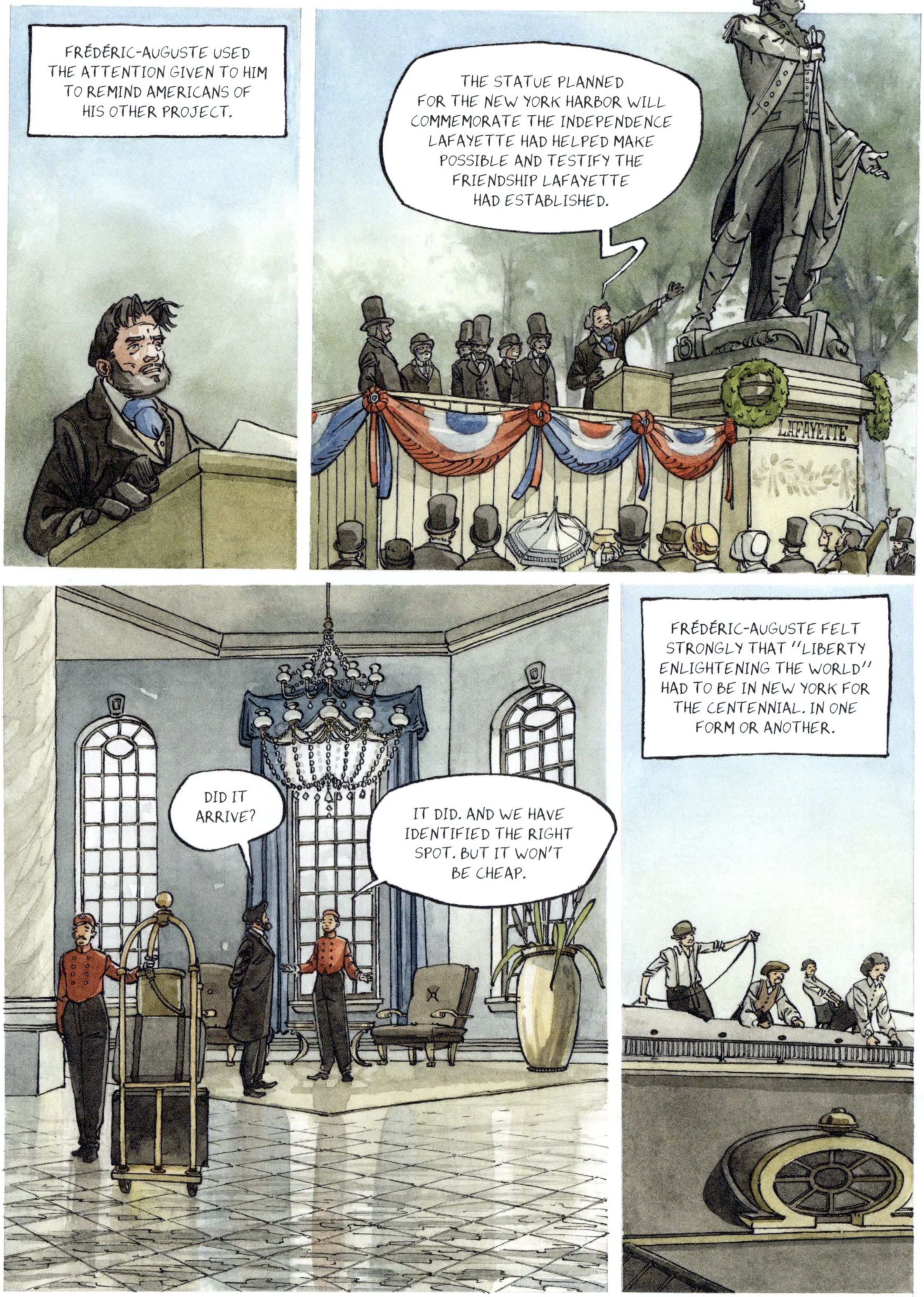
FRÉDÉRIC-AUGUSTE USED THE ATTENTION GIVEN TO HIM TO REMIND AMERICANS OF HIS OTHER PROJECT.
THE STATUE PLANNED FOR THE NEW YORK HARBOR WILL COMMEMORATE THE INDEPENDENCE LAFAYETTE HAD HELPED MAKE POSSIBLE AND TESTIFY THE FRIENDSHIP LAFAYETTE HAD ESTABLISHED.
LAFAYETTE
DID IT ARRIVE?
IT DID. AND WE HAVE IDENTIFIED THE RIGHT SPOT. BUT IT WON'T BE CHEAP.
FRÉDÉRIC-AUGUSTE FELT STRONGLY THAT "LIBERTY ENLIGHTENING THE WORLD" HAD TO BE IN NEW YORK FOR THE CENTENNIAL. IN ONE FORM OR ANOTHER.

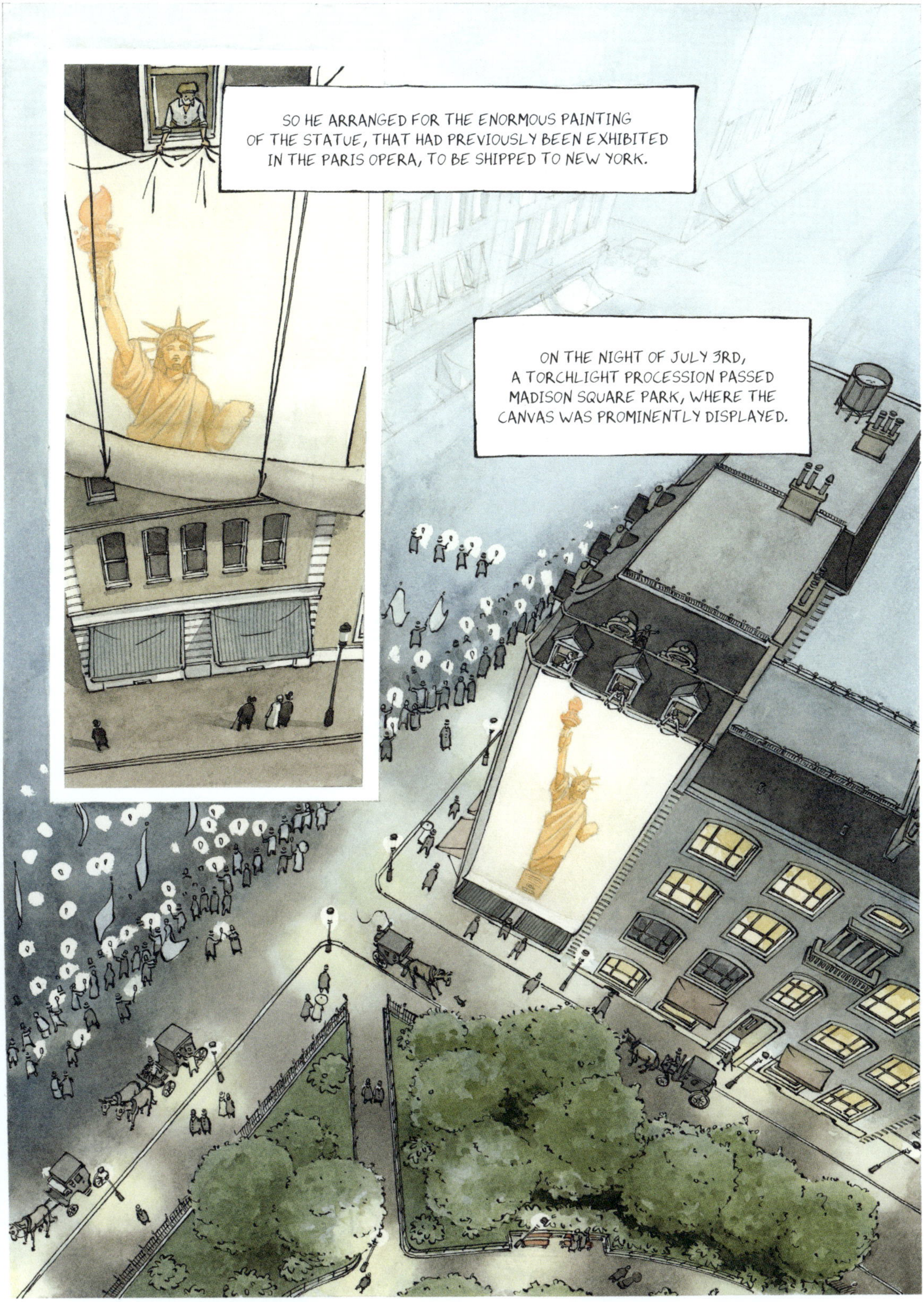
SO HE ARRANGED FOR THE ENORMOUS PAINTING OF THE STATUE, THAT HAD PREVIOUSLY BEEN EXHIBITED IN THE PARIS OPERA, TO BE SHIPPED TO NEW YORK.
ON THE NIGHT OF JULY 3RD, A TORCHLIGHT PROCESSION PASSED MADISON SQUARE PARK, WHERE THE CANVAS WAS PROMINENTLY DISPLAYED.

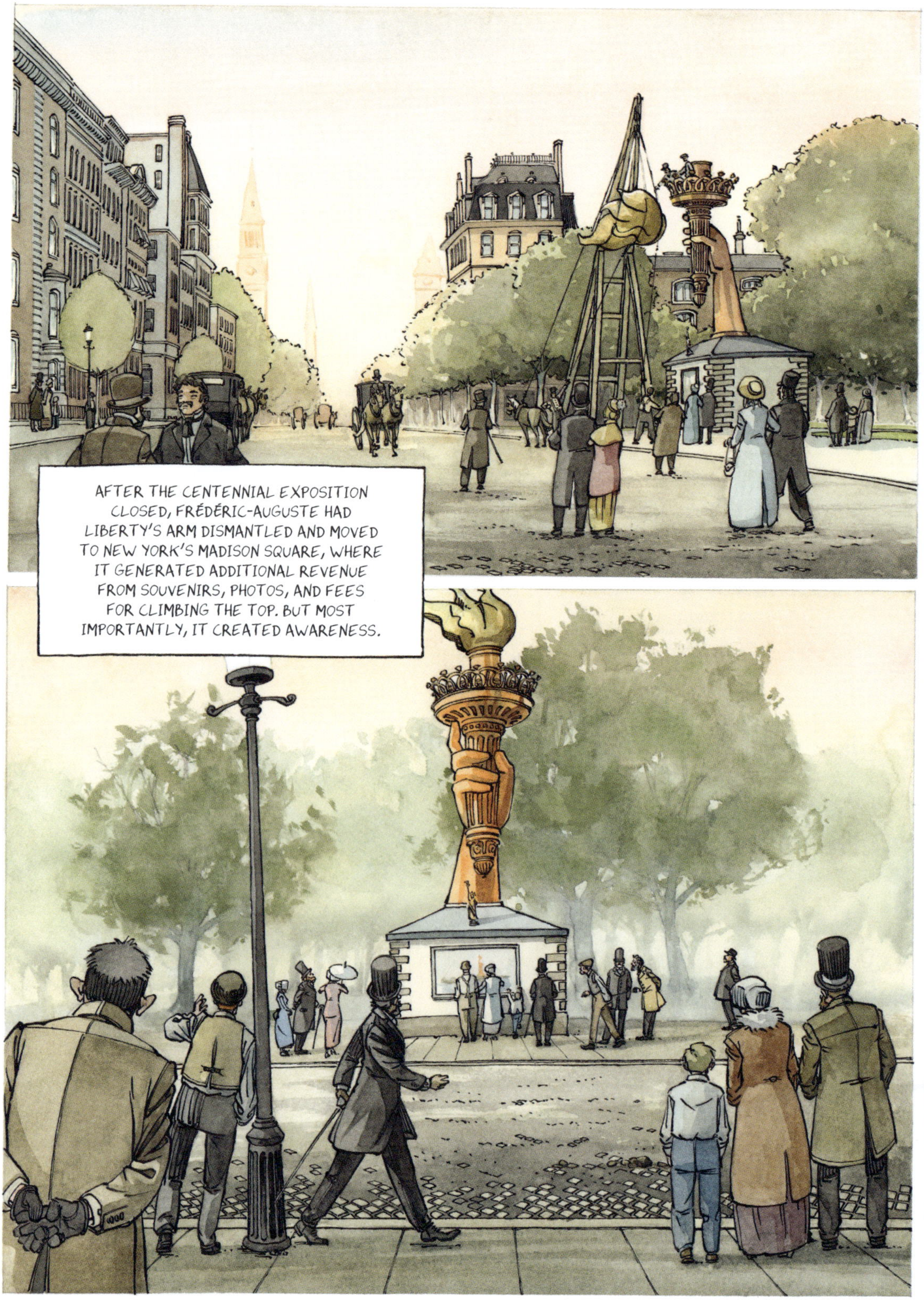
AFTER THE CENTENNIAL EXPOSITION CLOSED, FRÉDÉRIC-AUGUSTE HAD LIBERTY'S ARM DISMANTLED AND MOVED TO NEW YORK'S MADISON SQUARE, WHERE IT GENERATED ADDITIONAL REVENUE FROM SOUVENIRS, PHOTOS, AND FEES FOR CLIMBING THE TOP. BUT MOST IMPORTANTLY, IT CREATED AWARENESS.

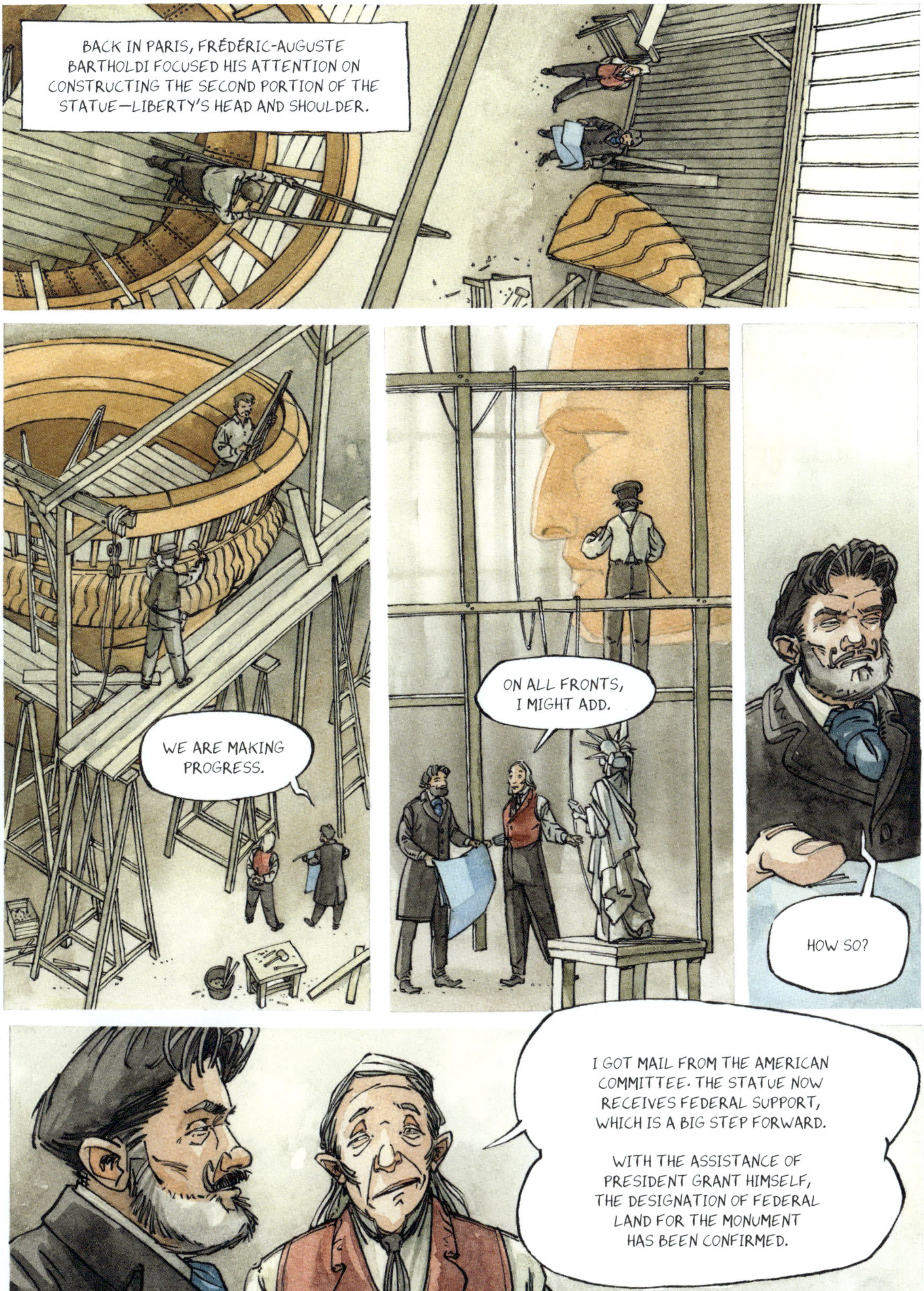
BACK IN PARIS, FRÉDÉRIC-AUGUSTE BARTHOLDI FOCUSED HIS ATTENTION ON CONSTRUCTING THE SECOND PORTION OF THE STATUE—LIBERTY'S HEAD AND SHOULDER.
WE ARE MAKING PROGRESS.
ON ALL FRONTS, I MIGHT ADD.
HOW SO?
I GOT MAIL FROM THE AMERICAN COMMITTEE. THE STATUE NOW RECEIVES FEDERAL SUPPORT, WHICH IS A BIG STEP FORWARD.
WITH THE ASSISTANCE OF PRESIDENT GRANT HIMSELF, THE DESIGNATION OF FEDERAL LAND FOR THE MONUMENT HAS BEEN CONFIRMED.

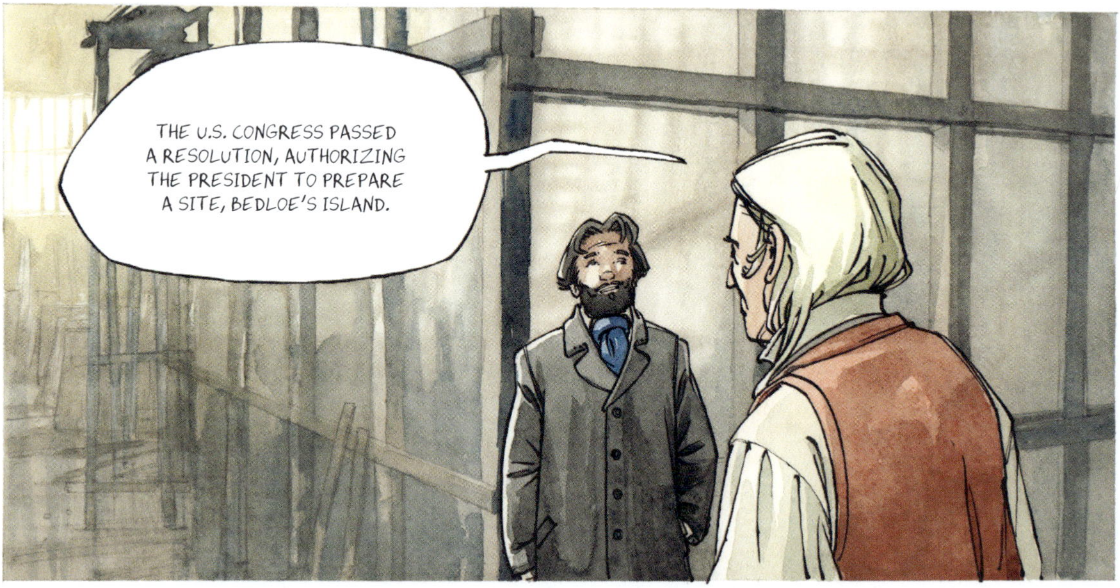
THE U.S. CONGRESS PASSED A RESOLUTION, AUTHORIZING THE PRESIDENT TO PREPARE A SITE, BEDLOE'S ISLAND.

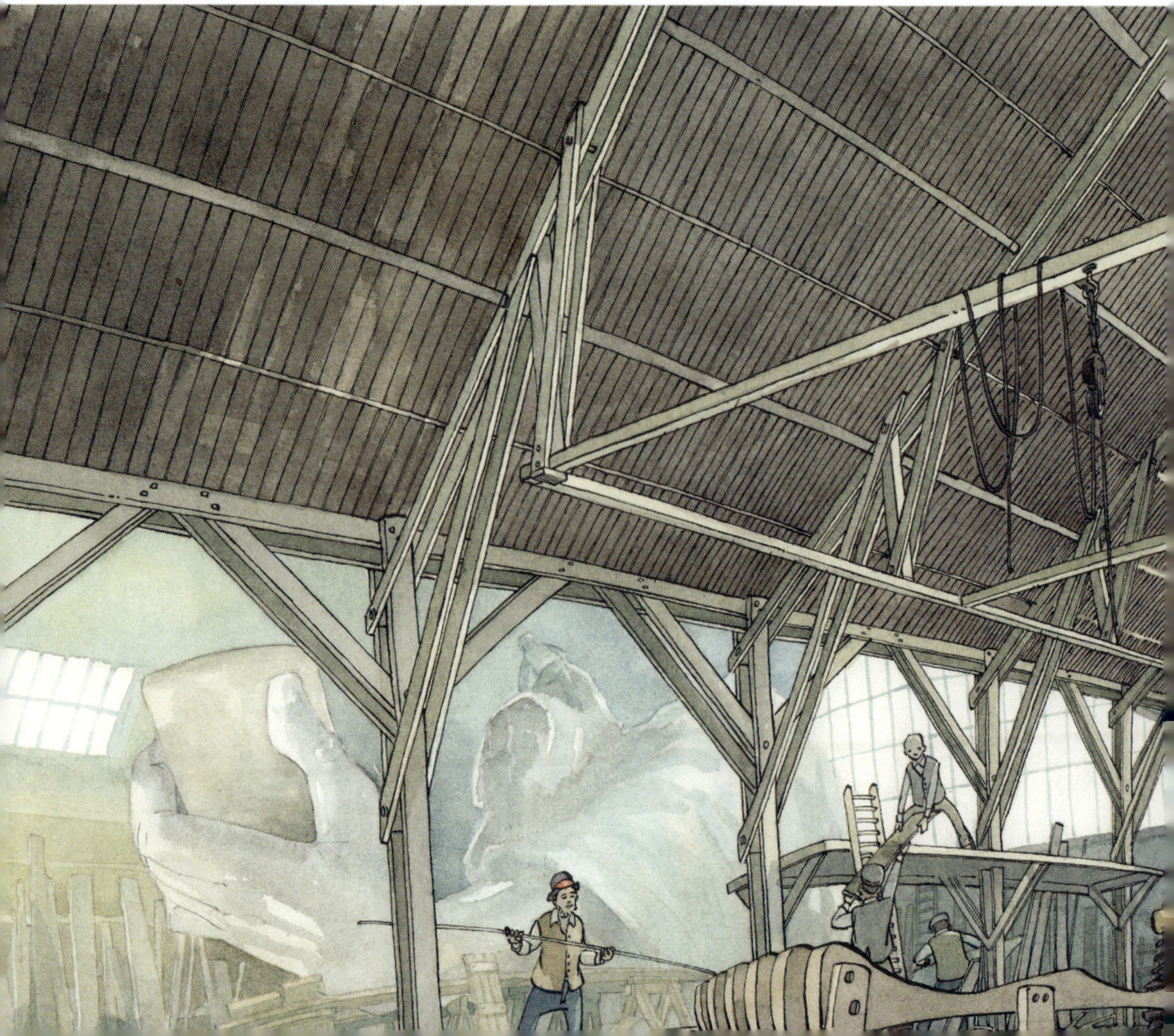

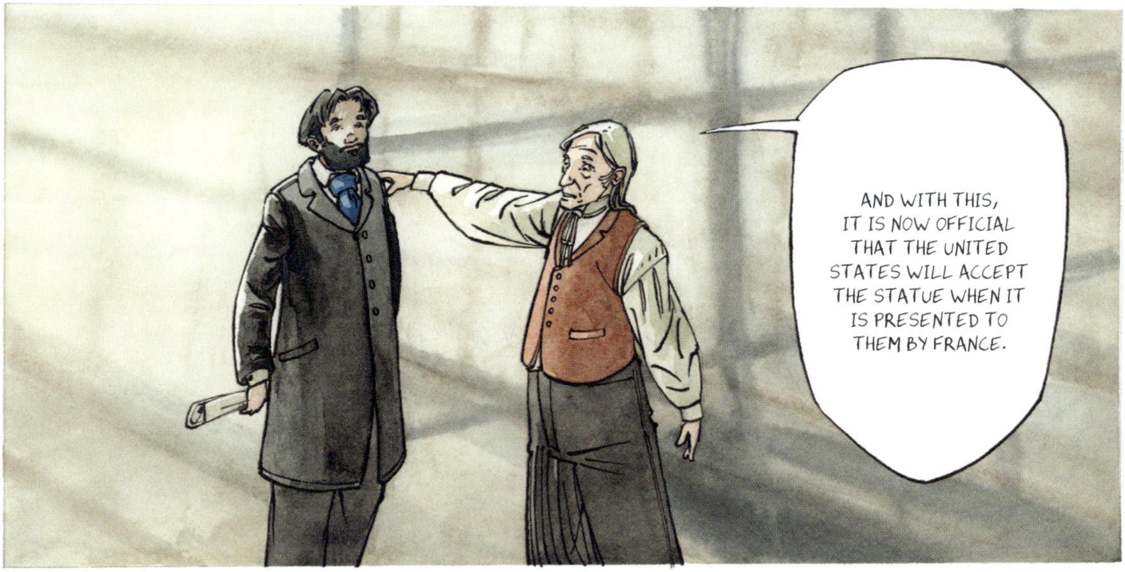
AND WITH THIS, IT IS NOW OFFICIAL THAT THE UNITED STATES WILL ACCEPT THE STATUE WHEN IT IS PRESENTED TO THEM BY FRANCE.

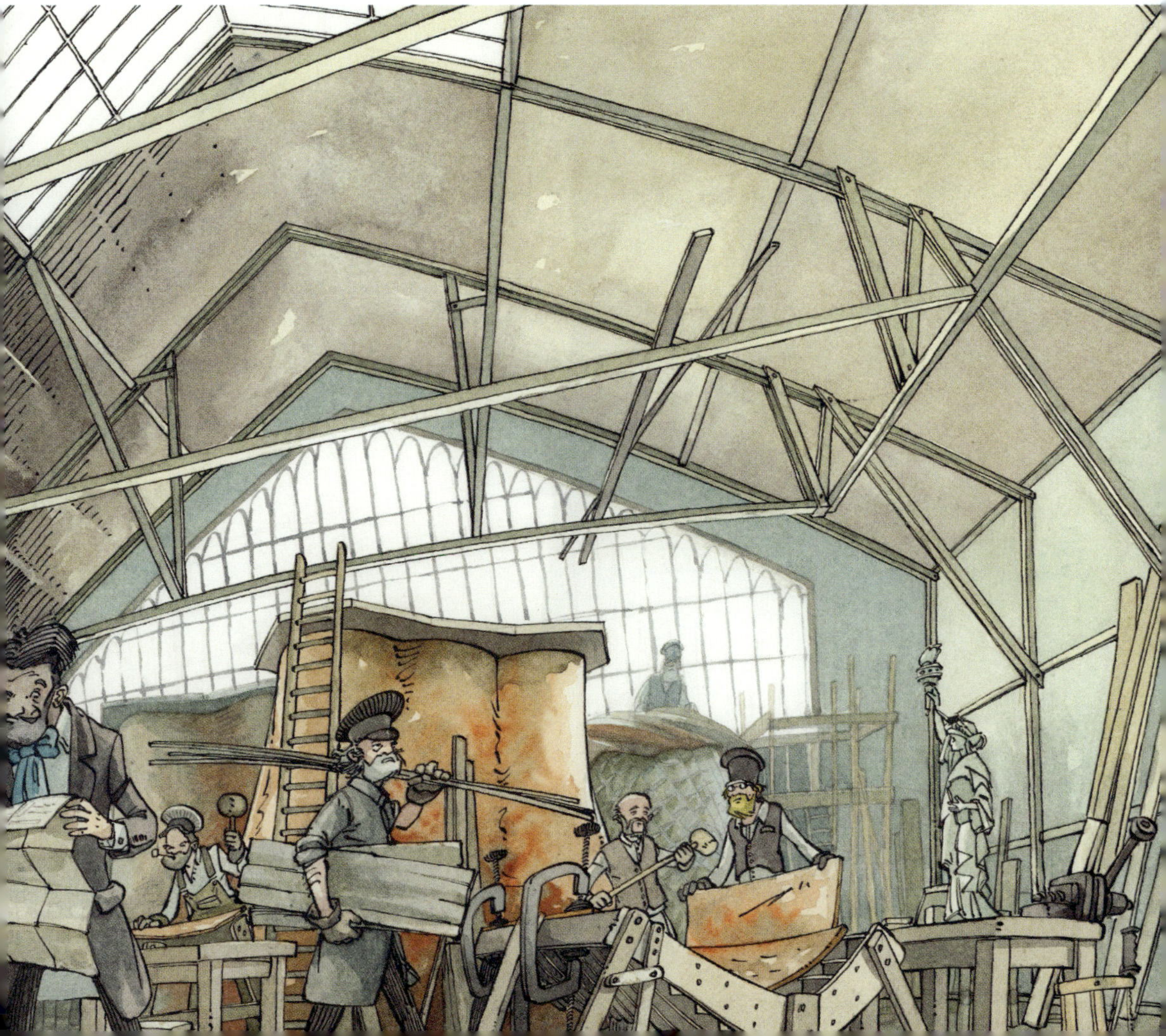

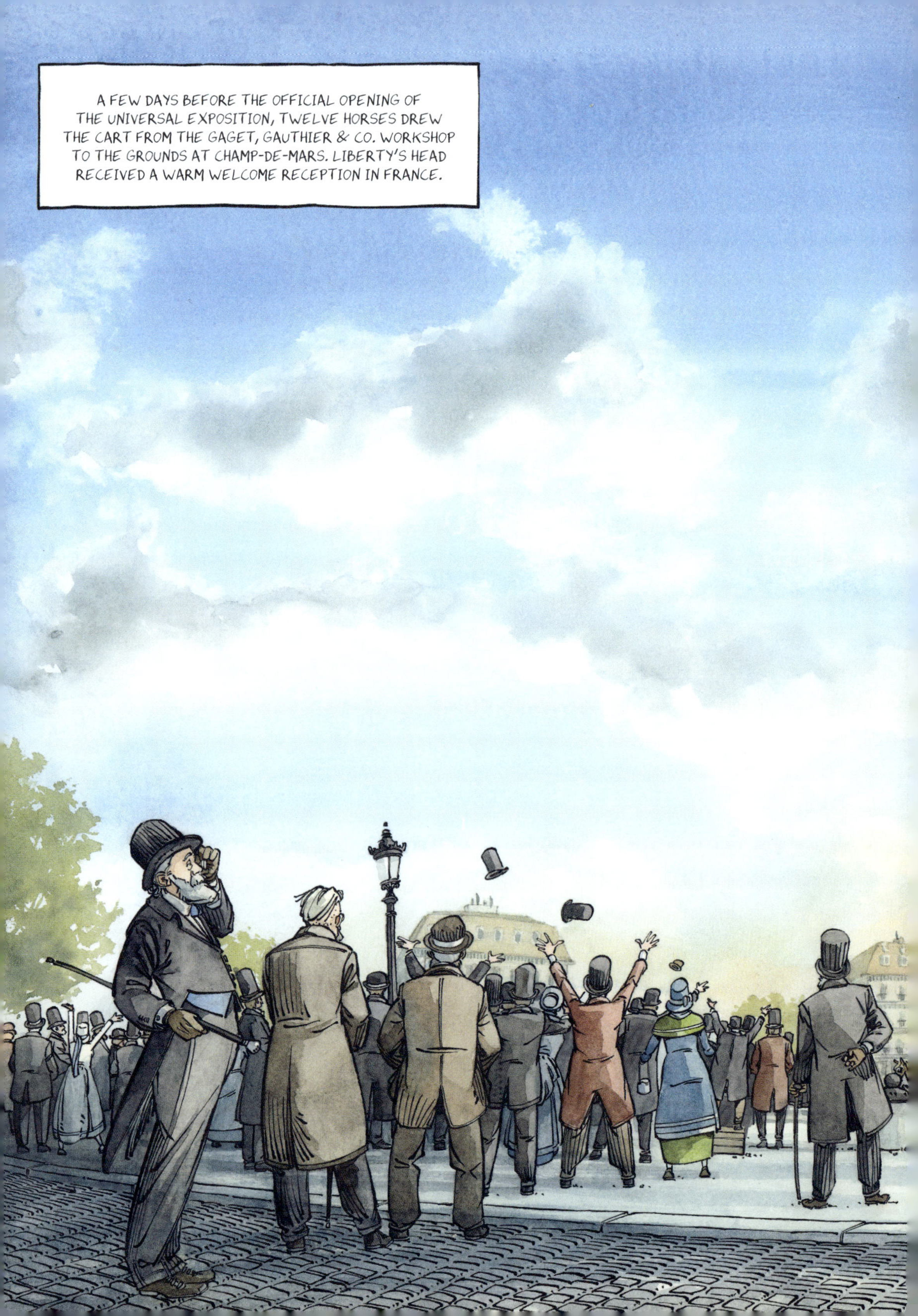
A FEW DAYS BEFORE THE OFFICIAL OPENING OF THE UNIVERSAL EXPOSITION, TWELVE HORSES DREW THE CART FROM THE GAGET, GAUTHIER & CO. WORKSHOP TO THE GROUNDS AT CHAMP-DE-MARS. LIBERTY'S HEAD RECEIVED A WARM WELCOME RECEPTION IN FRANCE.

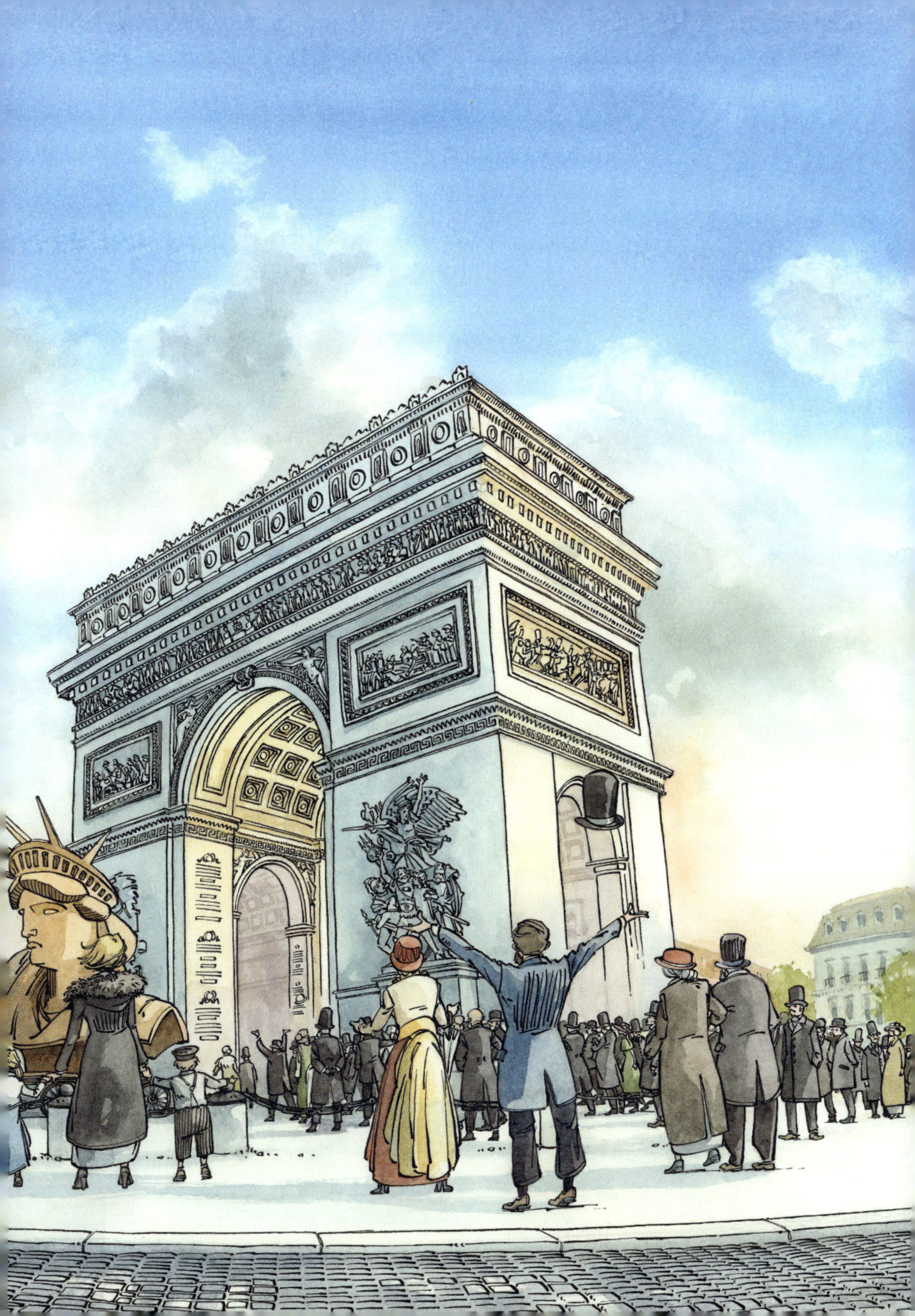

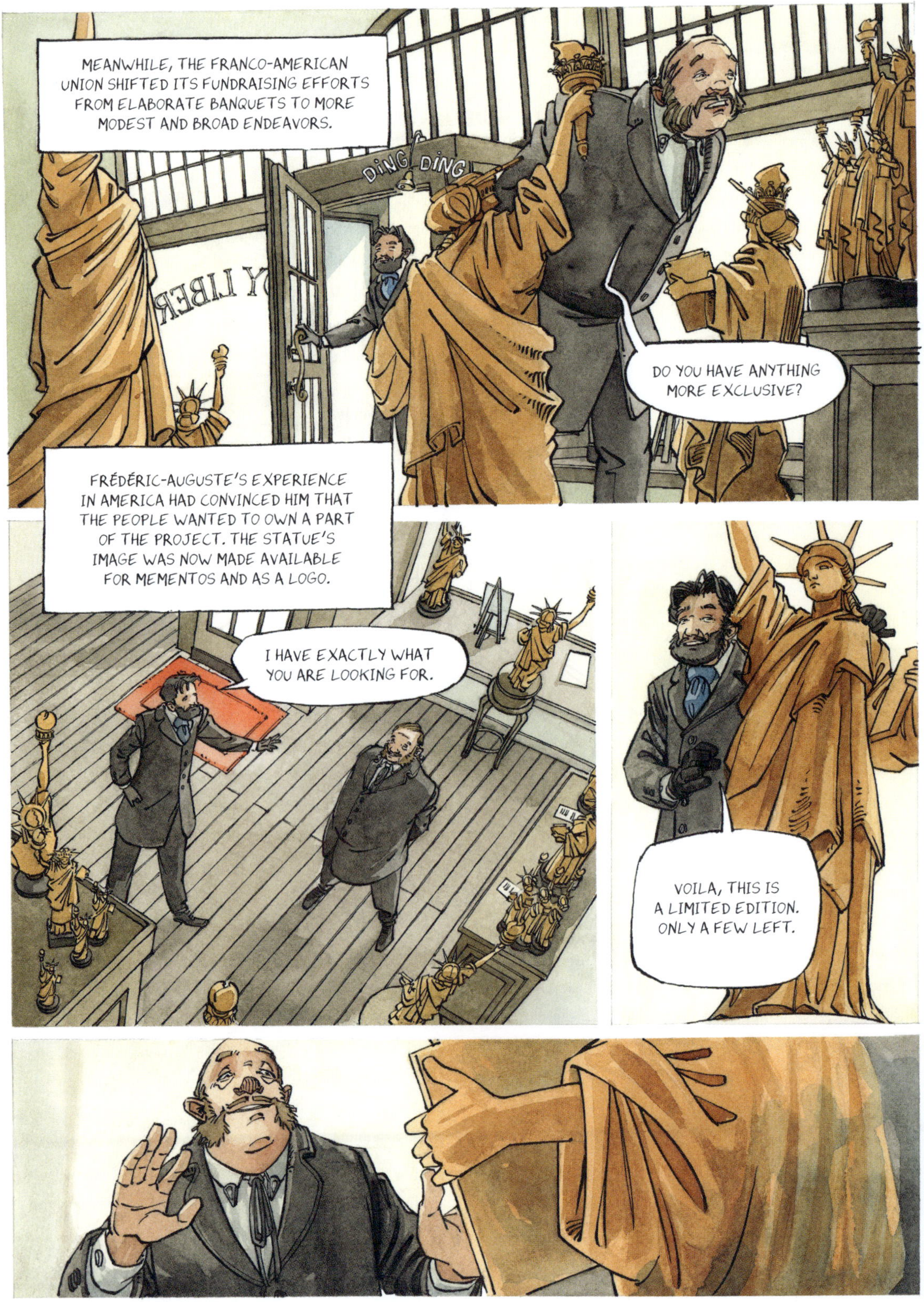
MEANWHILE, THE FRANCO-AMERICAN UNION SHIFTED ITS FUNDRAISING EFFORTS FROM ELABORATE BANQUETS TO MORE MODEST AND BROAD ENDEAVORS.
DING DING
DO YOU HAVE ANYTHING MORE EXCLUSIVE?
FRÉDÉRIC-AUGUSTE'S EXPERIENCE IN AMERICA HAD CONVINCED HIM THAT THE PEOPLE WANTED TO OWN A PART OF THE PROJECT. THE STATUE'S IMAGE WAS NOW MADE AVAILABLE FOR MEMENTOS AND AS A LOGO.
I HAVE EXACTLY WHAT YOU ARE LOOKING FOR.
VOILA, THIS IS A LIMITED EDITION. ONLY A FEW LEFT.

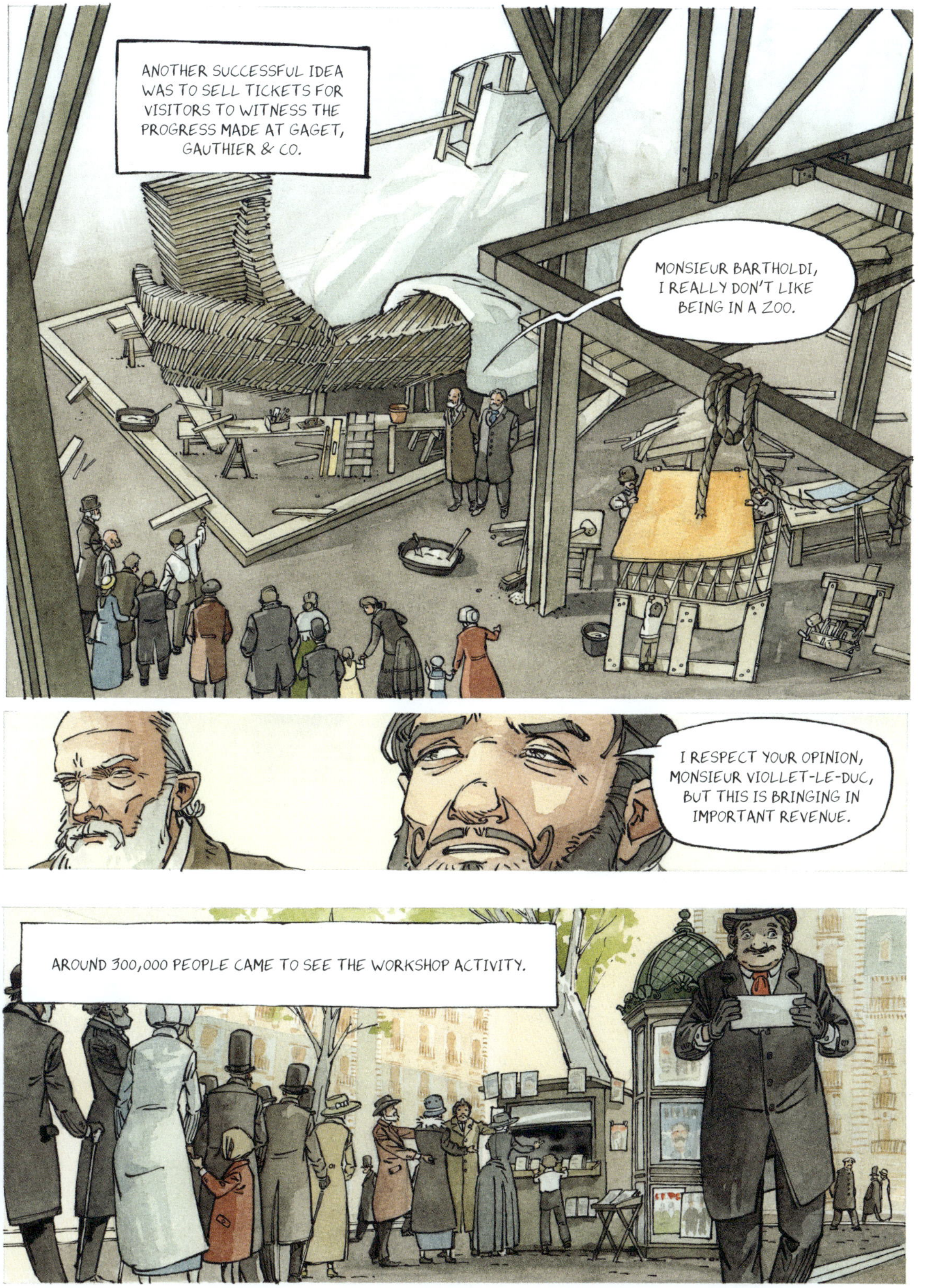
ANOTHER SUCCESSFUL IDEA WAS TO SELL TICKETS FOR VISITORS TO WITNESS THE PROGRESS MADE AT GAGET, GAUTHIER & CO.
MONSIEUR BARTHOLDI, I REALLY DON'T LIKE BEING IN A ZOO.
I RESPECT YOUR OPINION, MONSIEUR VIOLLET-LE-DUC, BUT THIS IS BRINGING IN IMPORTANT REVENUE.
AROUND 300,000 PEOPLE CAME TO SEE THE WORKSHOP ACTIVITY.

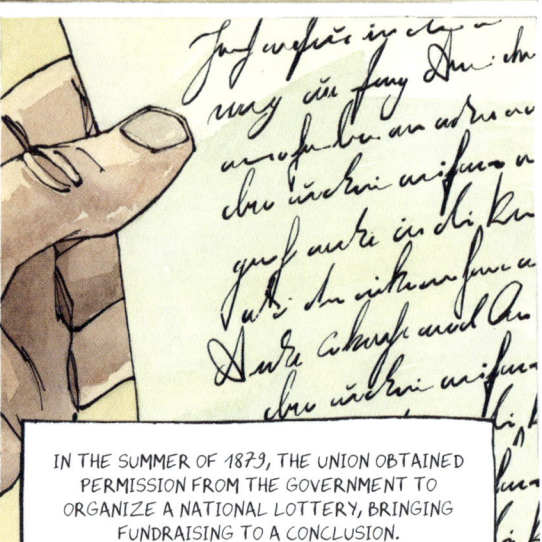

CRAC AH!

After nearly five years, the fundraising goal was reached. More than 100,000 individuals from 181 towns, and 10 chambers of commerce had contributed to the statue. It was truly becoming a gift from the French people to the American people.

In the summer of 1879, the union obtained permission from the government to organize a national lottery, bringing fundraising to a conclusion.

Congratulations, my friend!

Congratulations to you!

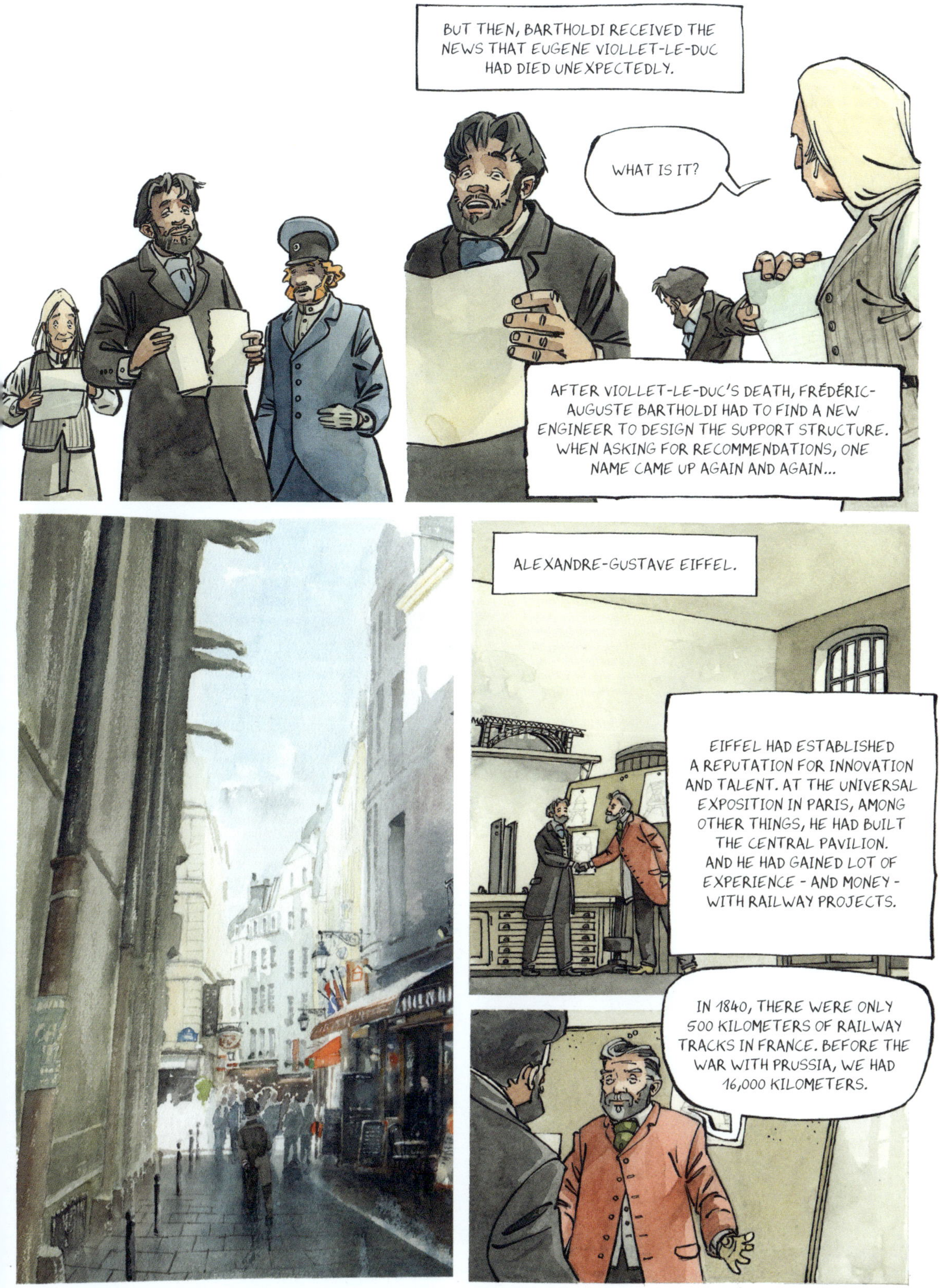
BUT THEN, BARTHOLDI RECEIVED THE NEWS THAT EUGENE VIOLLET-LE-DUC HAD DIED UNEXPECTEDLY.
WHAT IS IT?
AFTER VIOLLET-LE-DUC'S DEATH, FRÉDÉRIC-AUGUSTE BARTHOLDI HAD TO FIND A NEW ENGINEER TO DESIGN THE SUPPORT STRUCTURE. WHEN ASKING FOR RECOMMENDATIONS, ONE NAME CAME UP AGAIN AND AGAIN...
ALEXANDRE-GUSTAVE EIFFEL.
EIFFEL HAD ESTABLISHED A REPUTATION FOR INNOVATION AND TALENT. AT THE UNIVERSAL EXPOSITION IN PARIS, AMONG OTHER THINGS, HE HAD BUILT THE CENTRAL PAVILION. AND HE HAD GAINED LOT OF EXPERIENCE - AND MONEY - WITH RAILWAY PROJECTS.
IN 1840, THERE WERE ONLY 500 KILOMETERS OF RAILWAY TRACKS IN FRANCE. BEFORE THE WAR WITH PRUSSIA, WE HAD 16,000 KILOMETERS.

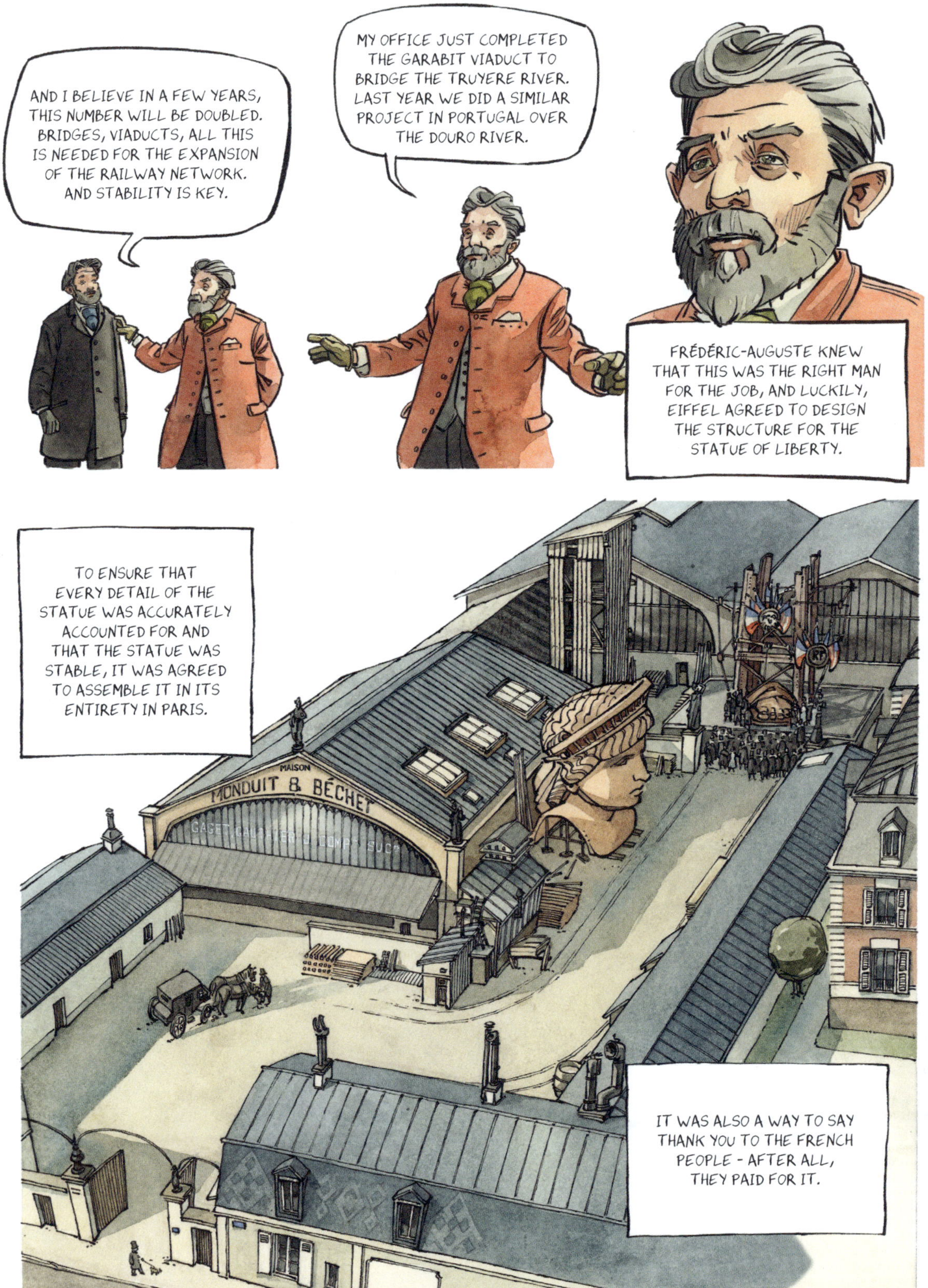
AND I BELIEVE IN A FEW YEARS, THIS NUMBER WILL BE DOUBLED. BRIDGES, VIADUCTS, ALL THIS IS NEEDED FOR THE EXPANSION OF THE RAILWAY NETWORK. AND STABILITY IS KEY.
MY OFFICE JUST COMPLETED THE GARABIT VIADUCT TO BRIDGE THE TRUYERE RIVER. LAST YEAR WE DID A SIMILAR PROJECT IN PORTUGAL OVER THE DOURO RIVER.
FRÉDÉRIC-AUGUSTE KNEW THAT THIS WAS THE RIGHT MAN FOR THE JOB, AND LUCKILY, EIFFEL AGREED TO DESIGN THE STRUCTURE FOR THE STATUE OF LIBERTY.
TO ENSURE THAT EVERY DETAIL OF THE STATUE WAS ACCURATELY ACCOUNTED FOR AND THAT THE STATUE WAS STABLE, IT WAS AGREED TO ASSEMBLE IT IN ITS ENTIRETY IN PARIS.
MAISON
MONDUIT & BÉCHET
IT WAS ALSO A WAY TO SAY THANK YOU TO THE FRENCH PEOPLE - AFTER ALL, THEY PAID FOR IT.

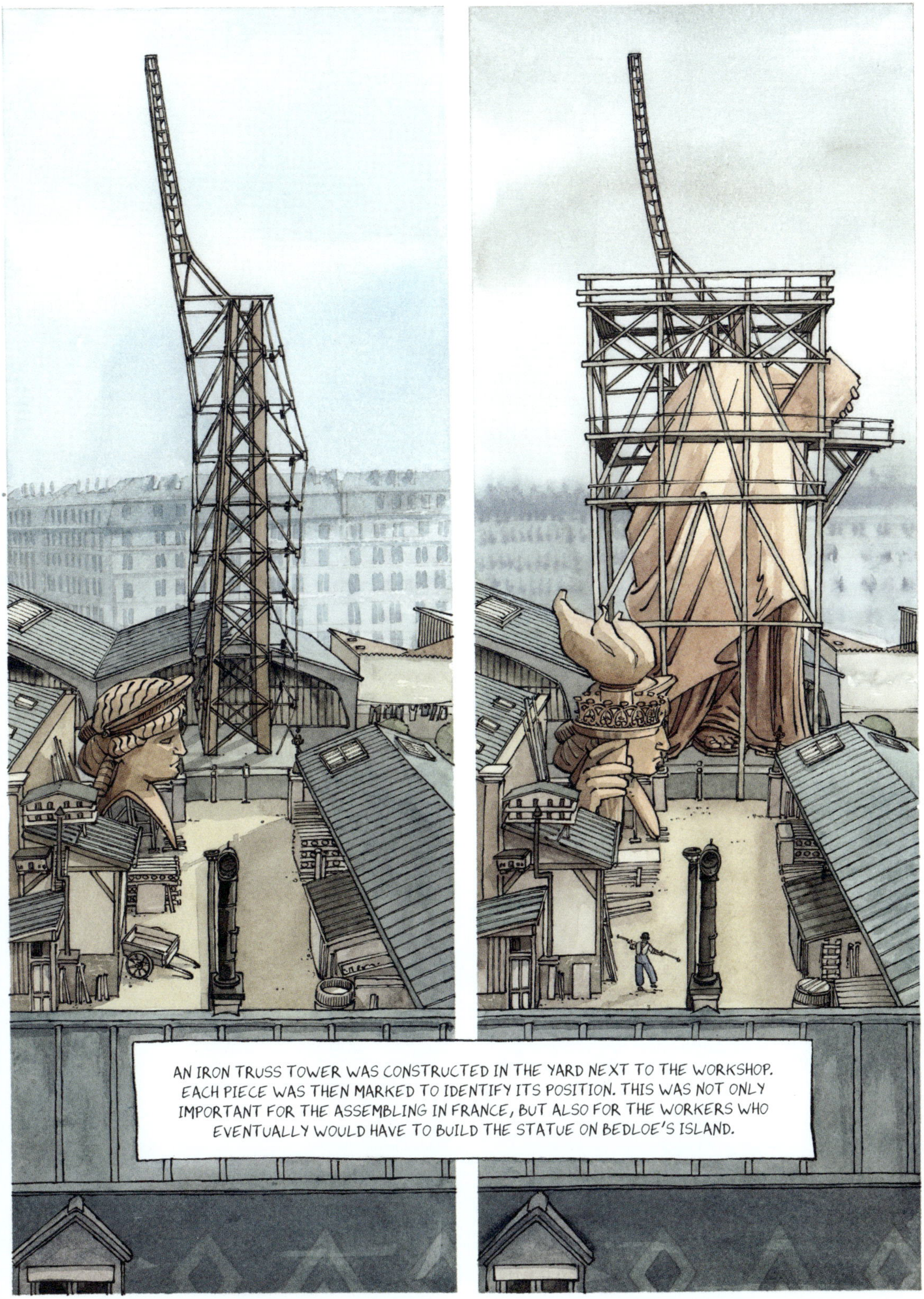
AN IRON TRUSS TOWER WAS CONSTRUCTED IN THE YARD NEXT TO THE WORKSHOP. EACH PIECE WAS THEN MARKED TO IDENTIFY ITS POSITION. THIS WAS NOT ONLY IMPORTANT FOR THE ASSEMBLING IN FRANCE, BUT ALSO FOR THE WORKERS WHO EVENTUALLY WOULD HAVE TO BUILD THE STATUE ON BEDLOE'S ISLAND.

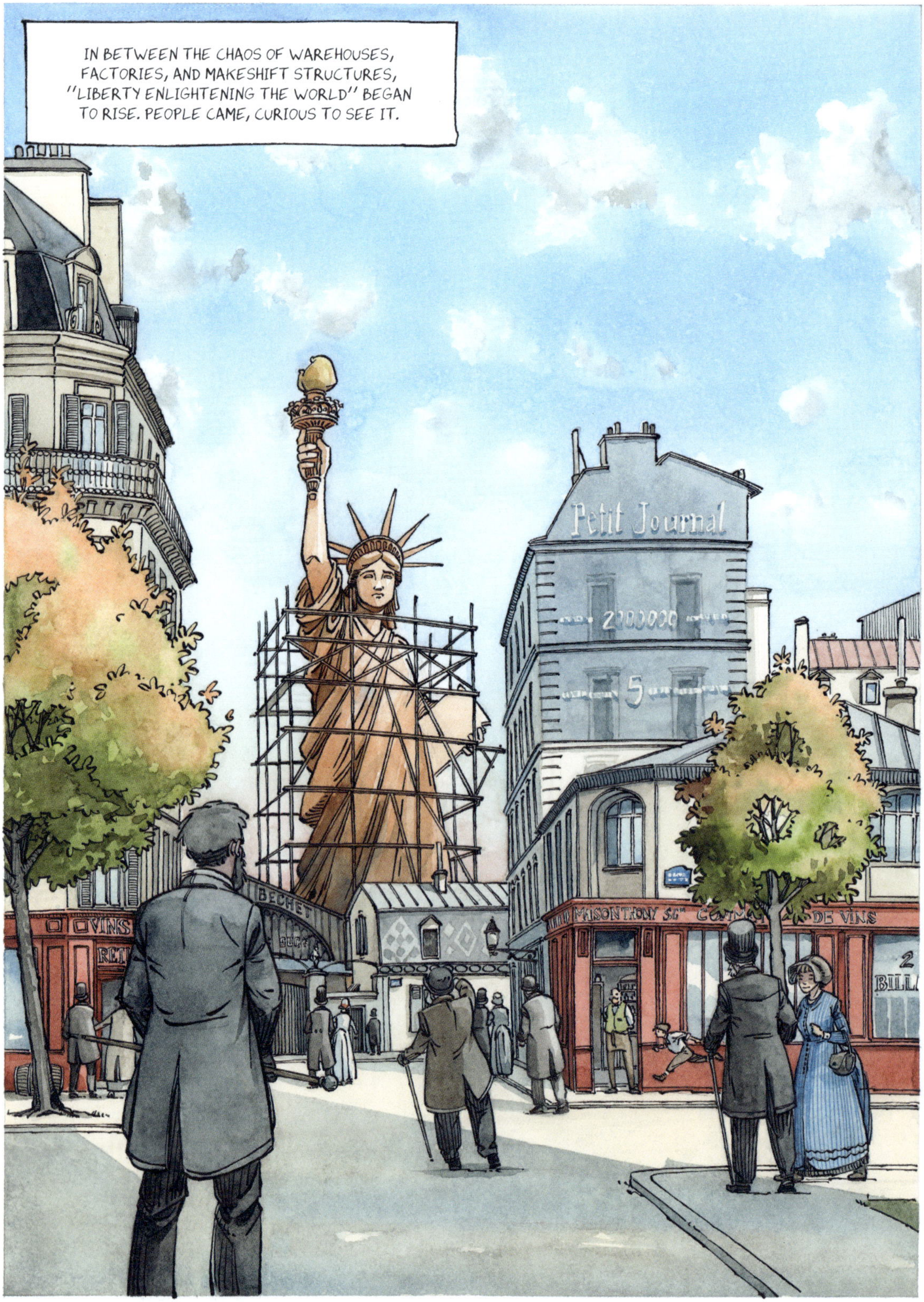
IN BETWEEN THE CHAOS OF WAREHOUSES, FACTORIES, AND MAKESHIFT STRUCTURES, "LIBERTY ENLIGHTENING THE WORLD" BEGAN TO RISE. PEOPLE CAME, CURIOUS TO SEE IT.
Petit Journal

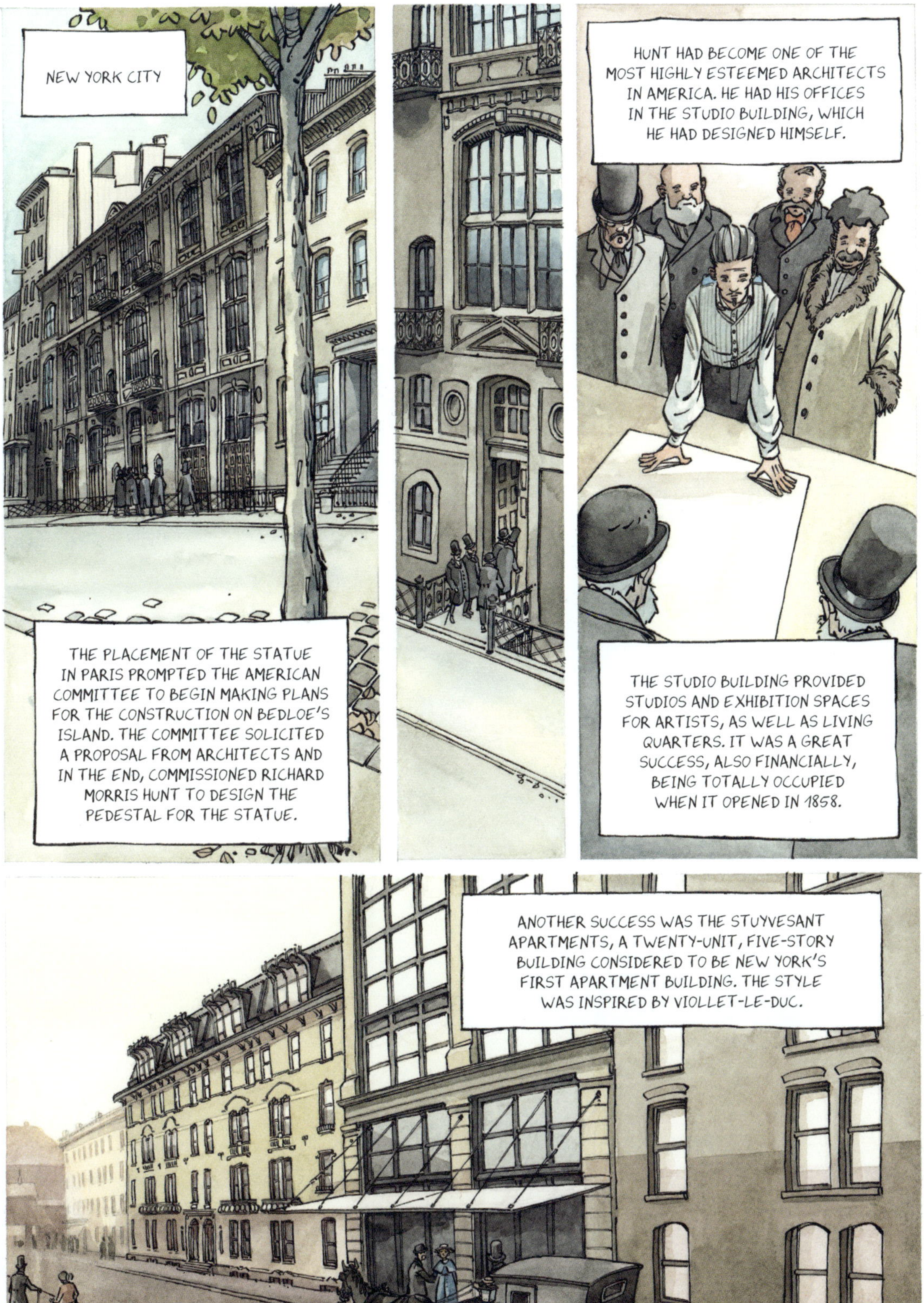
NEW YORK CITY
THE PLACEMENT OF THE STATUE IN PARIS PROMPTED THE AMERICAN COMMITTEE TO BEGIN MAKING PLANS FOR THE CONSTRUCTION ON BEDLOE'S ISLAND. THE COMMITTEE SOLICITED A PROPOSAL FROM ARCHITECTS AND IN THE END, COMMISSIONED RICHARD MORRIS HUNT TO DESIGN THE PEDESTAL FOR THE STATUE.
HUNT HAD BECOME ONE OF THE MOST HIGHLY ESTEEMED ARCHITECTS IN AMERICA. HE HAD HIS OFFICES IN THE STUDIO BUILDING, WHICH HE HAD DESIGNED HIMSELF.
THE STUDIO BUILDING PROVIDED STUDIOS AND EXHIBITION SPACES FOR ARTISTS, AS WELL AS LIVING QUARTERS. IT WAS A GREAT SUCCESS, ALSO FINANCIALLY, BEING TOTALLY OCCUPIED WHEN IT OPENED IN 1858.
ANOTHER SUCCESS WAS THE STUYVESANT APARTMENTS, A TWENTY-UNIT, FIVE-STORY BUILDING CONSIDERED TO BE NEW YORK'S FIRST APARTMENT BUILDING. THE STYLE WAS INSPIRED BY VIOLLET-LE-DUC.

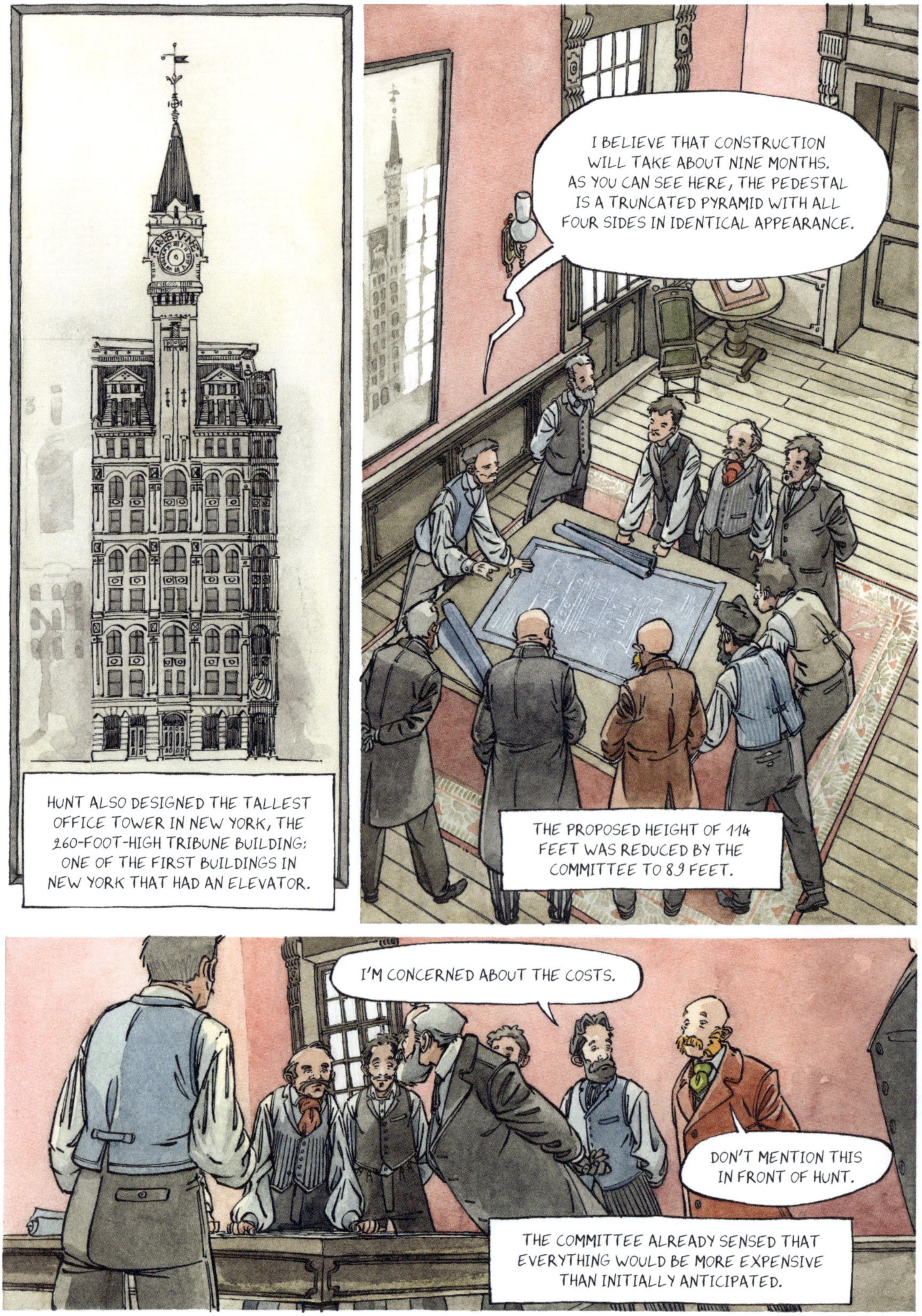
HUNT ALSO DESIGNED THE TALLEST OFFICE TOWER IN NEW YORK, THE 260-FOOT-HIGH TRIBUNE BUILDING; ONE OF THE FIRST BUILDINGS IN NEW YORK THAT HAD AN ELEVATOR.
I BELIEVE THAT CONSTRUCTION WILL TAKE ABOUT NINE MONTHS. AS YOU CAN SEE HERE, THE PEDESTAL IS A TRUNCATED PYRAMID WITH ALL FOUR SIDES IN IDENTICAL APPEARANCE.
THE PROPOSED HEIGHT OF 114 FEET WAS REDUCED BY THE COMMITTEE TO 89 FEET.
I'M CONCERNED ABOUT THE COSTS.
DON'T MENTION THIS IN FRONT OF HUNT.
THE COMMITTEE ALREADY SENSED THAT EVERYTHING WOULD BE MORE EXPENSIVE THAN INITIALLY ANTICIPATED.

IN PARIS, "LIBERTY ENLIGHTENING THE WORLD" WAS TOWERING OVER THE CITY. ITS TRUSS TOWER, THE TALLEST METAL STRUCTURE BUILT TO DATE, HINTED AT A NEW ERA.

THIS IS THE TALLEST STATUE IN THE WORLD.

AUGUSTE, I AM SO PROUD OF YOU.

THANK YOU, MOTHER.

ACTUALLY, IT IS NOT.

THE WORLD'S TALLEST STATUE KNOWN WAS THE 86-FOOT TALL HERMANNSDENKMAL IN GERMANY, COMPLETED IN 1875. IT WAS A SYMBOL OF GERMAN UNIFICATION AND STRENGTH, REPRESENTED BY A TRIBAL CHIEF WHO DEFEATED THE ROMANS IN 9 BCE.

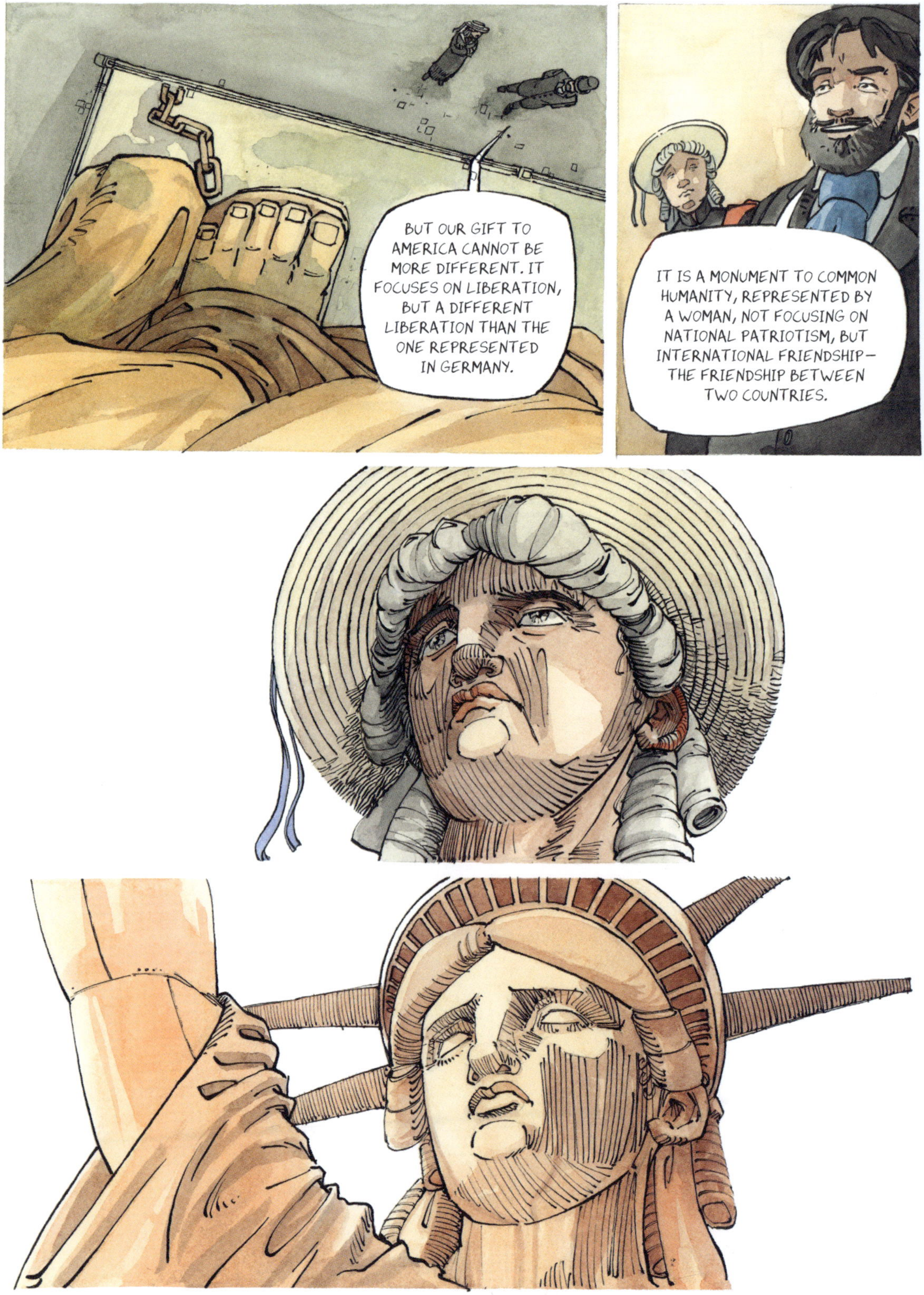
BUT OUR GIFT TO AMERICA CANNOT BE MORE DIFFERENT. IT FOCUSES ON LIBERATION, BUT A DIFFERENT LIBERATION THAN THE ONE REPRESENTED IN GERMANY.
IT IS A MONUMENT TO COMMON HUMANITY, REPRESENTED BY A WOMAN, NOT FOCUSING ON NATIONAL PATRIOTISM, BUT INTERNATIONAL FRIENDSHIP—THE FRIENDSHIP BETWEEN TWO COUNTRIES.

TO MARK THE COMPLETION, A CEREMONY WAS PLANNED FOR JULY 4, 1884.

I ACCEPT THE STATUE ON BEHALF OF U.S. PRESIDENT CHESTER ARTHUR AND THE AMERICAN PEOPLE. I ASSURE THE FRENCH NATION THAT THE AMERICAN PEOPLE RESPOND WITH ALL THEIR HEARTS TO THE SENTIMENT OF FRIENDSHIP. THIS STATUE WILL REMAIN FOR ALL TIME AN EMBLEM OF THE IMPERISHABLE SYMPATHIES UNITING BOTH COUNTRIES.

I WISH LABOULAYE WOULD BE HERE WITH US.

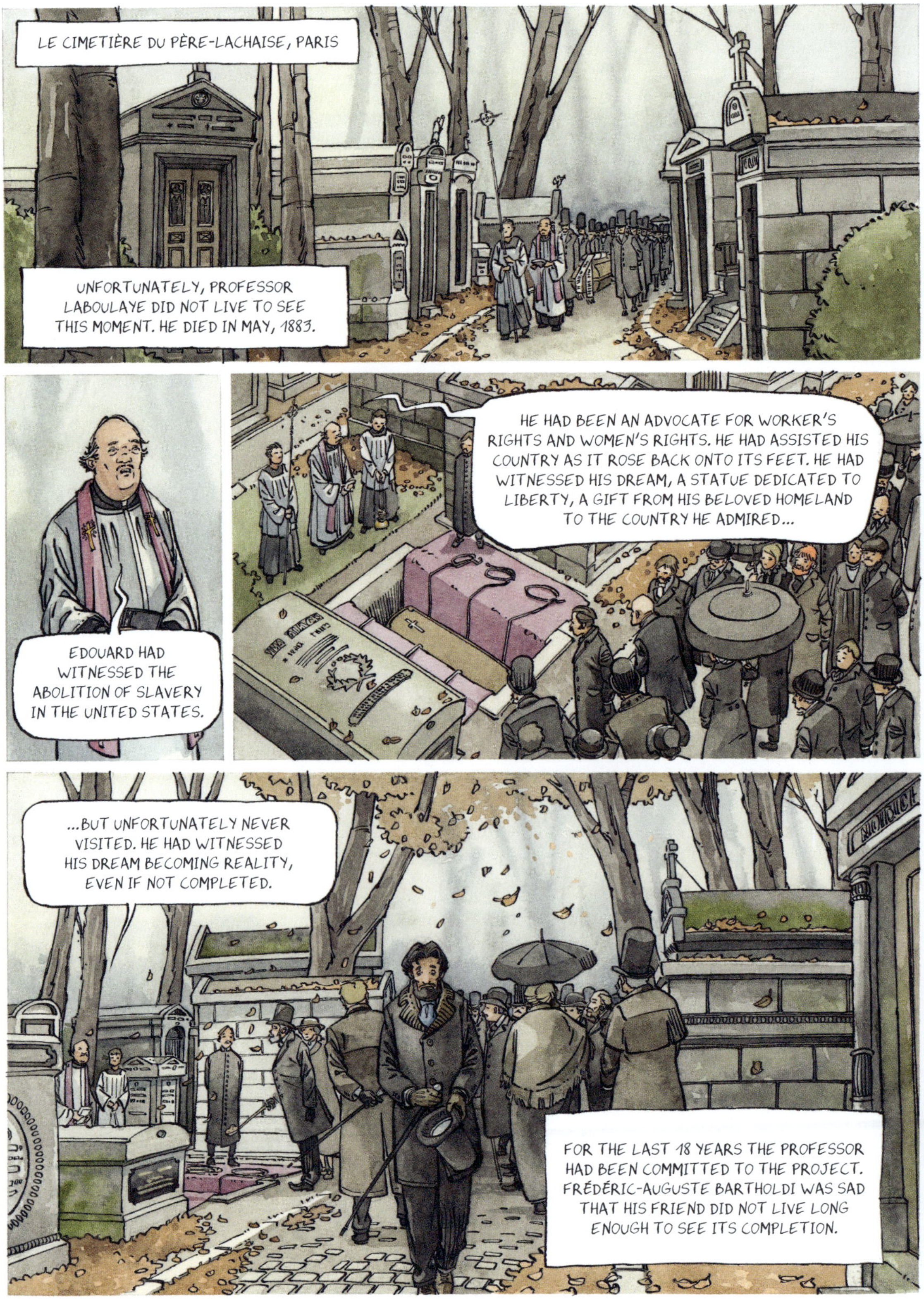
LE CIMETIÈRE DU PÈRE-LACHAISE, PARIS
UNFORTUNATELY, PROFESSOR LABOULAYE DID NOT LIVE TO SEE THIS MOMENT. HE DIED IN MAY, 1883.
EDOUARD HAD WITNESSED THE ABOLITION OF SLAVERY IN THE UNITED STATES.
HE HAD BEEN AN ADVOCATE FOR WORKER'S RIGHTS AND WOMEN'S RIGHTS. HE HAD ASSISTED HIS COUNTRY AS IT ROSE BACK ONTO ITS FEET. HE HAD WITNESSED HIS DREAM, A STATUE DEDICATED TO LIBERTY, A GIFT FROM HIS BELOVED HOMELAND TO THE COUNTRY HE ADMIRED...
...BUT UNFORTUNATELY NEVER VISITED. HE HAD WITNESSED HIS DREAM BECOMING REALITY, EVEN IF NOT COMPLETED.
FOR THE LAST 18 YEARS THE PROFESSOR HAD BEEN COMMITTED TO THE PROJECT. FRÉDÉRIC-AUGUSTE BARTHOLDI WAS SAD THAT HIS FRIEND DID NOT LIVE LONG ENOUGH TO SEE ITS COMPLETION.

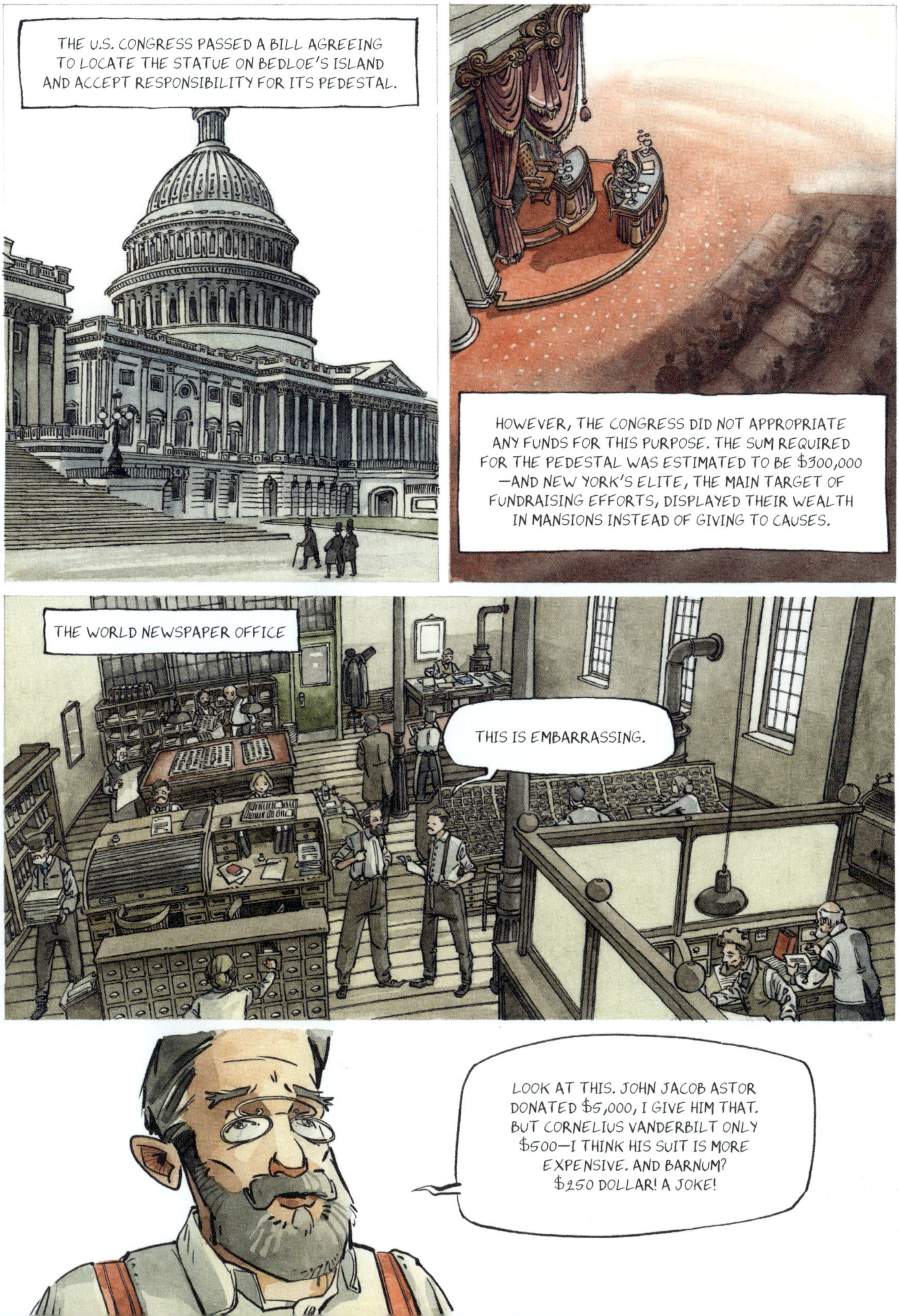
THE U.S. CONGRESS PASSED A BILL AGREEING TO LOCATE THE STATUE ON BEDLOE'S ISLAND AND ACCEPT RESPONSIBILITY FOR ITS PEDESTAL.
HOWEVER, THE CONGRESS DID NOT APPROPRIATE ANY FUNDS FOR THIS PURPOSE. THE SUM REQUIRED FOR THE PEDESTAL WAS ESTIMATED TO BE $300,000 —AND NEW YORK'S ELITE, THE MAIN TARGET OF FUNDRAISING EFFORTS, DISPLAYED THEIR WEALTH IN MANSIONS INSTEAD OF GIVING TO CAUSES.
THE WORLD NEWSPAPER OFFICE
THIS IS EMBARRASSING.
LOOK AT THIS. JOHN JACOB ASTOR DONATED $5,000, I GIVE HIM THAT. BUT CORNELIUS VANDERBILT ONLY $500—I THINK HIS SUIT IS MORE EXPENSIVE. AND BARNUM? $250 DOLLAR! A JOKE!

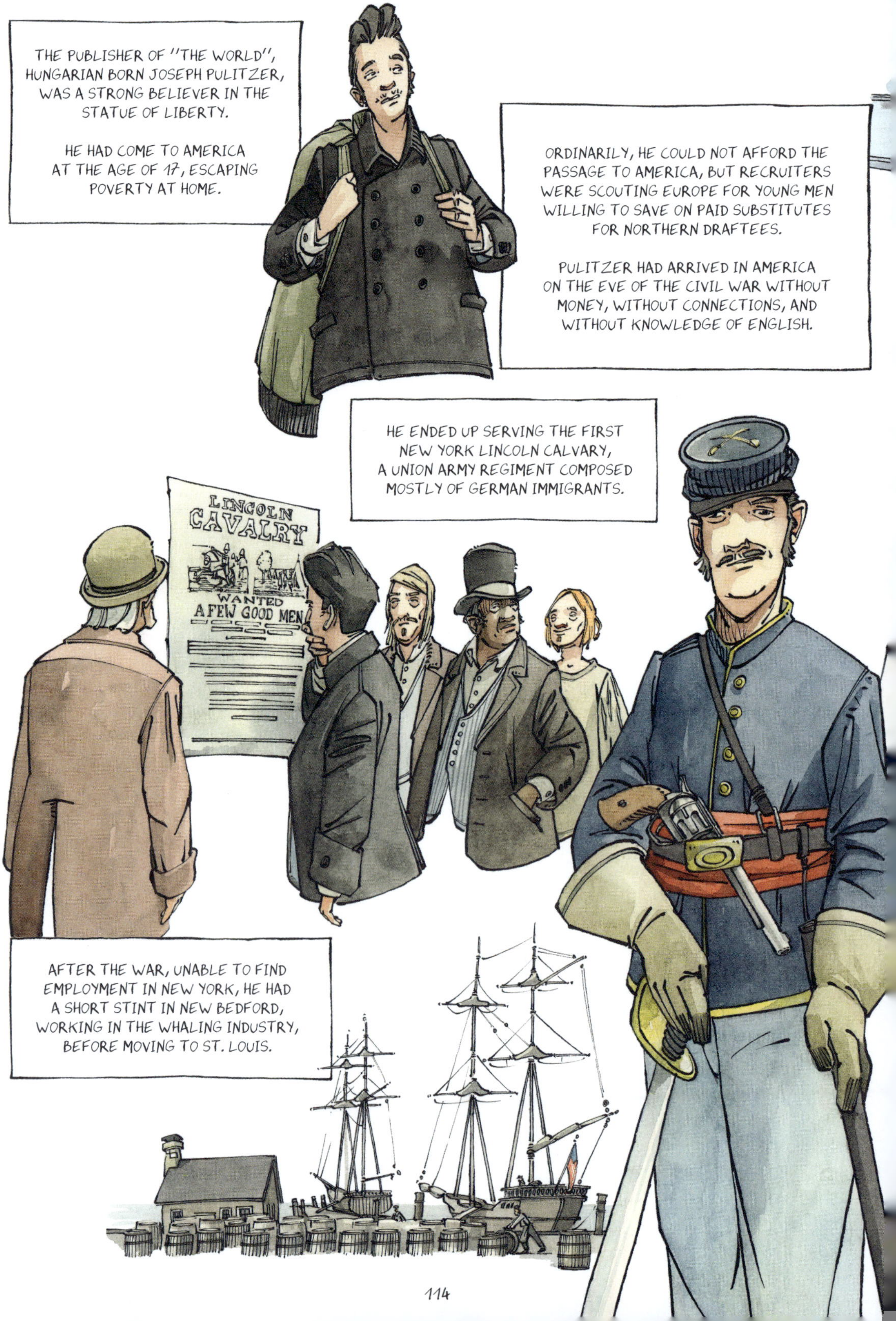

THE PUBLISHER OF "THE WORLD", HUNGARIAN BORN JOSEPH PULITZER, WAS A STRONG BELIEVER IN THE STATUE OF LIBERTY.
HE HAD COME TO AMERICA AT THE AGE OF 17, ESCAPING POVERTY AT HOME.
ORDINARILY, HE COULD NOT AFFORD THE PASSAGE TO AMERICA, BUT RECRUITERS WERE SCOUTING EUROPE FOR YOUNG MEN WILLING TO SAVE ON PAID SUBSTITUTES FOR NORTHERN DRAFTEES.
PULITZER HAD ARRIVED IN AMERICA ON THE EVE OF THE CIVIL WAR WITHOUT MONEY, WITHOUT CONNECTIONS, AND WITHOUT KNOWLEDGE OF ENGLISH.
HE ENDED UP SERVING THE FIRST NEW YORK LINCOLN CALVARY, A UNION ARMY REGIMENT COMPOSED MOSTLY OF GERMAN IMMIGRANTS.
LINCOLN
CAVALRY
WANTED
A FEW GOOD MEN
AFTER THE WAR, UNABLE TO FIND EMPLOYMENT IN NEW YORK, HE HAD A SHORT STINT IN NEW BEDFORD, WORKING IN THE WHALING INDUSTRY, BEFORE MOVING TO ST. LOUIS.

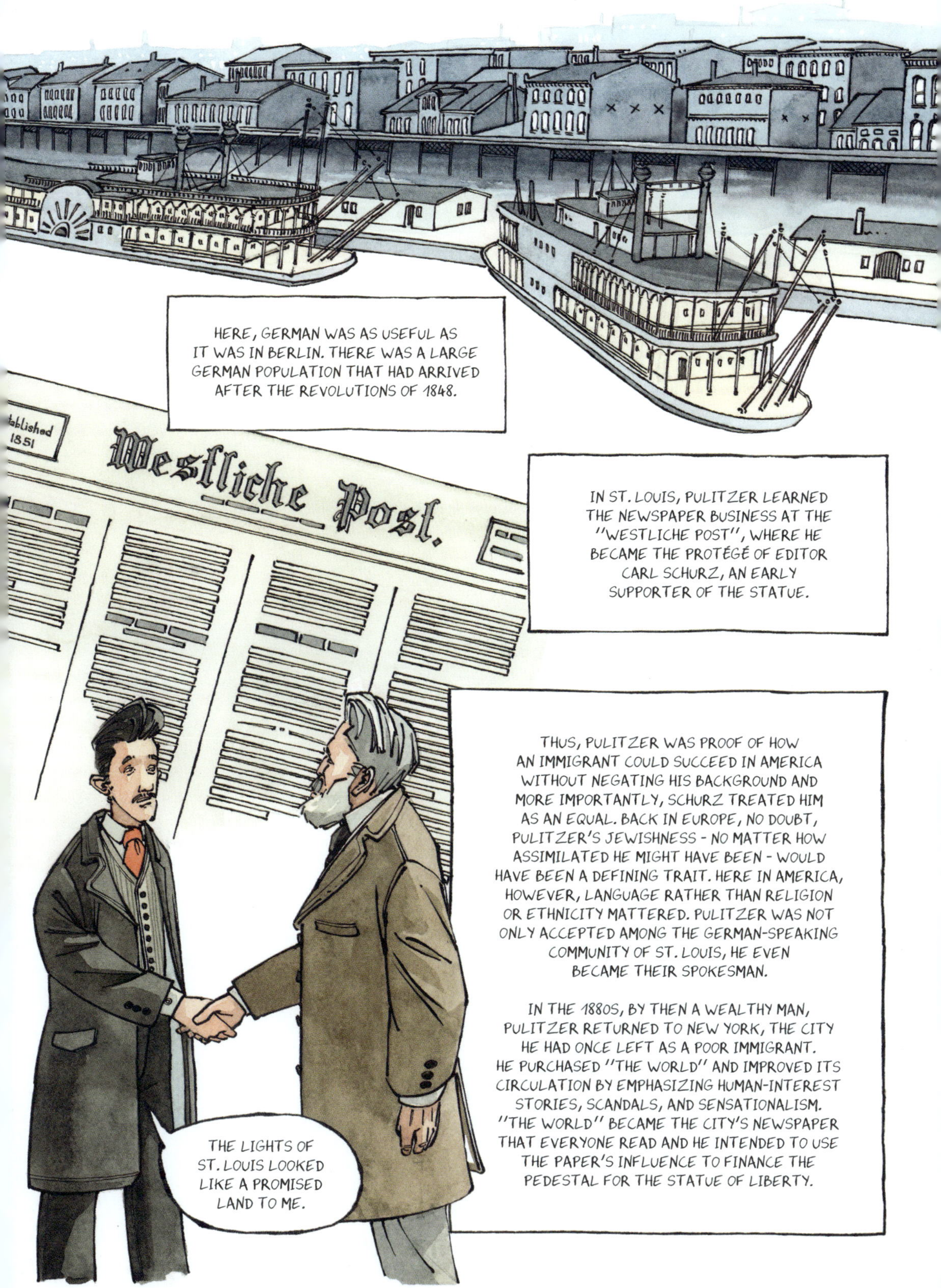
HERE, GERMAN WAS AS USEFUL AS IT WAS IN BERLIN. THERE WAS A LARGE GERMAN POPULATION THAT HAD ARRIVED AFTER THE REVOLUTIONS OF 1848.
Established 1851
Westliche Post.
IN ST. LOUIS, PULITZER LEARNED THE NEWSPAPER BUSINESS AT THE "WESTLICHE POST", WHERE HE BECAME THE PROTÉGÉ OF EDITOR CARL SCHURZ, AN EARLY SUPPORTER OF THE STATUE.
THUS, PULITZER WAS PROOF OF HOW AN IMMIGRANT COULD SUCCEED IN AMERICA WITHOUT NEGATING HIS BACKGROUND AND MORE IMPORTANTLY, SCHURZ TREATED HIM AS AN EQUAL. BACK IN EUROPE, NO DOUBT, PULITZER'S JEWISHNESS - NO MATTER HOW ASSIMILATED HE MIGHT HAVE BEEN - WOULD HAVE BEEN A DEFINING TRAIT. HERE IN AMERICA, HOWEVER, LANGUAGE RATHER THAN RELIGION OR ETHNICITY MATTERED. PULITZER WAS NOT ONLY ACCEPTED AMONG THE GERMAN-SPEAKING COMMUNITY OF ST. LOUIS, HE EVEN BECAME THEIR SPOKESMAN.
IN THE 1880S, BY THEN A WEALTHY MAN, PULITZER RETURNED TO NEW YORK, THE CITY HE HAD ONCE LEFT AS A POOR IMMIGRANT. HE PURCHASED "THE WORLD" AND IMPROVED ITS CIRCULATION BY EMPHASIZING HUMAN-INTEREST STORIES, SCANDALS, AND SENSATIONALISM. "THE WORLD" BECAME THE CITY'S NEWSPAPER THAT EVERYONE READ AND HE INTENDED TO USE THE PAPER'S INFLUENCE TO FINANCE THE PEDESTAL FOR THE STATUE OF LIBERTY.
THE LIGHTS OF ST. LOUIS LOOKED LIKE A PROMISED LAND TO ME.

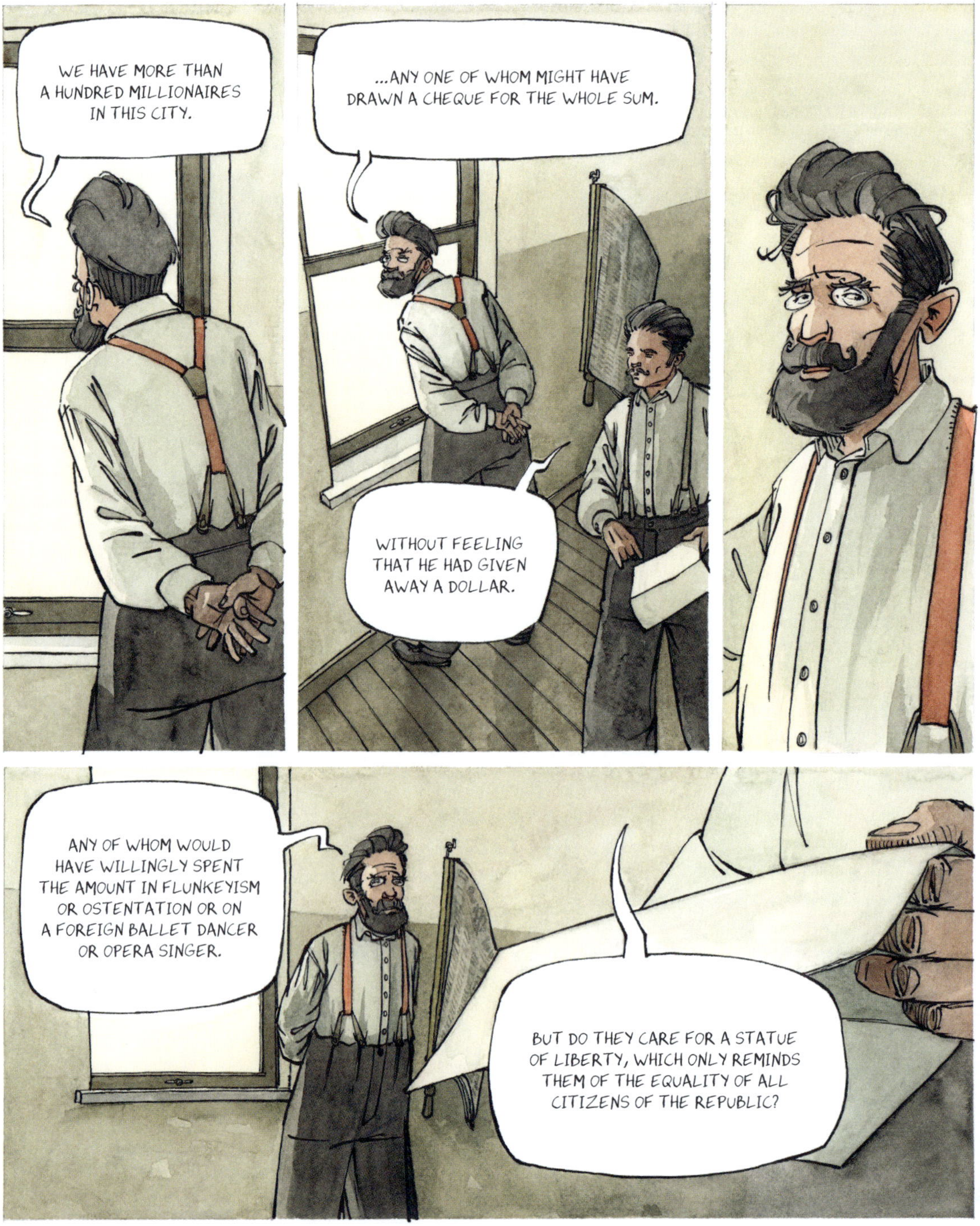
WE HAVE MORE THAN A HUNDRED MILLIONAIRES IN THIS CITY.
...ANY ONE OF WHOM MIGHT HAVE DRAWN A CHEQUE FOR THE WHOLE SUM.
WITHOUT FEELING THAT HE HAD GIVEN AWAY A DOLLAR.
ANY OF WHOM WOULD HAVE WILLINGLY SPENT THE AMOUNT IN FLUNKEYISM OR OSTENTATION OR ON A FOREIGN BALLET DANCER OR OPERA SINGER.
BUT DO THEY CARE FOR A STATUE OF LIBERTY, WHICH ONLY REMINDS THEM OF THE EQUALITY OF ALL CITIZENS OF THE REPUBLIC?

PART OF THE FUNDRAISING PROBLEM, HE KNEW, WAS THAT THE STATUE HAD NO PRECISE MEANING. FOR MANY AMERICANS, IT WAS A HOLLOW ICON AND NOT A LIKENESS OF A PARTICULAR PERSON OR A REPRESENTATION OF A SIGNIFICANT HISTORIC MOMENT. IN ADDITION, MANY BELIEVED THE WEALTHY SHOULD PAY FOR IT. THE INITIAL FUNDRAISING STRATEGY - LIKE IN FRANCE - TARGETED WEALTHY INDIVIDUALS WITH GALAS, CONCERTS, EVEN SPORTING BENEFITS. BUT THE CAPTAINS AND GRAND DAMES OF THE GILDED AGE WERE NOT GIVING AS MUCH AS HOPED.

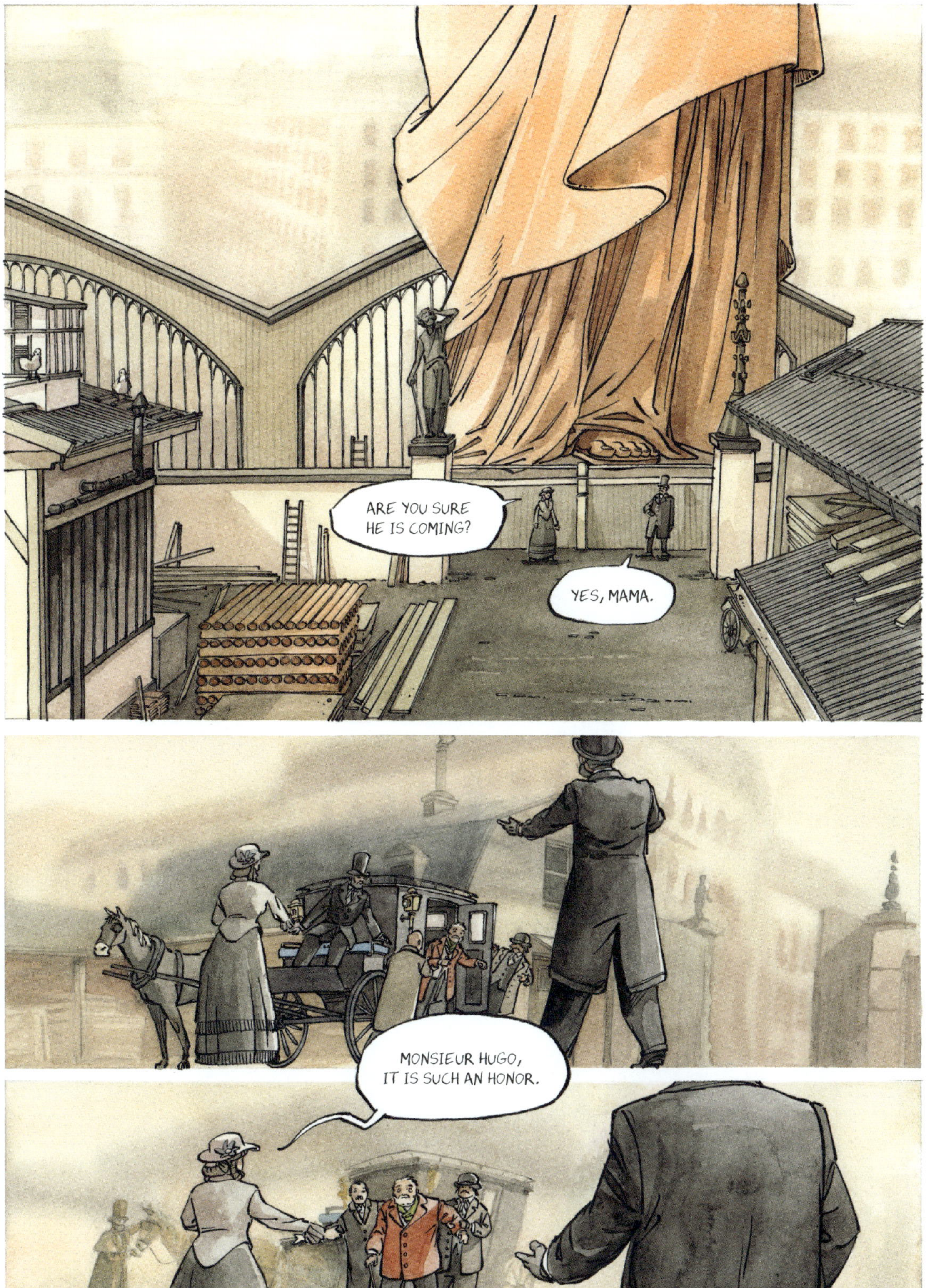
ARE YOU SURE HE IS COMING?
YES, MAMA.
MONSIEUR HUGO, IT IS SUCH AN HONOR.

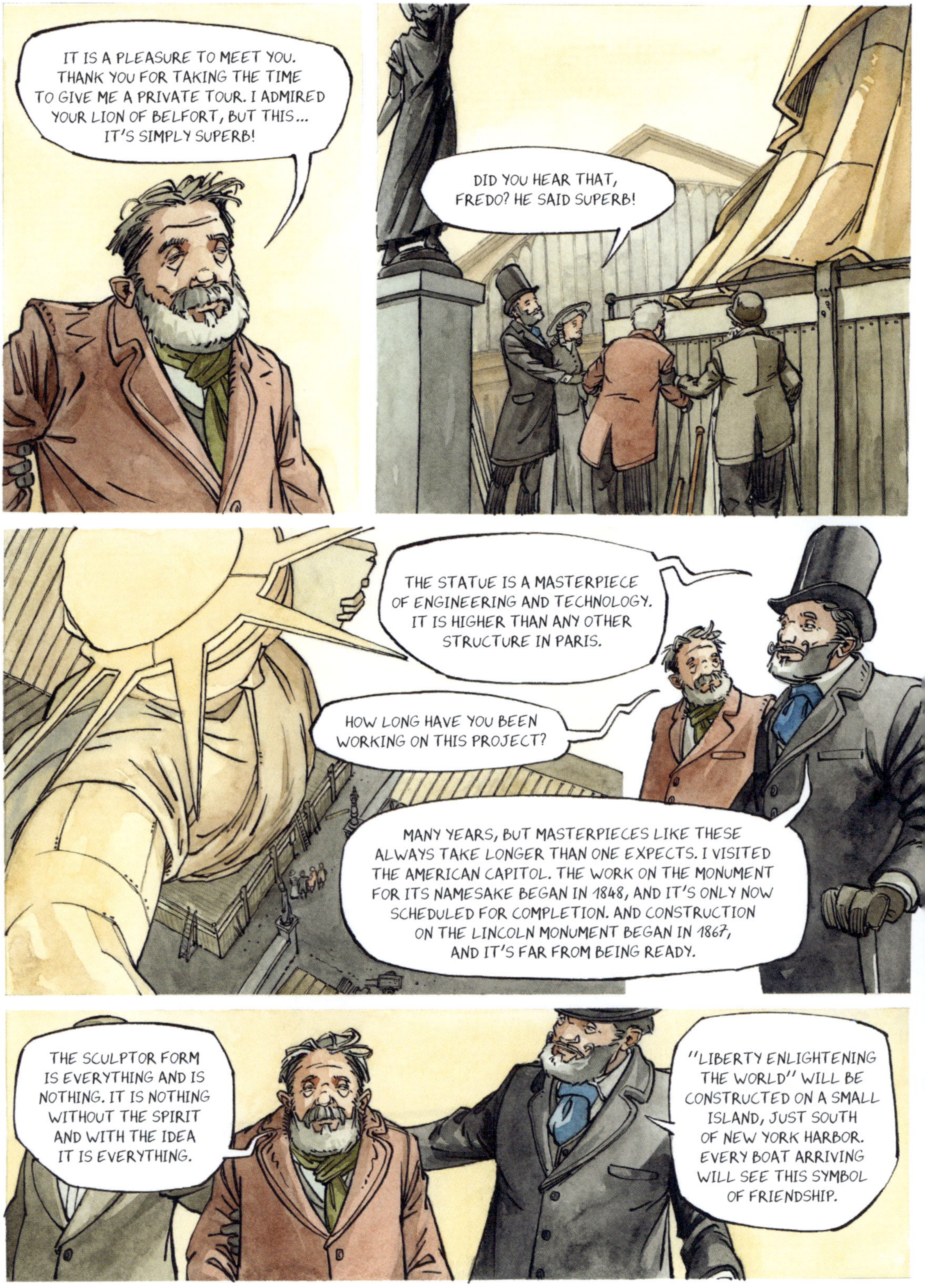
IT IS A PLEASURE TO MEET YOU. THANK YOU FOR TAKING THE TIME TO GIVE ME A PRIVATE TOUR. I ADMIRED YOUR LION OF BELFORT, BUT THIS... IT'S SIMPLY SUPERB!
DID YOU HEAR THAT, FREDO? HE SAID SUPERB!
THE STATUE IS A MASTERPIECE OF ENGINEERING AND TECHNOLOGY. IT IS HIGHER THAN ANY OTHER STRUCTURE IN PARIS.
HOW LONG HAVE YOU BEEN WORKING ON THIS PROJECT?
MANY YEARS, BUT MASTERPIECES LIKE THESE ALWAYS TAKE LONGER THAN ONE EXPECTS. I VISITED THE AMERICAN CAPITOL. THE WORK ON THE MONUMENT FOR ITS NAMESAKE BEGAN IN 1848, AND IT'S ONLY NOW SCHEDULED FOR COMPLETION. AND CONSTRUCTION ON THE LINCOLN MONUMENT BEGAN IN 1867, AND IT'S FAR FROM BEING READY.
THE SCULPTOR FORM IS EVERYTHING AND IS NOTHING. IT IS NOTHING WITHOUT THE SPIRIT AND WITH THE IDEA IT IS EVERYTHING.
"LIBERTY ENLIGHTENING THE WORLD" WILL BE CONSTRUCTED ON A SMALL ISLAND, JUST SOUTH OF NEW YORK HARBOR. EVERY BOAT ARRIVING WILL SEE THIS SYMBOL OF FRIENDSHIP.

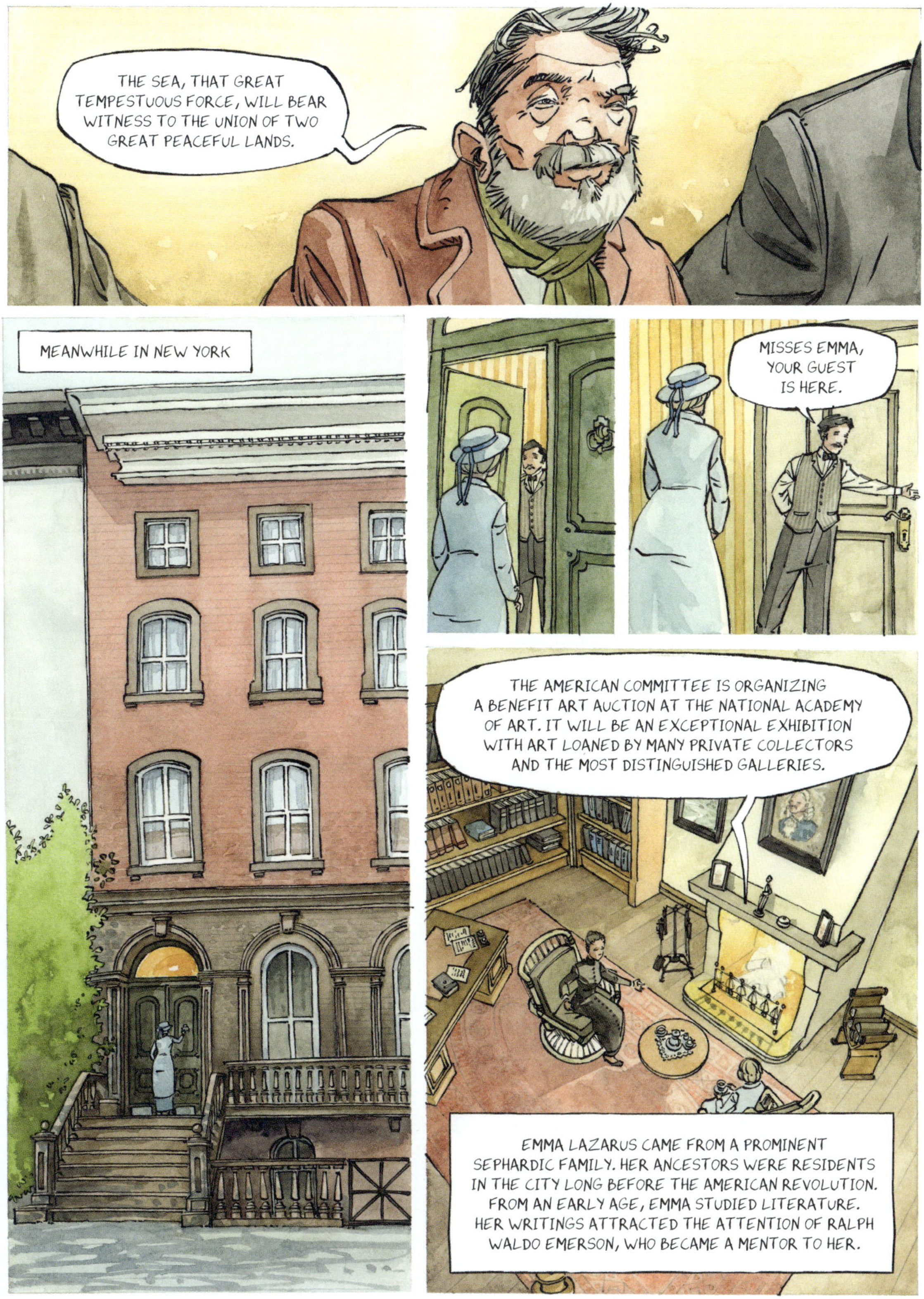

THE SEA, THAT GREAT TEMPESTUOUS FORCE, WILL BEAR WITNESS TO THE UNION OF TWO GREAT PEACEFUL LANDS.
MEANWHILE IN NEW YORK
MISSES EMMA, YOUR GUEST IS HERE.
THE AMERICAN COMMITTEE IS ORGANIZING A BENEFIT ART AUCTION AT THE NATIONAL ACADEMY OF ART. IT WILL BE AN EXCEPTIONAL EXHIBITION WITH ART LOANED BY MANY PRIVATE COLLECTORS AND THE MOST DISTINGUISHED GALLERIES.
EMMA LAZARUS CAME FROM A PROMINENT SEPHARDIC FAMILY. HER ANCESTORS WERE RESIDENTS IN THE CITY LONG BEFORE THE AMERICAN REVOLUTION. FROM AN EARLY AGE, EMMA STUDIED LITERATURE. HER WRITINGS ATTRACTED THE ATTENTION OF RALPH WALDO EMERSON, WHO BECAME A MENTOR TO HER.

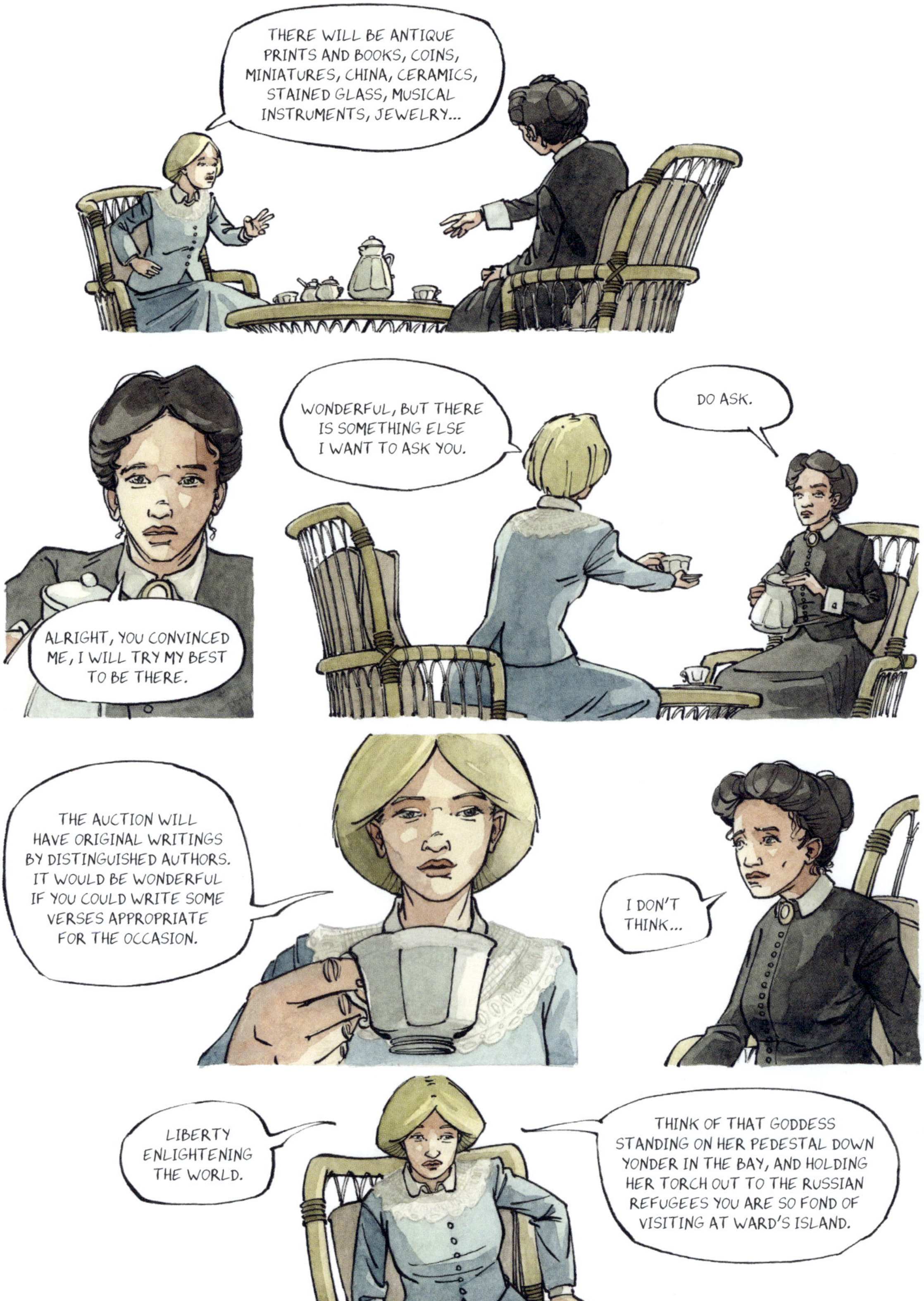
THERE WILL BE ANTIQUE PRINTS AND BOOKS, COINS, MINIATURES, CHINA, CERAMICS, STAINED GLASS, MUSICAL INSTRUMENTS, JEWELRY...
ALRIGHT, YOU CONVINCED ME, I WILL TRY MY BEST TO BE THERE.
WONDERFUL, BUT THERE IS SOMETHING ELSE I WANT TO ASK YOU.
DO ASK.
THE AUCTION WILL HAVE ORIGINAL WRITINGS BY DISTINGUISHED AUTHORS. IT WOULD BE WONDERFUL IF YOU COULD WRITE SOME VERSES APPROPRIATE FOR THE OCCASION.
I DON'T THINK...
LIBERTY ENLIGHTENING THE WORLD.
THINK OF THAT GODDESS STANDING ON HER PEDESTAL DOWN YONDER IN THE BAY, AND HOLDING HER TORCH OUT TO THE RUSSIAN REFUGEES YOU ARE SO FOND OF VISITING AT WARD'S ISLAND.

IN THE EARLY 1880S, THOUSANDS OF JEWS CAME TO NEW YORK, FLEEING POGROMS AND POVERTY IN RUSSIA. EMMA BECAME A LEADING ADVOCATE FOR THEM.

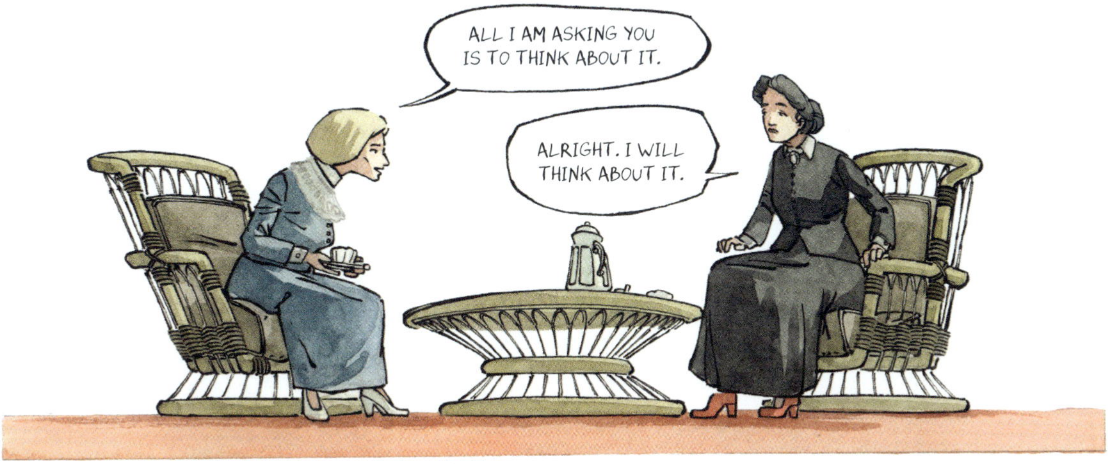
ALL I AM ASKING YOU IS TO THINK ABOUT IT.
ALRIGHT. I WILL THINK ABOUT IT.

IT WAS NOT THE FIRST TIME SHE HAD BEEN ASKED TO WRITE TO ORDER. BUT SOMETHING WAS DIFFERENT THIS TIME. DESPITE HER INITIAL HESITATION, EMMA WORKED ON A POEM.

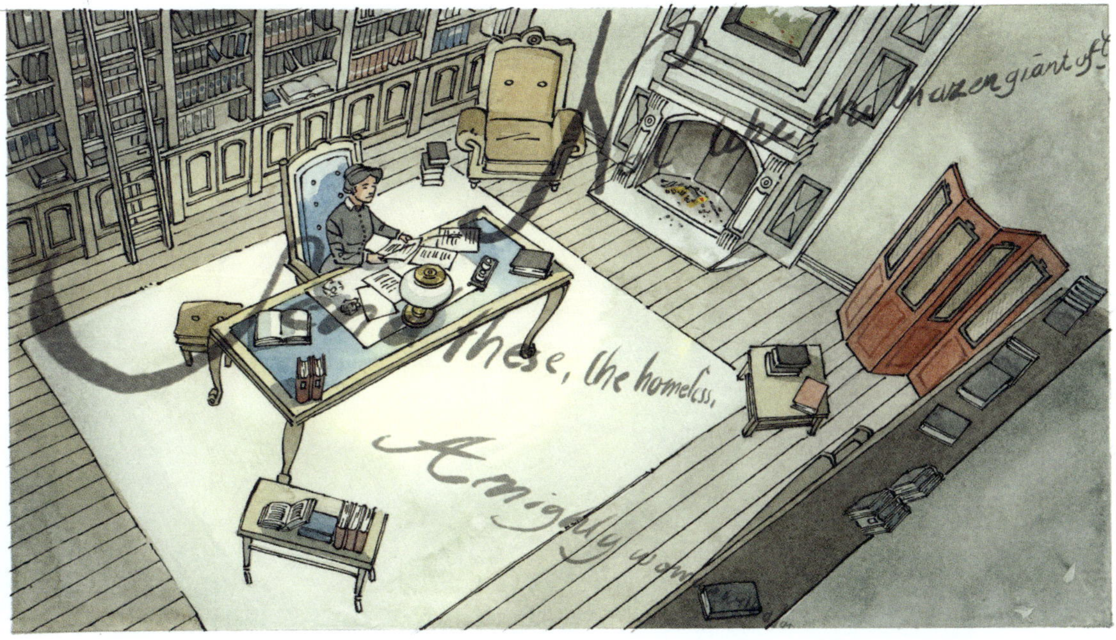
these, the homeless,

HER POEM WAS TITLED "THE NEW COLOSSUS." WITH IT, SHE WOULD GIVE THE STATUE A VOICE, MAKING LADY LIBERTY THE MOTHER OF ALL EXILES, WELCOMING IMMIGRANTS INTO THE LAND OF FREEDOM.

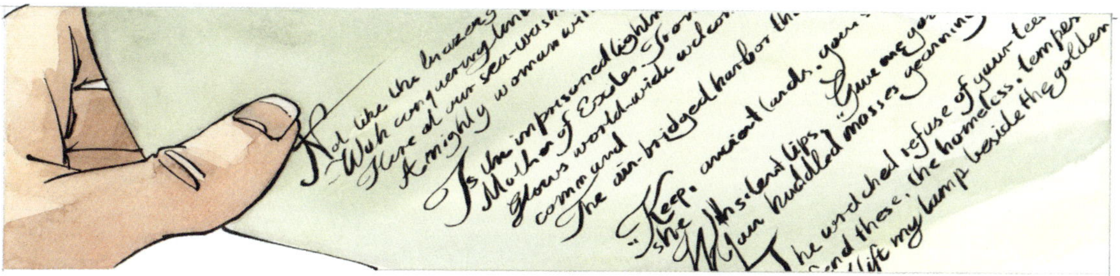

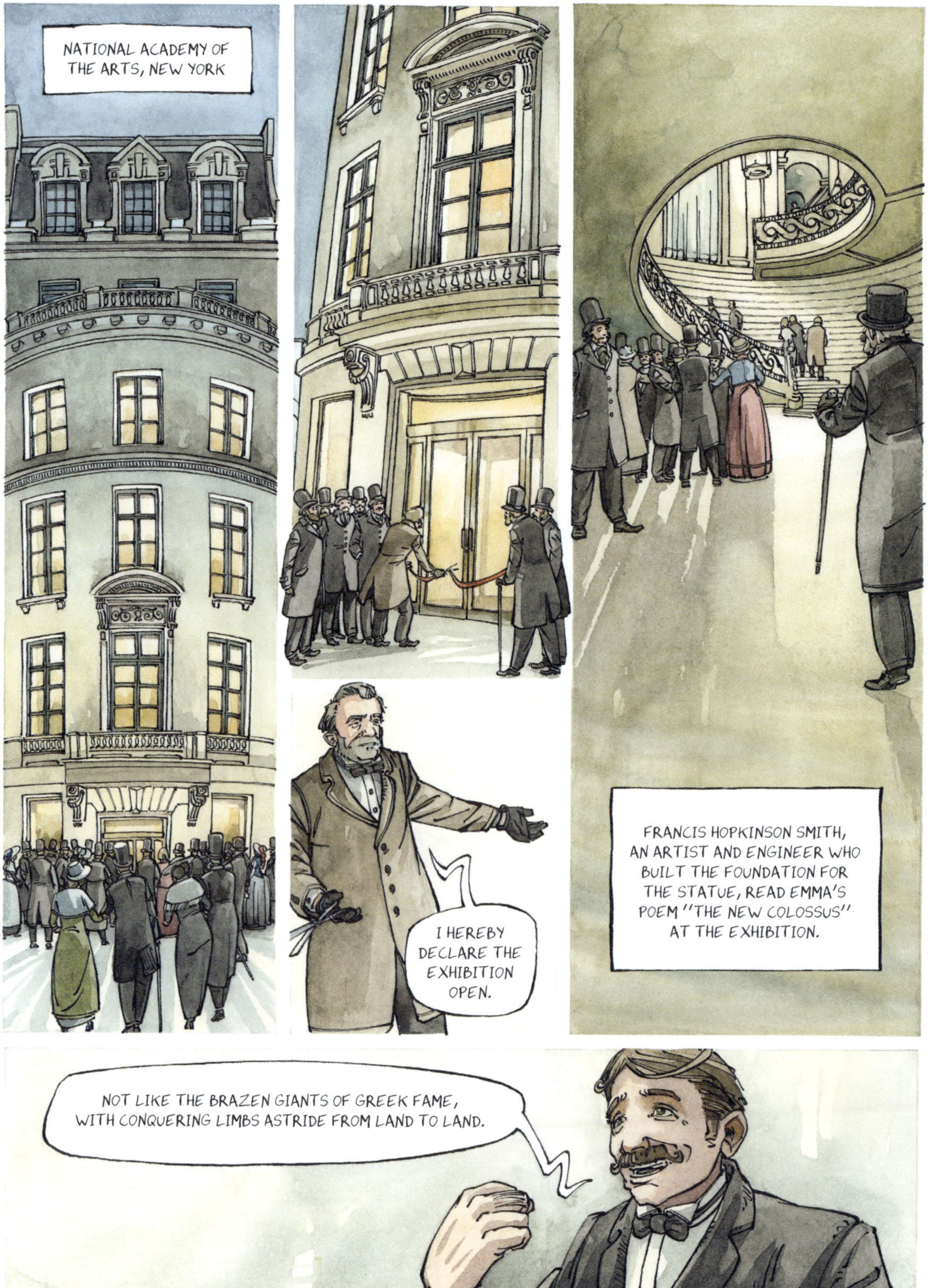
NATIONAL ACADEMY OF THE ARTS, NEW YORK
I HEREBY DECLARE THE EXHIBITION OPEN.
FRANCIS HOPKINSON SMITH, AN ARTIST AND ENGINEER WHO BUILT THE FOUNDATION FOR THE STATUE, READ EMMA'S POEM "THE NEW COLOSSUS" AT THE EXHIBITION.
NOT LIKE THE BRAZEN GIANTS OF GREEK FAME, WITH CONQUERING LIMBS ASTRIDE FROM LAND TO LAND.

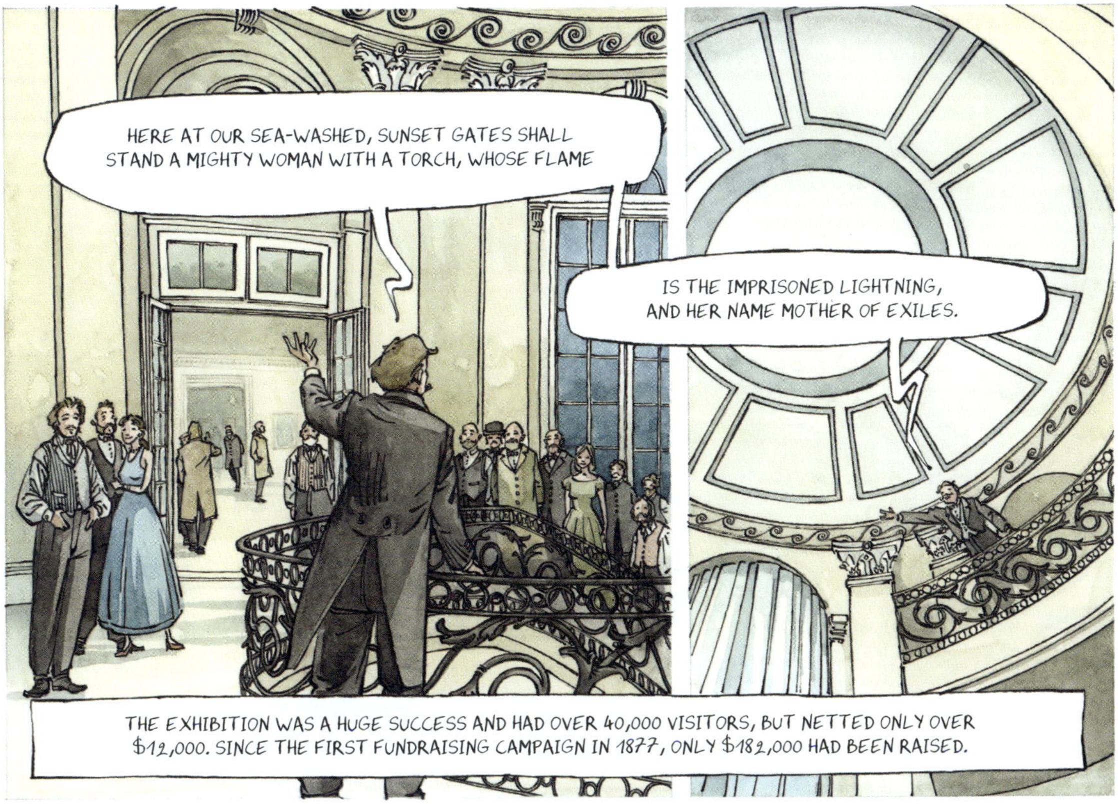
HERE AT OUR SEA-WASHED, SUNSET GATES SHALL STAND A MIGHTY WOMAN WITH A TORCH, WHOSE FLAME
IS THE IMPRISONED LIGHTNING, AND HER NAME MOTHER OF EXILES.
THE EXHIBITION WAS A HUGE SUCCESS AND HAD OVER 40,000 VISITORS, BUT NETTED ONLY OVER $12,000. SINCE THE FIRST FUNDRAISING CAMPAIGN IN 1877, ONLY $182,000 HAD BEEN RAISED.

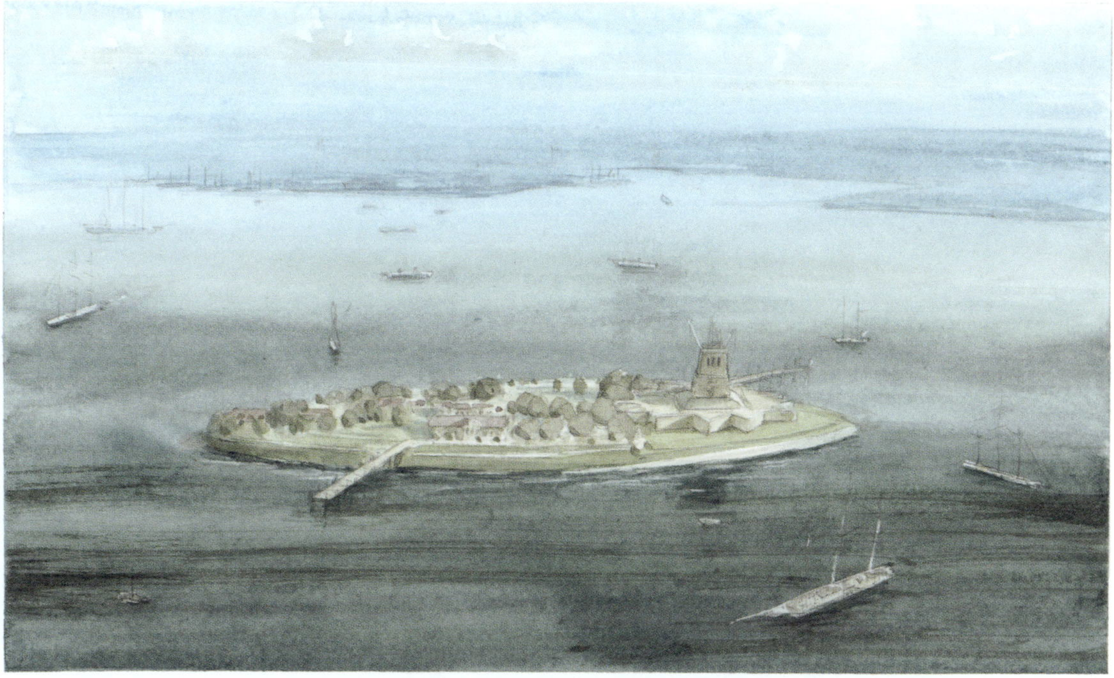

THE CONSTRUCTION OF THE PEDESTAL, MANAGED BY CHARLES POMEROY STONE AND ASSISTED BY CHARLES C. SCHNEIDER, WAS UNDERWAY. DAVID H. KING JR. OFFERED THE SERVICES OF HIS CONSTRUCTION COMPANY WITHOUT PROFIT. BUT THEN, IN MARCH 1885, THE AMERICAN COMMITTEE RAN OUT OF FUNDS.

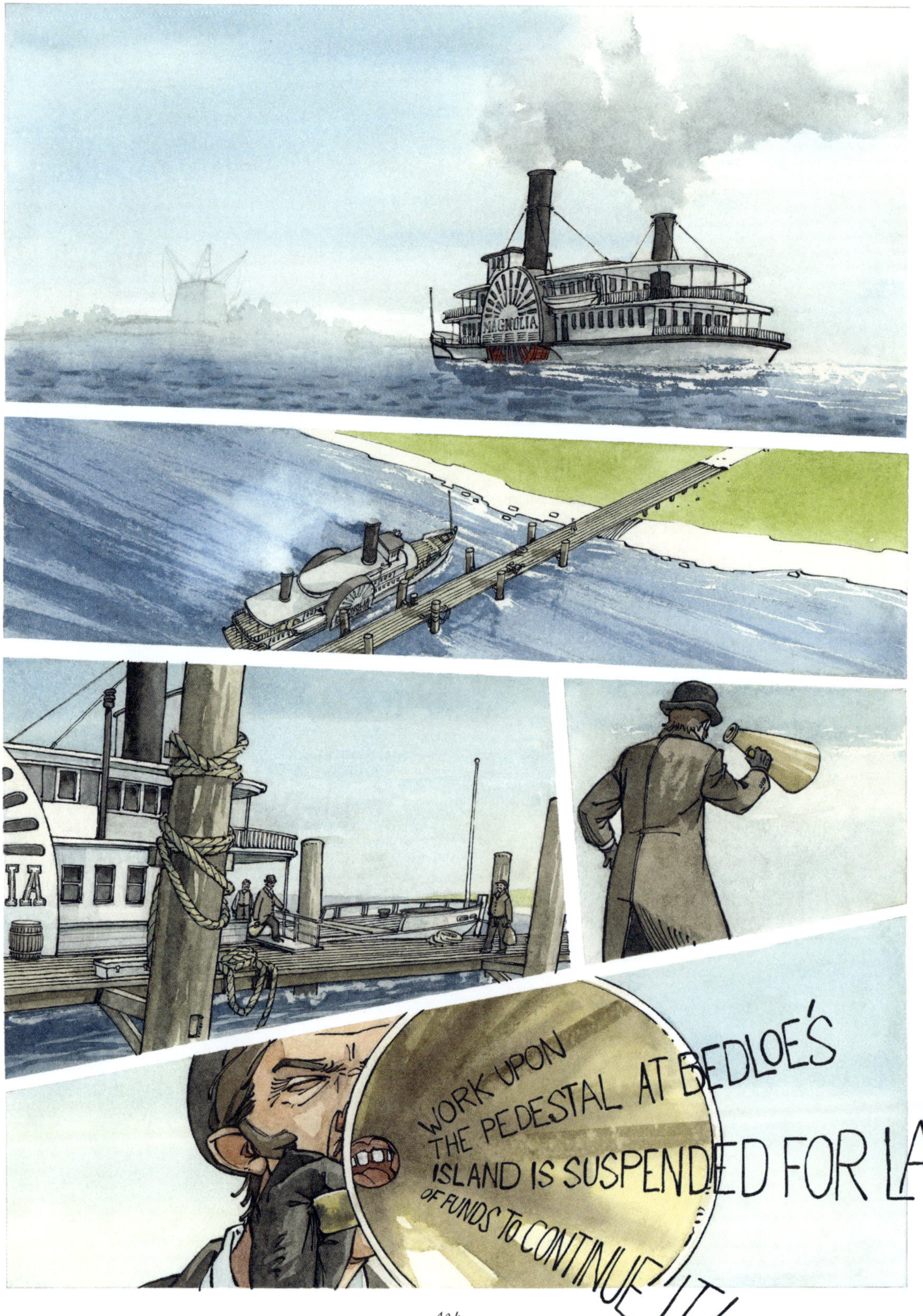
MAGNOLIA
WORK UPON
THE PEDESTAL AT BEDLOE'S
ISLAND IS SUSPENDED FOR LA
OF FUNDS TO CONTINUE IT!

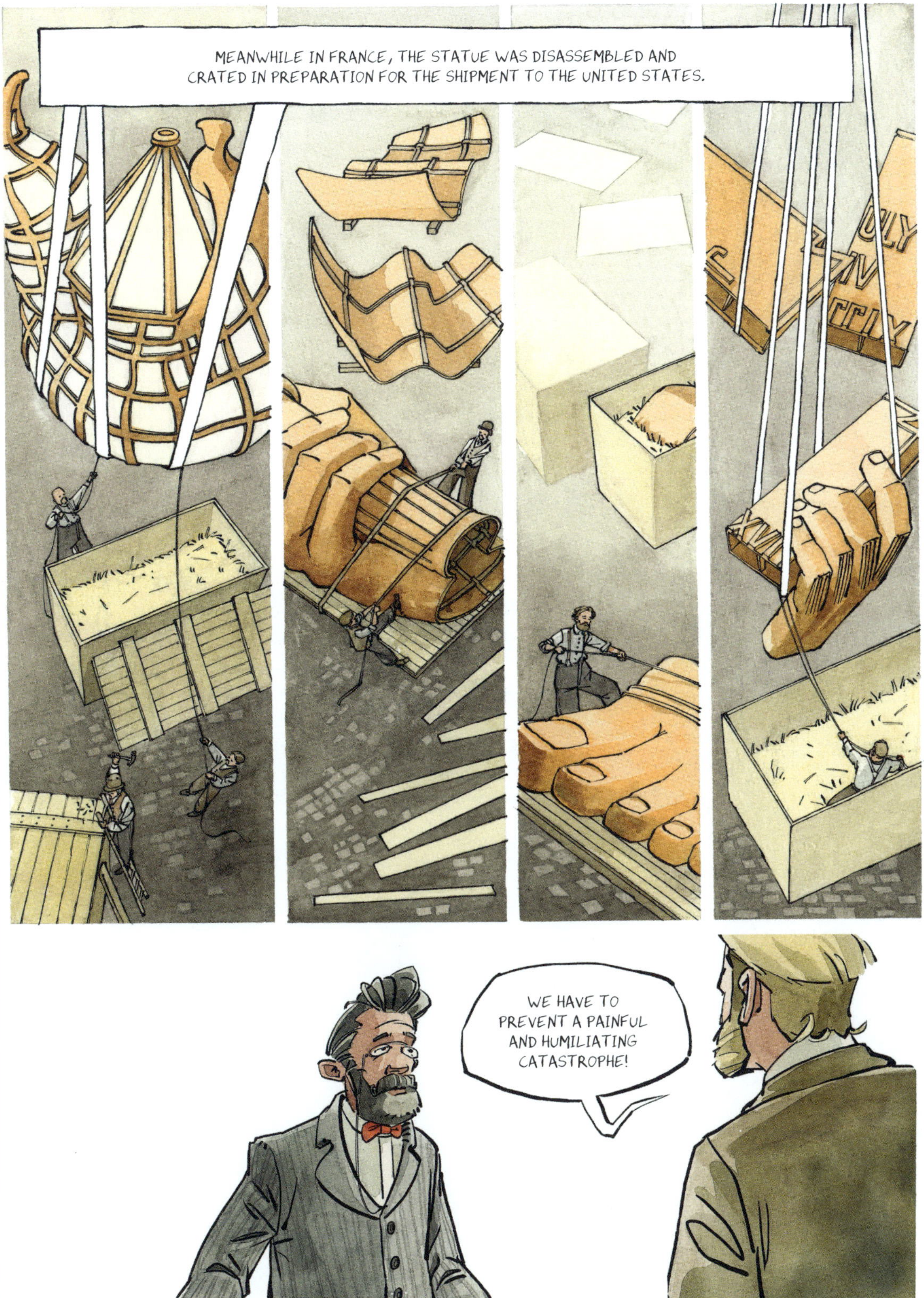
MEANWHILE IN FRANCE, THE STATUE WAS DISASSEMBLED AND CRATED IN PREPARATION FOR THE SHIPMENT TO THE UNITED STATES.
WE HAVE TO PREVENT A PAINFUL AND HUMILIATING CATASTROPHE!

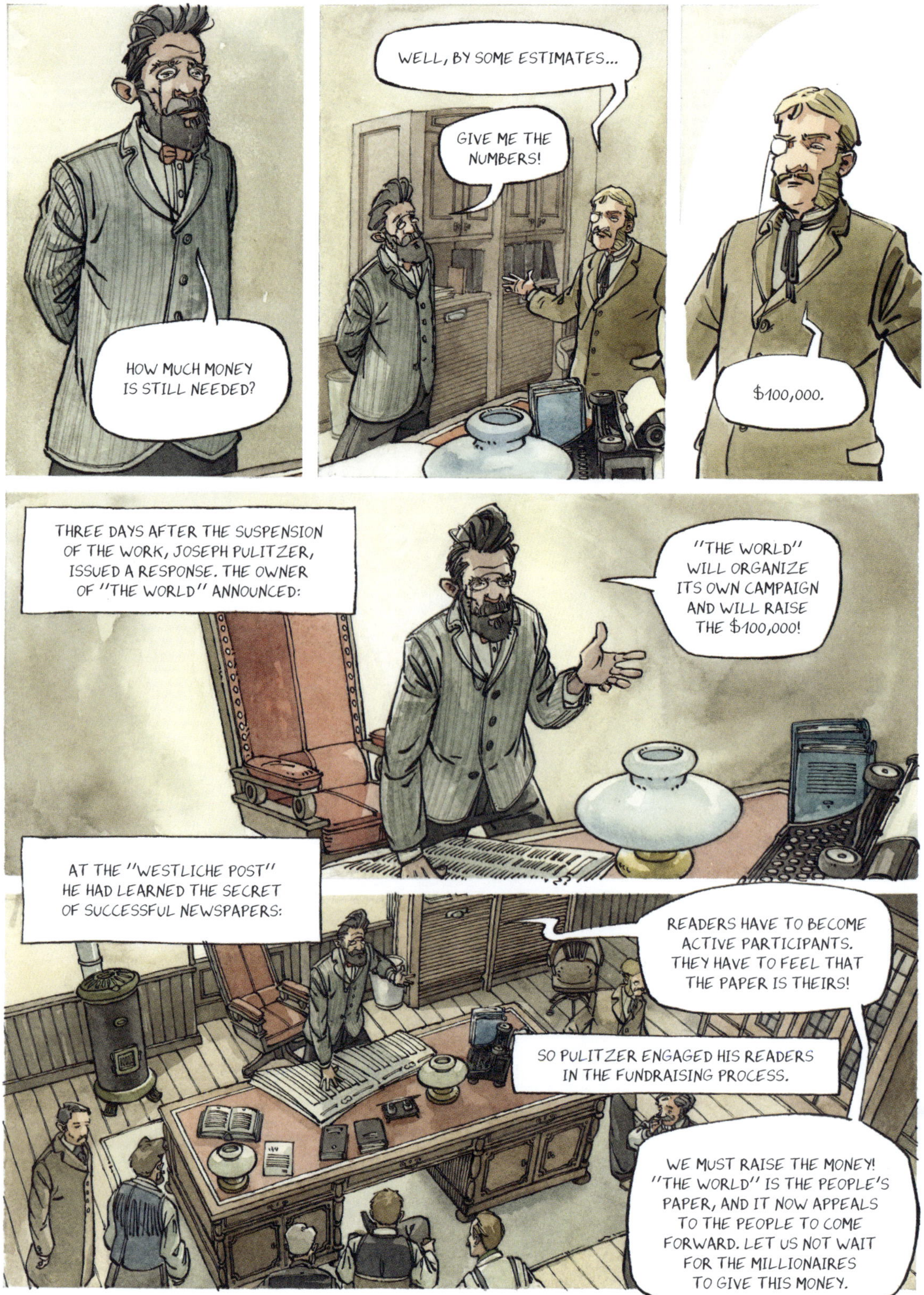
HOW MUCH MONEY IS STILL NEEDED?
WELL, BY SOME ESTIMATES...
GIVE ME THE NUMBERS!
$100,000.
THREE DAYS AFTER THE SUSPENSION OF THE WORK, JOSEPH PULITZER, ISSUED A RESPONSE. THE OWNER OF "THE WORLD" ANNOUNCED:
"THE WORLD" WILL ORGANIZE ITS OWN CAMPAIGN AND WILL RAISE THE $100,000!
AT THE "WESTLICHE POST" HE HAD LEARNED THE SECRET OF SUCCESSFUL NEWSPAPERS:
READERS HAVE TO BECOME ACTIVE PARTICIPANTS. THEY HAVE TO FEEL THAT THE PAPER IS THEIRS!
SO PULITZER ENGAGED HIS READERS IN THE FUNDRAISING PROCESS.
WE MUST RAISE THE MONEY! "THE WORLD" IS THE PEOPLE'S PAPER, AND IT NOW APPEALS TO THE PEOPLE TO COME FORWARD. LET US NOT WAIT FOR THE MILLIONAIRES TO GIVE THIS MONEY.

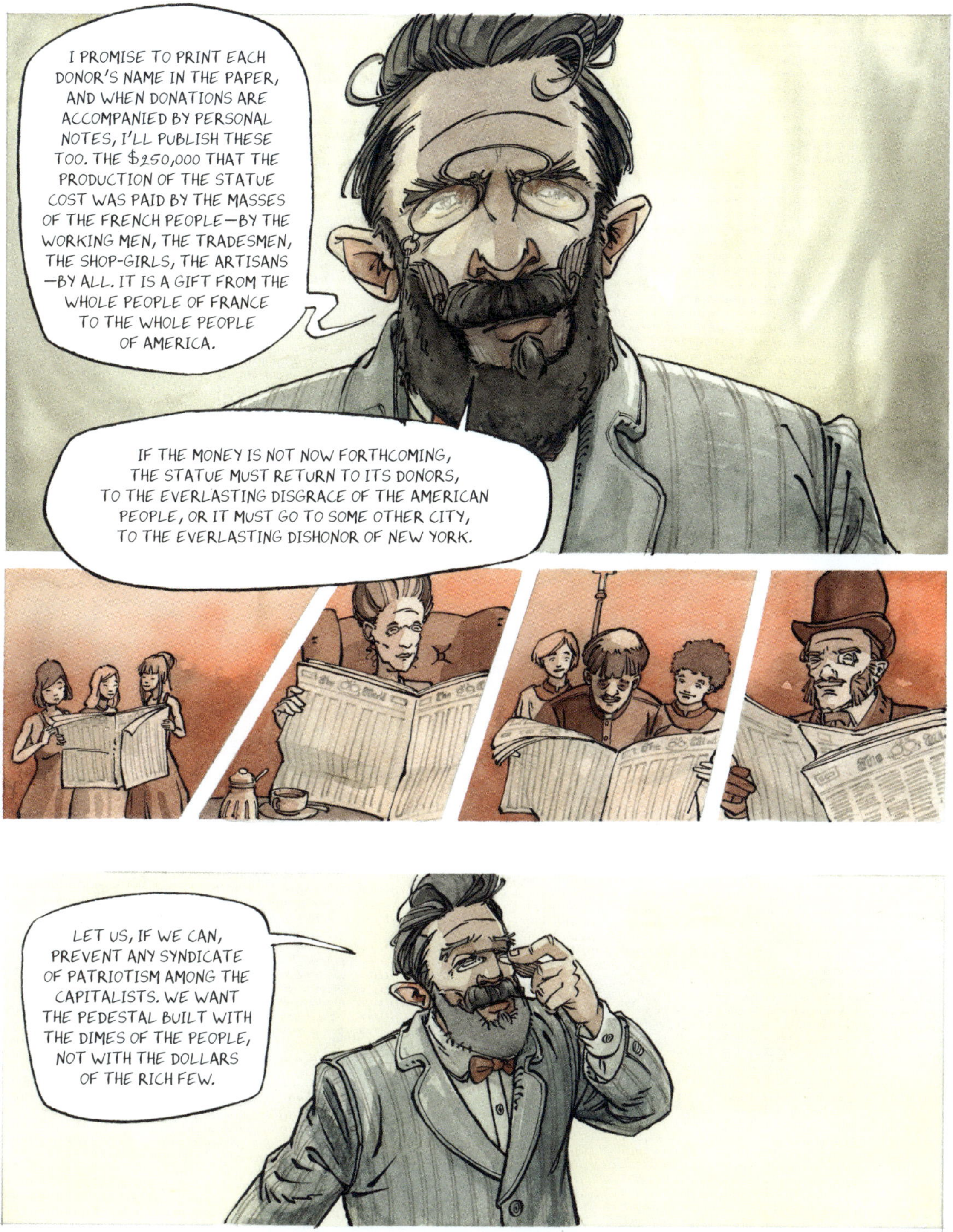

MORE THAN 120,000 PEOPLE—FARMERS, CLERKS, FACTORY WORKERS, POLICEMEN, IMMIGRANTS, HOUSEWIVES, AND CHILDREN—SENT MONEY. THE MAJORITY DONATED LESS THAN ONE DOLLAR.

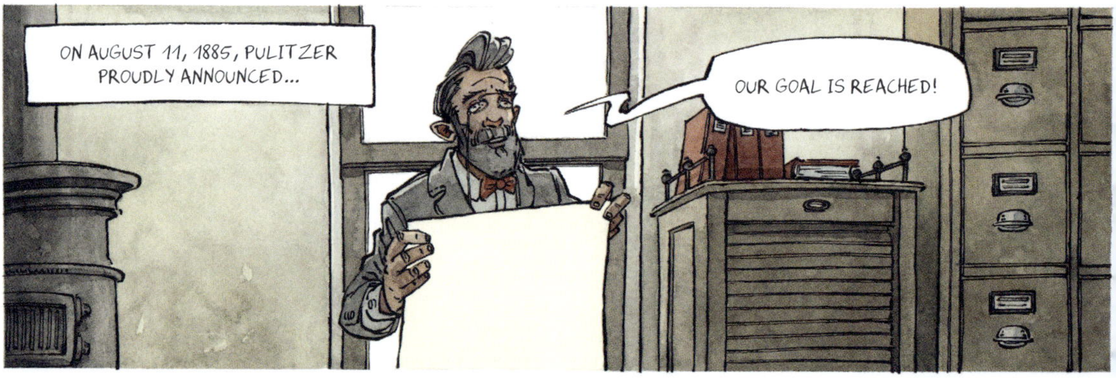
ON AUGUST 11, 1885, PULITZER PROUDLY ANNOUNCED...
OUR GOAL IS REACHED!

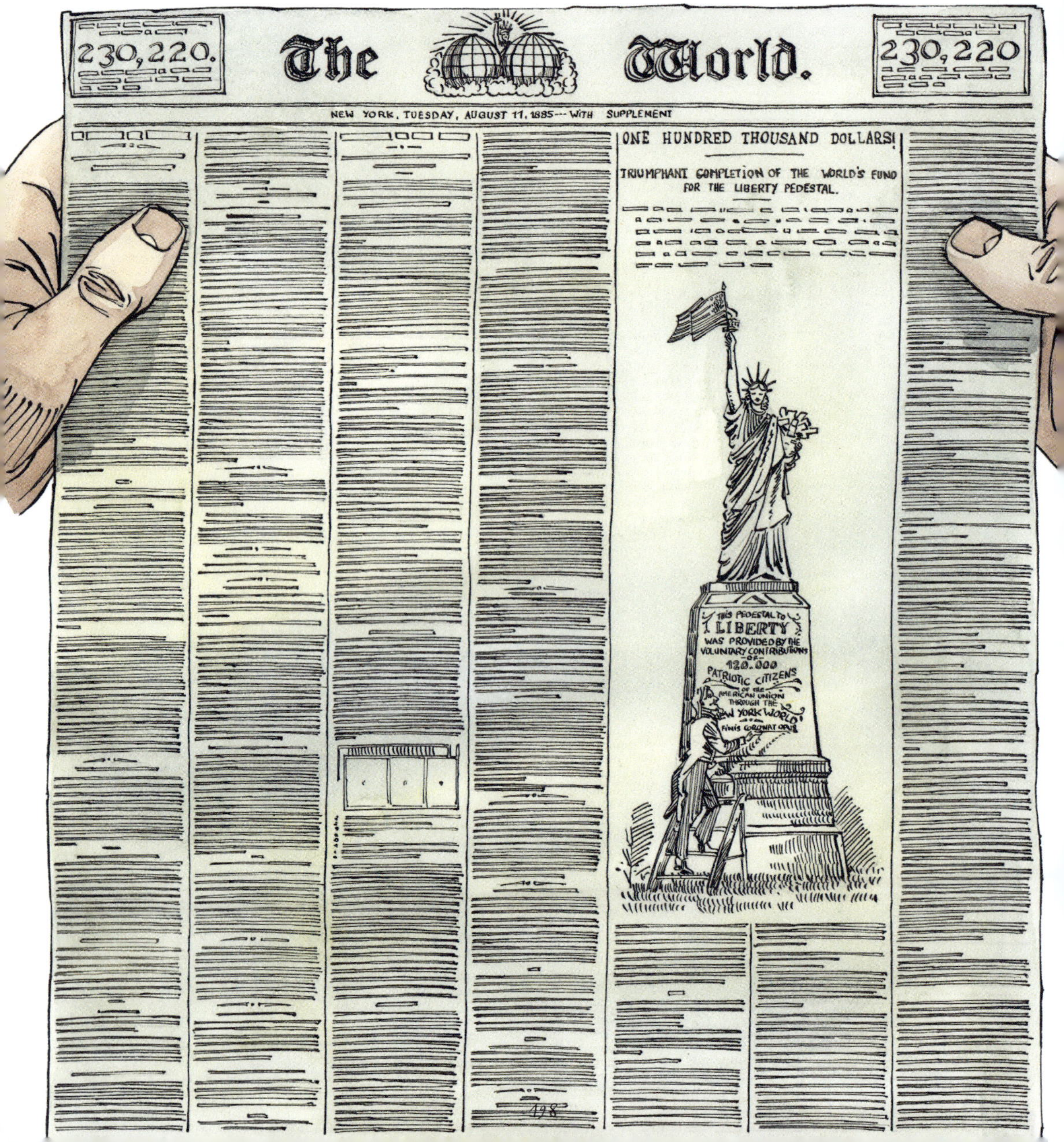
230,220.
The World.
230,220
NEW YORK, TUESDAY, AUGUST 11, 1885--- WITH SUPPLEMENT
ONE HUNDRED THOUSAND DOLLARS!
TRIUMPHANT COMPLETION OF THE WORLD'S FUND FOR THE LIBERTY PEDESTAL.
THIS PEDESTAL TO
LIBERTY
WAS PROVIDED BY THE
VOLUNTARY CONTRIBUTIONS
-OF-
120.000
PATRIOTIC CITIZENS
OF THE
AMERICAN UNION
THROUGH THE
W YORK WORLD
FINIS CORONAT OPUS

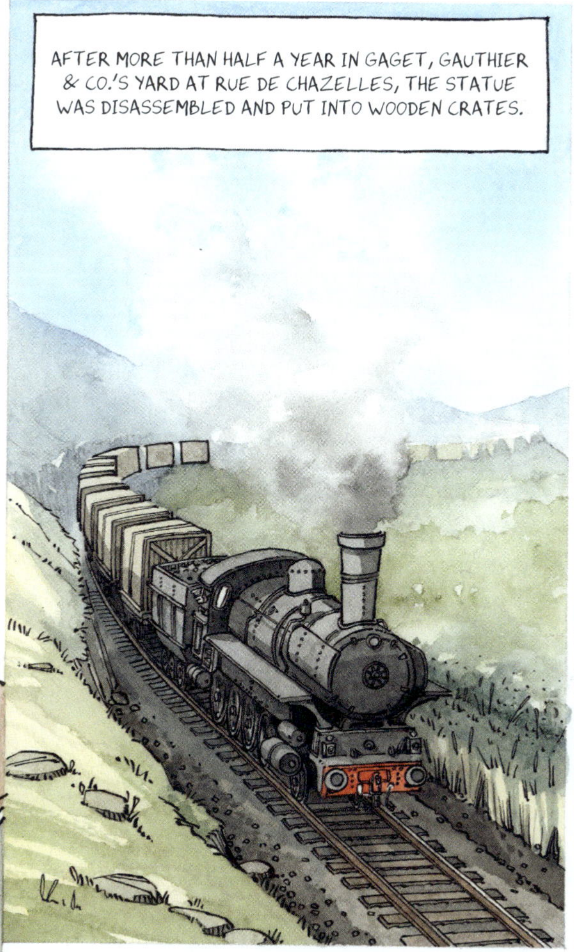
AFTER MORE THAN HALF A YEAR IN GAGET, GAUTHIER & CO.'S YARD AT RUE DE CHAZELLES, THE STATUE WAS DISASSEMBLED AND PUT INTO WOODEN CRATES.

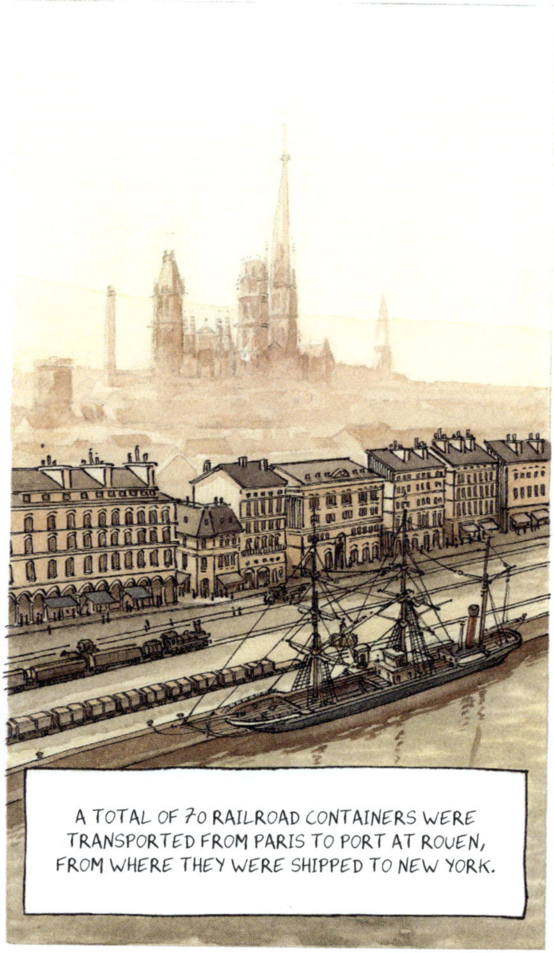
A TOTAL OF 70 RAILROAD CONTAINERS WERE TRANSPORTED FROM PARIS TO PORT AT ROUEN, FROM WHERE THEY WERE SHIPPED TO NEW YORK.

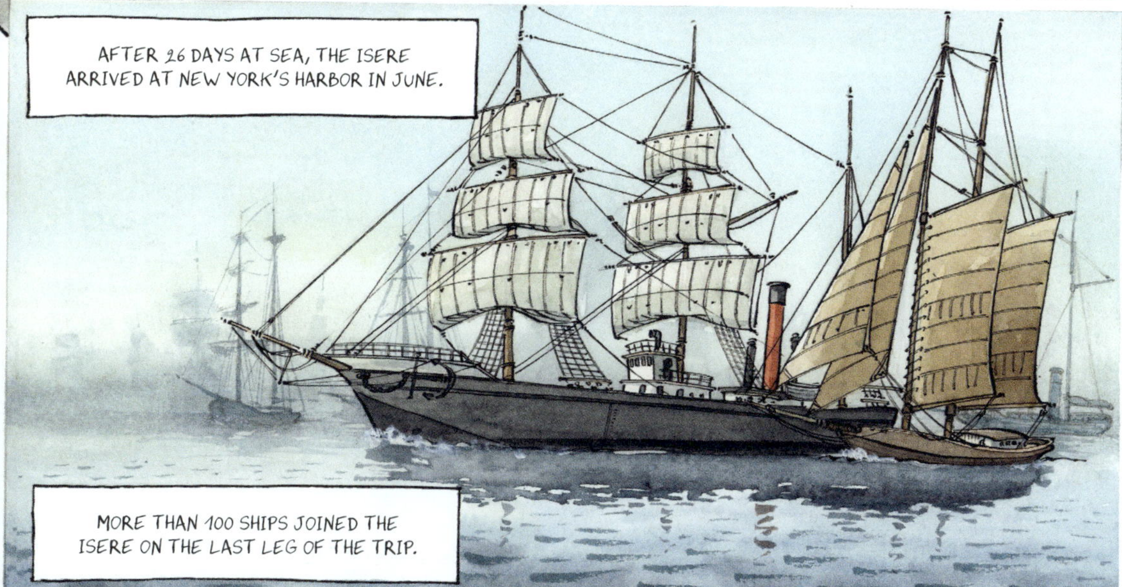
AFTER 26 DAYS AT SEA, THE ISERE ARRIVED AT NEW YORK'S HARBOR IN JUNE.
MORE THAN 100 SHIPS JOINED THE ISERE ON THE LAST LEG OF THE TRIP.

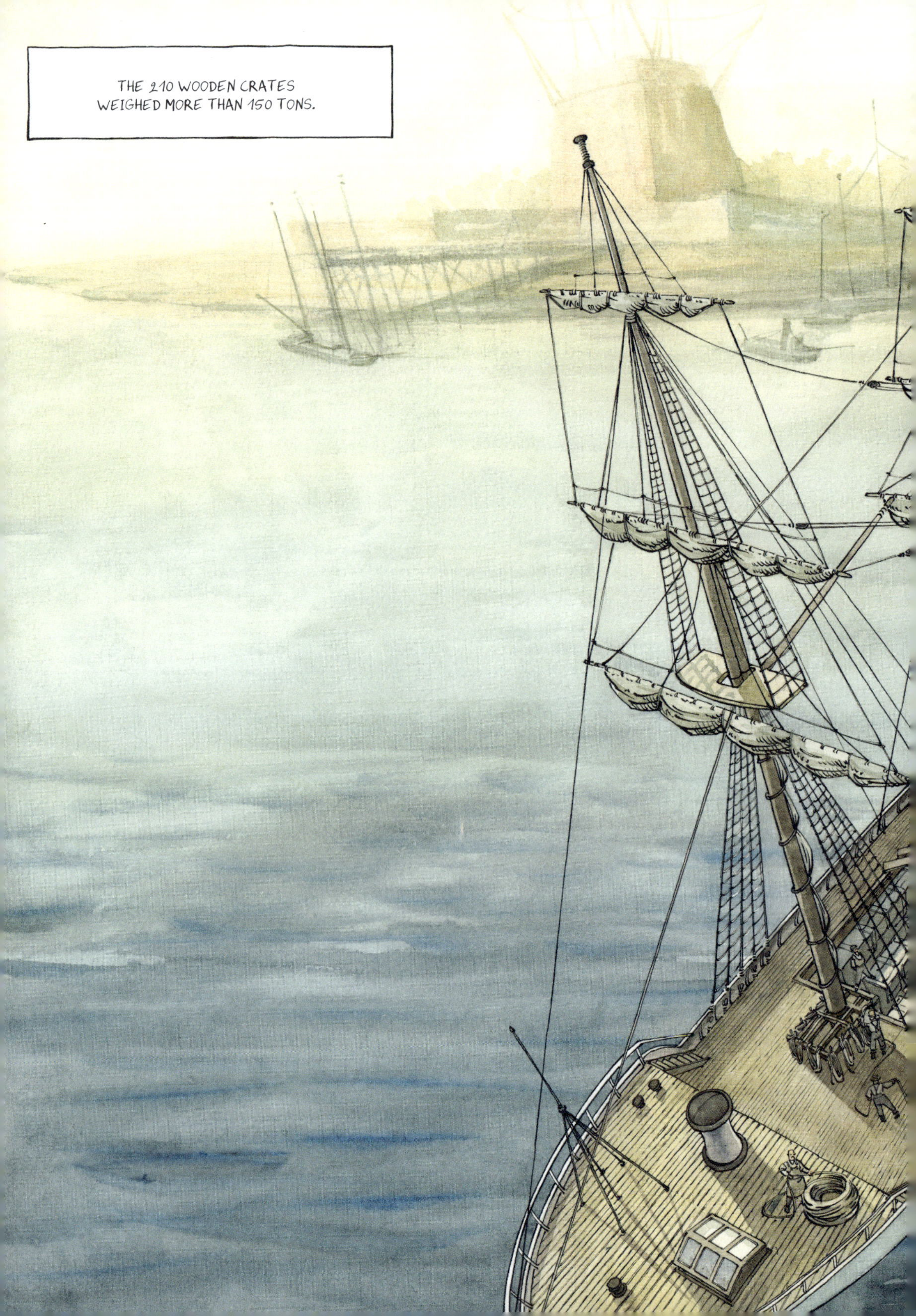
THE 210 WOODEN CRATES
WEIGHED MORE THAN 150 TONS.

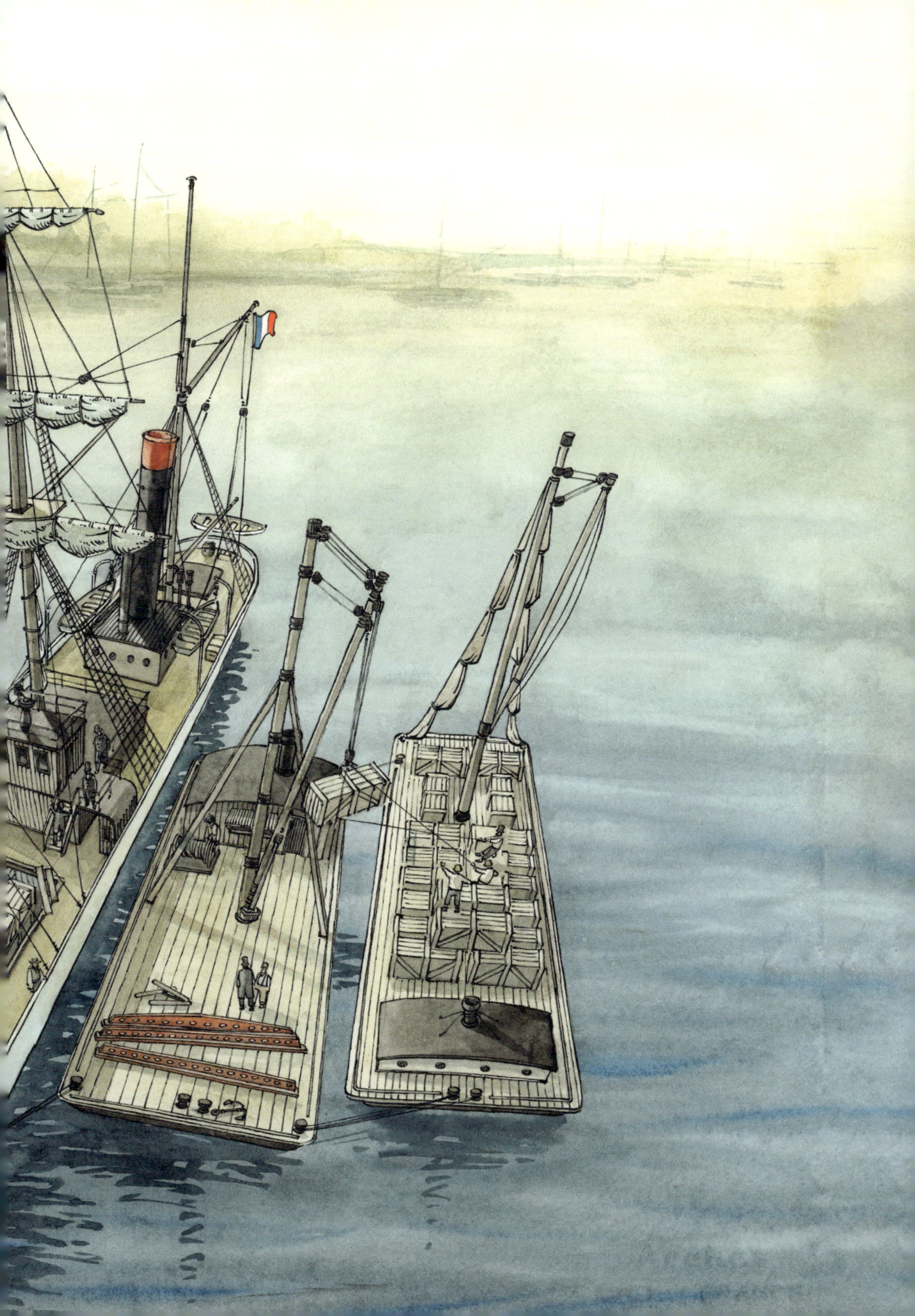

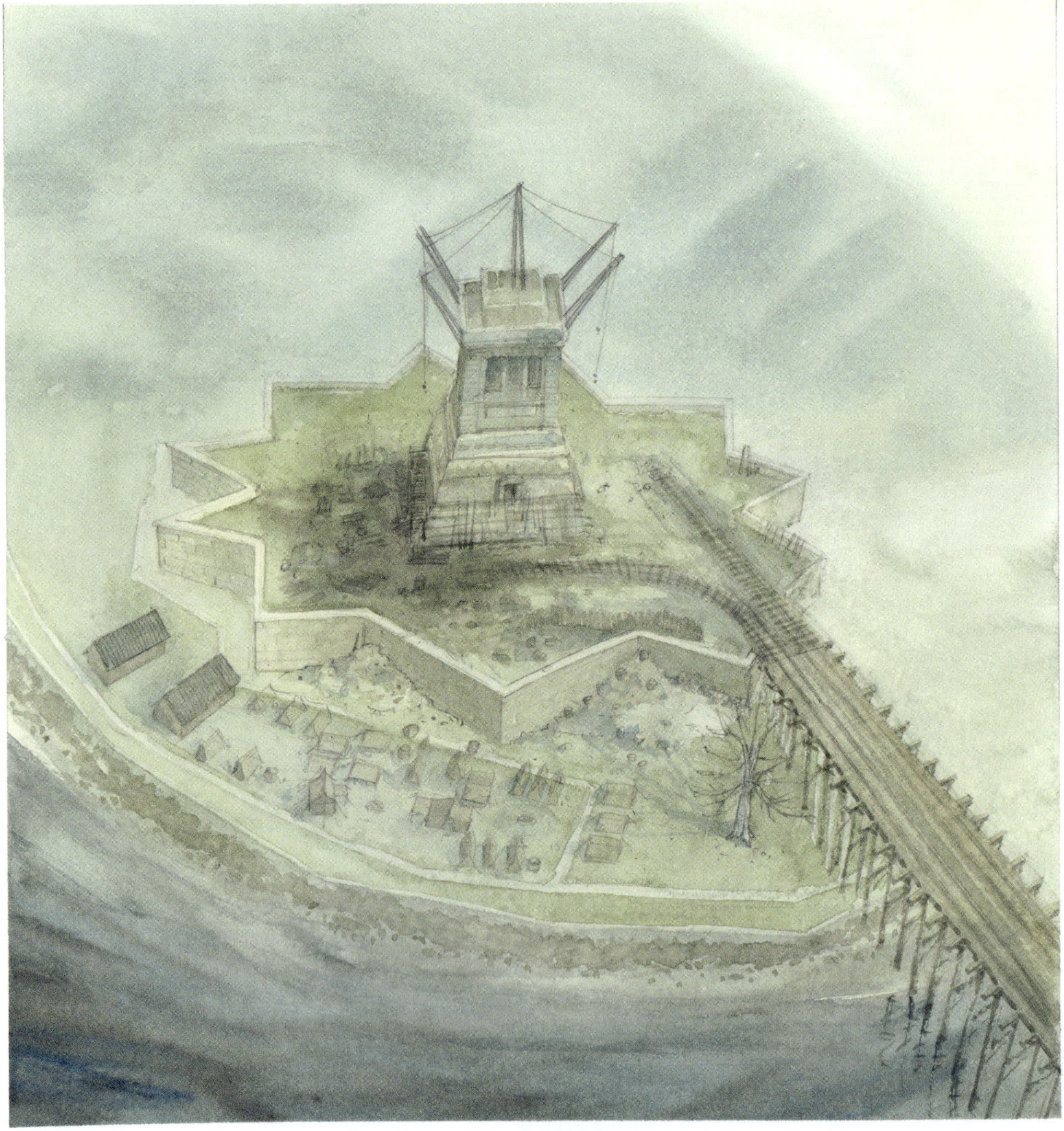

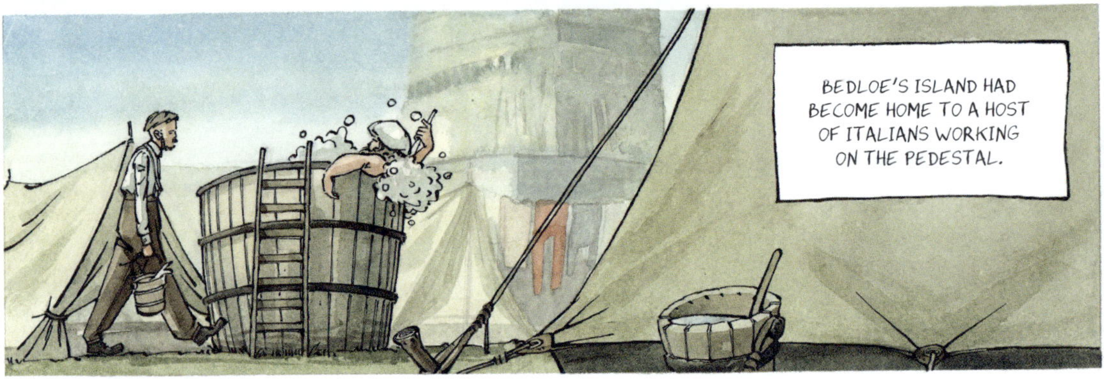
BEDLOE'S ISLAND HAD BECOME HOME TO A HOST OF ITALIANS WORKING ON THE PEDESTAL.

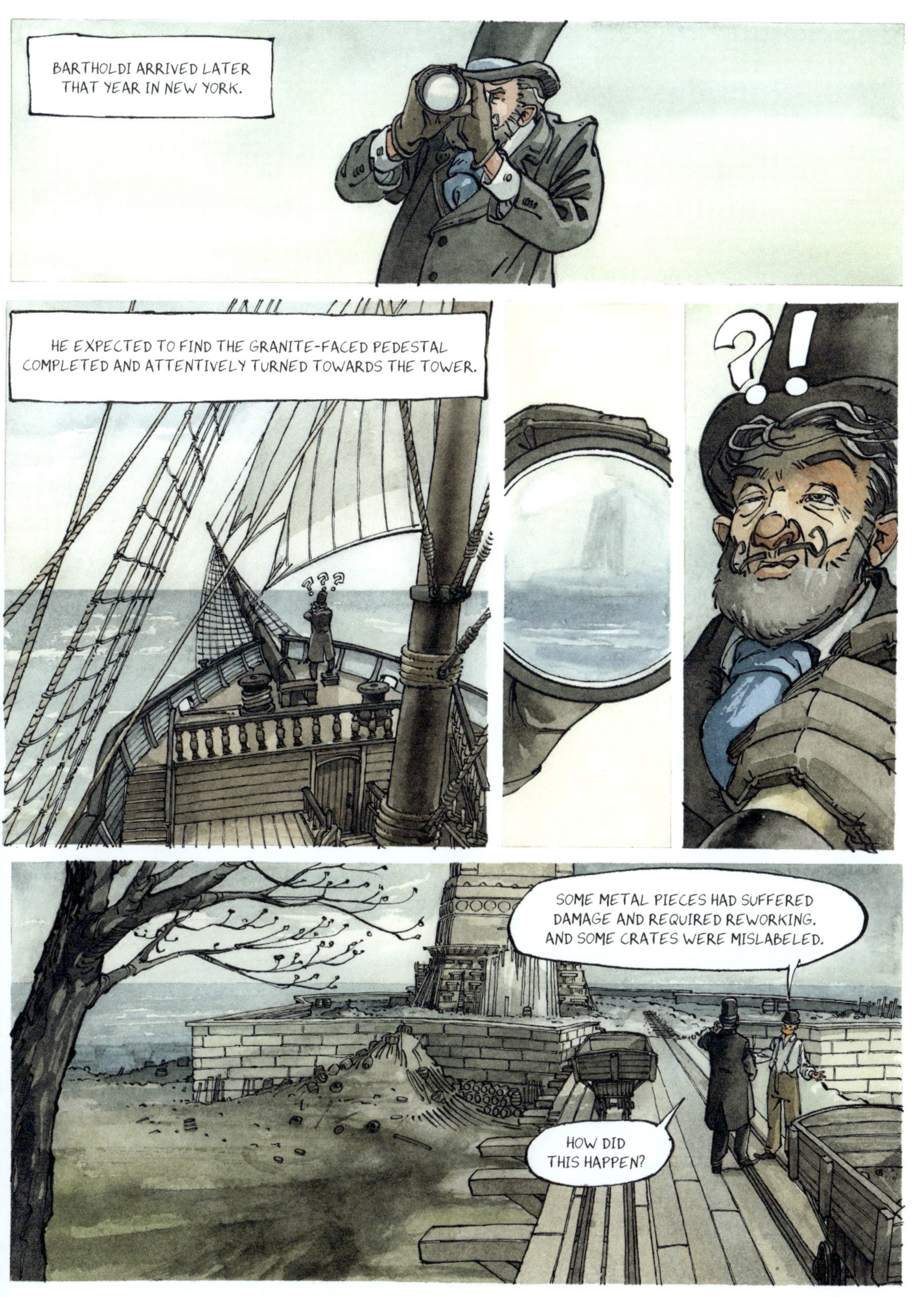
BARTHOLDI ARRIVED LATER THAT YEAR IN NEW YORK.
HE EXPECTED TO FIND THE GRANITE-FACED PEDESTAL COMPLETED AND ATTENTIVELY TURNED TOWARDS THE TOWER.
???
?!
SOME METAL PIECES HAD SUFFERED DAMAGE AND REQUIRED REWORKING. AND SOME CRATES WERE MISLABELED.
HOW DID THIS HAPPEN?

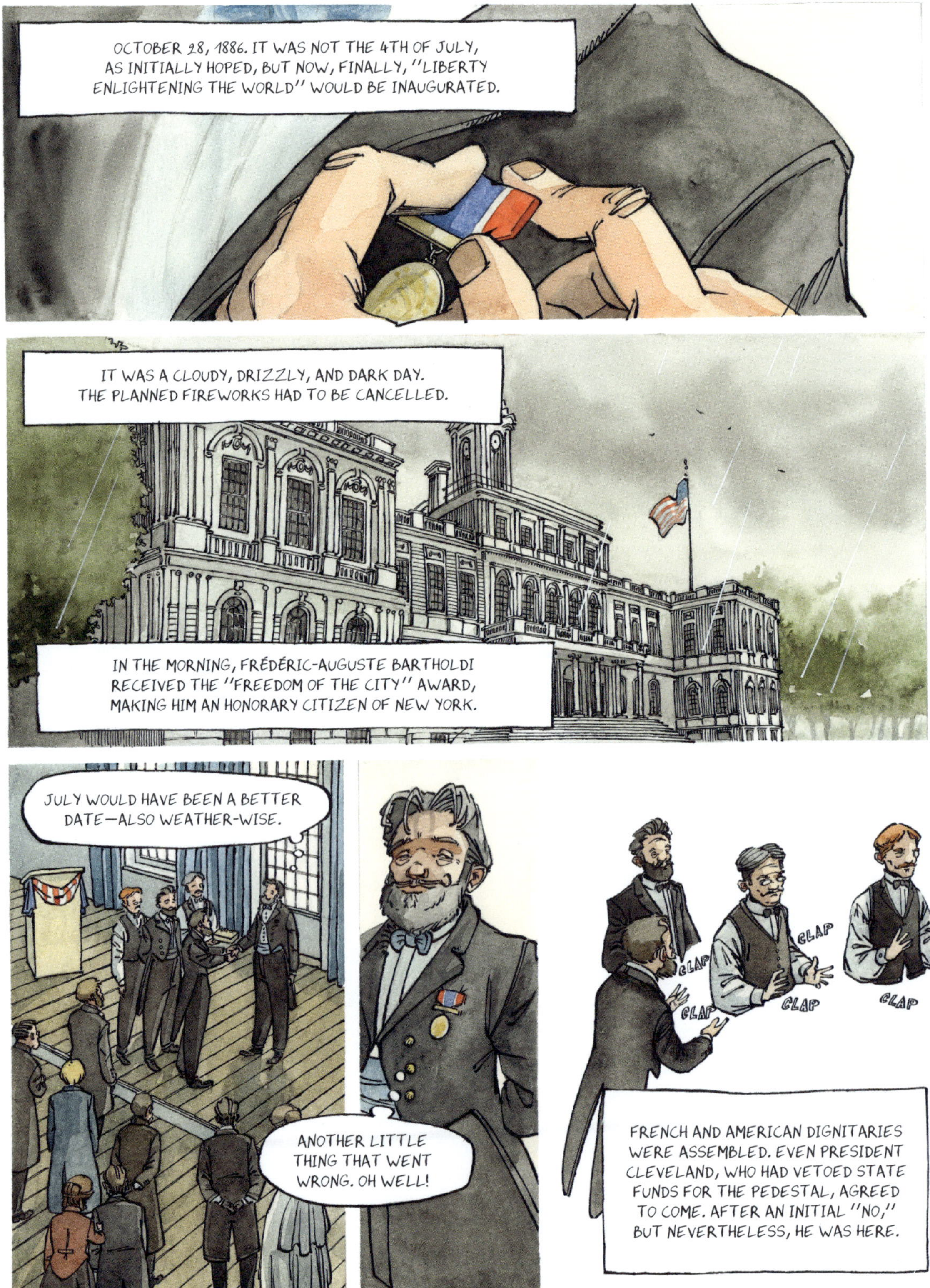

OCTOBER 28, 1886. IT WAS NOT THE 4TH OF JULY, AS INITIALLY HOPED, BUT NOW, FINALLY, "LIBERTY ENLIGHTENING THE WORLD" WOULD BE INAUGURATED.
IT WAS A CLOUDY, DRIZZLY, AND DARK DAY. THE PLANNED FIREWORKS HAD TO BE CANCELLED.
IN THE MORNING, FRÉDÉRIC-AUGUSTE BARTHOLDI RECEIVED THE "FREEDOM OF THE CITY" AWARD, MAKING HIM AN HONORARY CITIZEN OF NEW YORK.
JULY WOULD HAVE BEEN A BETTER DATE—ALSO WEATHER-WISE.
ANOTHER LITTLE THING THAT WENT WRONG. OH WELL!
CLAP
CLAP
CLAP
CLAP
CLAP
FRENCH AND AMERICAN DIGNITARIES WERE ASSEMBLED. EVEN PRESIDENT CLEVELAND, WHO HAD VETOED STATE FUNDS FOR THE PEDESTAL, AGREED TO COME. AFTER AN INITIAL "NO," BUT NEVERTHELESS, HE WAS HERE.

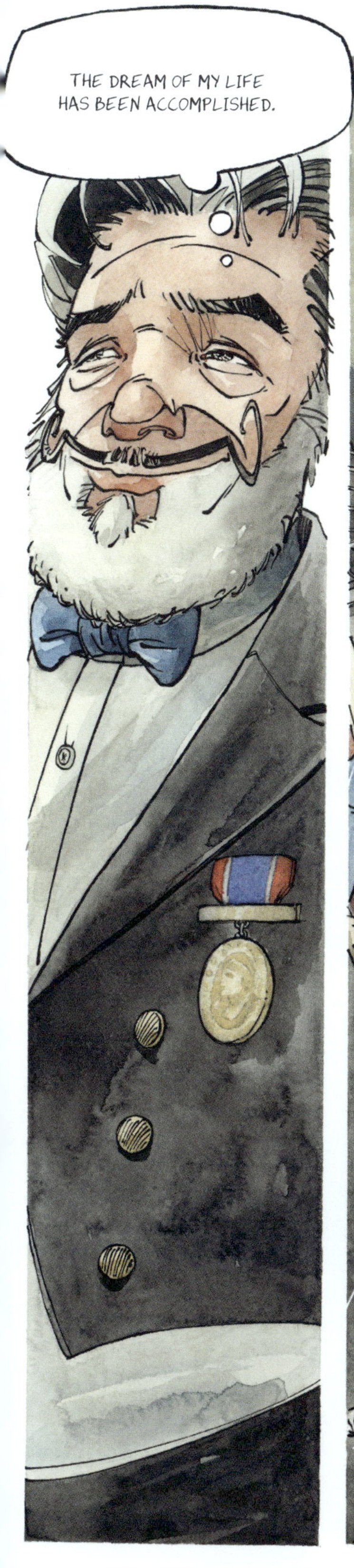
THE DREAM OF MY LIFE HAS BEEN ACCOMPLISHED.

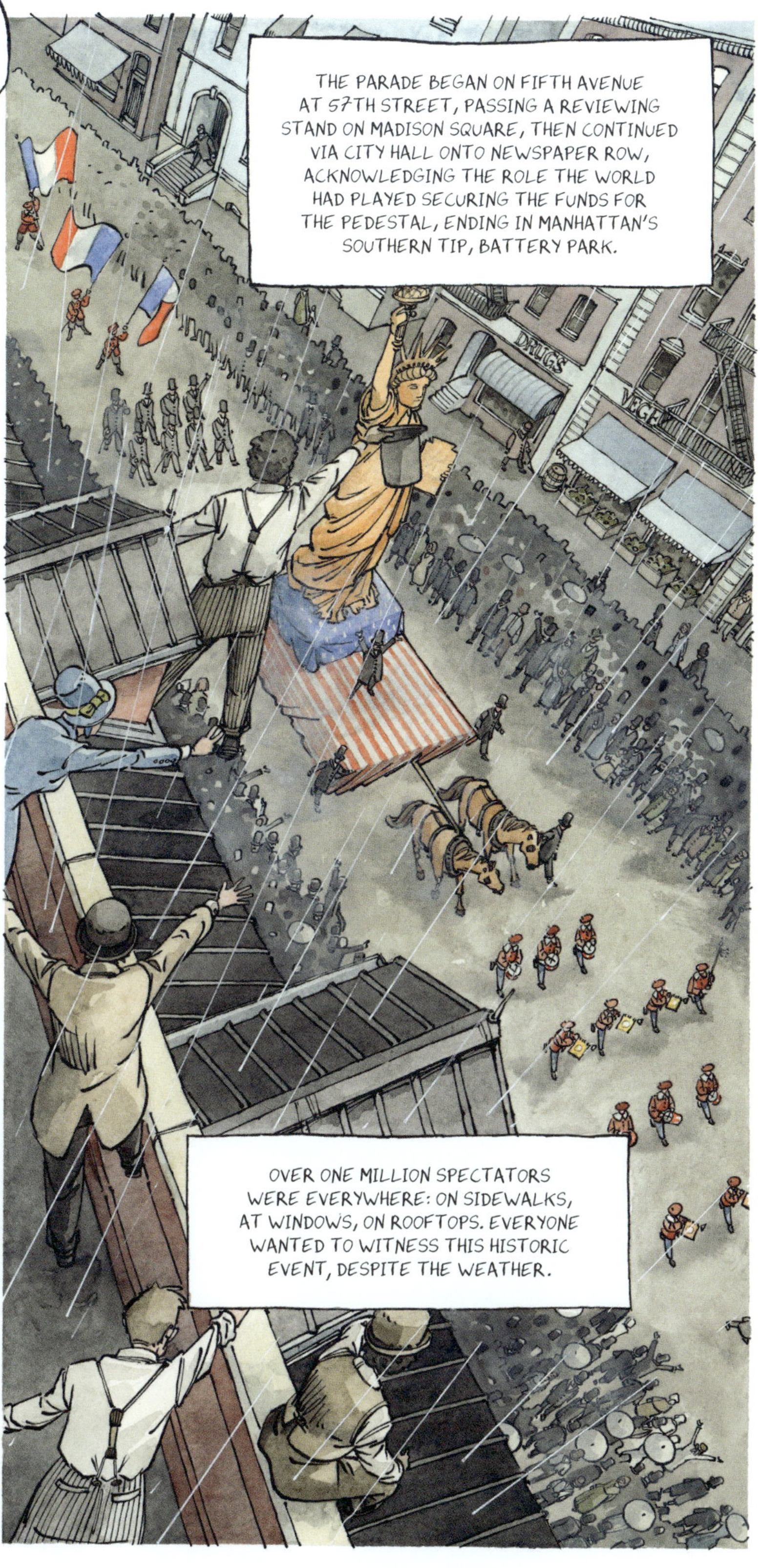
THE PARADE BEGAN ON FIFTH AVENUE AT 57TH STREET, PASSING A REVIEWING STAND ON MADISON SQUARE, THEN CONTINUED VIA CITY HALL ONTO NEWSPAPER ROW, ACKNOWLEDGING THE ROLE THE WORLD HAD PLAYED SECURING THE FUNDS FOR THE PEDESTAL, ENDING IN MANHATTAN'S SOUTHERN TIP, BATTERY PARK.
DRUGS
OVER ONE MILLION SPECTATORS WERE EVERYWHERE: ON SIDEWALKS, AT WINDOWS, ON ROOFTOPS. EVERYONE WANTED TO WITNESS THIS HISTORIC EVENT, DESPITE THE WEATHER.

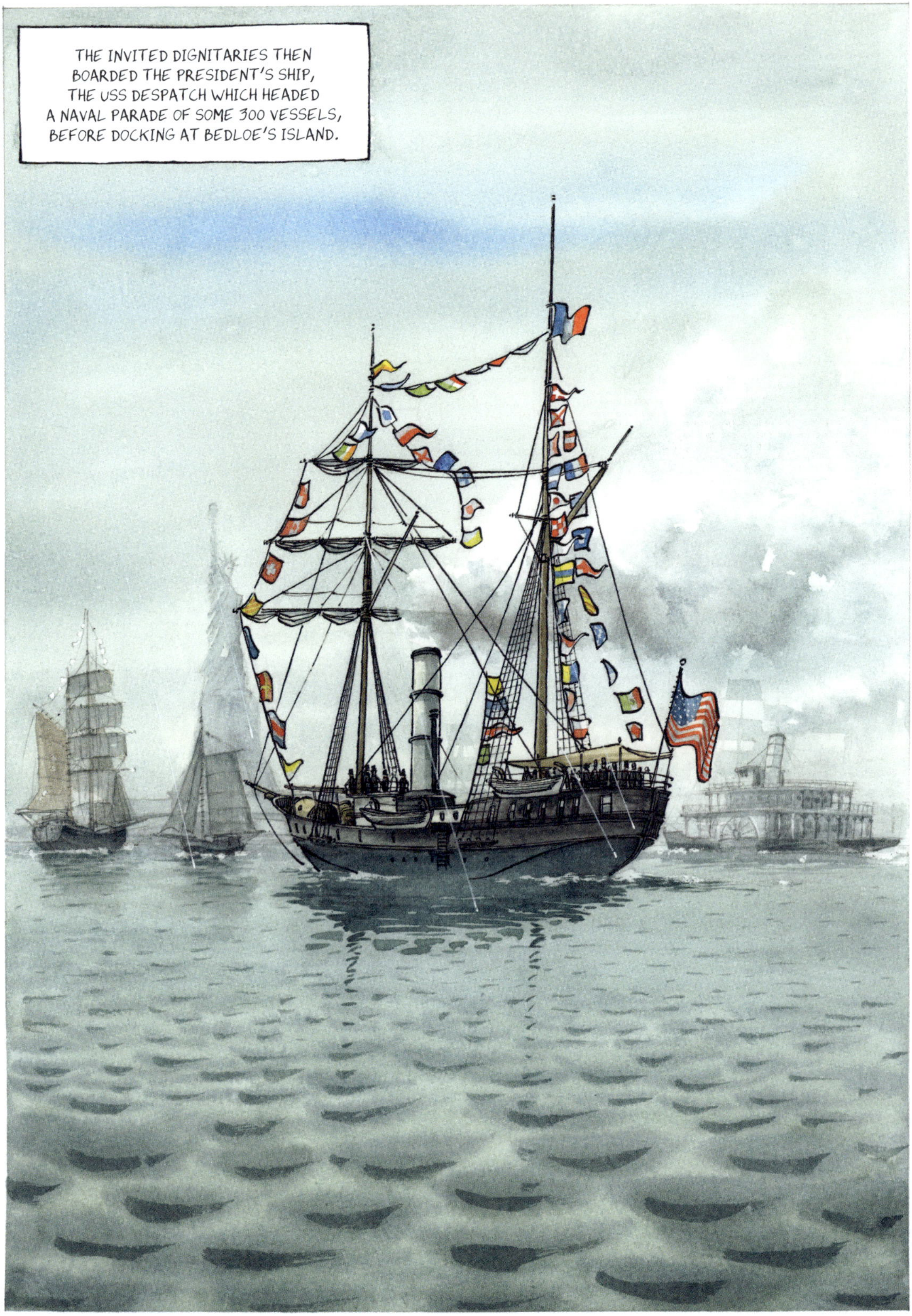
THE INVITED DIGNITARIES THEN BOARDED THE PRESIDENT'S SHIP, THE USS DESPATCH WHICH HEADED A NAVAL PARADE OF SOME 300 VESSELS, BEFORE DOCKING AT BEDLOE'S ISLAND.

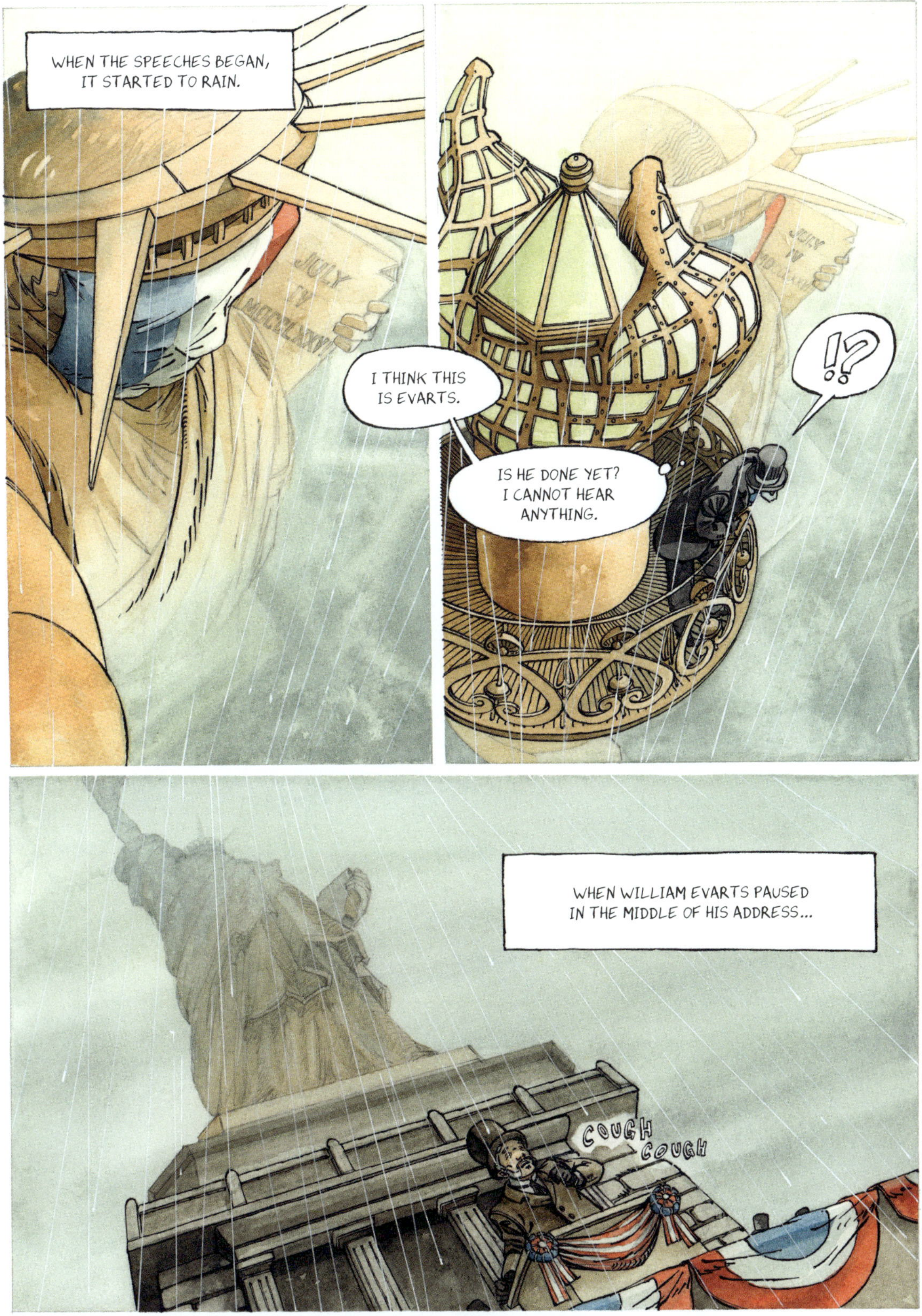
WHEN THE SPEECHES BEGAN, IT STARTED TO RAIN.
JULY IV MDCCLXXVI
I THINK THIS IS EVARTS.
IS HE DONE YET? I CANNOT HEAR ANYTHING.
!?
WHEN WILLIAM EVARTS PAUSED IN THE MIDDLE OF HIS ADDRESS...
COUGH COUGH

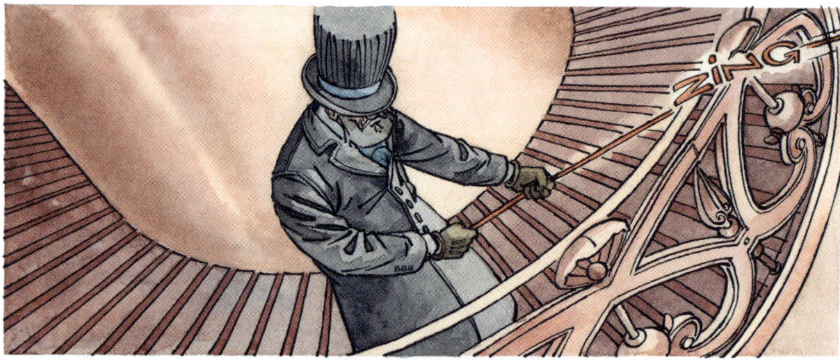
ZING
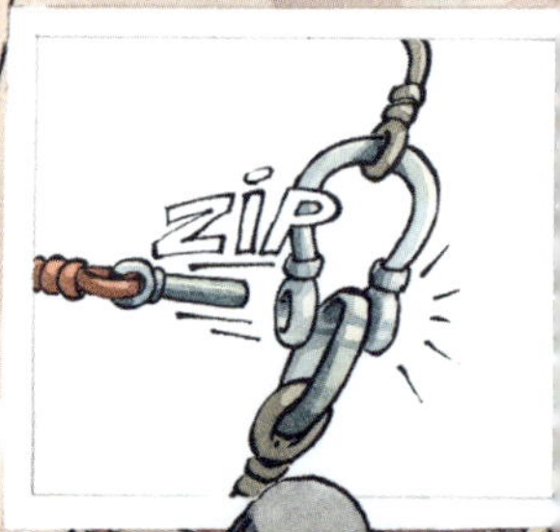
ZIP
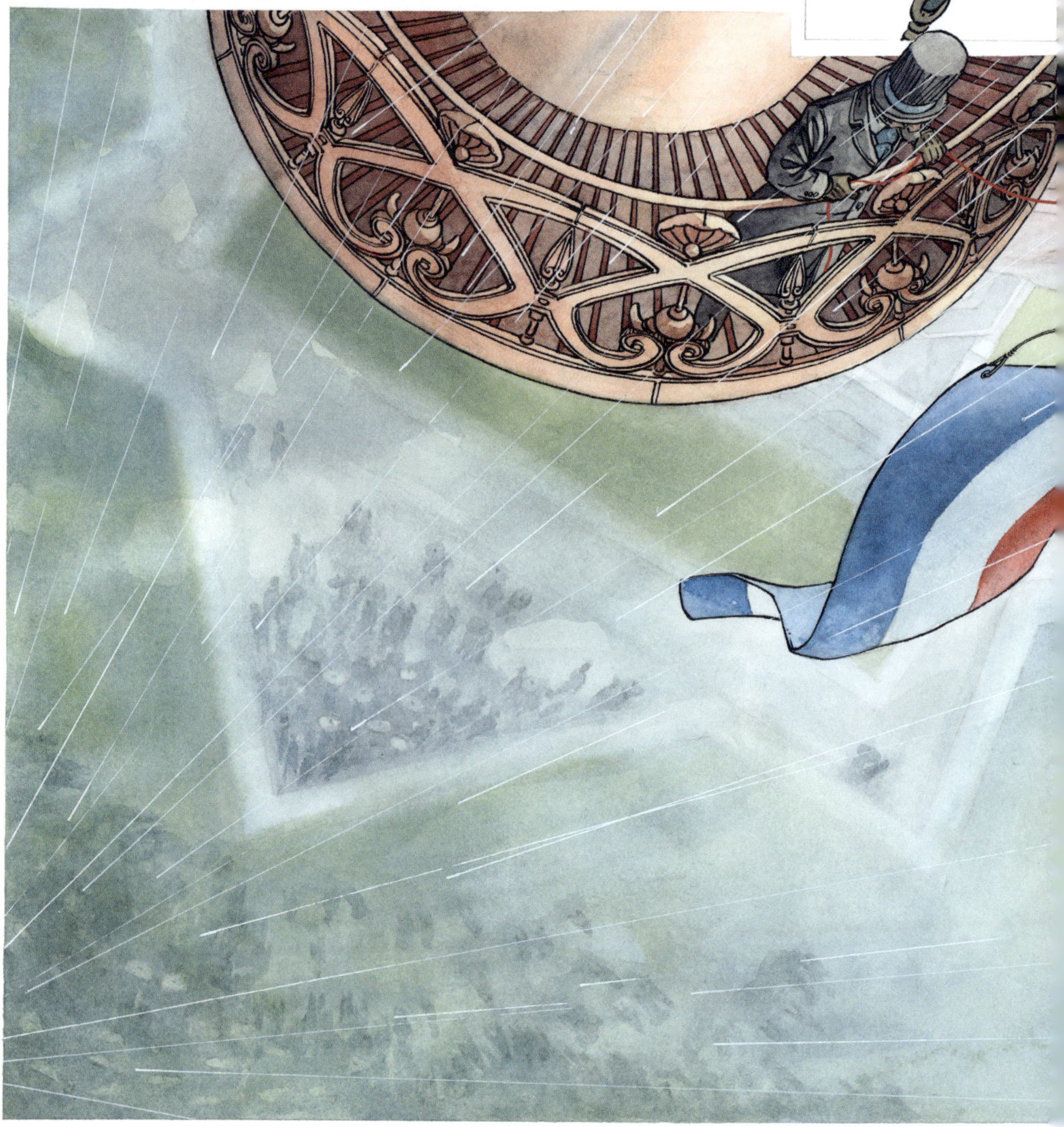

ZIP

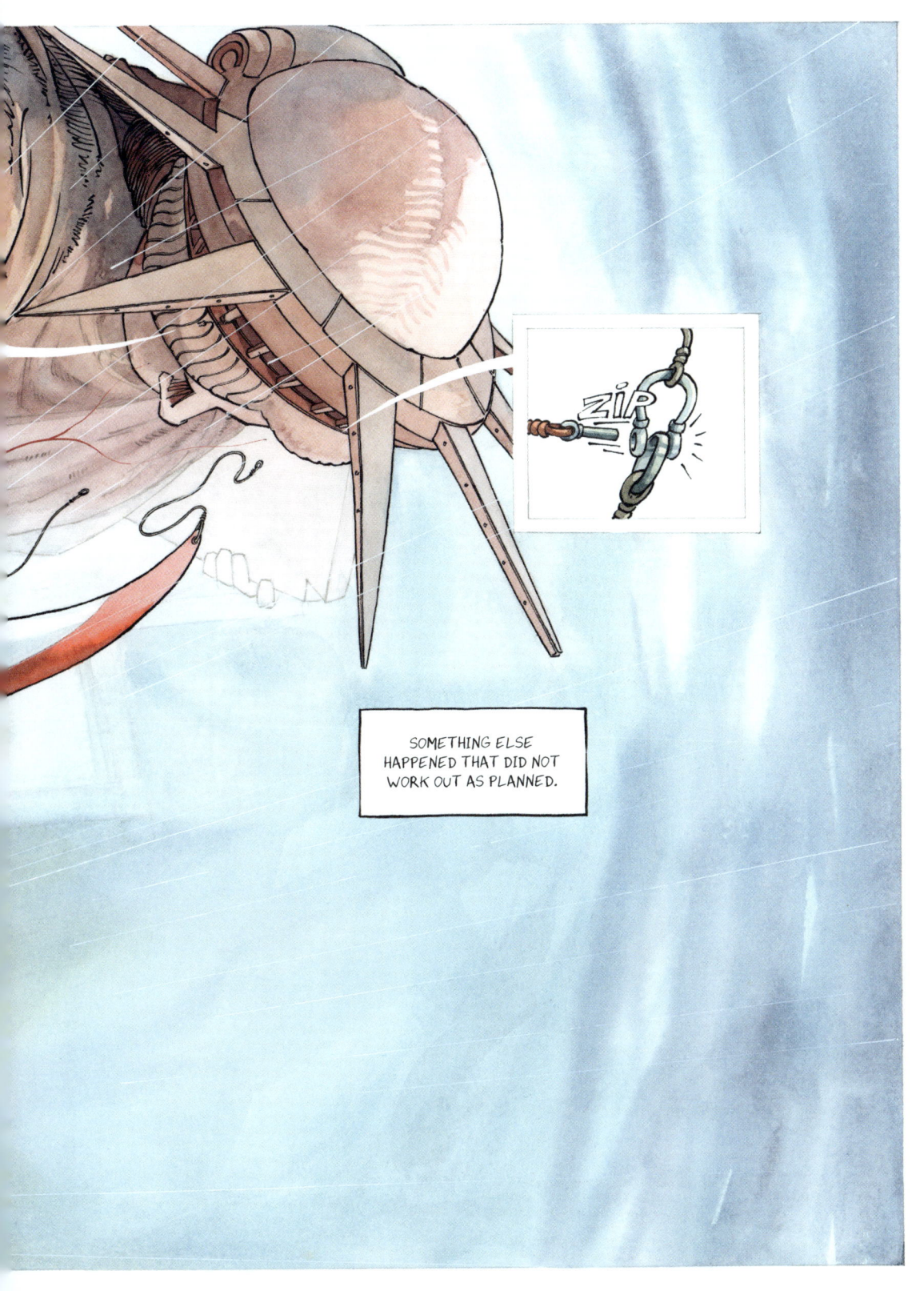

SOMETHING ELSE HAPPENED THAT DID NOT WORK OUT AS PLANNED.

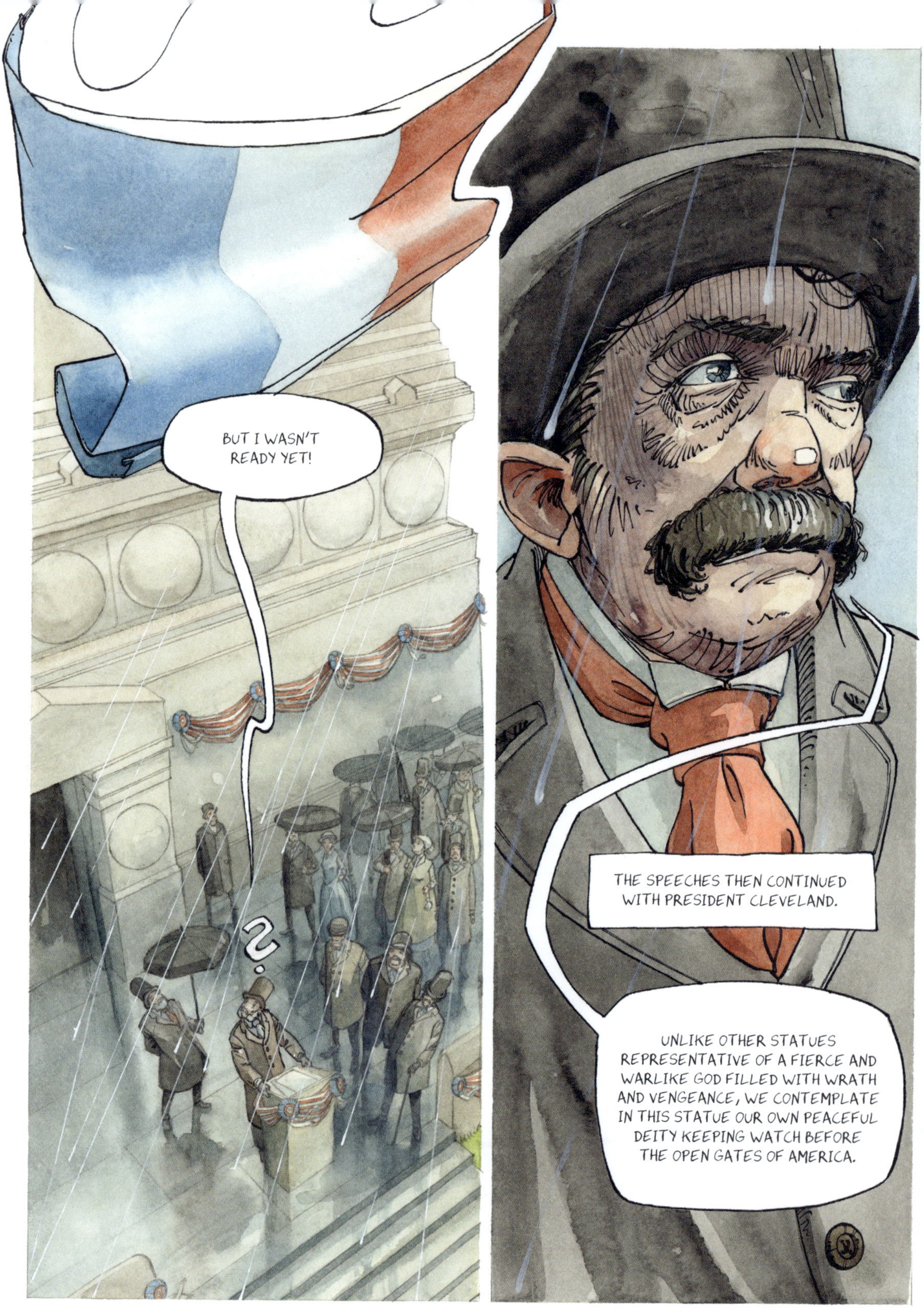
BUT I WASN'T READY YET!
?
THE SPEECHES THEN CONTINUED WITH PRESIDENT CLEVELAND.
UNLIKE OTHER STATUES REPRESENTATIVE OF A FIERCE AND WARLIKE GOD FILLED WITH WRATH AND VENGEANCE, WE CONTEMPLATE IN THIS STATUE OUR OWN PEACEFUL DEITY KEEPING WATCH BEFORE THE OPEN GATES OF AMERICA.

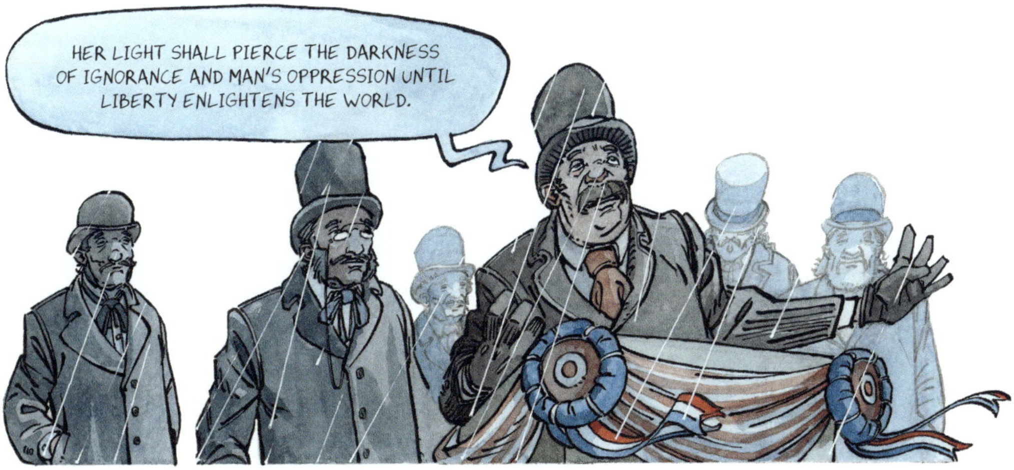
HER LIGHT SHALL PIERCE THE DARKNESS OF IGNORANCE AND MAN'S OPPRESSION UNTIL LIBERTY ENLIGHTENS THE WORLD.

W. ALBERT LEFAIVRE, THE FRENCH MINISTER TO THE UNITED STATES.

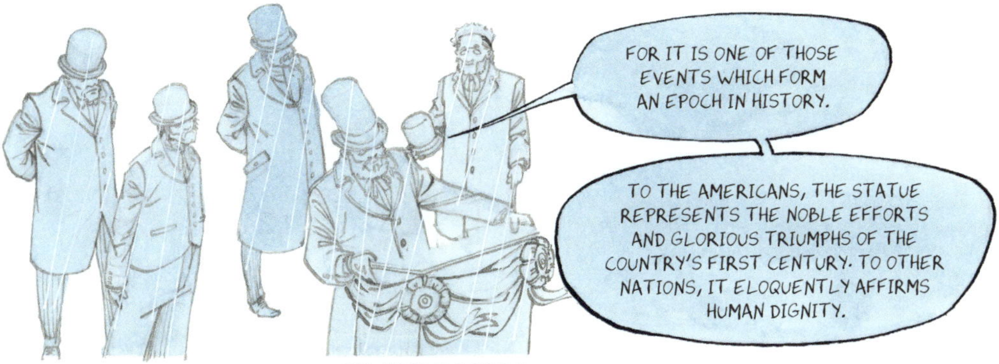
FOR IT IS ONE OF THOSE EVENTS WHICH FORM AN EPOCH IN HISTORY.
TO THE AMERICANS, THE STATUE REPRESENTS THE NOBLE EFFORTS AND GLORIOUS TRIUMPHS OF THE COUNTRY'S FIRST CENTURY. TO OTHER NATIONS, IT ELOQUENTLY AFFIRMS HUMAN DIGNITY.

CHAUNCEY M. DEPEW.

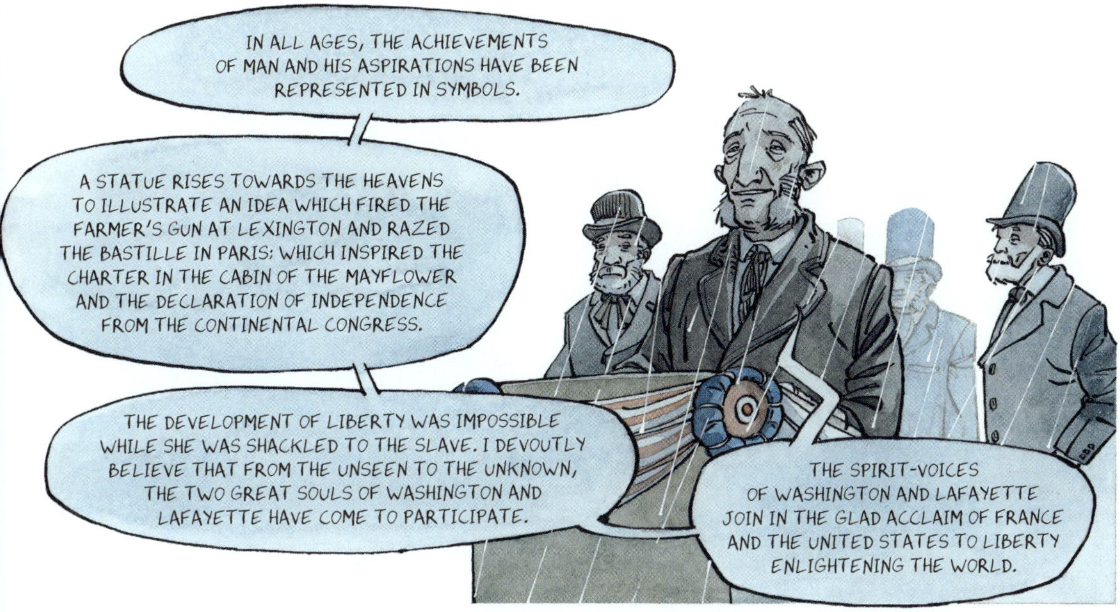
IN ALL AGES, THE ACHIEVEMENTS OF MAN AND HIS ASPIRATIONS HAVE BEEN REPRESENTED IN SYMBOLS.
A STATUE RISES TOWARDS THE HEAVENS TO ILLUSTRATE AN IDEA WHICH FIRED THE FARMER'S GUN AT LEXINGTON AND RAZED THE BASTILLE IN PARIS; WHICH INSPIRED THE CHARTER IN THE CABIN OF THE MAYFLOWER AND THE DECLARATION OF INDEPENDENCE FROM THE CONTINENTAL CONGRESS.
THE DEVELOPMENT OF LIBERTY WAS IMPOSSIBLE WHILE SHE WAS SHACKLED TO THE SLAVE. I DEVOUTLY BELIEVE THAT FROM THE UNSEEN TO THE UNKNOWN, THE TWO GREAT SOULS OF WASHINGTON AND LAFAYETTE HAVE COME TO PARTICIPATE.
THE SPIRIT-VOICES OF WASHINGTON AND LAFAYETTE JOIN IN THE GLAD ACCLAIM OF FRANCE AND THE UNITED STATES TO LIBERTY ENLIGHTENING THE WORLD.

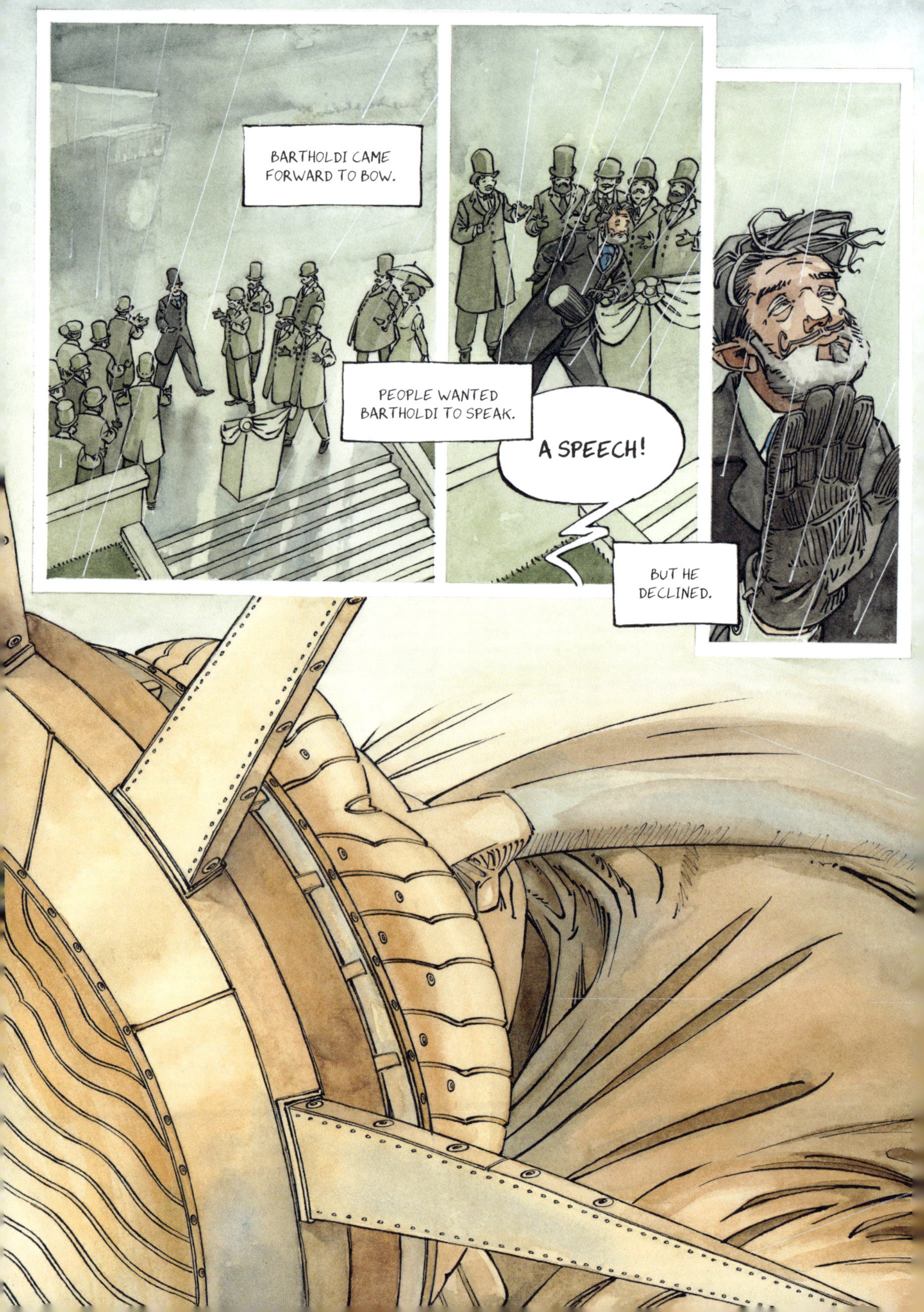
BARTHOLDI CAME FORWARD TO BOW.
PEOPLE WANTED BARTHOLDI TO SPEAK.
A SPEECH!
BUT HE DECLINED.

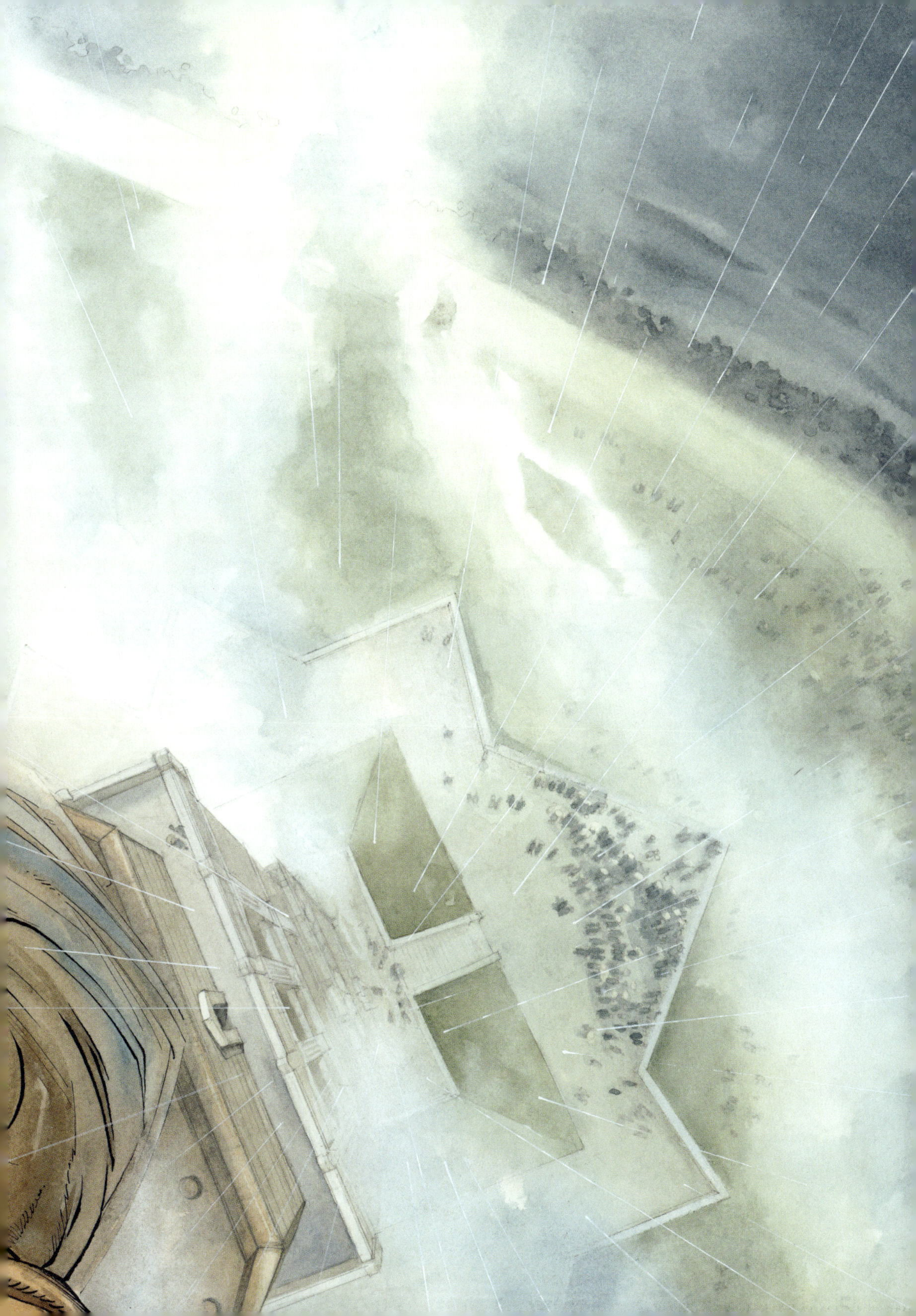

EPILOGUE

"The New Colossus" was not read at the dedication ceremony, nor was Emma Lazarus present. She died on November 19, 1887 at the age of only 38. Every New York newspaper reported on the death of the celebrated American poet.

The same year, Gustave Eiffel started his new venture: an iron tower that would become the centerpiece of the 1889 World Exposition in Paris.

Although a celebrated poet at her time, Emma's name was rather forgotten by the turn of the century, and so was her poem. The end of the nineteenth century was a time of mass immigration to the United States. America was changing, and so was New York. The city became a haven to immigrants from all over the world, hoping for a better life in the New World. Almost a million immigrants a year came from Europe, seeing "Liberty Enlightening the World" upon their arrival in the New York harbor.

In the spring of 1903, a memorial plaque engraved with "The New Colossus" was placed inside the pedestal of the Statue of Liberty.

The following year, Frédéric-Auguste Bartholdi died. The Statue of Liberty had become his legacy. The same way America was changing, the Statue was also changing. Soon it was forgotten that she was a symbol of the friendship between America and France. Lady Liberty became the Mother of Exiles, and like the immigrants becoming American, the French Lady became a symbol of her adopted country.

REFERENCE LITERATURE

Berenson, E. (2012). "The Statue of Liberty: A Transatlantic Story". Yale University Press: New Haven, CT.

Khan, Y. S. (2011). "Enlightening the World: The Creation of the Statue of Liberty". Cornell University Press: Itacha, NY.

Lebart, L., & Stourdze, S. (2017). "Lady Liberty". Firefly Books Ltd: Richmond Hill, Canada.

Mitchell, E. (2018). "Liberty's Torch: The Great Adventure to Build the Statue of Liberty". Atlantic Monthly Press: New York, NY.

YOU ARE HERE

You Are Here

You are Here
Copyright c 2021 by Seth Breitman

All rights reserved
Published by A Thousand Lifetimes Publishers
sethbreitman.com/YouAreHere
connect@sethbreitman.com
Princeton, New Jersey

No part of this book may be used or reproduced
in any manner without written permission of the publisher,
except in the case of brief quotations embodied
in critical articles or reviews.

ISBN: 978-1-7344136-1-8

Book Design
Camila Crespo - CALA studio
www.calastudio.design @cala.studio_

Illustrations
Jessie Lee Kent
jessieleekent.com

Final Proof Read
Joseph Donnelly

First Edition: March 2021

OUTLINE

1. Preface..........................1
   Ancient Babylon
   Development of the Human Ego
      Introduction......................15
   The Big Bang Until Today
   War or Opportunity

2. The Essence of the Wisdom.........19
   Fear of Death
   Our Unique Generation
   Two Forces, - & +
   Human Mind & Heart Development
   A Tiny Black Dot Inside
   Above to Below & Below to Above
   Attaining Eternal Fulfillment

3. yoU don't Have Free Will yet.........39
   Slaves to Our desires
   Pleasure and Pain
   Source
   Inner Software
   Internal Cause & Effect
   External Cause & Effect
   The Environment

4. The Purpose of
   the Wisdom............................57
   Human's Contemplative Power
   The Absolute Good, Bestowing Force in Nature
   Endless Receiving Force
   Purposeful Guidance
   Two Paths
   Recognizing Our True Nature

5. The Giving Force
   From Above............................77
   Endless Field of Forces
   Putting the Plus and Minus Together
   Our Root
   Becoming Like Our Root

6. The Mutual Guarantee
   From Below............................93

7. The Teaching of Wisdom
   and its Essence...................... 103
   Emotional Development to Feel Nature Face to Face
   Above to Below
   Below to Above
   The Thought of Creation
   Existence From Absence and Absorption of Light

8. Peace in the World.................. 121
   Everything Has a Right to Exist
   Ripening and Hastening the Ripening
   Two Governances
   Four Attributes
   Singularity
   Pleasure

9. The Last Generation................ 140
   The Will to Receive Pleasure
   Egoists & Altruists
   Communism
   Capitalism
   Democracy
   Nazism
   Marx, Lenin & Stalin
   Religion of Love
   Idealism & Religion
   The Religion of Love for the World
   Rebuilding the World
   The Middle Line

10. Love of Friends...................... 163

Chapter 1
Preface & Introduction

I CAN TELL YOU THAT
I LOVE YOU.

BUT WE'RE
EMOTIONAL CREATURES.

YOU NEED TO FEEL
MY LOVE TO KNOW
THAT IT'S REAL.

And all of this language, it is just
too poor to communicate what
needs to be said.

So what I've set out to do here in this book is
to give you a feeling. At least a hint of a feeling
of the true reality in which we live, a reality that
is filled with love.

How we can exit this life which is filled with sorrow?

How can we come to a good life of love?

For everyone.

What we are going to encounter in the following pages is no more and no less than the laws of nature that we exist in, that we are unaware of, until now.

A baby is born and doesn't know where she is. She doesn't know that there is night and day or such things as winter and summer. We are like those babies living in this world and we don't know what is happening to us.
The wisdom does exist but it is hidden in plain sight.

Therefore, my work is not to present anything new, but only to peel off the shells that conceal these concepts and present to you just the delicious fruit.

And if someone is not prepared to hear, then nothing will enter his ear.

A word of advice before we begin.

A skeptical reader is a good reader.

Skepticism will protect you from folly.

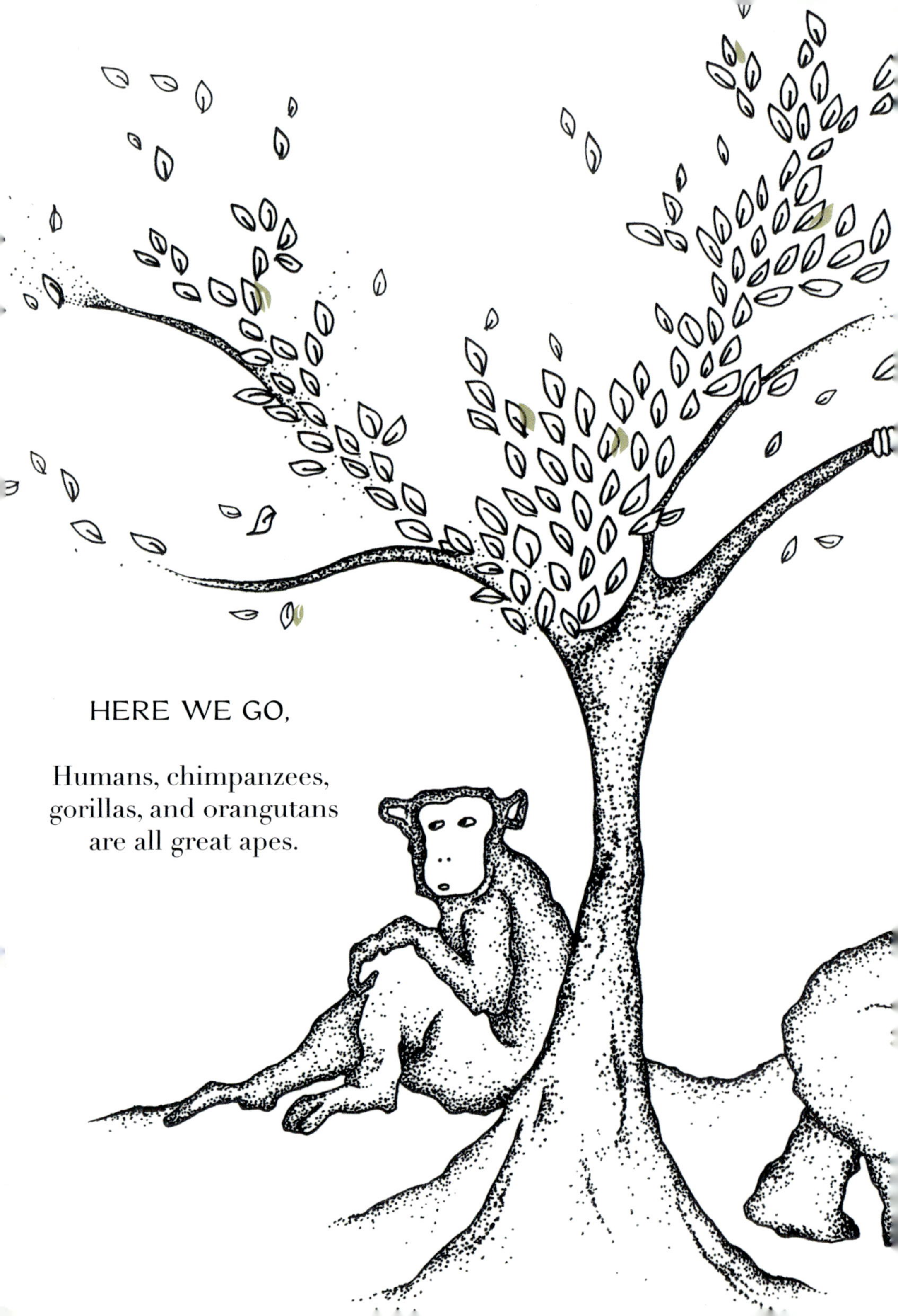

HERE WE GO,

Humans, chimpanzees,
gorillas, and orangutans
are all great apes.

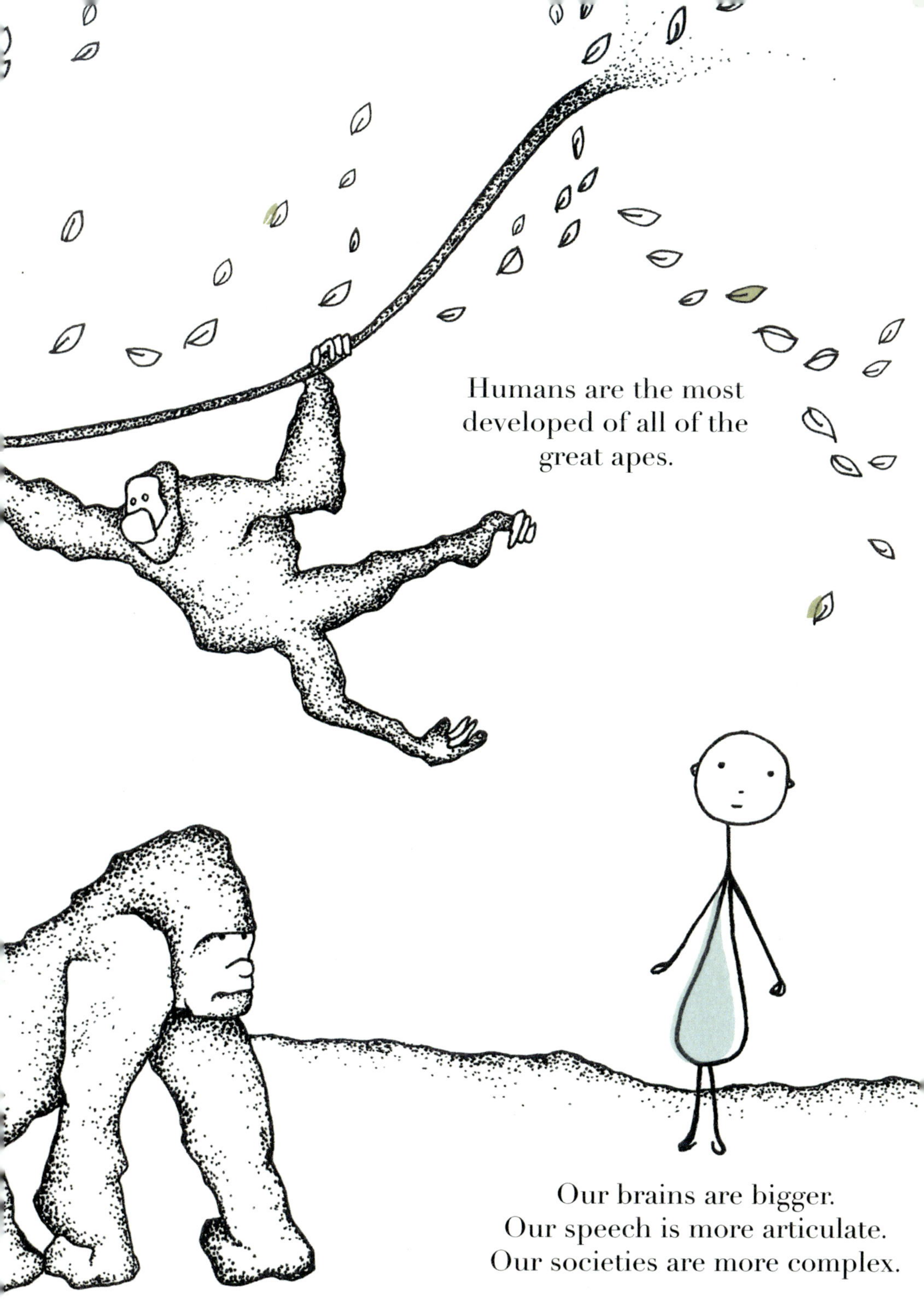

Humans are the most developed of all of the great apes.

Our brains are bigger.
Our speech is more articulate.
Our societies are more complex.

Unlike our primate relatives, our species started losing body hair and covering ourselves with garments. We started farming and building houses. And three thousand years ago between the Tigris and Euphrates rivers they made the first great civilization in Babylon.

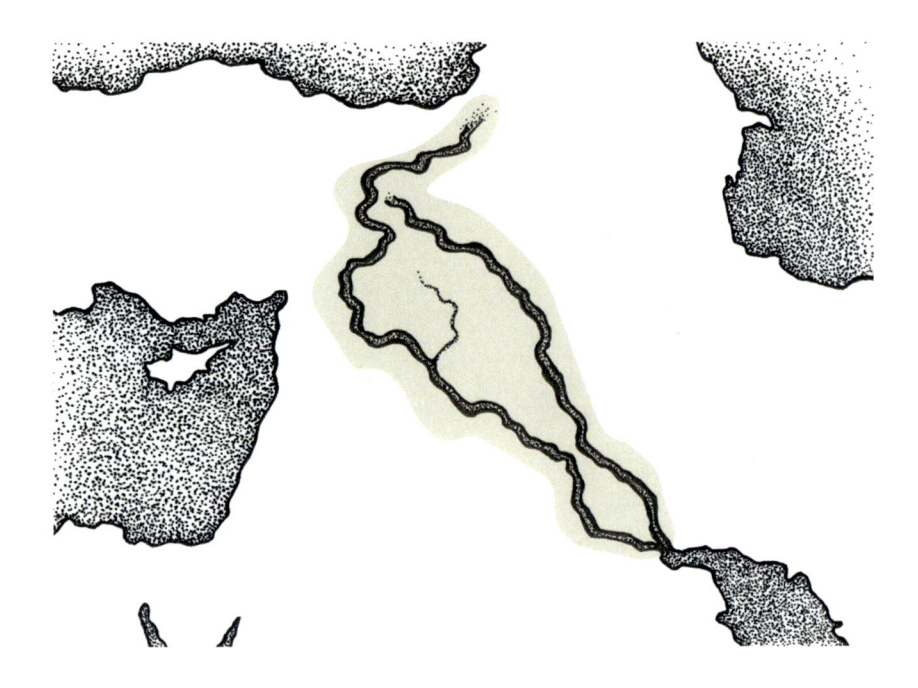

There, our ancient ancestors made discoveries in math, physics, and astronomy. We count 60 minutes in the hour because of them.
We count 60 seconds in a minute because of those Babylonians. They developed the wheel, the sailboat, writing and agriculture.

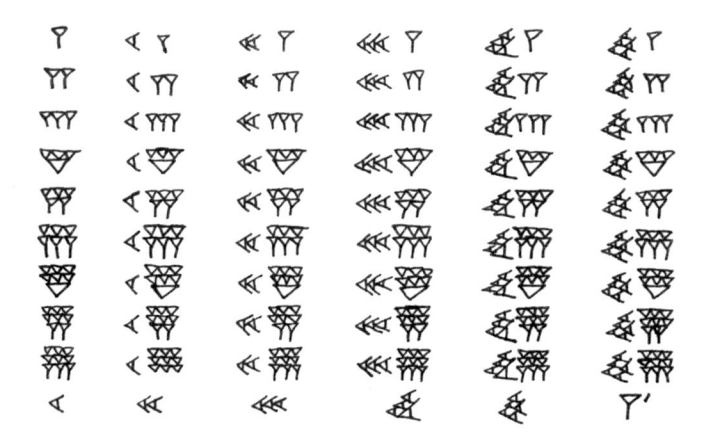

As they developed more and more they were becoming more alienated from each other, unable to relate and understand each other. We can relate to that. There was a small group who made discoveries and we have their writings, how they describe seeing through matter to the forces that connect everything. As if they were still animals that live instinctually and simultaneously humans, self aware of the whole system and all the parts and their interconnections. This wisdom didn't expand into society until they went through this great developmental leap.

Why? Well imagine that for a few hundred thousand years humans lived instinctually, like all animals. But human development isn't complete by just being an animal. There is some unique point in us that doesn't exist in the other animals, some point that drives us forward. In them developed new desires for architecture, art, transportation, trade, agriculture and mapping the stars. These qualities didn't appear overnight, but there was a great leap forward during this time.

As humanity moved away from instinct and moved more towards innovation, towards individuality, great clashes erupted. Conflicts and disputes. Alongside this natural development developed the method to unite above all of these differences. The differences between us are not bad for nature and they are not bad for us. We only have to learn how to arrange ourselves and use all of this development only for the good.

If we compare humanity today to humanity of thousands of years ago certainly we see how much more overdeveloped our egoistic qualities have become. Look at us today. Our development has led us to the disintegration of the family, the ecological devastation of our planet and world leaders posture for nuclear war.

It is not hard to see that we are far more self-centered, entitled and careless than those who came before us. From generation to generation, we are becoming more bellicose, hurtful, and more sophisticated in our malice.

Nature made us this way and it is not anyone's fault. And this may be the most unique part of this entire wisdom that we are opening up. While all religions and methods of the world suppress the ego, minimize the ego or criticize the ego, here we discover that this is how we are made, through no fault of our own after billions of years of development this is how nature made us. If a clay pot is flawed you go to the craftsman who made the pot, not to the pot itself. So we don't touch our egos.

But nevertheless we are all suffering! And we are suffering because of these egos. There is plenty of everything for everyone, yet everyone remains unfulfilled.

We need to study nature that developed us like this and understand what is actually going on here. All of the qualities that we find in humanity are all correct qualities. Our problem is we are using them all wrong. They are all aimed in exactly the wrong direction. The culture of ego has cut us off from the perception of nature's laws. The developed ego has corrupted everything, Einstein made a scientific discovery and the ego steals it to make an atomic weapon. Every great achievement of humanity has come as a result of incalculable suffering. Every endeavor of mankind is corrupted to the core, based on the exploitation of others.

Our work, as we will see soon, is only the correct connection and direction of the use of all of these egos.

We are not going to judge our egos as good or bad at all. We are just going to discover who we are, what forces are operating in us and what system we exist in.

Every person has desires and passions that belong to our animal nature. We are not responsible for these qualities that came to us at birth and through our upbringing. We don't praise a blue jay for eating so little and we don't condemn a lion for eating so much. Each creature according to its nature. But beyond that animal part of our existence is our human nature.

To live on the level that is uniquely human we have to do something that is uniquely human and that is to use our thoughts and desires to connect with each other in a good way.

INTRODUCTION

You won't find any philosophy or theory in this book. We will only delve into what you can feel.

OUR STORY BEGINS WAY, WAY BACK.

While there is a story of what happened before the **Big Bang**, we don't yet have any tools or senses to feel beyond time and space. Prior to the **Big Bang**, everything was one, in complete rest, no top and bottom, no forward and backwards. In complete rest, there is no concept of time. Time is essentially defined by us only as a sensation of movements.

So in the meantime we will leave what was before the **Big Bang** alone.

We will begin our work only with what we can perceive.

Part 1 Before the **Big Bang**, when all is one.

Part 2 The **Big Bang**, from absence to existence. Matter appeared in one tiny dot in the middle of empty space and it exploded outward.

Part 3 The expansion of all that material from a single point developing over billions of years.

Part 4 Started a few thousand years ago. We reached the complete development of our material reality. Now we enter into the development of the mind and the heart.

Every person in our world has to understand that we are in a process. There is a goal and we are moving towards it whether we like it or not. We are living inside of a system of unbreakable laws of nature and we are coming to a state where if we don't know the laws of nature, we will create a third world war and if that is not sufficient, even a fourth world war. A few millenia will pass, humanity will recuperate and some other forms of humans can emerge. Nature has no problem with time. We don't understand time, motion, the changes inside of us, what other forms and civilizations that used to exist. Today, now, we are a very special form and we have a wonderful opportunity before us.

Every person needs to receive an emotional and intellectual explanation that can stop the deterioration of humankind. The more that we are in good connections between people, the more that we adapt to the general developing force of nature which follows a plan, then we will rise above the chains of time and enter into a complete, whole and fulfilled life.

We have to advertise and make these things public as much as possible.

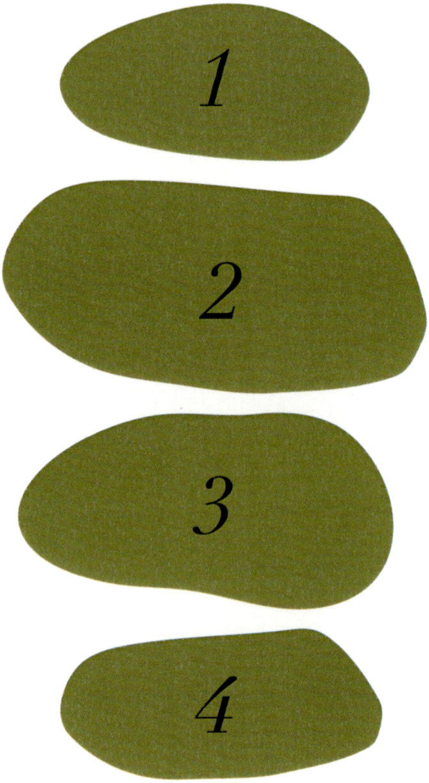
1
2
3
4

Chapter 2
The Essence of the Wisdom

The Essence of the Wisdom

is wider and deeper than the sea

What Does this Wisdom Revolve Around?

People are afraid of death
so throughout history we came up
with myths

    and stories
    to explain what's going on.

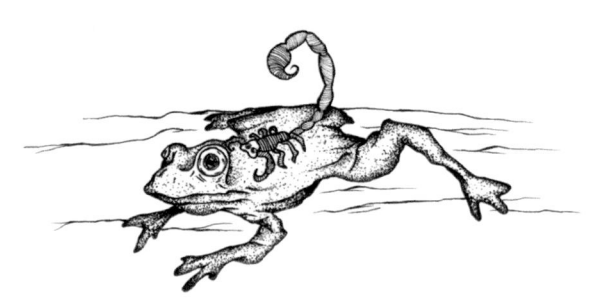

Why are things the way they are
and what happens when we die?

Depending on where on Earth we
grew up we had unique culture
and rituals to give us a way to deal
with the unknown. We receive
this as kids and live with it all of
our lives.

You and me are part of a new generation. We are like that ancient Babylonian generation. We are a big mixing of cultures and clans and tribes. Our generation has electricity, international travel and the internet. We're all mixed up and we are in another big leap. Nature is coming closer to us in a more revealed way.

We are not satisfied with folklore and superstition. We need to know why we live, what is the purpose of this life which is filled with

so **much** suffering?

Are we just running from one

Are we trapped in this maze,

fulfillment to the next until we die?

headed who knows where?

What we have in our hands
is a true wisdom.

We need to learn that all
that happens in our lives is
the result of two forces

− & +

and, they are in perpetual
war with one another.

Two legs propelling us forward, left foot and right foot.

All of the conflicts and disputes in our life are all part of nature's progression through time.

The hatred we feel. The rejection and the distance.
They set before us conditions by which we can advance. Whereby to the extent that we can accept what is happening to us with understanding, to that extent we can calibrate ourselves to nature's progression.

Everything in reality comes into being by this - & + war. Nothing comes in its finished form.

Earth, the home of humans in the universe was also born through this war. Before our planet was born, before she was land and water, she was a ball of fog. And then over spans of time that are so big we can't even comprehend, the gravity inside of that ball of fog concentrated the atoms until the ball of gas became a ball of fire.

Earth was fire. It was an epoch of terrible wars with the chilling force until it finally triumphed, cooling a thin crust around the surface.

Not still from the battle, the fire overpowered the crust and erupted from the bowels of the Earth. It shattered and melted the hard shell and a new era of wars began.

Eons interchanged before the liquids took their place in the bowels of the Earth. A new, thicker crust cooled on its surface and organic life took form.

These two opposing - & + forces manifest in the creation and formation of matter in four discrete degrees:

Speaking

Animate

Vegetative

Inanimate

By no effort of our own, we have landed on the top of this pyramid.

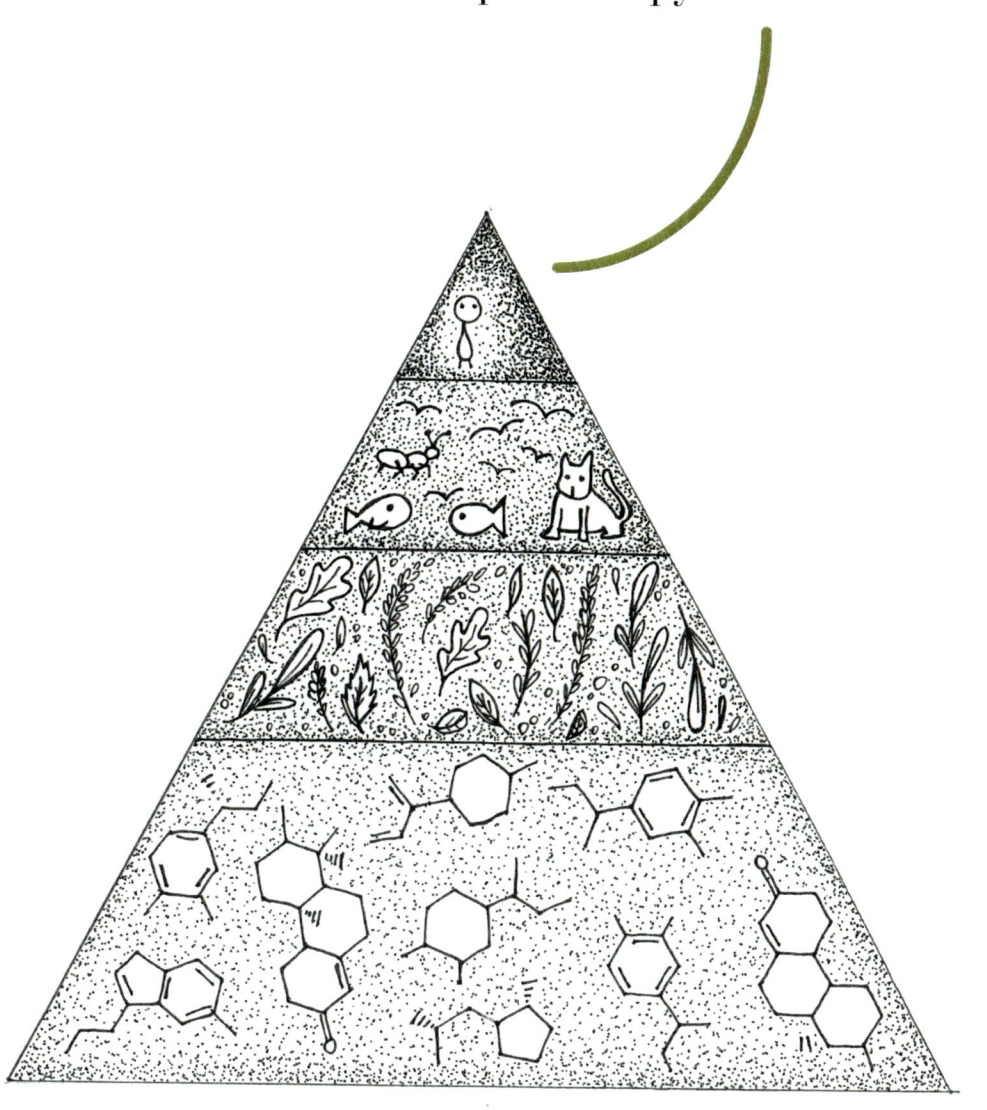

We are unique from all of the other animals. We have the power of the mind in us. It is thousands of times more valuable than the material power in us.

The human speaking degree must undergo a new order of gradual development. The - & + battle developed the prior 3 degrees of nature and that completed the material development. Now the battle that we are in is in our hearts and minds, not with our protein bodies.

We are in the midst of this mind and heart development, still given to the war between the negative & positive forces. They are faithful messengers and they will bring humanity to our final completion and perfection.

Everyone is always asking himself subconsciously about the purpose of life. What happens at the end of life? But usually we hide from these questions. We have to. If we had to focus on the emptiness of our lives, we'd rather be dead.

If we really looked at our life, is it worth being born at all? We are living with no true answers about ourselves.

We are flowing mindlessly in the current of life.

Our problem is that we are looking at our life and identifying our protein body as our self. But my protein body is not me. A person can change his liver, his kidney, his lung, even his heart. Or a hip or a knee. All of these parts are interchangeable and a person is still the same person.

But each person has an essence inside, a tiny black dot inside. A seed of a new desire, the desire to reveal the infinite reality that is outside of our skin.

We spend our lives chasing animal fulfillments and we continue to feel more and more empty. When that little black dot is planted in a good field, it is nourished and develops. By opening up this new reality we will feel everything.

There is a tsunami coming towards humanity. Viruses and climate problems, famine and war and there is nowhere to run to.

It is better for us to learn in what system of forces we are existing. We have the ability to escape from this life that is worse than death. Nature made a way to draw light into this black point inside of us and we will start perceiving a new reality. And when the black points connect with each other and the light fills that emptiness, that is called the feeling of eternal existence.

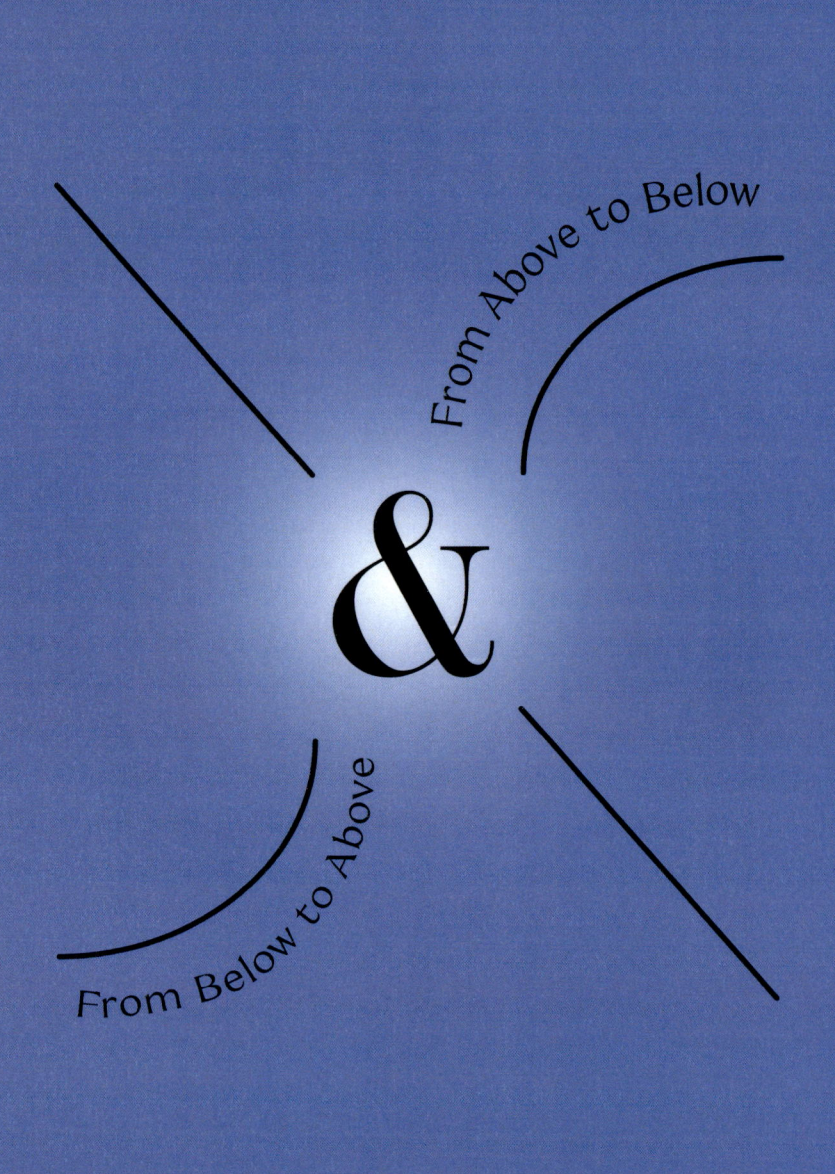

From Above to Below

&

From Below to Above

Now we are going to understand how this - & + system is specifically operating on us. We interact with these forces from two opposite directions, from two parallel orders. One order extends from 'above to below' and the other from 'below to above'.

What do we mean when we say there is an order that hangs down from above to below?

We are not talking about something hanging down from a cloud. We are talking about another dimension if you will.

Imagine that you were a stick figure living in a 2 dimensional reality. You can go right and left and forward and backwards. But then something awakens in you and you start to feel that there is another direction that you didn't even sense before.

The most important thing here is for us to start to get a sensation that there is more to life and that we want to see life in its true form.

Although we still can't see what it is, we want to discover it. Wanting to discover it is already enough to start to discover it.

Why is the world portrayed to us through these two parallel orders?

When a person wants to build a house, he starts with the most subtle form of the house, the initial thought of it. This is called 'above', in our head. Later we end with the physical house itself made of material. That is called "below".

And the opposite order is from below to above. By studying the house, its materials and design we can ascend up to understand the thought that contemplated this house.

As we study the fixed laws of nature in our world we start to reveal what "mind" thought of it, arranged it and created it. It's like a great scientist who has attained very lofty things in his thoughts. In order to convey them to a child below so that the child can absorb it, he as if lowers a ladder down to him.

We are now approaching that ladder to rise left (-), right (+) above our day to day animal existence, above a life of being pushed around senselessly by pleasure and pain.

HERE'S OUR PROBLEM

There is an endless source of energy that lights hundreds of billions of stars and pumps blood through billions of hearts. Endless energy. But living in that field of endless energy we feel endlessly empty. There is a condition for us to feel pleasure in our world. The pleasure needs to dress into something that we can feel. That spark of pleasure cannot be enjoyed as it is. It needs to lower itself and dress into food, dress into sex, into something that a person can feel, can ingest inside. If it remains outside of me I can't enjoy it. So I'm spending my life chasing tiny sparks. A tiny spark of pleasure in a coffee or in a smile from you and then I'm empty again.

We're never really actually attaining the essence of the pleasure, to climb above and partake in the flavors of the endless energy. Instead, some stimulation reaches one of our sensory organs. If I'm listening to a song and it's so beautiful that I cry, so what am I digesting here that enters me that makes me feel like this? That feeling is dressed in the musician's sounds. Sound waves enter my ear and collide with a small membrane which vibrates causing tiny electrical signals to fire which causes chemicals to be released into the body and this causes me to feel overcome with emotion and tears to flow from my eyes.

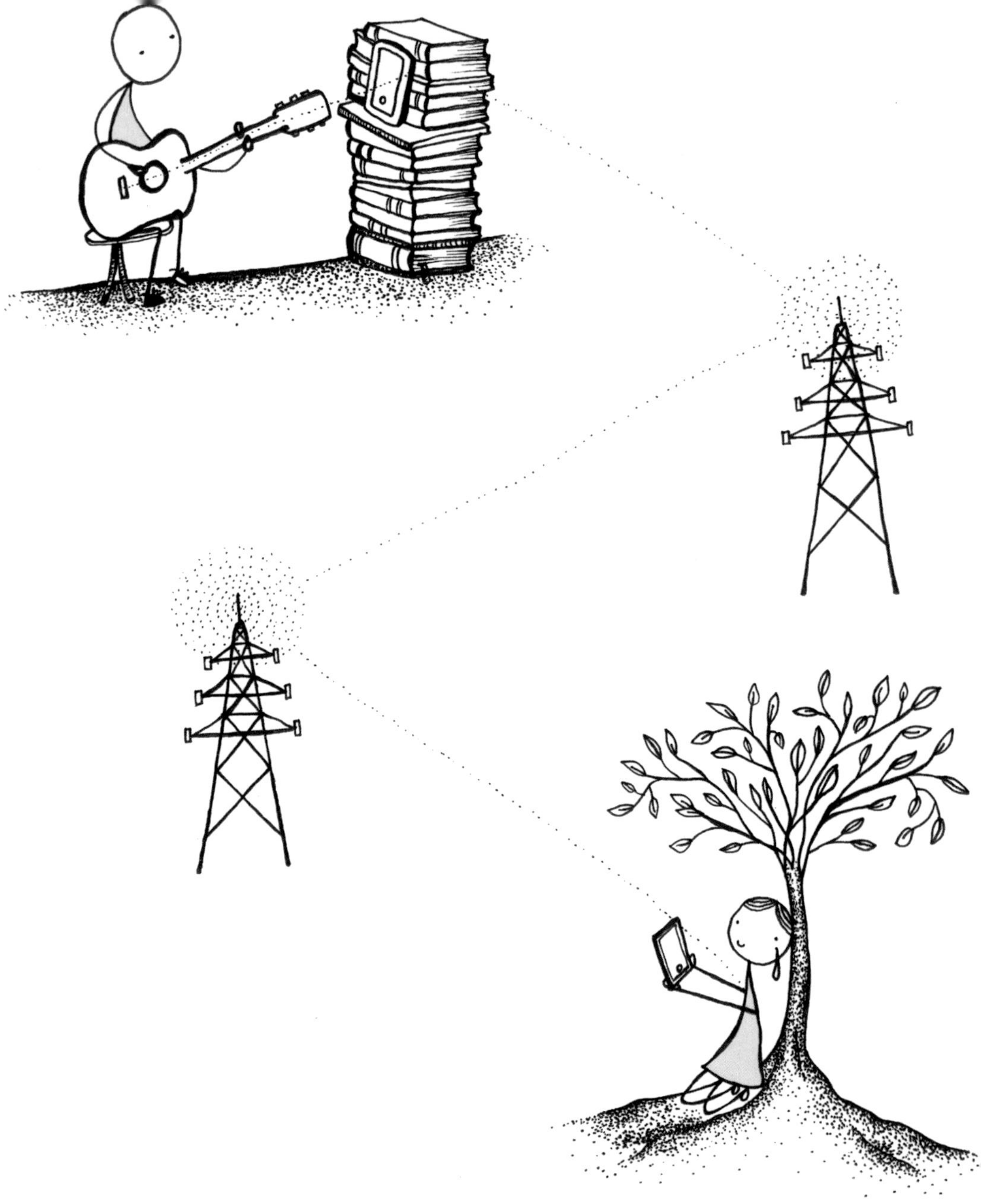

Our problem is that each of our senses can only ingest a small amount of the total possible pleasures.

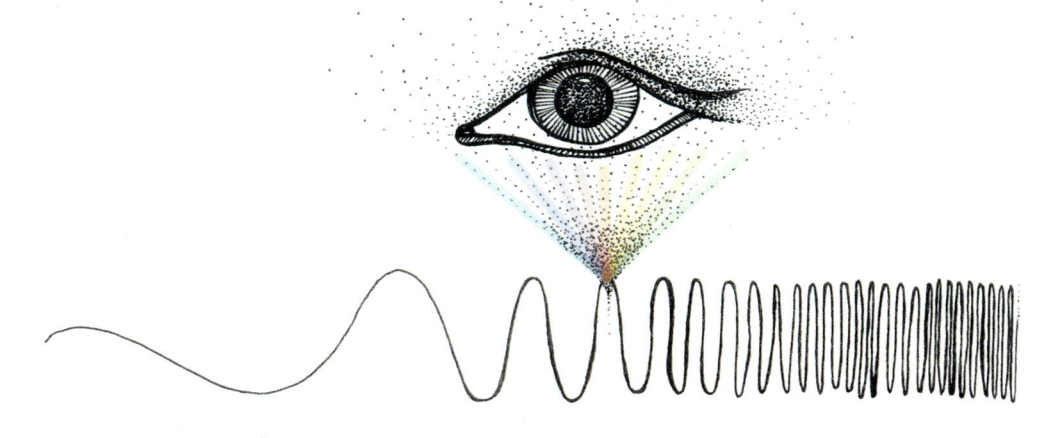

We have 5 senses in which to feel fulfillment.
However, the eternal fulfillment that we are searching for is not felt in our 5 bodily senses. Trying to fill our emptiness by filling our 5 senses will keep us feeling worse and worse. It's felt in a new sense. There are many religions and methods that teach a person to limit his desires. They say if you limit your desires you will suffer less when you don't fulfill them.
But that is not our work.

Nature is developing us not to be vegetative or animals but to enjoy all of reality endlessly.

Imagine if we had 5 **more** senses.
We will understand this soon.

We need to be like the stick figure. He used to live in his stick figure world with his stick figure house and his stick figure family and then he wakes up and starts to feel that there is much more happening here. He starts to feel and he can respond to it. When you feel fire on your skin, you know to move away. When you smell something delicious you know to come close. We also have other senses that we are discovering and with them we can feel direction and our purpose in life.

Speaking

Animate

Vegetative

Inanimate

Chapter 3
~~You~~ Don't Have Free Will ~~Yet~~

~~YOU DON'T~~ HAVE FREE WILL ~~YET~~

We are slaves to our desires.
I want food. I want sex.   I want money.
I want respect, knowledge and power.

Where do these desires come from?

And we are trapped between pleasure and pain.
Do we have any freedom in this life?
We are constantly checking ourselves. Move my
hand, scratch my cheek, check my phone.
This is how we are made.

PLEASURE AND PAIN

Our lives are simply governed by two forces.

1. To be drawn towards pleasure

2. To move away from pain

We are led around our entire life by these two reins. One pulling us towards pleasure and the other repelling us from pain.

We don't freely choose our clothes or what to eat or even our behavior.
We follow society that determines in us various habits according to shame and pleasure.

If we had no shame, we would say whatever we want to whomever we want and take whatever we want without asking.
Everyone acts without awareness being led by these two forces.

I know that this is hard to swallow for everyone, it doesn't matter if you are secular or religious.

And even more bewildering, if each person is being led by these desires, like reins on a horse, how can we even say that a person is selfish?!
So here we are.
With no accountability. Being led who knows where.

THE LAW OF CAUSE AND EFFECT

We feel independent.
We feel like we are acting on our own.

We feel unique and free.
When in fact, it is exactly the opposite.

Everything in reality abides by the law of cause and effect.

If we examine this in a purely scientific way, we'll see that each and every behavior that a creature follows in this world is pushed by ancient causes.

There is nothing in our world that just appeared from out of nowhere. Everything that emerges in our world, every object, every thought and every desire emerges from something that came before it.

Let's examine this process and see if we can locate some place in life where we can find free will.

EVERYTHING IN LIFE DEVELOPS THROUGH FOUR PHASES

1. PHASE ONE:
This is a thing's essence. In that essence lies the potential that will later be revealed as the form of the **source** emerges in the world.

2. PHASE TWO
This is the inner software that operates upon that **source**. Let's look at an example from nature, a stalk of wheat.

It grows all spring and summer and finishes in the fall. At that time the **source** of the wheat strips off its former clothing of a stalk. It takes on a new clothing, that of rotten wheat. After the seeds open, they are fit to clothe in another form.

The **source** of the wheat changes its clothing. It will never wear the clothing of a banana. It will always equalize again and become a stalk of wheat. This cycle of cause and effect, this wheat software is called phase two.

3. PHASE THREE
These are the things that the **source** encounters in the environment such as minerals in the soil, rain and sun that enter into the wheat and operate on the **source** to produce all of the differing quantities and qualities of wheat that can emerge.

4. PHASE FOUR
These are external forces that act upon the **source**. Like a weevil who comes and eats the wheat, or a farmer who cares for it and ensures its success.

These four phases happen in everything that emerges in the world. All of our desires, our thoughts and our actions contain these four factors which combine in us throughout our growth and determine what will become of our **source**.

SUMMER

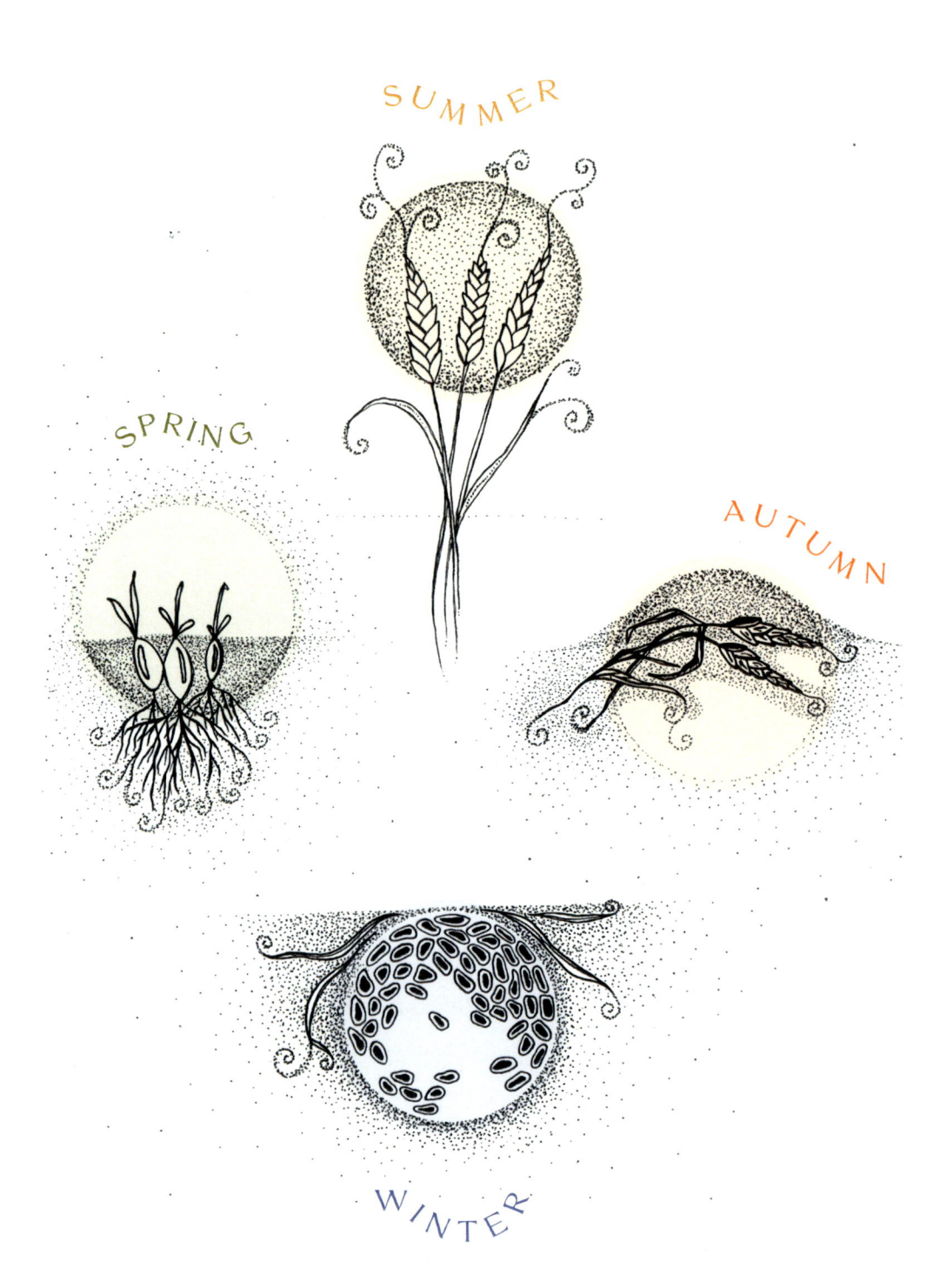

SPRING

AUTUMN

WINTER

HEREDITARY POSSESSIONS

You are created from a sperm from your father and an egg from your mother. The creation of a you is to a certain extent like copying from book to book. Matters that were accepted by your parents are copied into you. A child isn't born with the words and experiences that his parents have. The child receives these things in an abstract form.

It is like with the wheat. It contains in it what it needs to grow into a new stalk. But it is not ready for sowing until it has rotted, and it sheds its former shape.
So is the case with the drop of semen from which you were born. There is nothing in the drop that resembles you, only an abstract force.
The ideas of our parents, how they viewed the world, have turned into instincts that are passed to us. We are born and we don't even know what these are or why this happened.

Indeed, there are hidden forces that come to us from our ancestors. They appear in a certain part of our brain, as pictures in our subconscious.

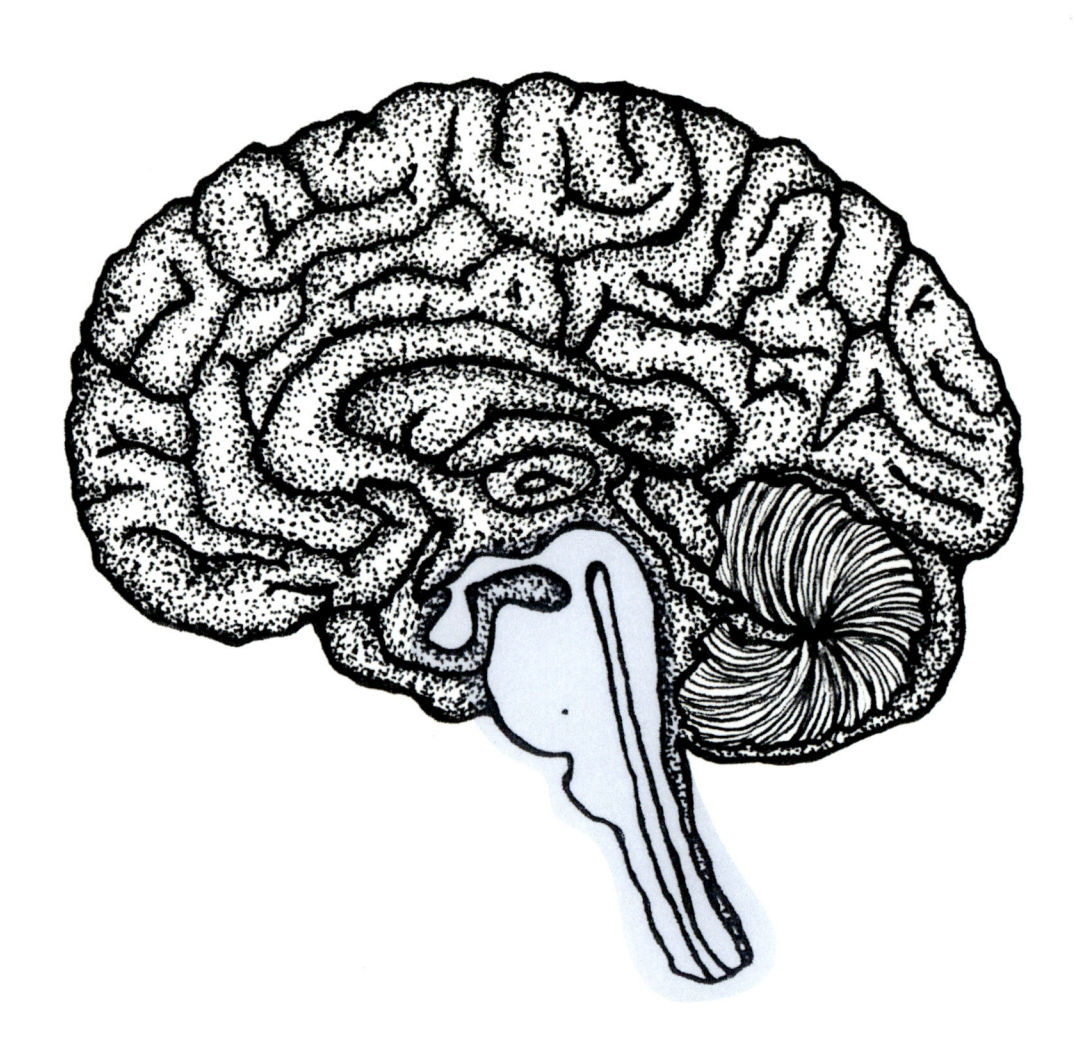

HABIT BECOMES SECOND NATURE

Now we can understand that a person inherits tendencies from his ancestors and from his environment and he turns them into the building blocks of his life. A good environment can shape these concepts for the good. Thus, through the cause and effect of his environment he can take a tendency that he had inherited from his forefathers and direct it. If I'm in the right environment I can make immense changes that can direct me.

Habit becomes second nature.
And sometimes through habit a person manages to completely uproot a bad tendency.

And in this we find something unique, above the rest of all of nature.

Humans can choose in which environment to plant themselves and by this change through the cause and effect of the environment.

In Summary

Every thought and idea that appears in us are only the fruit of these four factors.
And even if we were to sit and contemplate all day long, we won't be able to add or to alter what those four factors give us.

HERE IS OUR FREE CHOICE

When we examine these four factors, we find that we have no way to change the **source** of who we are. But we **can** protect ourselves against the other three factors of cause and effect which affect our source.

THE ENVIRONMENT

We can always add in the matter of choosing a good environment, meaning our friends, teachers and media. It is like a person who inherited a few stalks of wheat. From this small amount, he can grow dozens of stalks through his choice of the environment for his source. He chooses a field with fertile soil, with all the necessary minerals, sun and water that nourish the wheat abundantly.

The wise person will do well to choose the best conditions that impart good concepts and powers upon him and the fool is bound to fall into a bad environment and waste time on worthless things that are abundant and easy to come by.

Therefore, free choice exists for the person who continually chooses a better environment. And the benefit is not because of his good thoughts and deeds, which come to him without his choice, but because of his effort to acquire a good environment, which brings him these good thoughts and deeds.

All the praise and profit are to the environment where we plant our **source**.

Our desire has no freedom.

Our choice is the field where we plant it.

- Summer
- Autumn
- Winter
- Spring

Chapter 4
The Purpose of the Wisdom

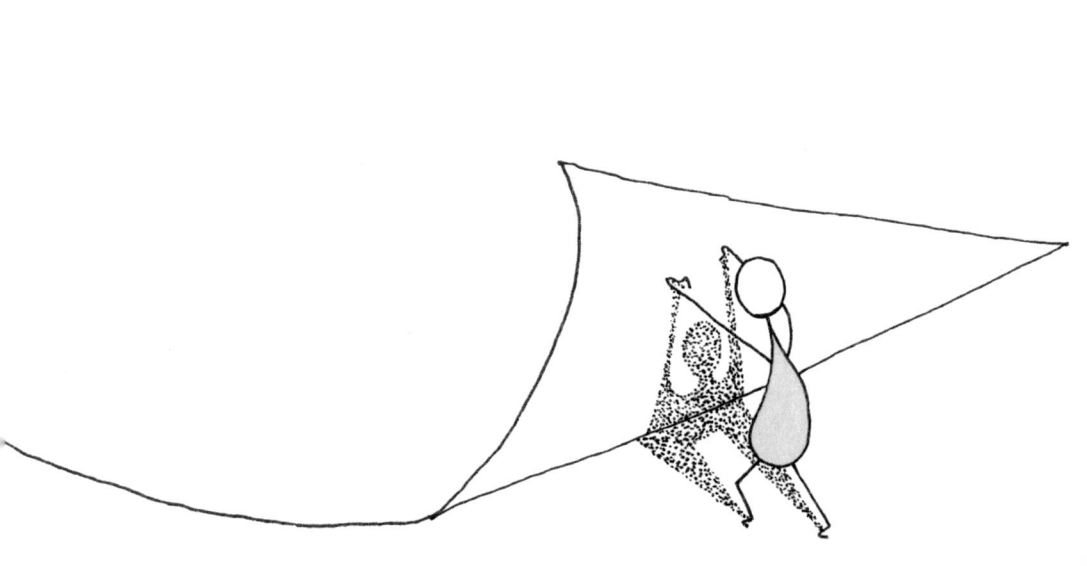

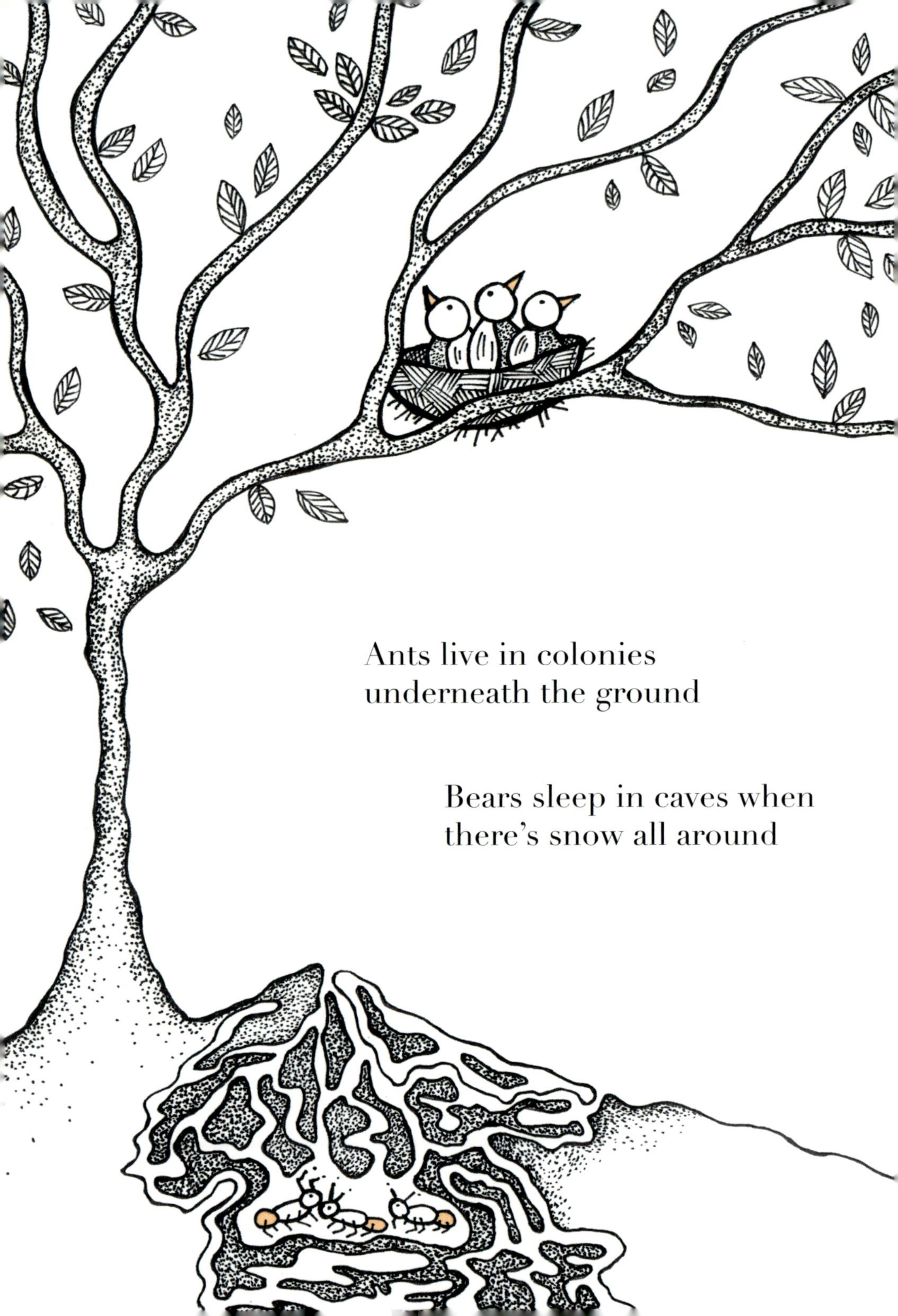

Ants live in colonies
underneath the ground

Bears sleep in caves when
there's snow all around

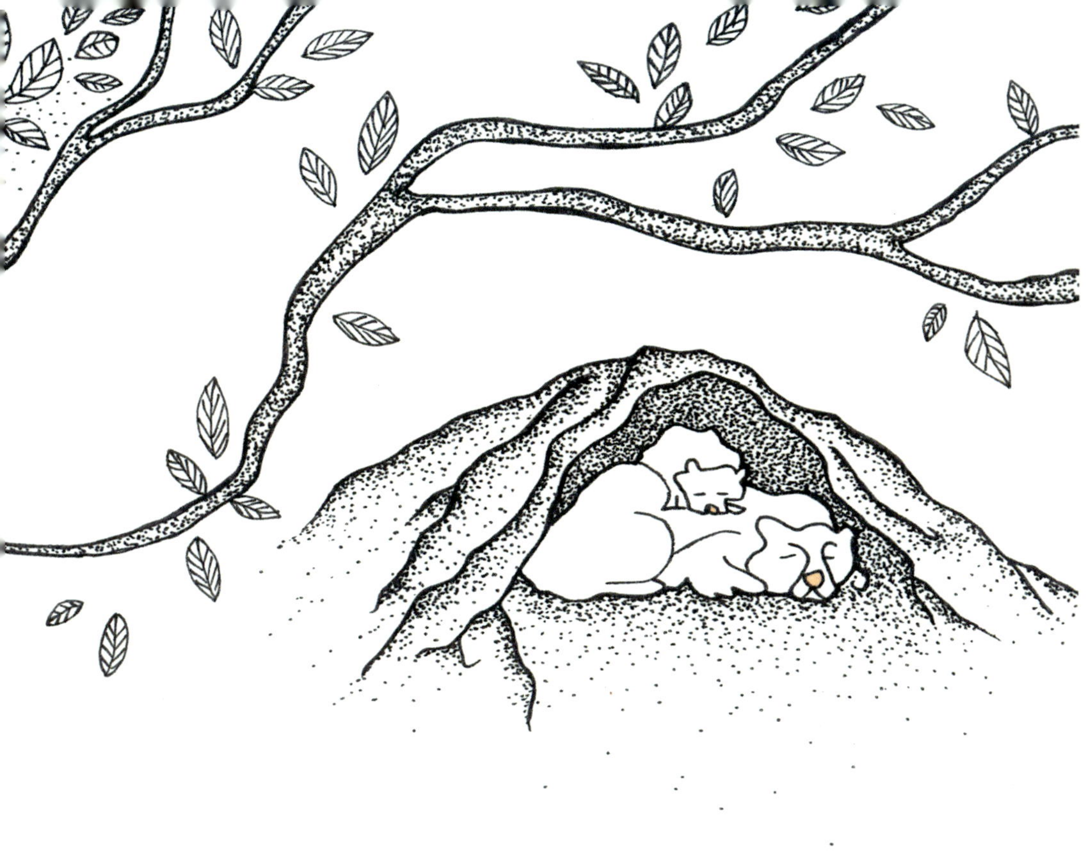

Blue bird boys and blue bird girls
make their blue bird nests in summer

You and me live in our homes
animals just like the others

Each animal lives according to the instinctual software installed in it from antiquity. What distinguishes human development from that of the other animals is our contemplative power. Human development does not end with our material development.

After the completion of the body comes the power of the mind. It is thousands of times more valuable than the material force in us and that brings us to our completion.

We are the most developed creatures in all of reality.

We are the ones who ask.

What is the purpose of my life?

And can I attain it while I live?

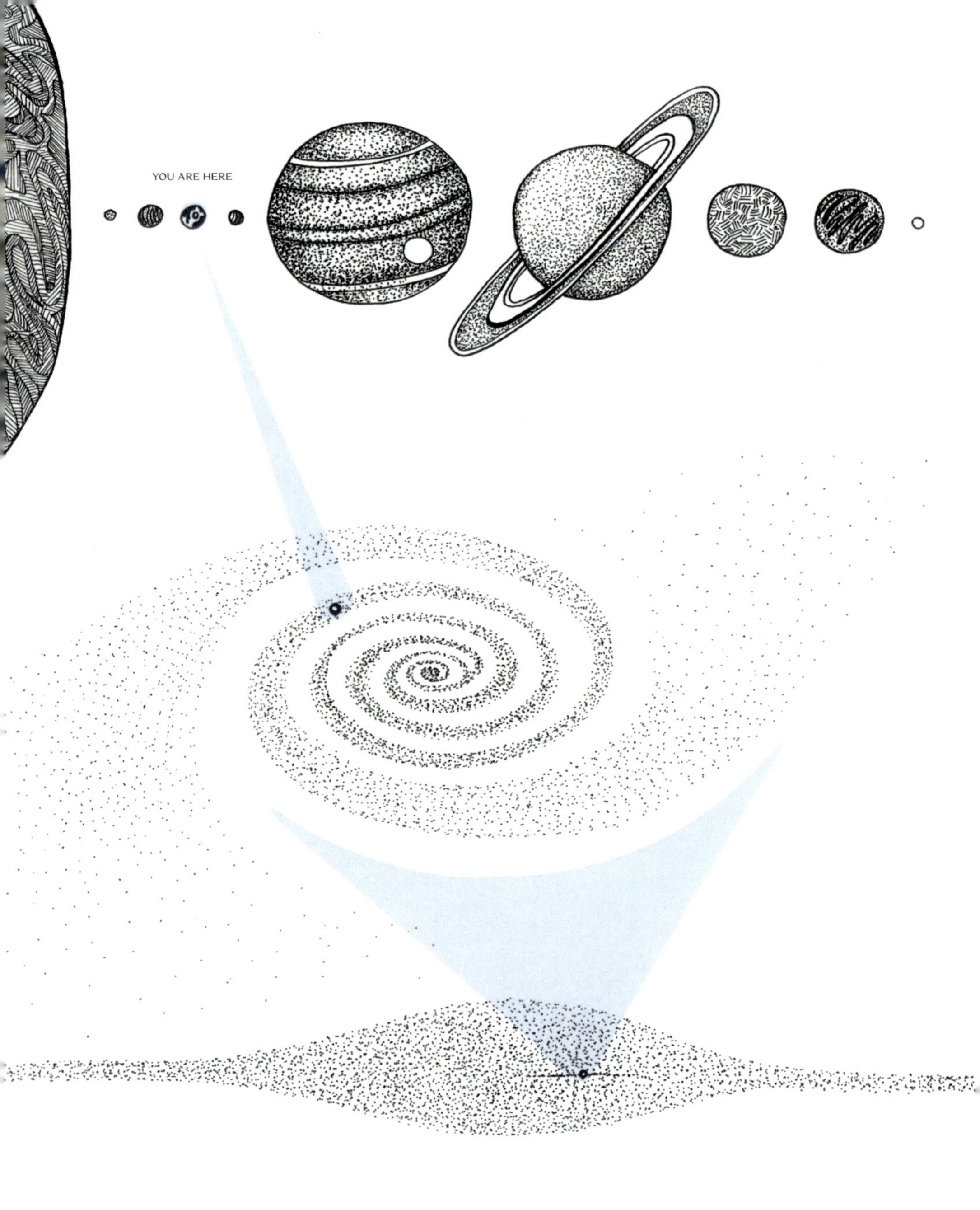
YOU ARE HERE

The Absolute Good, Bestowing Force in Nature

The universe is so big.

Our planet spins around among thousands of billions of stars in the Milky Way galaxy.
Besides our home galaxy, there are billions of other galaxies.
It is just impossible to comprehend what power came out of that Big Bang that to this day stars are still shining from the force that exited from that tiny point.

There is nothing to write about such a size.
We don't have any way to wrap our heads around something of that magnitude.

We can be impressed by a sunset, a great landscape, a famous person or a beautiful bird. But all of our planet and everything on it is no more than a small spec of sand on a spec of sand on a spec of sand compared to the expanse of the universe. And the universe we know is only the "known universe". The more we explore, the more we discover.
    There are countless planets that humankind does not use at all. The unknown does not contradict the known. Perhaps there is still, vegetative, animate and speaking on lots of planets. Nevertheless, here we are hurtling through space on a small rock that is full of all sorts of elements. Extract them, combine them release their power and we live by it. Clothed inside the heart of hearts of everything there is power. Endless power. Reality is permeated by this endless bestowing force of + energy. Opposite to the endless bestowing force in reality is material, which is an endless receiving force -. All of material reality from the smallest to the largest is no more and no less than a force of reception, receiving the force of bestowal.
That is the whole matter of our reality. And this matter runs a simple line of software:
    /* how can i receive the most fulfillment while exerting the least amount of energy)*/

This software runs in every atom, every molecule, every plant, every animal, every person, everything.

Think about it well

Think about it well Think about it well Think about it well
Think about it well Think about it well Think about it well
Think about it well Think about it well Think about it well
Think about it well Think about it well Think about it well
Think about it well Think about it well Think about it well
Think about it well Think about it well Think about it well
Think about it well Think about it well Think about it well
Think about it well Think about it well Think about it well
Think about it well Think about it well Think about it well
Think about it well Think about it well Think about it well
Think about it well Think about it well Think about it well
Think about it well Think about it well Think about it well
Think about it well Think about it well Think about it well
Think about it well Think about it well Think about it well
Think about it well Think about it well Think about it well
Think about it well Think about it well Think about it well
Think about it well Think about it well Think about it well
Think about it well Think about it well Think about it well
Think about it well Think about it well Think about it well
Think about it well Think about it well Think about it well
Think about it well Think about it well Think about it well
Think about it well Think about it well Think about it well
Think about it well Think about it well Think about it well
Think about it well Think about it well Think about it well
Think about it well Think about it well Think about it well
Think about it well Think about it well Think about it well
Think about it well Think about it well Think about it well
Think about it well Think about it well Think about it well
Think about it well Think about it well Think about it well
Think about it well Think about it well Think about it well
Think about it well Think about it well Think about it well
Think about it well Think about it well Think about it well
Think about it well Think about it well Think about it well

Purposeful Guidance

When observing nature's system, we see that everything is guided by a slow and gradual progression of causes and effect. Go ask a botanist how many phases a fruit undergoes from the seed until it becomes completely ripe. And not only do the early stages of the fruit show no evidence of its sweet and beautiful end, but as if to jest they show opposite qualities from the final outcome. The sweeter the fruit will be at its end, the more bitter it is at earlier stages of its development.

And so it is with us.

AT THE BEGINNING
WE DON'T UNDERSTAND

IN THE MIDDLE
WE DON'T UNDERSTAND

WE CAN ONLY UNDERSTAND WHY
THINGS ARE THE WAY THEY ARE AT
THE END OF THEIR DEVELOPMENT.

If you saw a baby horse and a baby boy being born you would see that from the start a horse already has some intelligence. He knows to avoid danger and knows where to suckle. The baby boy lays totally helpless unable to eat or take care of himself at all. We should conclude that the horse will be great and the baby boy lying senseless will be eaten by birds.

We must understand that there are phases of development which in the meantime prevent us from understanding their end which is always opposite to their initial shape.

One who is experienced can examine creation from its beginning to its end and can calm down and not fear the images that he sees as creation undergoes its phases of development. Instead he can already see its fine and pure end.

Two Paths Before Us

There are two paths of development before us. One is a long and painful path where one develops slowly by our own nature following a path of cause and effect until we decide to reject bad and choose good. And there is also prepared before us a pleasant and gentle way which qualifies us to advance to our good future quickly and painlessly.

Developing on the good path begins with consciously coming to recognize our true nature. It's time to turn away from imaginations and philosophies.

Our material nature is that desire to receive fulfillment that we learned about above.
That is it.
Every desire that we have is that **desire to receive fulfillment** expressing itself. And every thought that we have is serving those desires.

Every person is a creature just like all of the animals. He has unique desires and in this he is not praised or condemned. The qualitative difference between one person and the next is only the degree that one recognizes his true nature of wanting to receive for himself alone.

The undeveloped person doesn't sense his true nature, that he cares only about himself. This person lives unconsciously. He lives like an animal. He wakes in the morning and a desire arises to pee he pees, a desire to eat he eats. The wind blows him this way he goes this way, the wind blows him that way he goes that way. He doesn't recognize his egoistic nature that remains hidden within. He uses it openly without shame.

A more developed person senses this ego as bad and is ashamed to use it publicaly. But, he still commits these crimes in secrecy. Our modern world is full of wild animals dressed in nice clothes who exploit others to the best of their ability.

And those who are the most developed among us do not want to exploit others. They feel their egoistic self love is loathsome until they can't tolerate it anymore. Then there begins to emerge in them sparks of love of others.

We will always remain as receivers, that is the only matter in all of creation. We need to leave our animal nature as it is. Is a bird better than an ant better than a bear? But we are a unique creature. The ego on top of the animal is what we are speaking of. A bear eats his fill. A man is insatiable. A bird makes a nest. A man fills his home with excess. This is not about things, but about an attitude to life that we are never fulfilled, we are insatiable. And this is by design. So that we will not remain as animals but will learn to connect our endless desiring force with the endless fulfilling force.

Upon the revelation of our true nature as a desire to receive and by coming to see the futility of trying to fulfill this endless black hole, we become despaired of escaping from it. And then a new desire comes to rise above this system, a big bang inside of ourselves. Out of the endless emptiness begins to emerge sparks of love for others. And this wondrous love develops gradually. First comes the desire to bestow to those close to him and it expands to those around him and the circle widens and widens until he finally develops love for all of humanity.

South

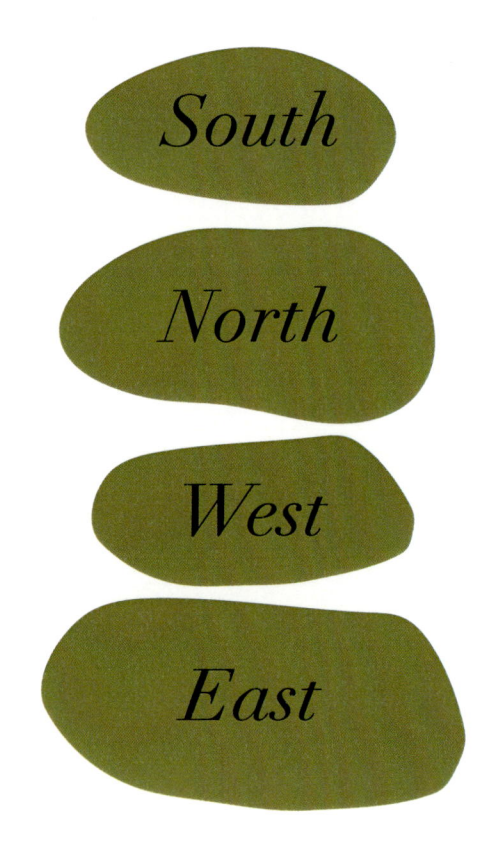

North

West

East

Chapter 5
The Giving Force
from Above

When I go to the beach in the summer I love playing in the water. My sons and I always play in the waves. We delight in it. We find a good place to stand where the waves break. When they come we have two choices. Either jump and ride up the front of the wave, feel weightless at the top and then land softly down. Or, we dive straight into the wave. When you dive into them the water glides past every inch of your skin. It rushes around every curve and down your sides. In your head you hear the muffled rumble and whoosh of sand turning around and the high pitched banging of the shells on the seafloor. And then the pressure overhead changes as the wave passes over. You're getting short of breath but you need to relax and wait. Then you aim up to the sky and swim up into the air with a deep breath. You are standing again on your feet and laughing out loud in joy.

There is a third thing we do, it's in it's own category. Sometimes we just stand there and let the waves crash on us. This gets us laughing the hardest. We let waves pummell us, knock us off balance, toss, flip and deposit us up on the beach with sand in every pocket and crease.

You can't stop waves.
If you study them you can determine in what patterns they come and where they will break. Feel the features on the seafloor that affect their shape.

Nature's laws don't discriminate.
They face all people on Earth equally.

Now we are going to learn about the singular law that contains all of the other laws. This is the bestowing power that gives life to all of reality.
Humanity is facing these waves of bestowal with no instruction book. Giant waves intended to lift us are pounding us.

There are so many forces acting upon us.

You've probably heard that your body is 70% water and that Earth is 70% water.

The moon's cycle pulls the water on Earth. Women's menstrual cycles are affected by the moon. Storms on the sun can affect our mood. Low atmospheric pressure can make your knees and elbows hurt. We are in a field of endless forces. So we wake up in the morning and are uncomfortable and irritable and we think it's because of the person next to us. Or it's the guy in traffic or this politician or that one. Meanwhile there is a symphony of forces crashing and acting upon us and we are completely unaware.

We don't have to study how the forces from each planet affects us and how weather affects us, etc. Each of these systems contain endless details. We don't need to become a computer scientist in order to use a mobile phone. We just need to pick it up and use it. It's prepared and ready. Nature's waves are ready to lift us up if we only know how to calibrate ourselves to them.

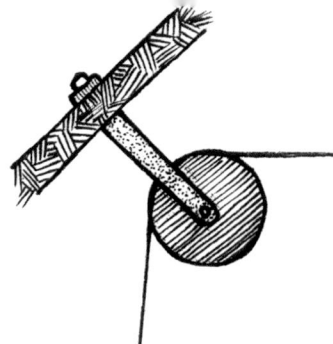

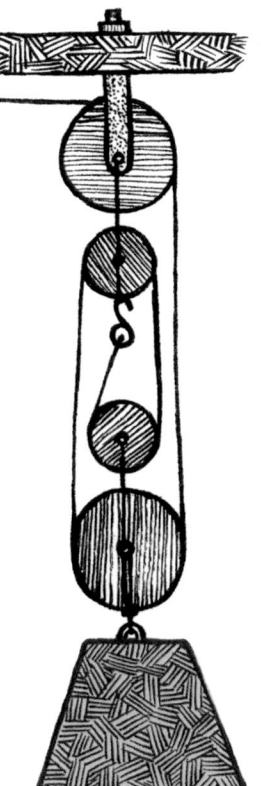

Gravity is still there, but you study it and study nature and then you ride on that force and make your effort in the correct place in the correct direction.

Gravity exists.

If you want to lift heavy rocks, for that the pulley was invented. With it you can lift 1000 pounds with your bare hands.

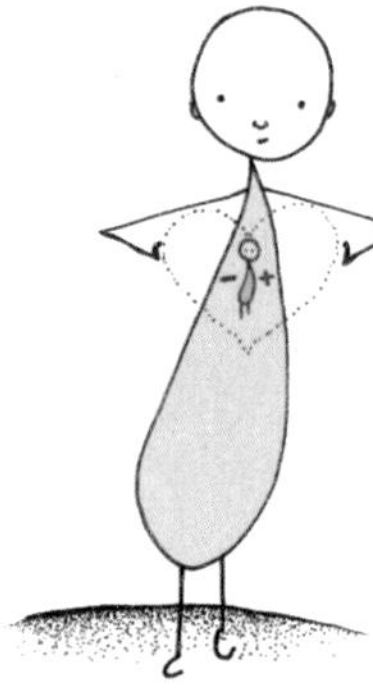

So now we will begin to learn how to balance the big invisible minus and plus inside of us. Just as we put two wires together in a device and it runs. We use those two forces, negative and positive in order to express ourselves, to make our actions similar to nature. The device that we build between the giant plus and minus is called a human.

And when we arrange the plus and minus we begin to feel new phenomenon. A new reality becomes tangible. Like the first person who imagined the wheel or imagined an airplane, it's called that a light shines in a person in a place that was dark before, in a place that we couldn't see before, now we see something new.

We are like a bird who spends all day trying to find worms in a hot, dry brick wall. At the end of the day he comes home exhausted, turns on the TV, smokes, drinks a beer and complains about his hard life.

Why is our life full of such burden?

Why weren't we created like a bird who already knows where to fly, where to find the worm?

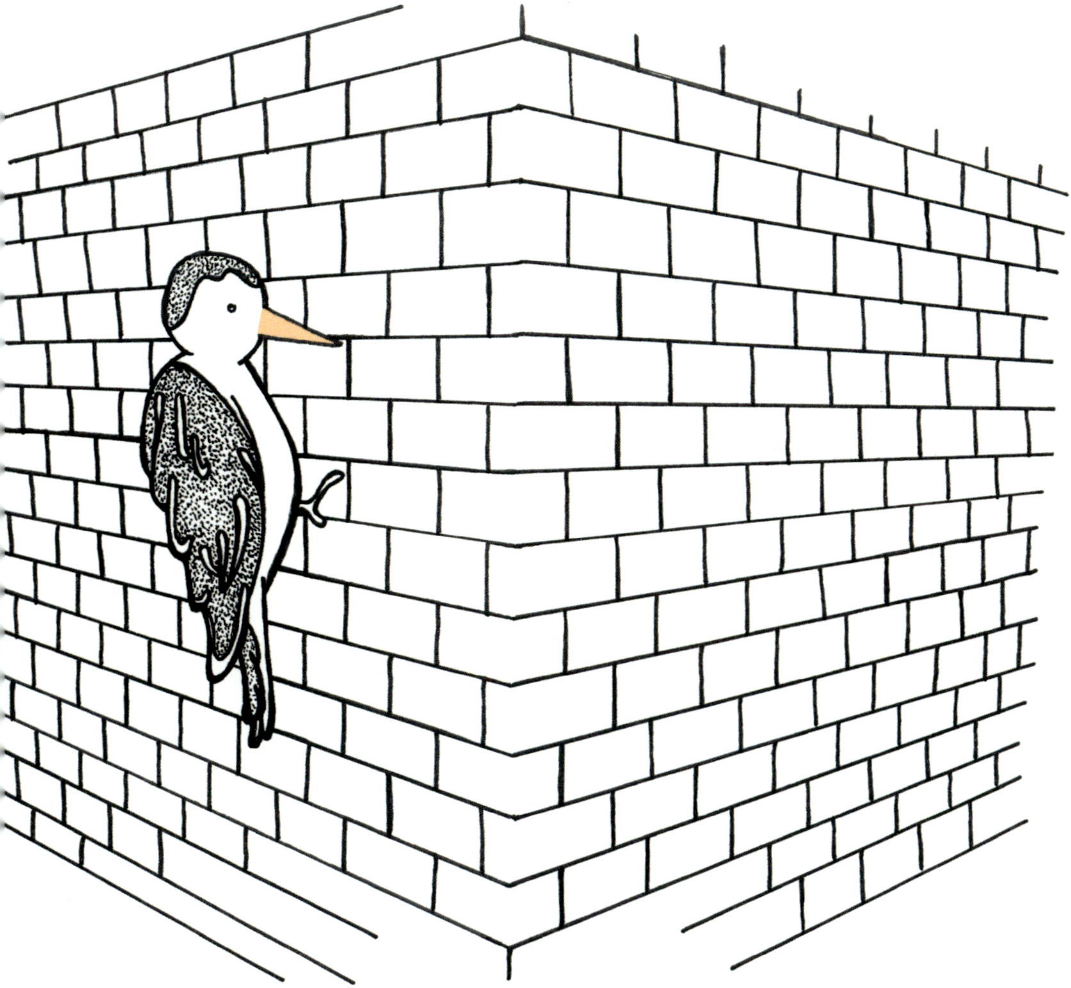

How does every bird know to take worms
from the soft earth?

BEFORE US IS A DOOR TO UNDERSTANDING THE SOURCE OF ALL OF THE PLEASURES AND PAINS IN THE WORLD.

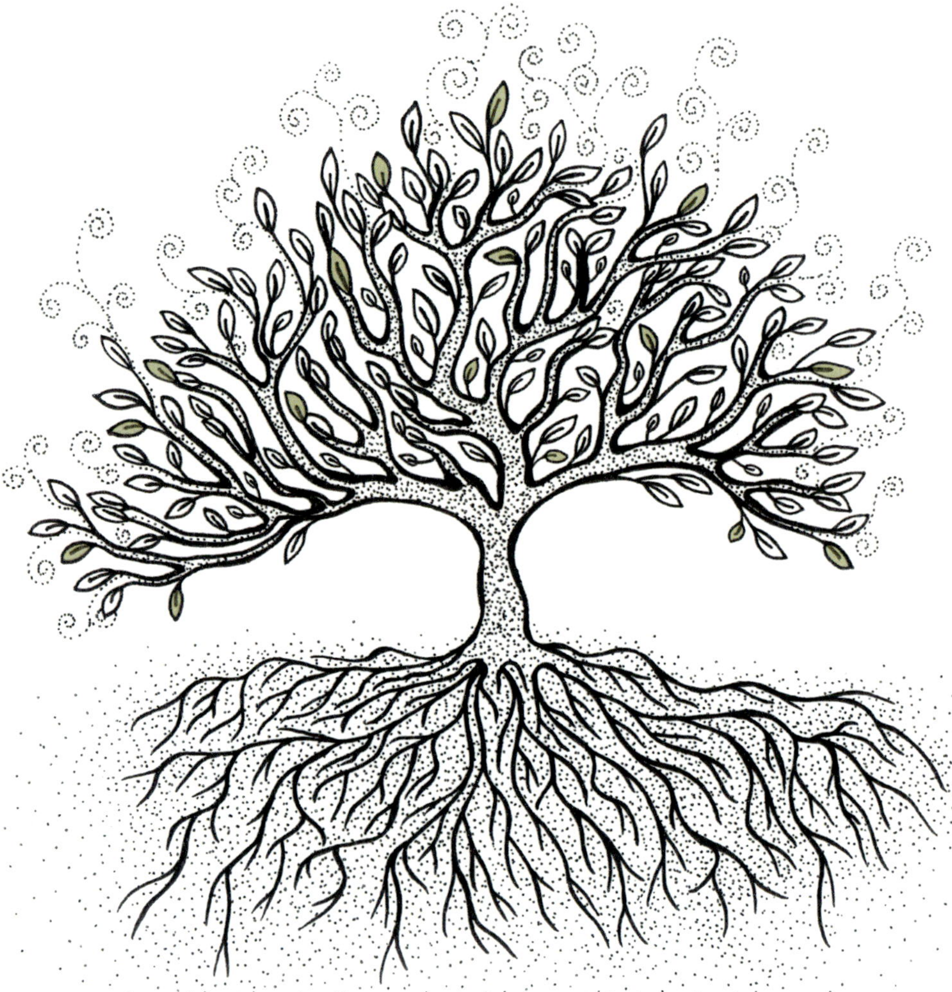

A branch bears the same nature as its root.

We find ourselves 14 billion years after the Big Bang from which our material life came. Material existence as we know it originated in that singularity. It is our root, containing everything, eternally. Thus we love rest, we love power, we love wisdom, we love strength and wealth and we hate their opposite, foolishness, weakness and poverty since they do not exist in our root at all. Our root is a bestowing force. This is why we feel shame and impatience when we receive charity from others because in our root, where we all extend from, there is no reception.

    All pleasure and sublimity naturally extend from our root.

    When we equate with our root we sense delight.

When a baby is born, she is in a state with no words, no past and future, no names, no borders. Where does Mom end and the wall begin? Everything is new for the first time. Every moment revolves around her feelings. Every movement a baby makes revolves solely around receiving for herself. She doesn't have a drop of care for others. As she grows, depending on her environment, she can start to get a small portion of bestowing love upon others. At first she loves others because they take care of her. If a person had to keep unconditional love, she would not be able to bear it. But as a person grows then she can hear how to love others in order to bestow and not just for the sake of self love. That means to make ourselves like our root which is bestowing. By this we become the same quality as the single law of nature.

By accostoming ourselves to keep this law in order to truly love, we gradually depart from the bosom of life. Nature spent billions of years of developing us to be greater and greater receivers and through great efforts we slowly rise and acquire a second nature. Meaning, we become a creator and build a second nature in ourselves, which is bestowing upon others. True love.

But we would never do this.
We would never forsake ourselves
and live to take care of others!

> So how can there be a law of nature,
> such an inclusive and important law
> that it is impossible for us to keep it?

And this is why we suffer as
the relentless waves of nature
pressure us to be like our root.

Fire

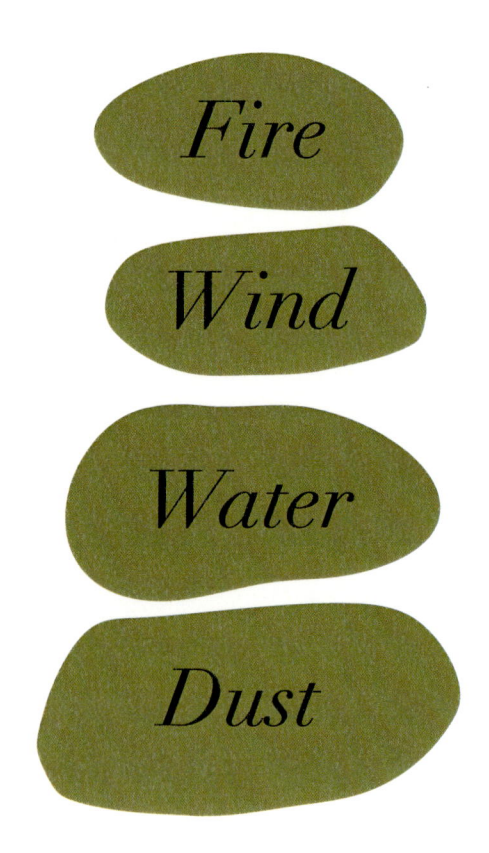

Wind

Water

Dust

Chapter 6
The Mutual Guarantee From Below

This is the most important chapter in explaining our role towards humanity.

    We learned already that our material existence extends from the Big Bang. All of reality was contained in that tiny dot, as one singularity. It exploded and shattered in every direction. As it developed, it did so in four cascading degrees.

By the time it gets to our senses, we perceive it as

1. *Inanimate*
2. *Vegetative*
3. *Animate*
4. *Speaking*

In each subsequent degree the quality of the matter moves further away from the starting point.

Today humanity has arrived at the end of that long chain of development, exactly opposite from that simple unity.

It turns out that all of the separation between us gives us the possibility to bring unity to all of creation.

We are like that small group in Babylon, a small group composed of friends from all of the nations of the world from every color and every size who have an inclination towards this. And everyone else who doesn't have this inclination will follow us after. We are connected in a network that is on a level above the level of our bodies. The minute that we begin to feel that we have an inclination towards this mutual guarantee, we enter the network. We shift from a personal feeling to a common feeling. From that feeling onward there begins to be this straight path and then the bestowing force of nature flows through this pipeline and it will enliven us. In this illumination we will see a new way and we will see how to carry it out, how everyone will help his friend.

The whole method that we are presenting is about attaining the unity of creation. We don't really know what it is. But nature promotes us like little children, leading us through all kinds of degrees just like the degrees children go through when they develop.

As we start connecting all the pieces back together, we start to understand the whole system of bestowal that we exist in. This is precisely what we are engaging in now.

All of the above mentioned four degrees of nature depend on this same mutual guarantee. Everything obeys fixed laws. This is how it is possible to measure the movement of a celestial object that is millions of light years away. Everything in reality follows rules and each part is connected to all of the other parts. All of the laws in physics, the way that electrons spin in the atom and how they build matter, all of these are laws of cause and consequence that keep the law of mutual guarantee. It is the essence of reality. As much as we keep it we will discover our own connection with the integral force of nature that enlivens us.

When we don't learn these laws, nature pressures us through all kinds of problems. Each disturbance is an opportunity to see where we need to work. In the place where we feel ourselves, there we need to feel all of our friends. From this new mind, the 5 parts of the mouth, the sounds we make, how we communicate knowledge, how we communicate intentions to each other. We convey a new reality to each other. That is why we are called the speaking degree.
By these actions we pacify the lower three degrees of animate, vegetative and inanimate. Everything returns to harmony.

In Chapter 5 we learned about the law of bestowal that operates on us from above. Our work is how to implement it, to understand why that primordial shattering happened, and then our conscious unification of the broken parts. In the process of calibrating ourselves to the force of bestowal, what we attain is the singular force, the unified law of all nature. We become adhered to it. There isn't a more important action in life. As we establish this form in our feelings life reveals a new color.

The diseases emerging from deep within the deforested forests and the viruses emerging from the melting ice where they were trapped for 10,000 years, they are trying to awaken us to this mutual guarantee. If we discover any malfunction in life, we correct it by increasing the mutual guarantee between us.

We are not starting this work with people who don't relate to it at all. Humanity is like a family. In a family the parents do everything for the sake of the children. We have a duty to start this work first by connecting with people who are close to us, who share the same goal and then with that great power and confidence we will advance the whole world to a state of love.

The purpose of Creation lies on the shoulders of the whole human race, black, yellow, red and white without any essential difference.

The world is judged by the majority.
On one hand of the scale are all of the benefits of loving others and on the other hand of the scale is all of the filthy mess of egoistic self love.

Eyes

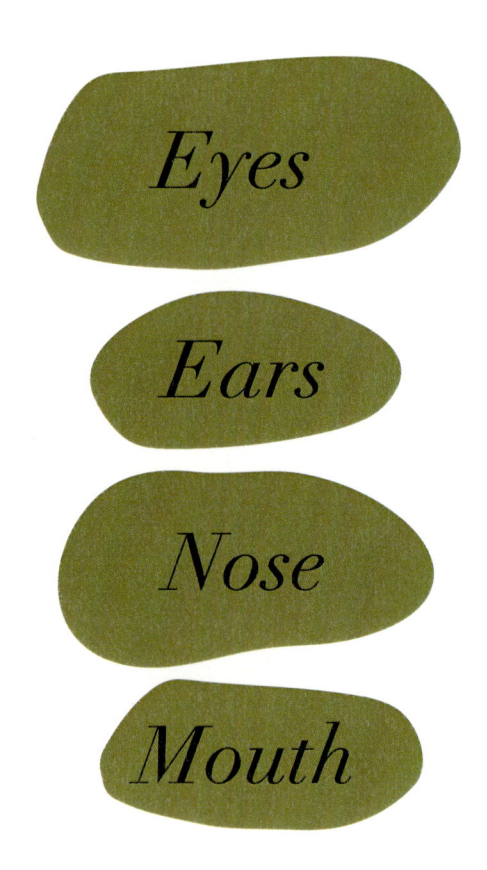

Ears

Nose

Mouth

Chapter 7
The Teaching of the Wisdom

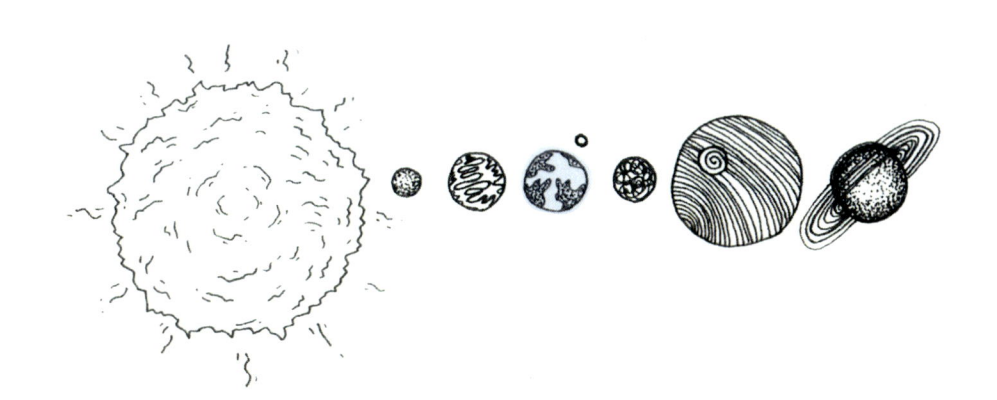

There are an estimated
1,000,000,000,000,000 ants
There are an estimated
3,500,000,000,000 fish
There are an estimated
400,000,000,000 birds

There are an estimated
8,000,000,000
unique speaking creatures

They have a special quality which makes them unique from all of the others. They are capable of feeling their own existence.

From feeling their own emotional existence they can learn how to discover the emotional existence of others.
And here is the true wonder. By accustoming ourselves to know and feel the desires of other people, we develop ourselves to be able to feel the forces in nature as if they are human sensations.
We will be able to relate to the laws of nature as if we are face to face with them. We will be able to converse with all of reality as if we were face to face with our beloved.

There are two special conducts in nature.

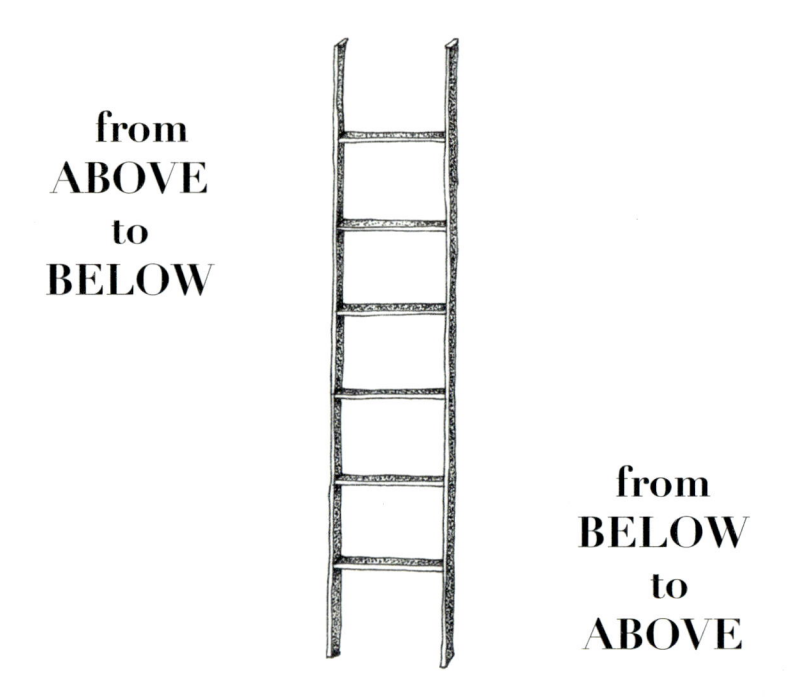

from ABOVE to BELOW

from BELOW to ABOVE

The degrees on the ladder are exactly the same in both directions. The higher we go, the more fine and pure and the lower we go the more coarse and physical. We learned this in Chapter 2, here we will open it up some more.

from ABOVE to BELOW

A desire arises in a person for something. Could be for anything. Let's say a person has a desire to have a house.

He begins to think, how will I feel there, what will it look like?

If he really wants it he will draw some plans or hire an architect and engineer to plan it out.

Next a person needs to collect building materials and tools.

Finally after all of that you can build a house. The process goes from light to heavy, from fine to coarse.

We started with a desire for a house that arises out of the air and we end with a house of wood and stone on the earth.

Our whole modern world is that built house.

Everything is already prepared.

from BELOW to ABOVE

Down here in the physical world we are in a universe that appears as it is expanding.
Let's imagine that we could rewind the movie, go backwards in time. So instead of the universe expanding and unfolding into the future, picture it going backwards. Imagine that everything is contracting back to the middle point. Go back before humans, before animals, before plants, before water, before Earth and the sun and the Milky Way galaxy and the universe. Go back before the Big Bang, before anything emanated from that tiny point. There was not even an empty space. Everything was one simple unity, even and equal.

And from the middle of that simple unity a thought arose to create a creature that could feel this eternal perfection, filling everything in every direction.

As soon as that thought arose, a black point appeared from out of nowhere in the middle of this endless light.

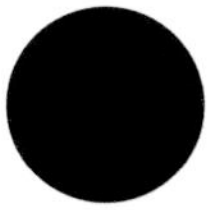

And it started to absorb the light.

As the light entered the black point it started to influence it, to make an impression inside of it.

The infinite light (0) cascaded down inside of this black dot and developed it through four distinct phases (1,2,3,4).

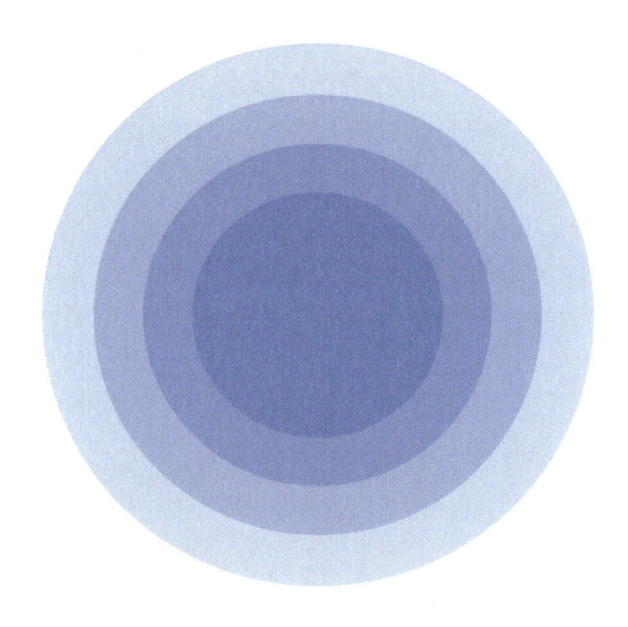

Before I was satisfied in this world. But then suddenly I felt that something was missing in my life, and I began to search for a place where I would feel better. What pushed me?

There is a tension that emerged, a delta between me and what is outside of me. I don't feel satisfied, I don't feel balanced.

The sensation of the surrounding light begins to influence and move me. Previously I was calmer but the surrounding light keeps pressuring me and I began to feel that the state I'm in is not good. I became increasingly sensitive to the light and it causes me to feel bad again! And again I began to search.

I began to move and transition into my next state. I began to look for answers. I tried in different places. I didn't succeed. And it formed in me a more accurate need. I grow this way, sorting everything in my mind and then I forget everything again and all that remains is a desire. I need to attain the truth of reality. I arrived at the center of the circle.

Thus I am pushed by the light every time. In essence, it's the light working on my desire, until I reach the very center.

THIS BLACK POINT
IS CALLED DESIRE.

IT IS CREATION.

It is everything that exploded from that big
bang. It is not considered good or bad. It is
no more and no less than a point that absorbs
light and develops by that absorption.

So what am I to do?

Now begins an order of work for humanity called **from BELOW UPWARDS**. These are like rungs of a ladder by which humanity can develop and climb up.

0
1
2
3
4
Inanimate
Vegetative
Animate
Speaking

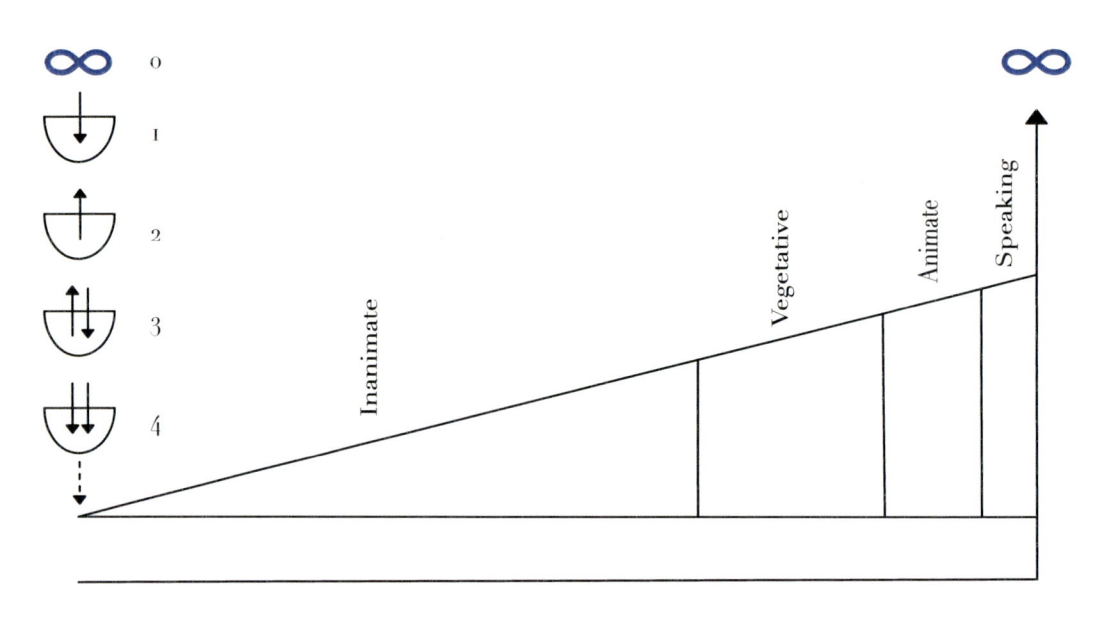

CLIMBING THE LADDER

As we climb this ladder, we move from matter, this house in which we live, this world in which we live and we rise degree by degree to the thought that came before material matter. As we climb up the ladder, as we approach the initial thought, our inner perception is illuminated. Our bodies remain on Earth and in new sensations we begin to traverse these degrees. Instead of the thought descending down and materializing into the material that is the house, we instead prepare a vessel in our inner sensations to feel the thought. We make inner disernments and measurements, relationships and connections, we unite opposites and we build a suitable vessel for the light to shine in.

Through this we reach a state where we begin to feel ourselves above time and space, exiting our egoistic nature, which all in all is the matter of creation.

Bones

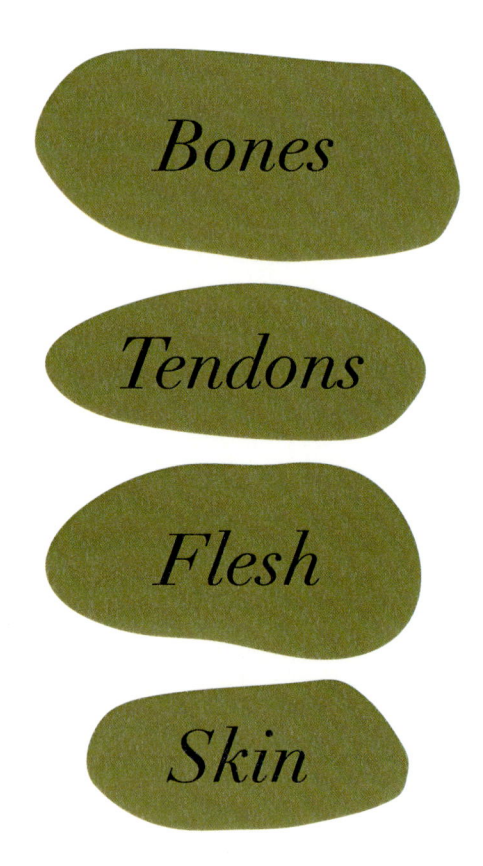

Tendons

Flesh

Skin

Chapter 8
Peace in the World

There are some people that see life as a broken machine that needs fixing.

Overthrow the elite! Save the environment!

Cleanse humanity of what is "bad" and only allow the good and useful to remain.

We must understand and be very careful when casting a flaw on anything. Did nature develop something for billions of years in order to be worthless?!

Here we can understand why everything must be evaluated according to where it is along the process of development.

IN REALITY, GOOD AND BAD, AND EVEN THE MOST HARMFUL IN THE WORLD, HAS A RIGHT TO EXIST.

For this reason, when a fruit tastes bitter at the beginning of its growth, it is not considered a flaw in the fruit. We all know that an unripe fruit has not yet completed its development. When something (or someone) appears as bad and harmful to us, we must also understand that it is still turning through time, counting the degrees that it must traverse until it completes its ripening. At that time the bad attributes turn to good like the fruit on the tree that counts the days until its sweetness will become evident to everyone.

THE WEAKNESS OF "WORLD REFORMERS"

Looking at nature's track record we can see clearly that nature doesn't want only what we call the "good and useful." World reformers want evil to disappear. They want to replace the damaged parts of the machine with good ones. Nature doesn't want this.
The "evil" force advances us. We need to take the evil forces of nature and build an opposite system that would compensate for it. And then through creating our own system of good that compensates for the evil, rise from both of these steps, like on the rungs of a ladder.

Nature builds the world from this evil force.
We on the other hand see it, get horrified and start fighting the evil. We must learn to compensate for it correctly, to use it as negative and then compensate with the positive charge as in electricity.
The evil exists.
And I must create a mountain of good to offset it.

FREEING OURSELVES FROM THE BOUNDARIES OF TIME

The law of ripening (of fruit, of a human, etc.) happens without asking our permission. One must go through many degrees which come heavily, slowly and stretch over a very long time before one reaches the end. And because we are sensing, living beings, we suffer great agony and pains in those states of development in order to develop up from a lower degree of an animal to a higher degree of a human. A pushing force of pain and torments accumulates until we can no longer tolerate it and then we advance.
We, however, are a special group of great apes.
Nature has handed us the ability to hasten the process, to be free and independent of the boundaries of time.
To understand this very simple concept we need to understand the two ways we can develop.
The first is our natural development through time which seems to be floundering along, ruthlessly carving its way through space.
In the second, we take the law of development upon ourselves. We greatly accelerate time freeing ourselves from its chains entirely and bringing ourselves to the completion of our ripeness. Thus we can set our hearts and minds to correct all of the bad attributes and turn them to good by our own will and thus hasten our development.

We learned in Chapter 4 that nature is a bestowing force. Opposite from that is our nature which is a will to receive that bestowing force. Our receiving nature makes us opposite from that eternal bestowing nature which is the source of life.

HOW DO WE EVALUATE GOOD AND BAD?

Before we examine the evil in the human species which needs correcting, we have to define what is "good" and what is "bad". Each and every person in society is like a wheel that is linked to several other wheels, inside of a machine. The single wheel has no freedom of movement. It always turns with the motion of the other wheels.

And if there is a breakdown in a wheel, the problem is evaluated according to how it affects the whole machine.
A person is considered good according to his service to the public good.
And a person is considered bad according to the harm he inflicts on the public.

*Everyone needs to understand
that his own benefit
and the benefit of society
are one and the same thing.*

The world is standing on four pillars
MERCY, TRUTH, JUSTICE, AND PEACE

Once we understand the desired attribute of goodness we should examine what we have to use to hasten that delight and happiness. With the inanimate, vegetative and animate degrees of nature there is no confusion about what is good or what is bad. For them everything is instinct, everything is clear, there are no questions. But we speaking creatures have constant doubts, uncertainty and blurriness. We're operated by forces which are unclear to us, we are always in confusion. We do everything to make life more comfortable according to our desires. We bring water where there is no water, we bring heat when it is cold outside. In this we have some qualitative advantage over the rest of nature. And from this we multiplied greatly.

We began to make connections between families and then between towns and states and then countries. Animals don't have such a thing.

In the last 100 years we have grown from 2 billion to 8 billion. There is no other species that does this. They build a place to hide some nuts, but not like people. They don't build power plants, fuel stations, they use the forces that they receive from nature and that is it. They don't improve on these forces and build with them a better and better world.

Animals live by instinct. Humans no. For this reason, throughout the generations human development has gradually advanced with four properties: **truth, mercy, justice, and peace** until they brought humankind to its current state. We want to take the law of development into our own hands and exit the torments that developmental history has in store for us, so let's study what these four gave us and what we should hope to get from them in the future.

TRUTH

Certainly there is nothing better than truth. However the majority in society does not accept the truth. First of all man feels that the world exists to serve him. This is what nature gives a person. It is a law of nature called ego that tells a person, you are special and you are allowed to take advantage of reality as much as you see fit. That's the truth.

Can you imagine if we lived like ants where everyone works all day for the sake of the society, with all of our might for the others. Man was created in the opposite way.

How can we organize our lives in such a way that we will not devour each other? Would we evaluate everyone equally, like ants, no one would look at how much anyone else works or doesn't work? Would we compel everyone to work equal hours and be compensated only according to his work?

But what if you are smarter than me so it's easier for you to do some job.

What if I'm stronger than you and it is easier for me to do some other job.

No one is the same, so we can't demand from everyone the same productivity.

From the outset we are different. In truth, each and every person feels that everyone else was created only to serve him, without him feeling any obligation to give anything in return. In short, the nature of each person is to exploit the lives of the others for his own benefit. He only gives to others out of necessity (although it is done cunningly so that the other will not notice). This is the absolute truth, the natural reality and it has a right to exist and there is no hope to eradicate it from the world. You can't rule the world with truth because one's truth is opposite to the truth of the others. The strongest, smartest, most nimble succeed and take advantage of the others.

TRUTH DIDN'T WORK TO ESTABLISH SOCIETY SO THEY TRIED TO ESTABLISH SOCIETY BASED ON MERCY, JUSTICE, & PEACE

No one wants to concede his view. Therefore humanity quietly leaves the truth aside, and let's behave as gentlemen, so we won't kill one another. With the animals, the sick and the weak would be eaten or starve. Humans on the other hand want to complement what nature didn't do in a good way. We see that the world is corrupted and we want to fix it. So we started to use mercy and justice. With these qualities, the world began its slow and clumsy climb towards organizing the lives of the collective. Systems developed to help the hungry, the sick, young couples, single mothers, the elderly. Under these conditions the weak and exploited increased in the world and they start quarrels and fights.

Those conditions brought society such strife that the "peacemakers" appeared. This is what caused division in society. Some adopted the attributes of mercy, they are the constructors, giving their possessions to others for the benefit of the collective. And some adopted the attribute of truth, meaning "what's mine is mine and what's yours is yours". By nature they are destructors.

HOPES FOR PEACE

The peacemakers are the powerful and courageous ones in society. They are seekers of truth. They assume control and renew social life based on conditions that they consider true. They defend their opinions firmly to the point of risking their lives and the lives of the people in society for their cause. This gives them power to prevail over those who seek mercy and charity, who are willing to give up their own good for the good of others. It turns out that seeking truth and the destruction of the world are one and the same. Therefore, we should not hope from the destructors to establish peace.

The proper conditions for peace for the individual and for the whole of humanity have not been established yet. As long as there is a minority in society who is unsatisfied with the conditions offered to them, there will always remain ready and willing fuel for a new quarrel and the new peacemakers that always follow. Thus we see how the hope for peace, which our generation so yearns for, is futile.

THE WELL-BEING OF A CERTAIN COLLECTIVE AND THE WELL-BEING OF THE WHOLE WORLD

Do not be surprised if I mix together the well-being of a part of society with the well-being of the whole world, because indeed, we have already come to such a degree that the whole world is considered as one collective society. Because each person in the world draws his life's marrow and his livelihood from all the people in the world, he is coerced to serve and care for the well-being of the whole world.

We have seen that the subordination of the individual to the collective is like a small wheel in a machine. In historic times that machine was small, one's family. A person was supported by his family and he worked for them.
In later times, families gathered into towns and counties.
Later towns and counties joined into states.
Until the individual was supported by all of his countrymen.

Therefore today, in our generation, when each person is aided for his happiness by the entire global village, it is necessary that to that extent, the individual becomes integrated into the whole world, like a wheel in a big machine.

In our time we must deal with just conducts that guarantee the well-being of the whole world because the benefit or harm of each and every person in the world depends and is measured according to the benefit of all the people in the world.
In our time nations are connected in the same way families used to be connected. That's why we can't worry about just one country. Although we know this and understand that our lives depend on the well-being of the whole world still it is not yet grasped properly. Why? Such is the conduct of development in nature, as we see with children. The act comes before the understanding.

IN PRACTICAL LIFE, THE FOUR ATTRIBUTES CONTRADICT ONE ANOTHER

If all of the above difficulties are not enough, we have a further mixup here. The four attributes contradict each other. The psychological makeup of each of us is unique and contradictory. Mercy, justice, truth and peace which come to us from our parents or by the environment contradict one another. The attribute of mercy for example contradicts all other attributes. What is the attribute of mercy? "What's mine is yours and what's yours is yours". And if all the people in the world were to behave by this quality, it would cancel all the glory of the attribute of truth, because if each and every one were naturally willing to give everything he had to others, and take nothing from another, then there would be nothing to gain from lying to one another. If there were no falsehood in the world, there would be no concept of truth.

Peace and justice contradict each other. If we divide all property justly, meaning give to the negligent and naive a substantial portion of the property of the nimble and the energetic, then these powerful and initiating people will certainly not rest until they overthrow the government that enslaves them and exploits them in favor of the weak. Therefore there is no hope for peace in society. Justice contradicts peace.

Etc., etc. all of the attributes contradict one another.

THE ATTRIBUTE OF SINGULARITY IN OUR EGOISM AFFECTS RUIN AND DESTRUCTION

Thus you see how our attributes collide and fight one another; and not only between parts of society, but within each person. The four attributes dominate us and fight within us until it is impossible for common sense to organize them. This is the reason why we cannot organize these things correctly. Our root is singular.

The still, vegetative and animate develop according to instinct. They don't reflect on their past like we do, they don't feel that they are special and can take advantage of reality as much as they can. A person unconsciously feels the singular source that is his root and he feels in his heart that he is unique and special. A person can feel brave if he comes from a lineage of warriors. Or a person can feel intelligent if he comes from a wise family. But here all of us extend from the same root if we go back to the start. Therefore we all feel that we are the most important. We want to be the wealthiest. We want to be the most famous. We want everything. We are all equal in that. Each one is ready to swallow the whole world for his own pleasure.

USING OUR NATURE OF SINGULARITY AS A SUBJECT OF OUR EVOLUTION

Now we shall understand the conditions that humanity will finally accept at the time of the appearance of world peace.

Q: How can it be that from the source of life from which every construction extends there can come something so corrupt that it brings all of the harm and ruin in the world? If nature is good, how can so much bad come from it? We can't leave this question unanswered.

A: It is because we use that special tool, our singularity in the opposite direction. From nature the singularity is a bestowing force, giving to all endlessly. From our side, the singularity is in a form of reception, to receive endlessly.

There are already people among us who use their singularity in forms of bestowal upon others. But they are still few. We are still in the midst of our path of development. When we come to the end of these degrees, we will all use our singularity only in a form of bestowal upon others and no one will use it in a form of self-reception.

We need to see role models of this to give us confidence amidst the waves of life. We need to see examples of bestowal upon others and not reception for oneself.

THE CONDITION OF LIFE IN THE LAST GENERATION

First, everyone must thoroughly understand and explain to his surroundings that the well-being of society, which is the well-being of the state and the well-being of the world, are completely interdependent. As long as the laws of society are not satisfactory to everyone, and leave a minority unsatisfied with the government, this minority will conspire and seek to overthrow the state.

And if its power is not enough to go head to head with the government, it will incite other countries to join. War is big business. At any given moment there are a vast amount of people who crave war and bloodshed.

Even the wealthy part of the society who lives well and is satisfied still has a lot to be concerned about for the safety of their lives. There are those that strive to overthrow them. If they understood the value of peace, they would be happy to adopt the conduct of life in the last generation.

We are in transition where if we don't accept the conditions of the last generation, we are facing war.

PAIN vs PLEASURE IN SELF-RECEPTION

I know this whole plan sounds imaginary and unrealistic.

But here's the thing, if we were to collect all the pleasures that we feel during our lives and put them all on one side of the scale, and collect all the pain and sorrow we feel and put it on the other side of the scale, it's clear the suffering would more than double the pleasure.

If we could see this, we would prefer not to have been born at all.

All we want is pleasure.

The whole reason why we **receive for ourselves** is because we desire pleasure. Food, sex, money, honor, power, it doesn't matter what flavor. All we want is pleasure. The difficulty is nothing but a psychological matter. To change our nature from enjoying when we **receive for ourselves,** to enjoying when **we bestow upon others.** We can live in a world where we feel that everything we give comes back to me. Everything belongs to me so I enjoy working.

Soon most of the labor jobs will be automated. Humanity will be free to engage in caring for each other. Humanity produces much more of everything than we need. There is abundance for everyone. Thus, if the direction were to change from self-reception to bestowal upon others, the individual will enjoy everything.

Mercy

Truth

Justice

Peace

Chapter 9
The Last Generation

A beast sees only from himself onwards with no intellect and no wisdom. A human can look into the past, like looking in a mirror and by that correct his future direction.

THE BASIS OF THIS WHOLE COMMENTARY IS THE WILL TO RECEIVE PLEASURE THAT IS IMPRINTED IN EVERY CREATURE.

The *will to receive* developed over billions of years from primordial stardust. It developed into more and more complex creatures until the proteins organized themselves into a human creature with a button that can detonate nuclear bombs and destroy the Earth.
And it is possible that wars will break out and the bombs will do their thing.
The relics that remain in that wasteland will finally agree that it is better for everyone to work for their own needs only as much as necessary and with all of their remaining forces, to work for the good of others.
And then then there will be no more wars.

There are two attributes in humanity:

1. **Egoist.** Egoist does not refer to caring for one's needs. All animals must take care of their needs. Our original animal nature is not considered "ego" and is not praised or condemned. The ego we are talking about is the ego that compels a person to hate and exploit others in order to make his own existence easier. All that he does, he does for himself. And if he ever does something for another, he must have a reward in return for his work.

2. **Altruist.** In the meantime altruist refers to those that are born with a tendency to want to give their lives for an "ideal", they want to fight for the benefit of others without any reward. The altruist's reward is when it is good for the other. There is always only a small minority in society with this 'altruist' nature. They've always been unsuccessful, they are too few and unable to endure. Even if they are successful to establish something, by the second generation it would be filled with egoists again.

We understand that life would be the best if everyone had what they need and everyone was happy and there were no wars. But how can we take billions of people who all feel unique and who want everyone else to serve them and build a system where everyone will be satisfied and happy without oppressing one another?

COMMUNISM

Communism starts with an altruistic ideal. The first communists before Karl Marx were unable to endure. When communism was able to spread successfully, it did so in an egoistic form. In order to get his ideal to take hold, the idealist incites and incorporates the poor & oppressed. He gets them to join with him for egoistic reasons (food, shelter, healthcare, money). Thus, communism spreads. The idealist with his poor & oppressed masses are powerful enough to overthrow the ruling government (which hates them both), but they can't sustain a cooperative government between them. Communism built on waves of hatred and envy only succeeds in overthrowing the ruling class, but not in benefiting the poor & oppressed. On the contrary, once the rulers are gone, the same idealists will turn the arrows of hatred against the workers.

Trying to implement communism prior to there being a group of altruists will lead to an absolute dictatorship. If communism is implemented before the public is ready for it, meaning before each one has proper fuel to work for the sake of the whole, then it only causes ruin.

Question: Why does communism fail?

Answer: In a communistic regime the worker is not rewarded for his diligence nor punished for his negligence. The worker knows that he will not be given more if he works more, or less if he works less. He doesn't have fuel to motivate himself. Labor productivity drops to zero. **No schooling in the world will help a human to work without fuel, without a reward.** Therefore, a communistic society must compel the workers to complete their share of the work through punishments. A government like this is worse than a capitalistic government.

We mustn't hope for any good future from the communists. Quite the contrary, we must fear the communists who lead according to their egoistic spirit and have no inhibitions about exploiting others to benefit themselves. They lie and depict a heaven on earth, and the plight of the public stays buried.

In a communist regime, the workers are defenseless and don't have the right to strike. The executives don't want them to discover the oppression they are under. They censor the media and public opinion and the masses can't uncover the evil deeds of the rulers. Universities will not let anyone speak who criticizes the ruling class. The government has full control and there will be no one to check them.

In a communist society supervisors watch over the workers to make sure everyone abides by the rules. The supervisors need to be paid more than the simple workers otherwise they would neglect their office and the state would be ruined. They therefore accumulate extra money. They will be able to save and invest. It seems that the supervisors in the communist regime should be considered as respectable capitalists. Thus, within a few decades, the government workers become millionaires strictly through exploiting the workers.

CAPITALISM

In the capitalist regime, free competition is the primary fuel for success. The diligent play and the winners are very happy. The losers suffer a bitter end on the street. In between is the working class, having no share in this game. Neither rising nor falling.

LEFT & RIGHT

On the Right: A capitalist regime is divided into two classes.
    1. The employers & leaders which are the minority.
    2. The workers & dependants which are the majority.

On the Left: A communist regime is divided into two classes.
    1. The supervisors & intellectuals which are the minority.
    2. The workers & the dependants which are the majority.

Ultimately, in both the communist and capitalist nations, the majority are unable to lead. Rather, they elect leaders from among the diligent with the hope that those they elect will not exploit them too much.

DEMOCRACY

In democracies various tactics are used to deceive the constituency. What happened to the Germans is one of nature's wonders. Hitler was elected by the vote of the majority. Along with the Volkswagen (people's car) and the Volkskühlschrank (people's refrigerator) the Third Reich subsidized the Volksempfänger (people's radio), one that every worker could afford, and with it, broadcasted daily sermons into every home. Think about it. They were the most civilized, well-mannered nation, and overnight they became savages, worse than even the most primitive nations in history. Several hundred years of education vanished like a bubble that pops and it's gone. When public opinion changed, education had nothing to rely on.

Even in the most civilized nation, the majority of the public is guided by their egos without any opinions of their own. They are promised this and that by politicians, they are guided this way and that way by the media and they go whichever way will give them more self-benefit.

It is possible that there can be good leadership. However, should some evil person come who is capable of uncovering the deceit that lives inside of people, and if he can use celebrities and create candidates that can be elected, then they can overthrow the fraudulent and elect the evil.

The world mistakenly thinks Nazism is an offshoot of Germany. In truth, Nazism is the offshoot of democracy and socialism that are left without manners, religion and justice.

Thus, all nations are equal in that and there is no hope at all that Nazism won't be adopted again by an advanced, civilized nation. Hitler was indeed elected democratically, and the majority of the public united behind him. Afterward, he uprooted all the idealists and did with nations as he wished. As the people wished.

Since the dawn of time, it has never happened that the majority of the public governed a state. The simple folk ruled only in the days of Hitler. He elevated public benefit to the level of devotion. He understood the beast that lives inside of a person and gave it the ability to unleash itself. For this they were willing to pay with their lives.

WHAT CAN WE LEARN FROM MARX, LENIN & STALIN

They must have been so happy when they thought that they could implement communism in Russia. It is such a big country, full of natural resources. In just a few years everyone could live comfortably and a government of justice and happiness would appear in the world. The capitalist governments would wither and quickly follow their example. But just the opposite happened! Not only was the ruling class not removed, it grew twice as big as it was before.

Marx was the first one to place the correction of the world on the working class. A very unique idea. (His theory took two forces into consideration, abusers and abused.) Rulership should come from the bottom up, not from the top down as it had been through history. It didn't occur to him to do it coercively, but rather democratically. The workers would have to be the majority, and then establish a government and its leaders would implement the motto, "everyone will work according to his strength and receive according to his needs."

Lenin added to it by forcing this minority opinion over the majority. His hope was that once the majority adopted it, then later they would conduct themselves altruistically. He needed an armed group of workers. So, just turn the soldiers into communists, destroy the property owners and take what is theirs.

However when he saw that it was not enough to destroy the property owners, but that millions of farmers must also be destroyed, he grew tired.
It is hard work to destroy half a nation.
Then came **Stalin**, who said that the end justifies the means.
He took upon himself the task of destroying the farmers, too.
He was successful.
None of them considered that human nature cannot be changed.
It is impossible that a person would work for another's needs without coercion.
To install altruism, you need the good will of the public.
And, even if you have the good will of the public, there is no certainty that the next generation will carry the flame.

What can guarantee that the flame will be passed from generation to generation?

...I'm hesitant to even write this word because the word has too many preconceived notions surrounding it and we probably need to find a new, better word, but in the meantime...
RELIGION. RELIGION can guarantee carrying the flame over to future generations.
The true RELIGION is the RELIGION of love. The most important thing that we need is to bring the world to good connections. The form of the RELIGION of love should first and foremost educate its members to bestow upon each other, to care about the good of the public as one cares for his own well-being.

Each religion of the world can stay with its customs and traditions. If you want to bow down before this thing or that, it does not
interfere with the RELIGION of love.

> You can go to the mosque on Friday.
> You can go to synagogue on Saturday.
> You can go to church on Sunday.
> You can practice one of the many African religions.

Leave the "uniqueness" of each nation in tact. Give full and complete confidence to each and every nation that their spiritual assets will be kept in full.
It does not matter as long as we are working on our good connections.

IDEALISM AND RELIGION

     The majority wants to work less than others and receive more than others, so they cannot yet realize love of others.   For this reason, the RELIGION of love helps inspire a person, guide a person, remind a person. Just as actors play with our imagination and can open our hearts and make us believe. They teach us about ourselves through their examples. Likewise, we expect the interpreters of the RELIGION OF LOVE to show us examples, to impress us and touch our hearts.
 The ideal of love of others has to ripen for at least three whole generations (grandparents, parents, kids) until love is taught and lived in the home and in society. The world will endure many more cycles before it comes to fruition, but there is no easier way to ripen than through RELIGION.

THE RELIGION OF LOVE FOR THE WORLD

One should work as much as one can for the well-being of the others until there is no one in the world who lacks his or her material needs. Everyone is committed to raising the standard of living ever higher so that all the people in the world will enjoy their lives and will feel more and more happiness. Our planet is rich enough for all of us so why are we fighting wars for generations. Let us share the labor and the produce and an end to all the troubles.

Tokens of due honors should be imparted upon those who contribute to society. The more one contributes, the higher the decoration one shall receive. And you will have to go out to the street for everyone to see such a medal on you. Why? Because by that you awaken envy in others to also be great like you and to bestow upon society. You don't do it to be proud. You walk down the street and everyone is pointing to you, saying this is not just any friend, this is a very special friend. They will say that you are so natural, you are so humble. You understand everyone and care about everyone. And you will have to suffer it because by this you give a good example to the others. Envy, lust and honor will help raise us to greater and greater degrees of bestowal.

What pleasure do b/millionaires have from their wealth? That they can buy protection for themselves and their family. In this new society they will have that and more. And if we say that their pleasure comes from the respect and honor they receive, don't worry, the gates of competition will never be locked. We must remember that the will to receive pleasure in us does not disappear. When we see that the people who contribute the most to society are the most honored and respected, then this will give us forces to also contribute.

The freedom of the individual must be kept as long as it is not harmful to society. And one who wishes to leave the society must not be detained in any way.

It is absolutely forbidden for any one from this altruistic government to turn to any of the remaining brute-force regimes or outside judicial establishments. All conflicts are to be resolved among the altruists. Judgments relying on force will be completely revoked. If there is one who makes trouble, he mustn't be brought to court forcefully. He must be reformed through explanations and clever arguments. If all of the counsels are to no avail, the public will turn away from him and disregard him. We are social creatures and we want to be accepted, we want to be appreciated and admired. So when a person exploits others, he will be treated like an outcast that no one wants to be around. Everyone will look down on this person as someone who is causing ruin. Public opinion shall condemn anyone who exploits the righteousness of his friend for his own benefit. There will still be courthouses, but they will only serve to sort out doubts, and they will not rely on any force. One who rejects the court's decision will be condemned by public opinion, and that is all.

Each nation, whose majority has been educated to bestow upon one another, will enter into an international altruistic framework. The surplus of a rich or diligent nation will improve the standard of living of a poor or needy nation, in materials and in means of production.

TO START THERE MUST BE A NATION OF ALTRUISTS

Until the public feels the value in world peace, it remains like unripe fruit. It is too early to try to reach this goal. It's a gradual process. Nevertheless this feeling of friendship and harmony must encircle the entire world. To start, there must be a nation of altruists. It will give an example to all nations on Earth. It will have all of the forms of government and infrastructure. Everyone will have food and a home, healthcare and education. Each and everyone will have what they need to live a healthy life. A person who hoards for himself will be thought of as some kind of thief.

     Neighbors will have a good influence on each other. In the media and in the mouths of the people will be praise upon those who are good to each other and condemnation of the egoists who exploit the righteousness of his friend.

LEADERS OF THE GENERATION

The public wants to believe that the leader has no personal commitments and interests, but that he has dedicated his private life for the common good. Indeed, this is how it should be. If the leader harms the public due to personal interest, he is a traitor and a liar. Once the public learns of it, they will immediately throw him out.

REBUILDING THE WORLD

Throughout history, the assertive, powerful ones evolved human society and the masses have followed like a herd. Then at the end of a long chain of different forms of governments came something for those masses. Democracy and socialism. When the masses finally open their eyes and take their fate into their own hands, they conclude that religion, manners, government, and justice serve the ruling class and harms all the others. They throw off the structures of those powerful and assertive people.

Thus, the majority has to build the world anew. However they don't have the ancestral inheritance of the assertive, powerful ones. In other words, they are like prehistoric people living in the modern world. They are virgin soil.

Everyone builds himself on the ruin of others. The more a person destroys, the more he becomes famous and praised. We don't even think of building anything new until we find a weakness to exploit in someone else. In Chapter 2 we learned about the struggle between the - & + forces that ruled the Earth with terrible destruction before the land took its place over the water. We shouldn't envy anyone who would live during that fiery hell. Rather it is much better to come into the world after the struggling materials make peace.

We are now at a crossroads and we can plunge into terrible wars between the left (-) & the right (+) in our home, in our town, in our nation and in our world. But now we can see that the land before us is vast. There is room for all views. There is no such thing as an "evil view", only an unripe view.

We need to build this new worldview in a way that it doesn't hurt other methods. Keep a normal life and maintain the freedom of the individual. In the end, we are merely building an economic structure.

We need not wait until all of the wrongs in society have been made right before we begin. As long as one feels satisfied, our body does not let us search. So don't be frightened by the feelings of dissatisfaction. This is our perception growing. Our field of awareness was 1 acre, now it is growing for example to 10 acres. We receive a new portion, but it appears to us unilluminated. It is dark and that does not feel comfortable. We have enough experience to know that it is suffering that causes us to search. Look at the changes that are happening today. People are losing their patience on the one side and bowing their head and asking what to do on the other side.

Bit by bit this is the work that nature is doing on our egos, and it is happening very fast. We thought, how will it be possible that nations can come together around a single goal. Look at what is unifying us! All of a sudden the entire world has the same problem and everyone starts speaking the same language. And this is how we will advance.

The world leaders having been sitting on wondrous stockpiles of weapons with the fear of certain ruin. They had no hope to be rid of these problems. The hungry multitudes are accumulating in terrible masses each day. The working class has almost completed its ripeness. Before the day of struggle comes, there is time for the mind to protect us from a complete ruin.

The Middle Line

Marx and everyone else only take two forces into account, the abusers and the abused. Everyone thinks they are correct and the other side is wrong.

Nature is especially showing us in a way that we can understand that only in the middle can the world come to connection. How can we reach the middle line? Imagine if there were a president that everyone loved. America is truly half and half. What kind of president can there be who is president of half the people? Today it's America, soon the same in France, in Germany, in all the nations where there are populations with different views, colors, the same will happen. This polarity between the left and right will rise even more. They will become even more opposite from the other. And through recognizing how opposite we are and how much we need this middle to come and help us, by that these forces of nature will explain to both sides in a soft language, how wrong they are and how each needs to rise above itself and reach connection. This middle force that comes from nature, it is not godliness or something up there, it is a force like the left and right are forces.

Humanity in our times is being educated by media that separates and incites us. We'll never achieve any good situation as long as they exist. Maybe the world will enter some kind of freeze. Unable to move forward, a new need will form in the people for connection.

The world will hear that there must be a middle line, and only in connection above our differences can humanity be saved. Love covers all crimes. We need to think about how to use all of the contradictions properly. We need to think about how to love.

This requires study, you need to educate humanity. Imagine the right all over the world and the left all over the world both being truly joyous.

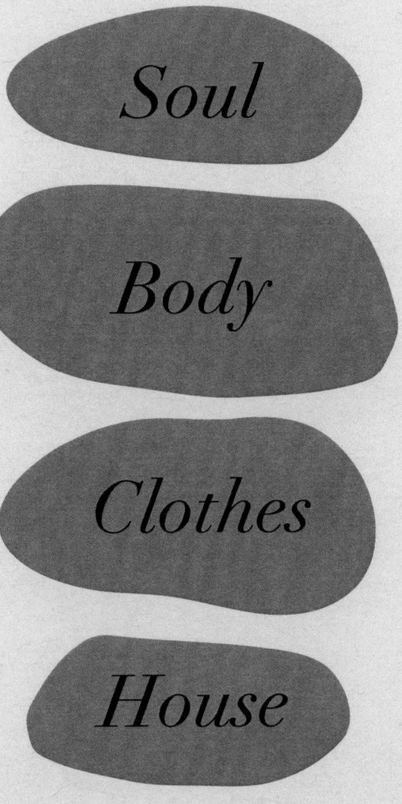
Soul
Body
Clothes
House

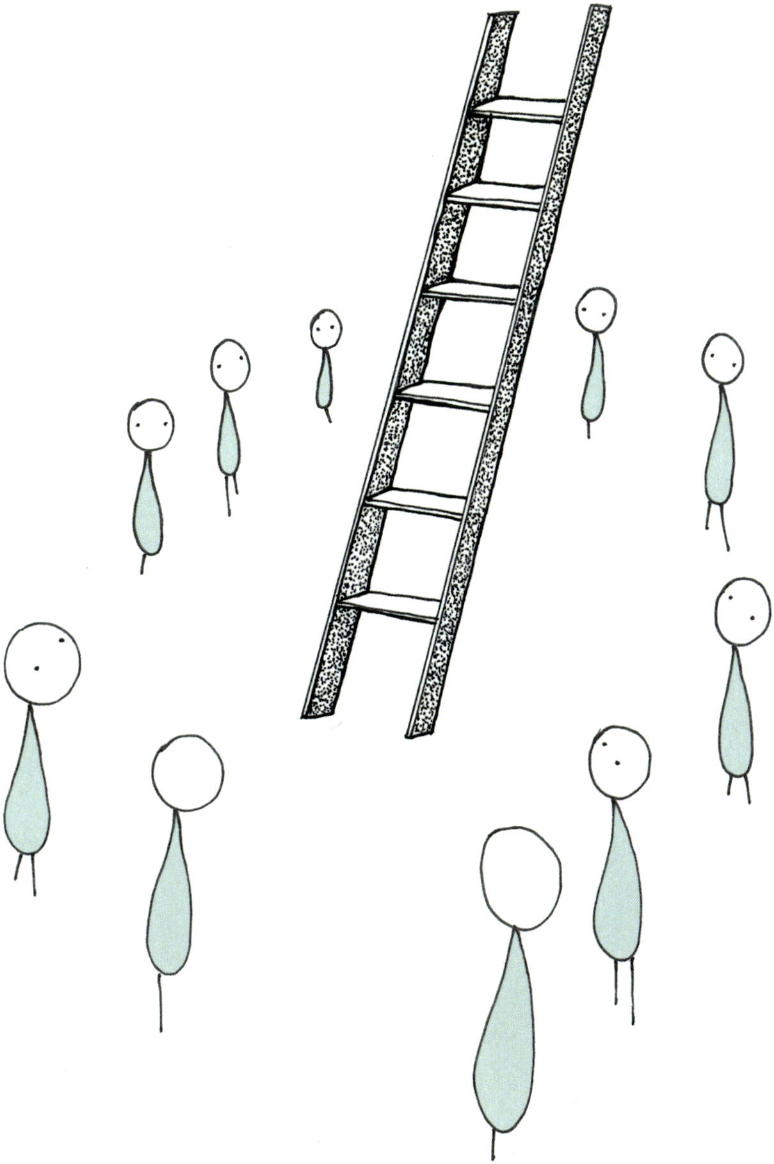

It's normal that we cry out.
We need a solution and we don't have one.
Say "now," not "later".
There is no cure for this distress, but only for those who need love and cannot go on without it, then strain to understand.

Exert in love of friends.

There is a great power hidden in it.
There are many sparks in each friend and when you collect all the sparks into one place, as brothers with love and friendship………….

*to express this in words,
we would need
1000s of books and it
wouldn't be any use.*

Each friend is not presenting himself to you, but through him you discover yourself.

Each flaw that I see in the other, I determine that it is a flaw in my perception.

It is known in psychology that what you value determines what you aim at
which determines what you perceive.

It means that now we are together and we already decided that we want to reach this exalted reality.

In spite of everything at this time, exert in love of friends. Upon this our right to exist depends. Upon this our near to come success is measured. Turn away from all of your imaginary engagements and set your hearts to thinking thoughts and devising proper tactics to truly connect your hearts as one and then you will see, then you will taste.

יהוה

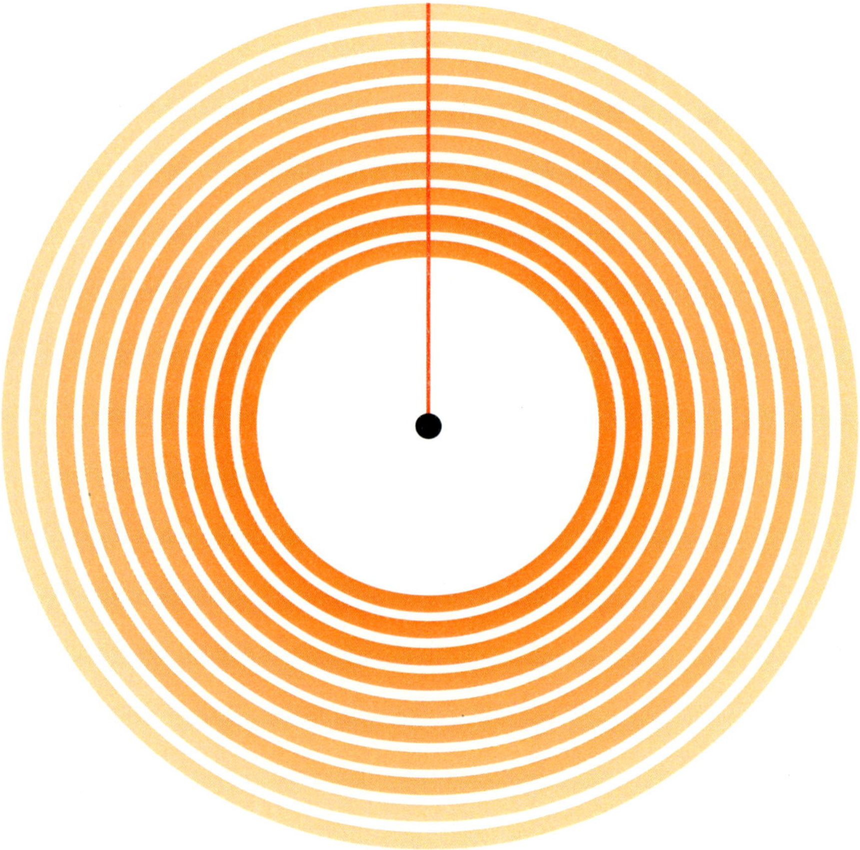

Acknowledgements

I am a small link in a long chain. I am barely a spec of sand compared to the greatness of those who discovered these things and passed them on to the generations. Everything in this book is based on the writings of Yehudah Leib HaLevi Ashlag (Baal HaSulam). While he lived he was able to see from one end of the world to the other. He described the inner workings of the body, of Earth and of the whole system of nature based on his inner attainment. His son and disciple, Baruch Shalom HaLevi Ashlag (Rabash) received it from him and taught the method of attainment to my teacher and guide, Michael Laitman, PhD (Rav). Rabash also gave my teacher permission to open this wisdom to everyone. That is how I arrived here. I have no words to express their greatness in my eyes. My soul is in their hands.

I am indebted to my beloved friends on this journey with me. Reliably you raise my spirits every morning and every night. I am nothing without you.

Thank you to Chaim Ratz and his team who translated and prepared all of the source texts into English by which I found this treasure.

These chapters are derived from the following articles of Baal HaSulam.

Chapter 2. The Essence of the Wisdom of Kabbalah
Chapter 3. The Freedom
Chapter 4. The Essence of Religion and Its Purpose
Chapter 5. Matan Torah
Chapter 6. The Arvut

Chapter 8. Peace in the World
Chapter 9. The Last Generation
Chapter 10. Love of Friends, Letter No. 13, Letter No. 47

If you are interested in discovering more about what is written in this book, find us at kabuconnect.com

Chapter 10
Love of Friends